If You're So Smart

Donald N. McCloskey

If You're
So Smart

The Narrative of Economic Expertise

The University of Chicago Press

Chicago and London

The University of Chicago Press, Chicago 60637
The University of Chicago Press, Ltd., London
© 1990 by The University of Chicago
All rights reserved. Published 1990
Paperback edition 1992
Printed in the United States of America

99 98 97 96 95 94 93 92   5 4 3 2

Library of Congress Cataloging-in-Publication Data

McCloskey, Donald N.
  If you're so smart : the narrative of economic expertise /
Donald N. McCloskey.
      p. cm.
  Includes bibliographical references.
  1. Economics literature.   I. Title.
HB199.M385   1990
330—dc20   90-33041
                                                      CIP

ISBN 0-226-55670-0 (cloth)
ISBN 0-226-55671-9 (paperback)

⊗ The paper used in this publication meets the minimum
requirements of the American National Standard for Information
Sciences—Permanence of Paper for Printed Library Materials,
ANSI Z39.48–1984.

Contents

Preface   vii

Introduction   1

Modernism narrowed the conception that economists had of their science.

1   Telling Stories Economically   10

Economics in fact uses metaphors, which is to say, models. But it also uses stories—stylized facts—about the weight of taxes or the rise of industry.

2   Plot and Genre in Economics   24

The analogy of economics with the writing of stories can be pushed far, from genre to the implied author.

3   The Politics of Stories in Historical Economics   40

If economists are storytellers they are historians. The stories of economics show in historical economics, such as that surrounding England's decline from Number One.

4   Economic Rhetoric in Aid of the Story Line   56

Every element of rhetoric supports the expert's story.

5   The Scholar's Story   70

A great historical economist told his story more self-consciously than most economists. One can unveil a rhetoric without invariably finding badness.

6 Metaphor Against the Story: Chaos and
   Counterfactuals   83

   *Metaphors and stories can get in each other's way, as in
   the hypothesis contrary to fact and in the telling of
   stories about explosive times.*

7 The Poetics and Economics of Magic   97

   *The story uncriticized by a metaphor or the metaphor
   uncriticized by a story is magic, against which
   economics warns.*

8 The American Question: If You're So Smart Why
   Ain't You Rich?   111

   *Get-rich-quick schemes, for example, with their reversal
   of status, are stories. But they are defective, magical.
   The mere critic cannot advise so well.*

9 The Limits of Criticism   123

   *Such criticism of criticism applies beyond economics.
   Economists and other social experts can tell wise stories
   of the past, but cannot profitably predict.*

10 Keeping the Company of Economists   135

   *Storytelling by an economic expert affects his character,
   and then his economics.*

11 The Common Weal and Economic Stories   150

   *The stories told well or ill govern policy. The story of
   American economic "failure" (a replay of the British
   story) is a dangerous example. Humans need stories,
   but they need them to be watched. A humanistic and
   interpretive economics, which keeps the mathematics
   but is aware of its stories, can do the watching.*

   Works Cited   165

   Index   177

Preface

*E*conomists tell stories in their science, which is no complaint. Everyone tells stories, the toddler telling about the scraped knee and the paleontologist telling about the panda's thumb. A story can be good or bad. When it is bad in economics or other fields of expertise it can do damage. In the worst case the storyteller views the story as "stylized facts" or "approximations of the good" or something else free from critical attention. The uncriticized story is not worth living.

The criticism here is literary, showing that economics and other human sciences rely on metaphors and stories, together. The one figure of speech can criticize the other, with better outcomes. Experts who recognized their literary devices would stop selling snake oil and would come back into the conversation of humankind. That is where they belong, back where we can watch them. The recommendation applies to all experts, economic or not. The economist, though, is a hard and rewarding case.

The book started from pieces written over the past few years, to various audiences, but the rewriting aims at the common reader. The Economics Program of the National Science Foundation supported part of the work, and the Manhattan Institute helped by awarding a national fellowship. The Michigan Institute for the Humanities provided a haven in a busy term. My personal debts are too embarrassingly numerous to record in full. The book is written by numberless economists and English professors of my acquaintance. One of the economists, Arjo Klamer of George

Washington University, a colleague at Iowa during the writing, has been unusually helpful, as is his wont. One of the English professors, Thomas Greene of Yale University, deserves special thanks for his astonishing summer course in 1988 on poetry and magic, at the Dartmouth Summer School of Criticism and Theory; it is his breadth of reference, not mine, that is reflected in Chapter 7. I must also thank Douglas Mitchell of the University of Chicago Press and Peter Dougherty of the Free Press, who saw a book and showed me how to extract it. Julie McCarthy of the University of Chicago Press improved the writing. My student Charles Abbott provided me with a list of stories in my own economics textbook, *The Applied Theory of Price,* which otherwise I would have had a hard time seeing.

I thank the following for permission to recast old metal: Routledge to use parts of "Storytelling in Economics," in Christopher Nash and Martin Warner, eds., *Narrative in Culture* (London: Routledge, 1989) in Chapters 1 and 2; Macmillan Press Ltd. to use parts of the articles "Continuity" and "Counterfactuals" in *The New Palgrave: A Dictionary of Economics* (London: Macmillan; New York: Stockton Press, 1987) in Chapter 6; *The American Scholar* to use parts of "The Limits of Expertise: If You're So Smart," 57 (Summer 1988), 393–406 in Chapters 8 and 9; and *The Cato Journal* to use parts of "The Rhetoric of Economic Development," 7 (Spring/Summer 1987), 249–54.

The context for my ruminations has been the Project on Rhetoric of Inquiry, known as "Poroi" (a Greek word meaning "ways and means"). Poroi is a group of one hundred or so professors of law, mathematics, accounting, literature, history, writing, engineering, philosophy, political science, communications, and a few dozen other fields at the University of Iowa and neighboring schools. The professors have gathered every two weeks winter and summer since 1980 to pursue what they call the Rhetoric of Inquiry, scrutinizing a colleague's paper line by precious line. They have discovered in the end something that should have been obvious at the beginning (professors can be slow, held back by learning)—that scientists and scholars, poets and politicians have in common at least the art of argument.

The art of argument has been studied for 2,500 years in "rhetoric," an ancient and latterly dishonored word. Rhetoric says that we can disagree sharply about politics or the balance of evidence, yet can still pause to note the forms of argument and to speak quietly together about improving them. Rhetoric is the art of a democracy and the science of a liberal education, the art and science of good people speaking well.

The book is dedicated to my good, humane, and learned colleagues at the University of Iowa. They and others are telling a new story, a pragmatic one suited to its Midwestern origins, about how honest argument fares among the people, even among the angry and distracted people of the academy.

Introduction

*I*t is pretty clear that an economist, like a poet, uses metaphors. They are called "models." The market for apartments in New York, says the economist, is "just like" a curve on a blackboard. No one has so far seen a literal demand curve floating in the sky above Manhattan. It's a metaphor.

The parallel proposition is not so clear, but is also true. The proposition is that the economist, like a novelist, uses and misuses stories. Once upon a time we were poor, then capitalism flourished, and now as a result we are rich. Some would tell another, anti-capitalist story; but any economist tells stories. Of course fact and logic also come into the economics, in large doses. Economics is a science, and a jolly good one, too. But a serious argument in economics will use metaphors and stories as well—not for ornament or teaching alone but for the very science.

Like other arts and sciences, that is, economics uses the whole rhetorical tetrad: fact, logic, metaphor, and story. Pieces of it are not enough. The allegedly scientific half of the tetrad, the fact and logic, falls short of an adequate economic science, or even a science of rocks or stars. The allegedly humanistic half falls short of an adequate art of economics, or even a criticism of form and color. Scientists and scholars and artists had better be factual and logical. But the point here is that they had also better be literary. The scientists had better devise good metaphors and tell good stories about the first three minutes of the universe or the last three months of the economy. A scientist with only half of the rhetorical tetrad is going to mess up her science.

It is easy to catch economists, as good scientists, in the act of using stories for their science. Outsiders will find this easier to see than the economists will, because the economists are trained to think of themselves as metaphor-makers instead of storytellers. That again is their happy obsession with models of supply and demand sitting up there in the sky.

Economists spend a good deal of time retelling stories that non-economists tell about the economy, such as: Once upon a time the economy seemed to be doing fine but had a secret monetary illness, then the illness broke out, and therefore everyone became poor. And to each other the economists tell other stories: Once upon a time there was a hog market out of equilibrium, then the sellers lowered the price, and as a result the market got back into equilibrium. Once upon a time the government cleverly reckoned it would drop taxes to achieve full employment, but the public had anticipated the move, and as a result the smart government was outsmarted. Once upon a time an East Asian country was poor, then it studied hard, saved a lot, and borrowed money and ideas from the rich countries, and therefore became rich itself. These stories are not going to dry up the market for *King Lear* or the New Testament, but anyway they are the stories that economists tell.

Not gods but people tell the stories. The stories are not facts made by nature. The artifice does not make the stories arbitrary; it merely makes them various. A paleontologist is constrained by what in fact happened to life and by what he thinks are relevant logics and metaphors. But nonetheless with the same facts he can tell the story in varied ways, as gradualist or catastrophist, for example, running the movie in dignified slow motion or in comic lurches. In geology the story of plate tectonics was told by disregarded cranks for decades before it became the dominant story. The same sort of thing happens in economics. The variety of stories does not make all the varieties equally good or important, no more than the variety of facts or logics or metaphors makes all of them equally good or important. To criticize the varieties of stories, though, you have to know that they are being told.

Stories can go wrong, which is hardly news. We swim all day in wrong stories told by liars, incompetents, and the self-deluded. In economics the wrong stories take a particularly dangerous form, which I shall call snake oil, the cure-all for what ails you. The customer wants the economist to be an expert forecaster, telling that simplest and most charming of economic stories: Once upon a time there was a newspaper reader who was poor; then she read a column by a wise economist, who for some reason was giving his valuable advice to her and two million other readers; and now as a result she is rich. Or: Once upon a time there was a kingdom with a people who did not like to study, preferring to sniff cocaine and watch videos on MTV; then the king hired an expert social engineer who had done much studying; and then as a result the people became prosperous, without of course having to do anything so painful as studying.

Economic snake oil sells, in other words, because the public wants it. The public wants it because of the fears that magicians and medicine men have always assuaged and because the public does not know the limits on economic storytelling. The economists, even many who do not look to a career in selling snake oil, are disabled by their training from knowing the limits. They do not know they are telling stories and therefore cannot distinguish good stories from bad.

One of the bad stories of modern life, in still other words, has a final scene in which the expert, such as the expert on the interest rate prevailing next month, keeps us warm and happy. The analogy with physical engineering, which recently *has* kept us warm and happy, is hard to resist. The social engineer promises to run the economy or the war or the culture with godlike expertise. But on the whole it is a wrong and naughty story, a wicked fairy tale.

And the tale of expert social engineering is unbelievable, really. It cannot answer the simplest folk skepticism: If You're So Smart, why ain't you rich?

The magical story that economists are asked to tell as advisors to governments or as social philosophers fit at best awkwardly and at worst disastrously with the metaphors they build elsewhere in their science. The metaphors, likewise, crash against sensible stories. Economic metaphors if pushed too far, as a 500-equation model of the American economy can be, produce storytelling nonsense. And stories, such as the story of America's tragic decline from Number One, contradict metaphors of maturity and international specialization that we know to be true. As during the 1960s, the badly used 500-equation metaphor can tempt us into trusting tricky policies rather than wise institutions. As in Britain a century ago, the bad story of America's rise and fall can tempt us into figurative and then literal war with our "competitors."

The literary solution to this literary problem in economic science is to use the stories and metaphors to criticize one another. Each part of the rhetorical tetrad, in other words, places limits on the excesses of the others. If you are fanatical about stories alone or about metaphors alone (or logics or facts alone, to finish it off), you will start saying silly and dangerous things in the other realm. The story of the Aryan Race, to take our century's plainest excess in storytelling, needed criticism. So on a lesser plane of evil did the metaphor of methodical accounting for bodies, hearts, and minds in Vietnam. It is better to be moderately, reasonably committed to the observing of true facts, together with the following of true logic, the telling of true stories, and the constructing of true metaphors, combined. It is boring and moderate but it is true. One part of the tetrad checks the other's rank immoderation. The combination yields truth for science and wisdom for policy.

The comic actor John Cleese says that he wants some day to do a scathing, utterly immoderate skit against immoderation. The argument here is a moderate, pluralist argument against monistic immoderation (most of the good arguments since Plato have been monistic and immoderate). Whether it is scathing or not remains to be seen. The proposal in any case is that economics and other expertise use all the resources of human reasoning, the whole rhetorical tetrad. The immoderation that recommends we narrow ourselves down to one piece of the tetrad has done us wrong. It has led us to build high-rise slums and high interest rate economies, and has been especially damaging since the 1950s.

Since those heady years economics has believed itself narrowed down to fact and logic. It shared then belatedly in the temporary narrowing of Western culture called "positivism" or "modernism" (Booth 1974; Klamer 1987b; the word "modernism" in literature means a unified rather than a "dissociated" sensibility, approximately the opposite of its meaning in other realms; see McGrath 1986, chap. 9). Modernism has roots as deep as Plato and Descartes, but in full-blown form it suits its name. Round about 1920 in the West certain philosophers came suddenly to believe that their whole subject could be narrowed down to an artificial language; certain architects came to believe their whole subject could be narrowed to a cube; certain painters came to believe that their whole subject could be narrowed to a surface. Out of this narrowness was supposed to come insight and certitude.

Insight did come (not certitude, alas). In philosophy after modernism we know more about languages lacking human speakers. In architecture we know more about buildings lacking tops. In painting we know more about pictures lacking depth of field. When news of modernism got out to economics around 1950 it yielded some worthwhile insight, too. In economics after modernism we know more about economic models lacking contact with the world.

On the whole, though, the narrowing did not work very well. The failure of modernism in economics and elsewhere in the culture does not say it was a bad idea to try. And it certainly does not say that we should now abandon fact and logic, surface and cube, and surrender to the Celtic curve and the irrational. We are all very glad to keep whatever we have learned from the Bauhaus or the Vienna Circle or the running of rats. It says merely that we should turn back to the work at hand equipped now with the full tetrad of fact, logic, metaphor, and story.

The modernist experiment in getting along with fewer than all the resources of human reasoning puts one in mind of the Midwestern expression, "a few bricks short of a load." It means cracked, irrational. The modernist program of narrowing down our arguments in the name of rationality was a few bricks short of a load. To admit now that metaphor and story matter also in human reasoning does not entail becoming less rational and less reasonable, dressing in saffron robes or tuning into "New Dimensions." On the contrary it entails becoming more rational and more reasonable, because it puts more of what persuades serious people under the scrutiny of reason. Modernism was rigorous about a tiny part of reasoning and angrily unreasonable about the rest.

Bertrand Russell, the master of modernism in philosophy, was a leading case in point (see Booth 1974). Santayana describes Russell during the First World War exploiting his retentive memory without a check of reason:

This information, though accurate, was necessarily partial, and brought forward in a partisan argument; he couldn't know, he refused to know everything; so that his judgments, nominally based on that partial information, were really inspired by passionate prejudice and were always unfair and sometimes mad. He would say, for instance, that the bishops supported the war because they had money invested in munition works. (1986, 441)

Modernists in philosophy or later in economics could not reason with most of their opponents; on most matters they could only shout and sneer. They would say: You are an unscientific fool if you do not believe that in building downtown Dallas the form should follow the function; or you are an ignorant knave if you do not believe that political science should be reduced to mathematics. We need now after modernism to grow beyond the sneers, getting more rigorous and more reasonable about the arguments, all at once.

Modernism seized the word "science" for its purposes. The word has for a long time been a club with which to beat on arguments the modernists did not wish to hear. English speakers over the past century and a half have used it in a peculiar way, as in British academic usage: arts and sciences, the "arts" of literature and philosophy as against the "sciences" of chemistry and geology. A historical geologist in English is a scientist; a political historian is not. The English usage would puzzle an Italian mother boasting of her studious son, *mio scienziato,* my learned one. Italian and other languages use the science word to mean simply "systematic inquiry" (as do for example French, German, Dutch, Spanish, Swedish, Polish, Hungarian, Turkish, Korean, Hindi, and Tamil). Only English, and only the English of the past century, has made physical and biological science (definition 5b in the old *Oxford English Dictionary* [Oxford 1933]) into, as the *Supplement* (1982; compare OED, 2d ed. 1989) describes it, "the dominant sense in ordinary use." It would be a good idea to claim the word back for reasonable and rigorous argument.

The English and modernist mistake, in other words, is to think of science and literature as Two Cultures. The Two-Cultures talk is not written in the stars, though common enough and encouraged by the deans. A dean of research at a large state university gave a talk a couple of years ago in which she spoke of the humanities as what is left over after the (physical and biological) sciences, and then after them the social sciences, have expended their eloquence. The humanities in her mind are a residuum for the mystical and the ineffable. The dean thought she was being good natured. The bad-natured remarks muttered from each side are worse: that if we mention metaphors we are committed to an arty irrationalism; that if we mention logic we are committed to a scientific autism.

One is tempted to shake them both and say, Get serious. The sciences, such as economics, require supposedly humanistic methods, right in the middle of their sciences; and likewise the arts and humanities require fact and logic, right in the middle of their own sciences. Newton used logic and metaphors; Darwin used facts and stories. Science is literary, requiring metaphors and stories in its daily work, and literature is scientific.

Speaking of a science such as economics in literary terms, of course, inverts a recent and guilt-producing hierarchy. But contrary to the century-long and English-speaking program to demarcate science from the rest of the culture—a strange program when you think of it—science is after all a matter of arguing. The ancient categories of argument are going to apply (for which see Perelman and Olbrechts-Tyteca 1969 [1958]; Perelman 1982; Booth 1974; Kennedy 1984; McKeon 1987; Nelson, Megill, and McCloskey, eds., 1987; Vickers 1988, among many others in the revival of rhetoric).

Stories are to be recognized in a complete psychology (Gergen and Gergen 1986; Bruner 1986); so too in economics after modernism (Klamer, McCloskey, and Solow, eds., 1988). A disciple asks his guru how the earth is supported in space. The guru answers readily, "On the back of a giant turtle." The disciple is at first satisfied, but then thinks of an objection. How is the turtle itself supported? The guru pauses, then replies: "On the back of a giant elephant." Good. But the disciple thinks of another objection. How is the elephant in turn supported? The guru reflects long and hard. Ah: "The first elephant is supported by another elephant, and the next by a next: you see, *it's elephants all the way down.*" Founding science on a turtle of certitude was a poor idea. Science is rhetoric, human argument, all the way down (Campbell 1987; Davis and Hersh 1987; Landau 1987; Bazerman 1987, 1988; Klamer 1987a; Carlston 1987; Galison 1987; Collins 1985).

Even ordinary arguing will sometimes use devices unintelligible to particular outsiders, "special topics" in the vocabulary of ancient rhetoric. Lawyers will use cases known only to themselves, and mathematicians will use special theorems. Any scientific community has its language, not to be dismissed as jargon, and its special topics.

At other points in the argument, though, the lawyers and mathematicians will use devices common to other people, "common topics." The appeal to precedent in law is a common topic, which is of course seen outside the law courts and the law journals. Similarly a mathematician makes daily the appeal to authority; but a non-mathematician makes it daily, too. Part of economics uses special topics. But some of its best arguments are common topics. Economic and other expertise shares human reasoning with other fields.

In my own economics or economic history I have many persuasive reasons for preferring a neoclassical, Chicago-school, free-market, quantitative, and mathematical way of telling the story of British economic decline in the late nineteenth century, say, and linking the story to the recent story of the United States. My Marxist, Austrian, institutionalist, non-Chicago, and non-economist friends sometimes do not like my way, and on this or that point they half persuade me, when I grasp their stories. But until the storytelling in economics and in other sciences is recognized we are going to find it hard to be reasonable. We will not know if we are so smart. And the snake oil, curing all our ills in Washington or Des Moines, will continue to be that deadly, secret poison.

1   Telling Stories Economically

Crabs have big molting glands, which makes them good subjects for studying glands in general (Spaziani et al. 1989). There seem to be at least two ways of understanding crab glands and other things: either by way of a metaphor or by way of a story, through something like a poem or through something like a novel. When a biologist is asked to tell why the molting glands of the crab are located just as they are, he has two possibilities. Either he can call on a model—a metaphor, an analogy—of rationality inside the crab, saying that locating them just *there* will maximize the efficiency of the glands in operation; or he can tell a story, organizing real or hypothetical time, about how crabs with badly located glands will fail. If he is lucky with the modeling metaphors he will discover equations with a simple solution. If he is lucky with the storytelling he will discover a true history of maladapted variety of crabs, showing it dying out. Metaphors and stories, models and histories, subject to the discipline of fact and logic, are the two ways of answering "why."

The metaphorical and the narrative questions answer each other. Suppose the biologist happens first to offer his metaphor, his ideal and hypothetical crab moving bits of its body from here to there in search of the best location for molting glands. The listener, still puzzled, asks, "But why?" The biologist will answer the new question with a story: he says, "The reason why the glands must be located well is that if crabs did a poor job of locating their glands they would die off as time passed." A story answers a model.

But similarly a model answers a story. If the biologist gives the evolutionary story first, and the listener then asks "But why?", the biologist answers now with a metaphor: "The reason why the crabs will die off is that poorly located glands would serve poorly in the emergencies of crab life." The glands would not be well located: that's why.

Among the sciences (in the recent English sense) metaphors dominate physics and stories dominate biology. The two can mix; that people regard metaphors and stories as answering each other will guarantee they do. Gregor Mendel's thinking in the 1860s about genetics was a rare case in biology of unmixed modeling, imagining inheritance to be "just like" the rolling of dice. Many decades later his metaphor was answered by the more usual story-telling, at which point people started believing it. In 1902 W. S. Sutton finally observed homologous pairs of chromosomes in grasshoppers. Sutton answered the question asked to a metaphor— "But *why* does the Mendelian model of genes work?"—with a story: "Because, to begin with, the genes are arranged along pairs of chromosomes, which I have seen acting out their little story of splitting and trading, one half from each parent."

The modes of argument are more closely balanced in economics. An economist explains the success of cotton farming in the South before the Civil War in static, modeling terms (he says: the South in 1860 had a comparative advantage in cotton) or he understands it in dynamic, storytelling terms (he says: the situation in 1860 was a natural selection from earlier successes). The best economics combines the two, the static model and the dynamic story, the economic theory and the economic history. For example, in 1920 the Austrian economist Ludwig von Mises wrote a paper on the impracticality of economic calculation under socialism. (The paper speaks to the late 1980s and the fall of socialism.) It was both a modeling of the ignorance that would plague any attempt in the future to replace the market and a story of the failures of War Communism (Lavoie 1985, 49).

The metaphors in economics and other fields have their own

comparative advantage. (I could use here either an evolutionary story from the history of science or a maximizing model from the sociology or philosophy of science.) Metaphors work best at making predictions of tides in the sea or shortages in markets, simulating out into a counterfactual world. In the seventeenth century the physicists gave up stories in favor of models, giving up the claim to tell in a narrative sense how gravity reached up and pulled things down. It just did, according to thus-and-such an equation; let me show you the model. Similarly an economist will argue that a price control on apartments will yield shortages. Don't ask how it will in sequence. It just will, according to thus-and-such an equation; let me show you the model.

On the other hand storytelling works best at understanding something that has already happened, like the evolution of crabs or the development of the modern corporation. The Darwinian story was notably lacking in models, and therefore in predictions. Mendel's model offered to explain the descent of peas and of man by a metaphor rather than by a story and was neglected for years, while natural selection was telling.

One can therefore talk about the models of economics as metaphors, as its "poetics" (McCloskey 1985a). A metaphor brings "two separate domains into cognitive and emotional relation by using language directly appropriate to the one as a lens for seeing the other" (Black 1962, 236). A story, on the other hand, sets down in chronological order the raw experience of one domain. It is a "presentation of a time-ordered or time-related experience that . . . supplements, re-orders, enhances, or interprets unnarrated life" (Booth 1988, 14). The combination of the two is more ambitious and more humanly satisfying. An allegory combines a metaphor (tortoises and hares are like human competitors) with a story (once upon a time the two raced, then the hare took a rest, then as a result the slow and steady tortoise won the race). Economics as a whole, for example, is an allegory of self-interest.

A story from an economist's life can sketch the poetics of economics at work. Shortly after the Second World War the agricultural economist Theodore Schultz, later to win a Nobel prize for the work, spent a term based at Auburn University in Alabama, interviewing farmers in the neighborhood (Schultz 1988). One day he interviewed an old and poor farm couple and was struck by how contented they seemed. Why are you so contented, he asked, though very poor? They answered: You're wrong, Professor. We're not poor. We've used up our farm to educate four children through college, remaking fertile land and well-stocked pens into knowledge of law and Latin. We are rich.

The parents had told Schultz that the *physical* capital, which economists think they understand, is in some sense just like the *human* capital of education. The children now owned it, and so the parents did, too. Once it had been rail fences and hog pens and mules. Now it was in the children's brains, this human capital. The farm couple *was* rich.

The average economist was willing to accept the discovery of human capital as soon as he understood it, which is in fact how many scientific and scholarly discoveries are received. It was an argument in a metaphor (or if you like: an analogy, a simile, a model). A hog pen, Schultz would say to another economist, is "just like" Latin 101. The other economist would have to admit that there was something to it. Both the hog pen and the Latin instruction are paid for by saving. Both are valuable assets for earning income, understanding "income" to mean, as economists put it, "a stream of satisfaction." Year after year the hog pen and the Latin cause satisfaction to stream out like water from a dam. Both last a long time but finally wear out when the pen falls down and the Latin-learned brain dies. And the one piece of "capital" can be made into the other. An educated farmer, because of his degree in agriculture from Auburn, can get a bank loan to build a hog pen; when his children grow up he can sell off the part of the farm with the hog pen to pay for another term for Junior and Sis up at Auburn, too.

So economists use metaphors in their science, like poets. An economist is a poet / But doesn't know it. The parallel proposition, the theme here, is that the economist is also a novelist and lives happily ever after. As the literary critic Peter Brooks said in *Reading for the Plot:* "Our lives are ceaselessly intertwined with narrative, with the stories that we tell . . . all of which are reworked in that story of our own lives that we narrate to ourselves. . . . We are immersed in narrative" (1985, 3). Or as the historian J. H. Hexter put it, storytelling is "a sort of knowledge we cannot live without" (1986, 8).

Economists have not lived without stories, not ever. Stories, as a working title had it, are "instruments of culture" (Nash and Warner 1989). It is perhaps no accident that economic science and the novel were born at about the same time (compare Brooks 1985, 5). It is perhaps no accident, either, that modernist stories of science flooded in as the sea of faith receded. We live in an age insatiate of stories.

Tell me a story, Dr. Smith. Why of course:

A pension scheme is proposed for the nation, in which "the employer will pay half." It will say in the law and on the worker's salary check that the worker contributes 5 percent of his wages to the pension fund but that the boss contributes the other 5 percent. The example is a leading case in the old debate between lawyers and economists. A law is passed designed (as people say) to have such and such an effect. The lawyerly mind goes only this far. According to the lawyer, under the pension scheme the workers will be 5 percent better off on balance, getting half of their pension free.

No economist, though, will want to leave the story of the pension plan in the first act, the lawyer's and legislator's act of laws designed to split the costs. Her suspicion is always aroused by things said to be free. She will want to go further into the little drama of pensions. She will say: "At the higher cost of labor the bosses will hire fewer workers. In the second act, consequently, the situation created by the law will begin to dissolve. At the old wage but with the pension added, more workers will want to get jobs than the boss wishes to give. Jostling queues will form outside the factory gate. The competition of the workers will drive down wages. By the third and final act a part of the 'boss's' share of the pension costs—maybe even all of it—will sit on the workers themselves, in the form of lower wages. The intent of the law," the economist will conclude with a smirk, "will have been frustrated."

Thus in Chicago when a tax on employment was proposed the reporters asked who would pay the tax. Alderman Thomas Keane (who later went to jail, though not for misappropriation of economics) declared that the City had been careful to draft the law so that only the employers paid it. "The City of Chicago," said Keane, "will never tax the working man." Ah, yes.

Thus again in 1987, when Senator Ted Kennedy proposed a plan for workers and employers to share the cost of health insurance, the newspapers reported Kennedy as estimating "the overall cost at $25 billion—$20 billion paid by employers and $5 billion by workers." Senator Kennedy will never tax the working man. The manager of employee relations at the U.S. Chamber of Commerce (who apparently agreed with Senator Kennedy's economic analysis of where the tax would fall) said, "It is ridiculous to believe that every company . . . can afford to provide such a generous array of health care benefits." The U.S. Chamber of Commerce will never tax the company.

The case illustrates a number of points about economic stories. It illustrates the pleasure economists take in unforeseen consequences, trick endings, a pleasure shared with other social scientists. It illustrates the selection of certain plots for special attention: an accountant or political scientist would want to hear exactly how the pension was funded, because the details of funding, which do not matter in the economist's way of storytelling, might affect the behavior of politicians or businesspeople in the future. It illustrates also the way that in telling their stories economists draw on typical scenes—the queues in front of the factory—and typical metaphors—workers as commodities to be bought and sold.

But most importantly here it illustrates the way stories support economic argument. Since Adam Smith and David Ricardo economists have been addicted to little analytic stories. (The addiction even has a name, "the Ricardian vice.") The economist says, "Yes, I know how the story begins in the first act; but I see dramatic possibilities; I see how events will develop from the situation at the start."

It is not controversial that an economist is a storyteller when she is telling the story of the Federal Reserve Board last year or the story of the industrial revolution in Britain last century. Plainly and routinely, 90 percent of what economists do is such storytelling. Yet even in the other 10 percent, in the part more obviously dominated by models and metaphors, the economist tells stories. Economists tell a lot of stories, and must practice therefore the art of telling.

Continuity and discontinuity, to give an example of the telling in detail, are devices of storytelling. The story of monetary policy over the past few months or the story of modern economic growth can be told as gradualist or catastrophist. How do you decide which is the better story? If stories are one part of economic science, how are they evaluated?

Consider one feature of the master story of modern life, the nature and causes of the wealth of nations. If the British industrial revolution was a "revolution," as it surely was, it happened at some time. There was a discontinuity, a before and after in the story. Various dates have been proposed, down to the famous day and year: such as the ninth of March 1776, when *The Wealth of Nations* provided an ideology for the age; or the five months in 1769 when Watt took out a patent on the high-pressure steam engine and Arkwright on the cotton-spinning water frame; or the first of January 1760, when the furnaces at Carron Ironworks, Stirlingshire were lit.

Such dating has of course an amateur air, part of a bad story. A definite date looks handsome on a plaque or scroll but the precision does not fit well with sophisticated storytelling. The discontinuity is implausibly sharp, drawing attention to minor details. The Great Depression did not start on 24 October 1929; the deregulation of

American banking was not completed with the repeal of laws restricting the payment of interest. The historical economist Nicholas Crafts (1977) has pointed out that the detailed timing of the industrial revolution should not anyway be the thing to be studied, because small beginnings do not come labeled with their probabilities of developing into great revolutions. He is identifying a pitfall in storytelling. The historical economist Joel Mokyr identifies another (1985, 44): rummaging among the possible acorns from which the great oak of the industrial revolution grew "is a bit like studying the history of Jewish dissenters between 50 B.C. and A.D. What we are looking at is the inception of something which was at first insignificant and even bizarre," albeit "destined to change the life of every man and woman in the West."

What is destined or not destined to change our lives will look rather different to each of us. Each historical economist therefore has his or her own dating of the industrial revolution, though varying in persuasiveness. Each sees another discontinuity. Elizabeth Carus-Wilson (1954 [1941], 41) spoke of "an industrial revolution of the 13th century": she found that the fulling mill was "due to scientific discoveries and changes in technique" and "was destined to alter the face of medieval England." A. R. Bridbury (1975, xix–xx) found in the late Middle Ages "a country traveling slowly along the road . . . that [it] traveled so very much more quickly in Adam Smith's day." In the eyes of Marxist writers the sixteenth century was the discontinuity, when capitalism set off into the world to seek its fortune. John U. Nef (1932), no Marxist, believed he saw an industrial revolution in the sixteenth century, centered on coal, though admittedly it slowed in the seventeenth century. A student of the seventeenth century itself, such as D. C. Coleman (1977), finds glimmerings of economic growth even in that disordered age. The most widely accepted period for the industrial revolution is the late eighteenth century, especially the 1760s and 1770s (Mantoux 1961 [1928]; Landes 1965, 1969), but recent students of the matter (Harley 1982; Crafts 1984) have found much to admire in the accomplishments of the early eighteenth century. W. W. Rostow

(1960) placed the "take-off into self-sustained growth" in the last two decades of the eighteenth century, but others have observed that even by 1850 the majority of British people remained in traditional sectors of the economy. And later still there was a second industrial revolution (of chemicals, electricity, and internal combustion) and a third (of electronics and biology).

Wider perspectives are possible, so wide as to encourage seeing continuity instead. Looking at the matter from 1907, Henry Adams could see a "movement from unity into multiplicity, between 1200 and 1900, . . . unbroken in sequence, and rapid in acceleration" (1931 [1906], 498). The principal modern student of the industrial revolution, R. M. Hartwell, appealed for continuity against the jostling throng of dates: "Do we need an *explanation* of the industrial revolution? Could it not be the culmination of a most unspectacular process, the consequence of a long period of economic growth?" (1967 [1965], 78).

Such questions of continuity and discontinuity are asked widely in economics, though sometimes only half consciously. The questions cannot be left to historians. Economics is mainly contemporary history and faces the problem of deciding when a piece of history has been continuous or not. For instance the discontinuity in the growth of big government, as Robert Higgs points out (1987), might be placed when the American institutions of big government were first thought up (1900–1918) or made (1930–45) or expanded (1960–70). Even recent and technical history in economics faces this storytelling problem. When, if ever, did the international alignment of prices and exchange rates break down in the 1970s? When did policy on antitrust alter to favor mergers? When did monetary policy last become expansionary? Where is the break? It is a question of stories.

The question has often been misconstrued as philosophical. The philosophical difficulty was first articulated in the fifth century B.C. by Parmenides and his student Zeno: that if everything is perfectly continuous, change is impossible (Korner 1967). Everything is, so to speak, packed too tightly to move. The economist will recognize the point as analogous to an extreme form of economic equilibrium; the physicist will recognize it as maximum entropy. If human nature doesn't "really" change, then history will be a string of weary announcements that the more things change the more they stay the same. If the economy is "really" in equilibrium all the time, then nothing remains to be done.

The economist and historian Alexander Gerschenkron noted that such a metaphysics would close the book of history (1962a, 12). A history or economics that began with the Parmenidean continuum would never speak. For purposes of social science Gerschenkron rejected the transition from the connectedness of all change to an absence of change. True, if you squint and fit a curve then no economic story looks discontinuous in the mathematical sense; but it is wrong then to deduce that "really" there is no change at all, or that the industrial revolution is a mirage. "Continuity" in the strict mathematical sense must be kept distinct from "continuity" in the storytelling sense.

Economists have often been muddled about this philosophical distinction, drawing surprising ideological implications from it. The great British economist of a century ago, Alfred Marshall, enshrined on the title page of his *Principles of Economics* (1890 and later edition) the motto *natura non facit saltum* (nature does not make a jump; Leibnitz and Linnaeus are early users of the phrase, which appears to date from Jacques Tissot in 1613). Marshall himself seems to have believed that the ability to represent behavior with mathematical curves that do not jump implies that the economic theory called "marginalism" is a good description of human behavior. (Marginalism says that humans calculate how far they should go.) One is less sure that Marshall believed that the lack of jumps in nature (quantum physics was about to make big jumps big news) implies that people should not jump either and should change society only gradually.

Anyway, both implications are commonly drawn and both are non sequiturs. Though both have been attributed to the modern mainstream in American economics, so-called neoclassical economics, neither one is necessary for it. Much bitter controversy has assumed that neoclassical economics depends on smooth curves and in consequence must advocate smooth social policies. There is a peculiar alliance in economics between discrete (jumpy) mathematics and Marxian economics, with its jumpy political program. There is an equally peculiar enthusiasm of some conservative writers for continuities in economic history. Gerschenkron cursed both their houses: the scientific storyteller should study change and continuity "unbothered by the lovers and haters of revolutions who must find themselves playgrounds and battle grounds outside the area of serious scholarship" (1962a, 39).

The main problems of continuity and discontinuity, however, are not solvable in seminars on philosophy. They are practical problems in the rhetoric of measurement and must be solved in the economic or historical workshop. When shall we say that the industrial revolution happened? Gerschenkron himself gave an answer confined to industry, for in common with most economic historians he regarded agriculture and services as laggards in economic growth. "In a number of major countries of Europe. . . . after a lengthy period of fairly low rates of growth came a moment of more or less sudden increase in the rates, which then remained at the accelerated level for a considerable period. That was the period of the great spurt in the respective countries' industrial development. . . . The rates and the margin between them in the 'pre-kink' and the 'post-kink' periods appear to vary depending on the degree of relative backwardness of the country at the time of the acceleration" (1962a [1968, 33–34]).

The level at which such discontinuity is to be observed is at choice. As Gerschenkron remarked, "If the seat of the great spurt lies in the area of manufacturing, it would be inept to try to locate the discontinuity by scrutinizing data on large aggregate magnitudes such as national income. . . . By the time industry has become bulky enough to affect the larger aggregate, the exciting period of the great spurt may well be over" (34–35). Inept, he says. The story would be badly told. In a footnote to these sentences he deals with his bête noire, Walt Whitman Rostow (a stage theorist as an economic historian, one of the first appliers of modern economics to history and, less happily, an advisor to presidents). Rostow's "failure to appreciate this point has detracted greatly from his concept of the take-off [Rostow's set of metaphors about the discontinuity], which in principle is closely related to the concept of the great spurt as developed by this writer."

The point is a good one and applies to all questions of continuity in aggregate economics, or aggregate anything. Small (and exciting) beginnings will be hidden by the mass until well after they have become routine. Recall Crafts and Mokyr on eighteenth-century industry. Mokyr has put it as a matter of arithmetic: if the traditional sector of an economy is growing at a slow 1 percent per annum and starts with 90 percent of output, the modern sector growing at a fast 4 percent per annum will take three-quarters of a century to account for as much as half of output (1985, 5). It's just the arithmetic. We may call it the Weighting Theorem (or the Waiting Theorem, for the wait is long when the weight is small to begin with). There are parallel points to be made elsewhere in economics and in social science generally. In the branch of mathematical economics called growth theory, for instance, as was noticed shortly after its birth, a century of theoretical time is needed in most models for a shift to yield growth of as much as 90 percent of its final, "steady" state. More generally, economists have long recognized the tension between microeconomic explanations and macroeconomic things to be explained. In stable models the small beginnings stay small for a long time.

The point about small beginnings is not confined to economics: sociologists quarrel in the same way, using even the same jargon of micro and macro. The search for discontinuity in an aggregate curve raises the question of the level at which we should do our social thinking, the so-called aggregation problem. It would apply to literary history, too: is Romanticism best studied in Blake or Browning, in its small beginnings or its full career?

Gerschenkron himself, unfortunately, did not answer the storytelling question well by his own standards and was in the end hoist by his own petard. In an important work examining Italian industrial output Gerschenkron placed the "great spurt" in the period 1896–1908 and wished to explain it with the great banks founded about the same time, in the 1890s. Stefano Fenoaltea, fleetingly a student of Gerschenkron (until the student contradicted the master), applied the Weighting Theorem to the case (Fenoaltea, n.d.). Surely, Fenoaltea reasoned, the components of the industrial index—the steel output and the chemical output—are the "real" units of economic analysis. (People talk this way, incidentally, when they want to make a storytelling point but do not want to defend it explicitly. The rhetoric of "reality" is used nowadays by some economists to coerce other economists into giving micro foundation for all of their macroeconomics.) Fenoaltea noted that if the little components started accelerating *before* the great banks appeared, becoming bulky only later, then the banks could not have been the initiating force.

Unhappily, the little components did just this. They spoil Gerschenkron's bank-led story of Italian industrialization: the components accelerated not in the nineties but in the eighties, not after but before the banks made their mark. To paraphrase Gerschenkron on Rostow, by the time the progressive components of industry had become bulky enough to affect the larger aggregate, the exciting period was well over.

Yet the moral is still Gerschenkron's: that continuity and discontinuity are tools "forged by the historian rather than something inherently and invariantly contained in the historical matter. . . . At all times it is the ordering hand of the historian that creates continuities or discontinuities" (1962a, 38). Gerschenkron nodded, but the nodding makes the point. The multiple datings of the industrial revolution make it, too. So does any choice of smoothness or suddenness in economic storytelling.

The point is that history, like economics, to say it again, is a story we tell. Continuity and discontinuity are narrative devices, to be chosen for their storytelling virtues. Niels Bohr said once that "It is wrong to think that the task of physics is to find out how nature is. Physics concerns what we can say about nature" (Moore 1985 [1966], 406). It is *our* say. We can choose to emphasize the continuous: "Abraham begat Isaac; . . . begat . . . begat . . . and Jacob begat Joseph the husband of Mary, of whom was born Jesus." Or the discontinuous: "There was in the days of Herod, the king of Judea, a certain priest named Zacharias." It is the same story, but its continuity or discontinuity is our creation, not God's.

Economists spend a lot of time worrying whether their metaphors—they call them "models"—meet rigorous standards of logic. They worry less whether their stories—they call them "stylized facts," a phrase that makes tiresome trips to the library unnecessary—meet rigorous standards of fact. The choice to have high standards of logic, low standards of fact, and no explicit standards of metaphor and story is itself a rhetorical one. It depends on the audience of economic scientists. If economists become economists by way of the Department of Mathematics, for example, it will not be surprising when they bring along a rhetoric of logic-is-enough; if by way of the Department of History, a rhetoric of facts-are-enough. Few economists become economists by way of the Department of English or of Communications, and so not many know they are telling stories.

2 Plot and Genre in Economics

*A*ny moderately broad conversation like economics, then, will involve the rhetorical tetrad—fact, logic, metaphor, and especially story.

Telling the stories in economics as matters of beginnings, middles, and ends has many attractions. A proper scientific treatment would start with pure plot, breaking 100 economic stories down into their components as the Russian folklorist Vladímir Propp did in 1928 for 100 Russian folk tales (1968 [1928], 19–24). In economics they would be the capitalization-of-Iowa-corn-prices tale, the exit-from-and-entry-to-computer-selling-in-the-1980s tale, the correct-burden-of-the-Kennedy-health-insurance tale, the great-oaks-from-little-acorns-grow tale, and so forth. The tales would then be analyzed into "functions" (Propp's word for actions). And, to Proppize it entirely, one would ask whether the sequences of functions prove to be constant, as they are in Russia.

The task sounds bizarre. But actually economics is too easy a case. It is not hard enough to make it scientifically worthwhile to go searching for structure in economic stories. Economics is already structural, as the linguist Ferdinand de Saussure pointed out long ago (1983 [1916], 79, 113). The actions of an economistic folklore are few: entry, exit, price setting, orders within a firm, purchase, sale, valuation, and a few more. It is indeed this self-consciously structural element that makes economics so irritating to outsiders. Economists say over and over again, "action X is just like action Y"—labor is just like a commodity, slavery is just like capitalization, children are just like refrigerators, and so forth.

The economist's favorite phrase should please literary intellectuals, who look for hidden structure below the surface of things: "underneath it all." Underneath it all, international trade among nations is trade among individuals and can be modeled in the same way. Underneath it all, an inflated price is earned by someone as an inflation wage, leaving average welfare unchanged. Underneath it all, we owe the national debt to ourselves (the people who pay the taxes might wonder about this one). In such a highly structured field, whose principles of storytelling are so well known by the main storytellers, it would be surprising to find as many as thirty-one distinct actions, as Propp found in his 100 Russian folk tales (1968 [1928], 64). He found seven different characters (80). That seems more likely: the early English economist David Ricardo (the one who brought Ricardian vice into the world) got along in his economic tales with three—the worker, the landlord, and the farmer.

Tale-telling in economics follows the less formal constraints of fiction, too. The most important is the sense of an ending, as in the story of the pension scheme. Go all the way to the third act. In notably economic language the Bulgarian-French literary critic Tzvetan Todorov asserted that "the minimal complete plot consists of the transition from one equilibrium to another" (quoted in Prince 1973, 31). Gerald Prince used some ingenious mental experiments with stories and non-stories to formulate a definition of the "minimal story," which has

three conjoined events. The first and third events are stative [such as "John was poor"], the second is active [such as "then John found a pot of gold"]. Furthermore, the third event is the inverse of the first [such as "John was rich"]. . . . The three events are conjoined by conjunctive features in such a way that (a) the first event precedes the second in time and the second precedes the third, and (b) the second event causes the third. (31)

Prince's technique isolates what it is about the tales that we recognize as stories. Is this a story?

A man laughed and a woman sang.

No, it does not feel like one—in the uninstructed sense we learned at our mother's knee (anything of course can be a story after Joyce and Kafka, not to speak of writers of French detective stories). The following sounds more like a story:

John was rich, then he lost a lot of money.

At least it has the claim of sequence or consequence, "then." And it has the inversion of status ("rich . . . poor"). But it doesn't quite make it. Consider:

A man was happy, then he met a woman, then, as a result, he was unhappy.

Right. It feels like a complete story, as "generally and intuitively recognized" (5). Contrast:

John was rich and he traveled a lot, then, as a result, he was very happy.

Something is screwy. What is screwy is that his status is not inverted from what it was.

One can use Prince's examples to construct stories and non-stories in economics. Test the pattern:

Poland was poor, then it adopted capitalism, then as a result it became rich.

The money supply increased this year, then, as a result, productivity last year rose and the business cycle three decades ago peaked.

A few firms existed in chemicals, then they merged, and then only one firm existed.

Britain in the late nineteenth century was capitalistic and rich and powerful.

The pattern is story/non-story/story/non-story.

Stories end in a new state. If the story of the pension scheme ended with a 5 percent gain by the worker the economist says "it is not an equilibrium." "Not an equilibrium" is the economist's way of saying that he disputes the ending proposed by some untutored person. Any descendant of Adam Smith, left or right, by way of Marx or Marshall or Menger, will be happy to tell you a better story. Many of the disagreements inside economics turn on this sense of an ending. To an eclectic Keynesian, raised on picturesque tales of economic surprise, the story idea "Oil prices went up, which caused inflation" is full of meaning, having the merits that stories are supposed to have. But to a monetarist, raised on the classical unities of money, it seems incomplete, no story at all, a flop. As the economist A. C. Harberger likes to say, it doesn't make the economics "sing." It ends too soon, halfway through the second act: a rise in oil prices without some corresponding fall elsewhere is "not an equilibrium."

From the other side, the criticism of monetarism by Keynesians is likewise a criticism of the plot line, complaining of an ill-motivated beginning rather than a premature ending: where on earth does the money you think is so important come from, and why? The jargon word is "exogenous": if you start the story in the middle the money will be treated as though it is unrelated to, exogenous to, the rest of the action, even though it's not.

There is more than prettiness in such matters of plot. There is moral weight. The historian Hayden White has written that "The demand for closure in the historical story is a demand . . . for moral reasoning" (1981, 20). A monetarist is not morally satisfied until she has pinned the blame on the Federal Reserve. The economist's ending to the pension story says, "Look: you're getting fooled by the politicians and lawyers if you think that specifying the 50-50 share in the law will get the workers a 50 percent cheaper pension. Wake up; act your age; look beneath the surface; recognize the dismal ironies of life." Stories impart meaning, which is to say worth. A *New Yorker* cartoon shows a woman looking up anxiously from the TV, asking her husband, "Henry, is there a moral to *our* story?"

The sense of adequacy in storytelling works in the most abstract theory, too. In seminars on mathematical economics a question nearly as common as "Haven't you left off the second subscript?" is "What is your story?" The story of the pension scheme can be put entirely mathematically and metaphorically, as an assertion about where the pension tax falls, speaking of supply and demand curves in equilibrium thus:

$$w^* = - [E_d/(E_d + E_s)]T^*.$$

The mathematics here is so familiar to an economist that he will not need explanation beyond the metaphor. (It says that the tax is shared between demanders of labor and suppliers of labor depending on how sensitive they are to wages.) But in less familiar cases, at the frontier of economic argument, the economist will need an explanation. That is, he will need a story. Like the audience for the biologist explaining molting glands in crabs, at the end of all the mathematics he will ask insistently *why*. In advanced seminars on economics "What is your story?" has become a technical phrase. It is an appeal for a lower level of abstraction, closer to the episodes of human life. It asks for more realism in a fictional sense, more illusion of direct experience. It asks to step closer to the nineteenth-century short story, with its powerful and non-ironic sense of Being There.

And of course even the most static and abstract argument in economics, refusing to become storylike and insisting on remaining poetic and metaphorical, is part of "that story of our own lives which we narrate to ourselves." A scholar has a story in which the work in question is an episode. This is why seminars in very abstract and metaphorical fields, such as mathematics and parts of economics, so often begin with "how I came to this subject." The fragment of autobiography gives meaning to it all. You will hear mathematicians complain if a seminar has not been "motivated." The motivation is a story, frequently a mythic history about this part of mathematics or about this speaker. The audience wishes to know why the argument might matter to the speaker and therefore to the audience itself. The story will then have a moral, as all good stories do. Listen, my children, and you shall hear / Of the marketing life of an auctioneer.

Economics-as-story provides a place to stand from which to look at the plots of economics. To repeat, the author must be a novelist or a poet, a user of either a story or a metaphor. But the reader, too, figures in economic thought. A useful distinction has been drawn by the literary critic Louise Rosenblatt (1978) between aesthetic and efferent reading. In efferent reading (from Latin *effero*, I carry off) the reader focuses on what she will carry off from the reading. Efferent reading is supposed to characterize model building and science. Model building and science is supposed to be useful for something outside itself. In aesthetic reading, by contrast, the reader focuses on her experience at the time of reading. The aesthetic is supposed to characterize storytelling and art.

Yet an aesthetic reading of a scientific text commonly clinches the argument. The feeling "Yes: this is right" in the last stanza of Yeats' poem "Among School Children" resembles the feeling that comes from the ancient proof that the square root of 2 cannot be expressed as the ratio of two whole numbers. Rosenblatt supposes that "To adopt an aesthetic stance . . . toward the directions for constructing a radio is possible, but would usually be very unrewarding" (34). Well, usually. Yet the computer repairman takes an aesthetic attitude toward the schematics for a Murrow computer: "A nice little machine," he says, and smiles, and is brought to this or that solution. The Nobelian physicist Steven Weinberg argues that aesthetic readings govern the spending of millions of dollars in research money (1983). His own theory, ugly before some new results arrived, came to be reckoned beautiful enough to test with $40 million (four times the National Science Foundation's budget for all of economics, by the way). The pleasure of the text is sometimes its meaning, even in science.

Rosenblatt anticipates such an argument, noting that theories of literature that do not stress the reader's role are left puzzled by pleasurable nonfiction, such as *The Decline and Fall of the Roman*

Empire or, one might add, the best applied economics, as that of Ronald Coase or A. C. Harberger. The reader's response gives a way of keeping track of the aesthetic readings when they matter. The naive theory of scientific reading asserts that they never do.

The telling of artful stories has its customs, and these too may be brought to economics. Take for instance the bare notion of genre, that is, of types of literary production, with their histories and their relations to each other. Poets have epic and lyric, pastoral and narrative. The scientific report is itself a genre, whose conventions have changed from time to time. Kepler wrote in an autobiographical style, spilling his laboratory notes with all their false trails onto the page; Galileo wrote urbane little dramas. It was Newton, in other ways also an unattractive man, who insisted on the cramping literary conventions of the Scientific Paper (Medawar 1964; Bazerman 1988). An economist should be aware that he adopts more than a "mere style" when he adopts the conventions of a genre.

Pure theory in economics is similar to the literary genre of the marvellous (following here Tzvetan Todorov's distinction between the "marvellous," where the laws of nature are plainly violated, and "fantasy"—what would be called "horror fiction"—where the reader hesitates between realism and the marvellous, uncertain and afraid [1977 (1971), 156; 1973/75 (1970), chap. 2]). Like the marvellous the genre of economic theory violates the rules of "reality" for the convenience of the tale, and amazing results become commonplaces in a world of hypothesis. That animals exhibit the foibles of human beings is no surprise to a reader brought into a world in which animals talk. "Romance" is the older word. One of the earliest among modern literary theorists, Clara Reeves, gave in 1785 a definition of romance (quoted in Scholes and Kellogg 1966, 7) which would suit the latest production in the *Journal of Economic Theory:* "The Romance in lofty and elevated language, describes what never happened nor is likely to happen."

No blame attaches. The task of pure theory in economics is to invent marvels that have a point, the way *Animal Farm* has a point.

The plots and characters of pure theory have the same relation to truth as those in *Gulliver's Travels* or *Midsummer Night's Dream*. Pure theory confronts reality by disputing whether this or that assumption drives the result, and whether the assumption is realistic. Economists have long quarreled over the realism of this or that assumption. The literary analogy puts the debate in a strange light. It is the talking animals or the flying carpets that makes *The Arabian Nights* "unrealistic?"

Economists would do well to know what genre they are reading or writing, to avoid misclassifying the marvellous. Speaking of pure theory as marvellous, I repeat, does not put it at a low value. *Gulliver's Travels* is marvellous, too, but pointed, instructive, useful marvels for all that. Knowing the genre, though, is necessary for the critic and helpful for the artist. Economic and other theorists usually know what genre they are writing. They show it in their little jokes, of "turnpikes" along the way to economic growth and "bliss" points when you get there.

Yet the marvellous and romantic can be given too free a rein. Auden noted that "What makes it difficult for a poet not to tell lies is that, in poetry, all facts and all beliefs cease to be true or false and become interesting possibilities" (quoted in Ruthven 1979, 175). Some fields of economics consist mainly of interesting possibilities. The hundredth possible world of international trade theory gives the impression of an allegorical poesy gone whacko.

Good empirical work in economics, as already noted, is like realist fiction. Unlike fantasy, it claims to follow all the rules of the world. (Well . . . all the *important* ones.) But of course it too is fictional. The applied economist can be viewed as a realistic novelist or a realistic playwright, a Thomas Hardy or a Henrik Ibsen. The analogy on its face seems apt. Economics is a sort of social history. For all the brave talk about being the physicists of the social sciences, economists do their best work when looking backwards, the way a paleobiologist or geologist or historian does.

A certain kind of empirical work in economics, to continue the analogy, is like horror fiction, Todorov's "fantasy." Unlike the marvellous, it follows all the rules of the world except one, catching the reader unaware. Dr. Frankenstein is a wholly believable and ordinary figure except for his ability to make humanoids. A policy experiment may be wholly believable except for its introduction of a radical new policy, the reduction of the income tax form to a single page, say, or the elimination of securities regulation.

But wait a minute. To all this the modernist schoolmasters so long in charge of our intellectual life would reply crossly that it is my analysis that is the fantasy and fiction. The proper scientist *finds* the story. No fiction about it.

The answer to such an assertion has long been understood. The storyteller cloaks himself in Truth—which is what annoyed Plato about alleged imitations of life in sculpture or poetry. Just "telling the story as it happened" evades the responsibility to examine the point of view. Realist fiction does this habitually—which shows another use for the literary analogy, to note that realist fiction in science can also evade declaring a point of view. The sociologist Michael Mulkay notes in the epistolary arguments of biologists a Rule 11: "Use the personal format of a letter. . . . but withdraw from the text yourself as often as possible so that the other party continually finds himself engaged in an unequal dialogue with the experiments, data, observations and facts" (1985, 66). The evasion is similar in history: "the plot of a historical narrative is always an embarrassment and has to be presented as 'found' in the events rather than put there by narrative techniques" (White 1973, 20).

The suppression of the "I" in scientific writing is more significant than one might think. In the modern novel the suppression of the authorial "I" has resulted in a technique peculiar to literature, "represented speech and thought." Grammarians call it "unheralded indirect speech," the French *style indirect libre*. Any page or two of Jane Austen serves: "Sir Walter had taken a very good house in Camdenplace, a lofty, dignified situation, such as becomes a man of consequence" (1965 [1818], 107, Sir Walter's words ["dignified

. . . a man of consequence"] in Austen's mouth); "Could Anne wonder that her father and sister were happy? She might not wonder, but she must sigh that her father should feel no degradation in his change" (108; Anne's words ["sigh . . . no degradation"] in Austen's mouth).

The parallel technique in science might be called "represented Reality" or "unheralded assertion" or *style indirect inévitable.*" The scientist says: It is not I the scientist who make these assertions but reality itself (Nature's words in the scientist's mouth). Scientists pretend that Nature speaks directly, thereby effacing the evidence that they the scientists are responsible for the assertions. It's just there. The result is similar in fiction: "We [as readers] cannot question the reliability of third-person narrators. . . . Any first-person narrative, on the other hand, may prove unreliable" (Martin 1986, 142). Thus Huck Finn, a narrator in the first person, misapprehends the Duke, and we the readers know he does. The scientist avoids being questioned for his reliability by disappearing into a third-person narrative of what really happened.

Yet, to say it once more, nothing is given to us by the world in story form already. The poet and critic J. V. Cunningham noted the limits of sheer observation: "it is not the direct observation of murders and of the process of detection that leads to the construction of a detective story. . . . What a writer finds in real life is to a large extent what his literary tradition enables him to see and to handle" (1976, 182). Or the critic Northrop Frye: "To bring anything really to life in literature we can't be lifelike: we have to be literature-like" (1964, 91).

We tell the stories just as we make the metaphors (and in truth, we decide on the logic and we construct the scientific facts, subject to the hints the world leaves in our path), as in the choice of continuity. John Keegan illustrates the general point in his military history, *The Face of Battle.* He speaks of the "rhetoric of battle history" (1978 [1976], 36) as demanding that one cavalry regiment be portrayed as "crashing" into another, a case of "shock" tactics. Yet an observant witness of such an encounter at Waterloo reported that "we fully expected to have seen a horrid crash—no such thing! Each [line of cavalry], as if by mutual consent, opened their files on coming near, and passed rapidly through each other" (149). Horses, it turns out, will not crash into each other, or into people, and so the usual story is falsified. A story is something told to one another by human beings according to human rhetorical conventions, not something existing ready-told in the very rocks or cavalry regiments or mute facts themselves.

Stories, in other words, are selective, the selection being done by their authors. In this they are similar to metaphors and models, which must select, too. We cannot portray anything literally completely, as Niels Bohr once illustrated to a class. He asked his students to *fully* describe a piece of chalk, to give every fact about it. The students found the task impossible. Description has to be radically selective. We cannot know the history of every atom in the chalk or the location of every atom that bears any relation to the atoms in the chalk. We decide what matters, for our purposes, not God's or Nature's.

The fictional writer selects like the scientist and invites the reader to fill in the blanks. Stories or articles can give only a sample of experience, because experience is overwhelmed with irrelevance: taking out the garbage, bumping the table, scratching the back of one's head, scanning the title of a book one was not looking for. What distinguishes the good storyteller or the good scientific thinker from the bad is a sense of pointedness. One damned thing after another is not a pointed story, or good science (cf. Bruner 1986).

The parsimony of scientific stories is not the result of some philosophy commending parsimony. It is a result of the way we read science, our ability to fill in the blanks, telling pointed stories in our culture. An economist can read the most unreadable and compressed production of a fellow economist if she participates in the same community of speech.

Wholly fictional stories are parsimonious in the same way. Skillful fiction, whether in the form of *Northanger Abbey* or *The*

Origin of Species, "stimulates us to supply what is not there," as Virginia Woolf remarked of Austen. "What she offers is, apparently, a trifle, yet is composed of something that expands in the reader's mind and endows with the most enduring form of life scenes which are outwardly trivial" (1953 [1925], 142). Remarking on her remark in turn, the critic Wolfgang Iser put it this way: "What is missing from the apparently trivial scenes, the gaps arising out of the dialogue—this is what stimulates the reader into filling the blanks with projections [the image is of the reader running a motion picture inside his head, which is of course why novels can still compete with television]. . . . The 'enduring form of life' which Virginia Woolf speaks of is not manifested on the printed page; it is a product arising out of the interaction between text and reader" (1980, 110–11).

As Arjo Klamer (1987a) has shown for the postulate of economic rationality, scientific persuasion, too, is like that. Persuasion of the most rigorous kind has blanks to be filled at every other step, whether it is about a difficult murder case, for example, or a difficult mathematical theorem. The same is true of those difficult pieces of recent economic history called economic policy. What is unsaid—but not unread—is more important to the text as perceived by the reader than what is there on the page. As Klamer puts it, "The student of the rhetoric of economics faces the challenge of speaking about the unspoken, filling in the 'missing text' in economic discourse" (175).

The running of different motion pictures in our heads is going to produce different texts as perceived. Todorov asks: "How do we explain this diversity [of literary readings]? By the fact that these accounts describe, not the universe of the book itself, but this universe as it is transformed by the psyche of each individual reader" (1980 [1975], 72). And elsewhere: "Only by subjecting the text to a particular type of reading do we construct, from our reading, an imaginary universe. Novels do not imitate reality; they create it" (67f.) Economic texts also are made in part by the reader. Obscure texts are often therefore influential. The crafty John Maynard

Keynes, for example, most influentially in *The General Theory of Employment, Interest and Money*, left many opportunities for readers to run their own internal motion pictures, filling in the blanks.

Well, so what? What is to be gained by thinking this way about economics? The big answer is the burden of the rest of the book: that by seeing their stories and metaphors together the economists and their audiences can resist the many charms of snake oil, and see that economists are wise, but not so smart. That is why an outsider to economic expertise might care that the experts kept their metaphors and stories lined up.

But consider one minor and internal answer: storytelling makes it clearer why economists disagree. Disagreement among scientists is suggestive for the rhetoric of science in the same way that simultaneous discovery is suggestive for its sociology.

The non-economist does not realize how much economists agree, back in the seminar room or the office. But he is not entirely wrong in thinking that they also disagree a good deal. Economists separate themselves into long-lasting schools, allegedly more typical of the humanities than the sciences (though any recent history of a science will give the lie to the journalistic assumption that science is agreement: such as Gould 1989, 19: "we [paleontologists] certainly do not agree about very much," a remark he documents in the rest of the book). A journalist will commonly end his television story about a new tax by complaining that the economists he has interviewed appear to disagree. He is not surprised that a story about a far-reaching change in economic policy evokes more disagreement than a story about a fire in the Holiday Inn. But if economics is a science, dammit, why can't economists agree?

One cause of disagreement is an oversimplified theory of reading. The theory of reading adopted officially by economists and other scientists is that scientific texts are transparent, a matter of "mere communication," "just style," simply "writing up" the "theoretical results" and "empirical findings." Communication is seen as the transmission of unaltered little messages through inter-mental pipes, in the manner of the hydraulic tube at the drive-in bank, or a sewer. The pipes occasionally get clogged up. That's a "communications problem." Then a Roto-Rooter of "let's be clear" reams out the pipes and lets the flow surge through.

If reading were so free from difficulties as this then naturally the only way our readers could fail to agree with us, after we have reamed out the pipes, would be on account of their dimness or their ill will. (Set aside the unlikely possibility that we the writers are the dim ones.) It's sitting right there in black and white. Don't be a dunce.

A better theory of reading sees scientific prose as being like liter-ary prose, complicated and allusive, drawing on a richer rhetoric than a narrow demonstration. The better theory is the one a good teacher uses with students. She knows well enough that the text is not transparent to the students, and she does not get angry when they misunderstand. God likewise does not get angry when his students misunderstand His text. In fact, like scientists and schol-ars, God writes difficult texts to ensnare us. St. Augustine, as the literary critic Gerald Bruns has noted, viewed the obscurity of the Bible as having "a pragmatic function in the art of winning over an alienated and even contemptuous audience" (1984, 157). The contrived obscurity is not nice but is not rare in science and re-ligion. Bruns quotes Augustine (who might as well be justifying the obscurities of a mathematical economist proving the obvious): "I do not doubt that this situation was provided by God to con-quer pride by work and to combat disdain in our minds, to which those things which are easily discovered seem frequently to be worthless" (157).

Even with a sophisticated theory of reading, though, the econo-mists would differ, because they come from different literary cultures. A scientist will come from a certain background, sup-plied with a language. Unless her reader knows roughly the same language—that is, unless he has been raised in approximately the same community as she has—he will misunderstand and will be unpersuaded. The misunderstanding is no more unforgivable than being non-French or non-Balinese. The reader comes from another culture, with a different tongue.

And even if the foreign culture is understood it may be rejected. A foolishly sentimental poem has the same irritating effect on a reader as does a foolishly libertarian piece of economics. The reader refuses to enter the author's imaginative world, or is unable to. A literary critic said, "A bad book, then, is a book in whose mock reader we discover a person we refuse to become, a mask we refuse to put on, a role we will not play" (Gibson 1980 [1950], 5). The reader therefore will of course misread the text, at least in the sense of violating the author's intentions. We do not submit to the authorial intentions of a badly done greeting card or of a scholarly argument written in a culture hostile to ours. In a well-written novel or a well-written scientific paper we agree to submit to the authorial intentions, so far as we can make them out. The entire game in a science such as biology or chemistry or economics is to evoke this submission by other scientists to authorial intentions. The general public submits in turn. The great chemist Linus Pauling for a long time commanded attention, and his readers submitted to his intentions, at least outside of vitamin C; the great economist Paul Samuelson likewise does so, at least outside of investment advice.

The argument can be pushed further. An economist expositing a result creates an "authorial audience" (an imagined group of readers who know this is fiction) and at the same time a "narrative audience" (an imagined group of readers who do not know it is fiction). As the critic Peter Rabinowitz explains (1980 [1968], 245), "the narrative audience of 'Goldilocks' believes in talking bears." The authorial audience realizes it is a fiction. The Roto-Rooter theory and the one-unified-culture theory cannot accommodate such an obvious point about real writing, that the authorial and narrative audiences (and authors) are different (compare Booth 1988, 105).

The difference between the two audiences created by the author seems less decisive in economic science than in explicit fiction, probably because we all know that bears do not talk but we do not all know that the notion of "marginal productivity" in economics is a metaphor. The narrative audience in science, as in "Goldilocks," is fooled by the fiction, which is as it should be. But in science the authorial audience is fooled, too (and so incidentally is part of the literal audience, the actual readers as against the ideal readers the author appears to want to have). Michael Mulkay, again, has shown how important is the inadvertent choice of authorial audience in the scholarly correspondence of biochemists. Biochemists, like other scientists and scholars, are largely unaware of their literary devices and become puzzled and angry when their literal audience refuses to believe in talking bears (1985, chap. 2). They think they are merely stating facts, not making audiences. Small wonder that scientists and scholars disagree, even when their rhetoric of "What the Facts Say" would appear to make disagreement impossible. Science requires more resources of the language than raw sense data and first-order predicate logic.

Taking economics as a kind of writing, then, explains some of the disagreements of economists and other academic folk. The explanation shows that the fact-logic half of the rhetorical tetrad does not suffice for human reasoning. Economists go on disagreeing after the "theoretical results and empirical findings" have been laid out for inspection not merely because they are differentiating their product or suffering from inflammation of the paradigm but because they read a story or a scientific paper written in an unfamiliar language ignorantly, yet do not recognize their ignorance. They are like the imperious British visitor to Florence who believes firmly that Italians really do understand English and can be made to admit it if one speaks slowly and loudly: WHERE . . . IS . . . YOUR . . . STORY??!

3   The Politics of Stories in
Historical Economics

*I*f economists told stories about the economy they would be historians. Well, they do and are. They are not social engineers, though they want to be. They are social philosophers and above all social historians. Much of what they do is history in another key.

Stories of British Failure

An accessible and important instance is the story of British economic "failure" after 1870. The debate has flipped and flopped since the 1920s between prosecutions and defenses of the Victorians. The sons of Victorian fathers, prominent among them John Maynard Keynes, attributed Britain's difficulties between the wars to Victorians long dead. Around 1940 the charge was stated at length by historians such as Duncan Burn. During the early 1960s the case for the prosecution, thrice told, was brought to a peak of eloquence by historians such as David Landes. In the late 1960s and 1970s, unexpectedly, the Victorians acquired defenders, mainly Americans trained in technical economics, including myself. Around 1980 the prosecution was renewed by a new group of historians and historical economists, among them William Lazonick and Martin Wiener. And by the late 1980s the defense too had been renewed. The cycle of revision makes the head ache, but no more so than fifty other long-running economic controversies.

Because British history guides other histories the choice of metaphors and story lines in British economic history has more than academic interest. The continuity or discontinuity of the British

industrial revolution still shapes our ideologies. The British en-
closure movement of the eighteenth century is still viewed as a
model or anti-model for land reform. The British experience with
imperialism in the nineteenth century is still taken as typical. And
the British experience of being first in manufacturing and then dis-
gracefully "failing" is still supposed to contain a moral for us all.
Britain was the first industrial nation, and the first to become mature—some would say, with charming ageism, senile. Britain's
past looks to many like the world's future. We are all British in the
end. And if capitalism works, as others would claim, it should certainly have worked in Britain, most of all in the grand old days of
laissez faire, in that late Victorian age.

The economists Bernard Elbaum and William Lazonick, who
are dubious about the health of advanced capitalism and are
among the recent critics of Victorian businesspeople, favor medical metaphors of what went wrong. They speak of an "affliction,"
the "British disease," and "diagnosis" (Elbaum and Lazonick
1986, 1). The historians David Landes and Martin Wiener, who
argue that the culture of a mature economy favors leisure over
work, prefer the more bourgeois metaphor of a race (Landes
1969; Wiener 1981). Their metaphors of "leadership" in the
"race" appear for example in Landes's chapter headings, "Closing
the Gap" and "Short Breath and Second Wind"—and a military
version in "Some Reasons Why," taken from a poem about a cavalry charge.

The story is stated in a few pages of Landes's classic work of
1965, containing a conference paper of 1954, reprinted and extended as a book in 1969, *The Unbound Prometheus: Technological Change and Industrial Development in Western Europe from
1750 to the Present*. The main question of the middle third of
Landes's book is, "why did industrial *leadership* pass in the closing decades of the nineteenth century from Britain to Germany?"
(1969, 326, italics added). His answer is in brief: "Thus the Britain of the late nineteenth century basked complacently in the
sunset of economic hegemony. . . . Now it was the turn of the third

generation, the children of affluence, tired of the tedium of trade and flushed with the bucolic aspirations of the country gentleman. . . . They worked at play and played at work" (336).

Landes notes that the way the European story is usually told justifies the talk of footraces and cavalry charges among iron-masters and insurance brokers, and of the sunset of economic hegemony. The balance of power in Europe since Peter the Great is supposed to have depended on industrial leadership. Waterloo and the Somme are supposed to have been decided on the assembly line and trading floor. The supposed link between the lead in war and the lead in the economy became a commonplace of political talk before World War I and has never since left the historical literature. To think otherwise, says Landes, is "naive" (327).

The link, it needs to be pointed out, is doubtful. After all, a large enough alliance of straggling, winded followers could have fielded more divisions in 1914. The case again of Soviet Russia in 1942 or North Vietnam in 1968 suggests that military power does not necessarily follow from economic power. Landes is speaking a truth but an irrelevancy true by definition when he quotes a forward-thinking Frenchman of 1788: "The people that last will be able to keep its forges going will perforce be the master; for it alone will have arms" (326). The remark is literally true—no forge, no bayonet. But it is true by chemistry and definition, in the way that H_2O is 2 of H and 1 of O, with no substitution allowed. It is not true by economic fact and military history. In an economy there are substitutes for blood and iron, even if there are not in chemistry. The French in fact imported iron from their chief enemy throughout the Napoleonic Wars.

The literal extinction of forges has seldom caused defeat, notwithstanding the hardy myth that blockades and strategic bombing win wars (Olson 1963). The Union sacrificed more men than the entire United States did in any other war to put down a rebellion by a less populous section that it outproduced in 1860 by 30 to 1 in firearms, 24 to 1 in locomotives, and 13 to 1 in pig iron (McPherson 1988, 318). In World War I the shovel and barbed wire, hardly the most advanced fruits of industry, locked the Western Front. Strategic bombing, using the most advanced techniques and the most elaborate factories, failed in World War II, failed in Korea, and was therefore tried again with great fanfare, to fail again, in Vietnam. The equation of military power with economic power is good newspaper copy but poor history.

What is most wrong about the metaphor of leadership in a race of industrial might, though, is that it assumes silently that first place among the many nations is vastly to be preferred to second, or twelfth. Leadership is number-one-ship. In the motto of the great football coach, Vince Lombardi: "Winning isn't the most important thing; it's the only thing."

Landes reports correctly that "within fifteen years [of cheering the Prussian victory over perfidious France in 1870] . . . the British awoke to the fact that the Industrial Revolution and different rates of population growth had raised Germany to Continental hegemony and left France far behind" (1969, 327). He is correct that in fact the British in the 1880s did fret about German "hegemony" and did speak of the necessity to "awaken." The British at the time certainly did believe the Lombardi motto, *numero uno* or nothing.

It is the usual panic of the intellectuals, the sort we are seeing now in the United States vis-à-vis Japan and Europe. The journalists and professors are enchanted by the image of foreign trade as a football game. Yet historians do better to resist the sporting and military metaphors they find in their sources. Landes here yields to the magic, asserting unconsciously the importance of coming first *and only first*. For example: "To be sure, it is easy to demonstrate the exaggeration of these alarms. Germany's gains still left her far *behind* Britain as a commercial power. . . ." (328, italics added). Landes was not thinking critically about his historical sources or his economic story. The metaphors of disease, defeat, and decline are too harshly fixated on Number One to be right for an economic tale. The Lombardi motto governs narrowly defined games well enough. Only one team wins the Super Bowl.

The fixation on Number One, though, forgets that in economic affairs being Number Two, or even Number Twelve, is very good indeed.

The sporting metaphor, in other words, is not a good theme for the story of the British economy in the late nineteenth century. Its forty-five million souls were not trying to score points on Germany or the United States. They were trying to earn a living and gain the pearly gates, on their own, making individual choices daily with no collective goal in mind. In the century after 1870 the residence of the souls in Britain—or, better, in a world economy integrated from the mid-nineteenth century on—gave them steadily expanding choice; and they had been relatively rich at the outset. The prize for second in the race of economic growth was not poverty. The prize was great enrichment, if rather less enrichment than certain other groups of people, mainly poorer people. Since 1870, in other words, Britain has grown pretty damned well, from a high base.

By contrast, the diseases of which the pessimists speak so colorfully are romantically fatal; the sporting or military defeats are horribly total; the declines from former greatness irrevocably huge. An historian can tell the recent story of the first industrial nation as a failure, and be right by comparison with a few countries and a few decades. The historian would sell plenty of books to Americans in the last years of the twentieth century, because Americans—or at least the Americans who write the newspaper articles and frame the trade policies—are experiencing a new anxiety about "loss of leadership."

On a wider, longer view, however, the metaphor of failure in a race is strikingly inapt. Before the British the Dutch were the "failure." The Dutch Republic has been "declining" practically since its birth. With what result? Disaster? Poverty? A "collapse" of the economy? Not at all. The Netherlands has ended small and weak, stripped of its empire, no longer a strutting power in world politics, a tiny linguistic island in a corner of Europe—yet fabulously rich, with among the highest incomes in the world (now as in the eighteenth century), a domestic product per head quadrupling since 1900, astoundingly successful by any standard but Lombardi's.

Though inapt, the pessimistic story is the dominant one. Failure to keep up in technological change, it is said, explains why British growth dropped after 1870, in comparison with its mid-century pace and in comparison with that of the new industrializing countries. The failure in turn is said to have caused British shares of world markets to fall. Martin Wiener's pessimistic storytelling, for instance, has Britain "surrendering a capacity for innovation and assertion" by 1901 (1981, 158). Such a remark jars in the alternative and optimistic story, which tells of a necessarily less bulky Britain engaging nonetheless in such innovation and assertion as radar, the Battle of Britain, jet engines, and the structure of deoxyribonucleic acid.

The way of telling stories, then, shape one's opinion about Victorian failure. The narrative circle—namely, that one needs the moral to tell the story, and yet the story makes the moral—is similar to the "hermeneutic circle" on the reader's side (that one needs to know the context to know the details, but the details to know the context). It is not breakable. The stories that Wiener or Landes or Lazonick or I want to tell about the Victorian economy will alter if not determine the stories we do tell, because on both sides the wished-for story will decide which of the infinity of facts are relevant. Elbaum and Lazonick want the story to be one of penalties incurred from an early start, as in a more sociological vein do Landes and Wiener. The story of the tortoise and the hare has lasting appeal.

The optimists like me want the story to be one of "normal" growth, in which "maturity" is reached earlier by Britain. The failures were by international standards small, say the optimists, even in the industries such as steel and chemicals in which Britain is supposed to have done especially badly. Everyone concedes that in shipbuilding, insurance, bicycles, and retailing, Britain did well. But whether it "did well" or not, its growth did not depend importantly on keeping right up with Number One. Britain in 1890 could have been expected to grow slower than the new industrial nations. The British part of the world got there first, and was therefore "overtaken" in rate of growth by others for a time. Belgium was another early industrial country and had a similar experience of relative decline, seldom noted. On the whole, with minor variations accounted for by minor national differences in attention to detail, the rich nations converge.

Nothing awful happens to Britain in this story, and no neurotic blame or xenophobic hysteria is in order. The falling British share of markets was no index of "failure," any more than a father would view his falling share of the poundage in the house relative to his growing children as a "failure." It was an index of maturity.

The main British story since the late nineteenth century is the more than trebling of British income as others achieved British standards of living or somewhat beyond. A 228 percent increase of production between 1900 and 1987 is more important than an 8 percent "failure" in the end to imitate German habits of attention to duty. Looked at from India, Britain is one of the developed nations. The tragedy of the century past is not the relatively minor jostling among the leaders in the front of industrial nations. It is the appalling distance between the leaders at the front and the followers at the rear.

The story can be told statistically, from the tables of the leading student of world growth and trade, Angus Maddison. He assembled recently the statistics of national output for thirty-one countries from 1900 to 1987. Expressed in the purchasing power of 1980, some of the countries are given in table 1.

To use the image of the racecourse, the whole field, followers as well as leaders, advanced notably—usually by factors of three or more since 1900 in real output per head. The main story is this general and surprising advance. The tripling and more of income per head relieved much misery and has given life-affording scope to many people otherwise submerged: think of your great-grandparents. Out of Maddison's thirty-one cases, Japan was a follower

Table 1   The Statistical Fate of Nations: Rich and Poor in 1900 and 1987
(in dollars of 1980 purchasing power)

Country	National Product per Head		Factor of Increase
	1900	1987	
	Rich Countries		
United Kingdom	$2,798	$9,178	3.2
Belgium	2,126	8,769	4.1
France	1,600	9,475	5.9
Germany	1,558	9,964	6.4
United States	2,911	13,550	4.6
	The Newly Rich		
Japan	677	9,756	14.4
	The Enrichening		
South Korea	549	4,143	7.5
USSR	797	5,948	7.5
	The Newly Poor		
Argentina	1,284	3,302	2.6
	The Poor		
India	378	662	1.8
Mexico	649	2,667	4.1

Source: Angus Maddison (1989, 19).

that became a leader, Argentina a leader that became a follower.
South Korea and Taiwan have exhibited such astonishing growth
recently (output per head growing by a factor of eight since 1950)
that they fit in a special class, on the Japanese model. Excluding
these four cases the race has been run as shown in table 2.

It was not until around 1980 that the followers finally reached
the post the leaders had passed eighty years before, for reasons
that economists still do not adequately understand (except to understand that the lag is not a matter of imperialist extortion). It
would seem that one quarter of the growth in the rich countries
from 1900 to the present might be assigned to special advantages

Table 2   Product per Head has Increased Everywhere Since 1900, Though
More Among the Rich than the Poor

	1900	1987	Factor of Increase 1900 to 1987
Leader Countries (15)	$1,893	$10,235	5.4
Follower Countries (13)	573	2,270	4.0
Factor of Difference at One Date	3.3	4.5	

Source: Maddison (1989).
Note: Leaders: Australia, Austria, Belgium, Canada, Denmark, Finland, France, Germany, Italy, [setting aside Japan], Netherlands, Norway, Sweden, Switzerland, United Kingdom, United States. Followers: Bangladesh, China, India, Indonesia, Pakistan, Philippines, [excepting South Korea and Taiwan], Thailand, [excepting Argentina], Brazil, Chile, Colombia, Mexico, Peru, USSR.

the rich countries earned or acquired. But three quarters of their growth (which is 4 times $1,893 divided by the end-state of $10,235 per head in the rich countries) is attributable to worldwide forces, forces powerful enough to overcome even the obstacles to growth in the average poor country.

In other words, the trouble with the pessimistic choice of story in the literature of British failure is that it describes the happy outcome of Britain's growth as a tragedy. Such talk is at best tasteless in a world of real tragedies—Argentina, for example, once rich, now subsidizing much and producing little; or India, trapped in poverty after much expert economic advice. At worst the pessimism about Britain is immoral self-involvement, nationalist guff accompanied by a military band playing "Land of Hope and Glory." The economists and historians appear to have mixed up the question of why Britain's income per head is now six times that of the Philippines and thirteen times that of India—many hundreds of percentage points of difference which powerful forces in sociology, politics, and culture must of course contribute to explaining—with the more delicate and much less important questions of why British income per head in 1987 was 3 percent less than the French or 5 percent more than the Belgian.

In the face of a world-girdling explosion of incomes the fixation on a trivial "lag" of Britain behind some of the other leaders demands itself a story. Probably the fixation arises from the pride of first place, à la Lombardi. Many in Britain bemoan the loss of Empire and delight in describing a powerful industrial nation of fifty-five million people as "a small island." The common man feels less important without an Empress of India at Buckingham Palace, and the intellectuals mope around the club regretting a lost vocation for instructing the natives. Many American leaders of opinion adopt the British despair and indulge in sage talk that "we must do better." Soon enough it will be stiff upper lips, old chaps, eh, what? In spoofing this lugubrious Anglo-Saxon attitude no one has improved upon Sellars and Yeatman, in their classic of sixty years ago, *1066 and All That*. Their précis of memorable English history from blue Celts and Boadicea to modern times ends abruptly on page 115, after the Great War—because then "America became Top Nation and history came to a. [full stop]"

Meta-stories

The conventions of storytelling have affected the literature of Victorian failure in another way. The stories have ideological significance. The meta-narratives of politics can remain tacit, as in Wiener's writing or my own, or can be declared openly. Elbaum and Lazonick are admirably open: "In historical perspective, however, state activism must be absolved from bearing primary responsibility for Britain's relatively poor economic performance" because, after all, the poor performance by their story dates far back into the age of laissez faire (1986, 11). They end their chapter by attacking the Thatcher government for its "supposition that there are forces latent in Britain's 'free market' economy that will return the nation to prosperity." They express confidence instead in "the economic benefits of industrial planning" (16).

And the story of the scholarly literature itself matters. To repeat: "Our lives are ceaselessly intertwined with narrative, with stories that we tell and hear told, . . . *all of which are reworked in that story of our own lives that we narrate to ourselves"* (Brooks 1985, 3). Control over the historiography is as important as control over the history itself. Economists and historians tell stories of their own scholarly lives and attempt to impose them on others (a brilliant recent development of the theme in technical economics is Weintraub 1991).

In the academic story about Victorian economic stories the ruling metaphor, as in other essentially contested areas of economics or history, has not been steady accumulation of knowledge but conflict. Elbaum and Lazonick begin their edited volume of 1986 with an account of the wicked neoclassical economists arrayed against the rest, and in particular against the brave Marxists. Thirteen years earlier McCloskey and Sandberg (1971) had done the same with a different set of heroes and villains. It is not hard to guess how the stories were framed in both cases: this essay, both said, is the culmination of the long struggle against Error.

The historical writer must place himself at the end of a story that makes dramatic sense. Thus another contributor to the debate over Victorian economic failure, Robert Allen, who follows McCloskey more closely than is profitable to say, devoted the opening pages of an otherwise technical article imitating McCloskey's work to an intellectual history putting distance between himself and McCloskey (Allen 1979). In mathematics such remarks are the motivation, the story of our own lives, how God led me, His prophet, into the light.

Since historians and economists are trained to be ignorant of their rhetoric they do not notice themselves making a story of their own lives. In particular they do not apply the same standards they would apply to the history itself. Economists are especially inept here, because they get no self-conscious training in the telling of plausible stories. Other scientists, believing themselves to be nonhistorical, share the ineptness. A chemist's understanding of even the recent history of chemistry will consist of whiggish just-so stories about true enlightenment dawning. It is not surprising to find that historical geologists and paleontologists and the historians

The literary critic Northrop Frye has written that literature "has somewhat the same relation to the studies built out of words, history, philosophy, the social sciences, law, and theology, that mathematics has to the physical sciences. . . . Pure mathematics enters into and gives form to the physical sciences, and . . . the myths and images of literature also enter into and give form to all the structures we build out of words" (1964, 127). Frye's stripping away of mathematics from the human sciences is two-culture talk and unnecessary. Economics is a human science and yet properly mathematical. But he is right about the other leg of the argument. Stories in economics take much from literature, broadly conceived, choosing continuity or discontinuity, delighting in the ironies of the tortoise and the hare, ranging intellectual armies against one another, telling a story of our own lives that makes us heroes in the end. Economists and other experts are going to resist historical fact and historical argument, unwisely, until they recognize that they themselves are historians, tellers of stories, in their economics and in their lives.

4   Economic Rhetoric in Aid
of the Story Line

*E*conomic stories depend on rhetoric. The point is not to expose the rhetoric and then condemn it for being rhetoric. Rhetoric is unavoidable. An economist or historian cannot avoid writing rhetorically since any argument has a rhetoric, a style of argument, taking "argument" to mean "any designs on the reader." A collection of random facts and assorted bits of logic does not add up to an argument; but as soon as a writer advocates a model or a story in which the facts and logic are to fit he has begun to argue. If one is to argue in favor of this or that story there is no way of being non-rhetorical. "Just give me the facts" is itself a rhetoric, Sergeant Friday arguing his case by claiming not to. Writing rhetorically is no more a crime than breathing rhythmically.

Matters of form, usually viewed as ornament, are commonly in fact matters of argument. Even in poetry, Paul Fussell notes, "The meter conducts the argument. The meter is the poem. The art of poetry is the art of knowing language and people equally well. It is an art whose focus is in two directions. . . . The knowledge of the way the reader will react when a technical something is done to him is what controls the poet's manipulation of his technique. To do something to the reader is the end of poetry" (1979, 104).

In explicitly historical work, of course, such as that on Victorian failure, much of the technical rhetoric is directed at the story, which carries much of the argument.

Ethos

Consider the first principle of rhetoric, that the presumed character of the writer affects how the words are read by an audience. The Greek word is *ethos*, which is to say, "habit," "character," "moral impression." Economic and historical writers lard their prose with ethical appeals. That is no surprise or scandal. We pay more attention to the President than to a congressional aide, more attention to the boss than to the assistant. A writer will of course present himself as worthy of scientific attention. Non-economists make ethical appeals in historical writing to the character of The Sophisticated Professional or The Historian. Everyone makes an appeal to ethos, if only an ethos of choosing never to stoop to such matters as ethos.

Some of the complexity in economics and therefore in historical economics amounts to the appeal, usually a risible one, to the ethos of The Scientist. Complicated machinery of intellect, *Dasein* or demography, fascinates everyone. Unhappily, obscurity in argument pays. A book by a French historian famous for his profound obscurity was recently translated into plain English. When thus made clear it turned out that his argument was simple, even a little simple-minded. The historian in his eminence was outraged by the lucidity of the translation. It did not capture, he complained, "*ma profondité.*"

An appeal to the character of The Profound Thinker is sweet indeed. The education of an economist drills into him the ethos of The Scientist Dealing With Super Profound Matters. The historical economist William Kennedy, for example, has argued in profound terms that in Victorian Britain engineering and other progressive sectors should have grown faster: "the conservatively estimated gains from such counterfactual sectoral shifts of economic activity . . . [are] on the order of 25 percent to 50 percent of British GNP in 1913" (1982, 105). Shuffling around could have increased the output of the British economy by a quarter to a half. That seems remarkable.

The remarkable conclusion comes from a profound calculation: "The aggregate average rate of growth may be defined as a weighted sum of the average rates of the component sectors of the economy [equations follow defining the rate of growth of a whole as the growth rate of its parts]. . . . It is possible to transform the accounting identity defined in equation (1) to allow ready consideration of counterfactual possibilities as follows" (equations follow showing what happens to the growth of the whole when the growth of one sector rises). He then calculates the "counterfactual" with much effort in four large tables to five digits of accuracy.

Kennedy's argument assumes its conclusion, more directly than is usual even in economics. The argument begins and ends this way: If certain production had grown faster *without other production growing slower,* then British production would have been larger. Startlingly, that is all the difficult-sounding machinery of "may be defined" and "transforming identities" and "counterfactual possibilities" amounts to. The economics is literally that if 2 + 3 = 5, then 5 will grow if 2 does. The economic idea of scarcity—that a growing 2 might have to take some labor or machinery from 3—does not appear in his economics. If a professor wrote more books *and did not teach fewer hours* his combined output would be larger. If you watched more television *and did not spend less time at other activities* your day would be longer.

The argument is a "counterfactual" in a somewhat special sense. It does not ask what might reasonably have happened if our world had been modified in small ways; it contemplates a world of free lunches, in which British engineering could grow faster without other sectors having to pay. If more production could come from nothing, then Britain could have been richer. Well, yes. But if 25 or 50 percent richer, why not 100 or 500 percent, or 10,000 percent? All we need to do is to imagine a "counterfactual possibility" (engineering growing at 300 percent a year, say) and then confuse ourselves and others impressed with *profondité* by putting the number into a sum of many terms transformed by arithmetic. Complicated arguments have this danger, that the complexity will conceal violations of good sense even from the framers. The point is a commonplace in scientific argument: "Mr. Brown's argument is so complex that it must be mere sand-in-the-eyes." Among economists for example the point has killed the large-scale statistical model, at least for scientific as against policy-making purposes. If one constructs a 500-equation model that cannot be reduced to simpler terms then one cannot hold any of its reasonings in mind. It ceases to be humanly persuasive. True, one can say, "Believe me: the model just works." The appeal persuaded economists twenty years ago. It no longer does (except again for certain tasks of prediction for policy). No one doubts a calculation on how to fly a spacecraft to Mars, despite its complexity, because we have great confidence in the law of gravity inside the calculations (though in fact perturbation theory in celestial mechanics has doubt-provoking complexities). But everyone doubts a blindingly complex calculation when the laws of motion are less well understood, as in economics.

Complexity has therefore also been used in the literature on Britain as the opposite of an authoritative ethos, as evidence of disauthority. This is the rhetorical plan in an essay by the historical economist Stephen Nicholas in 1982. Nicholas doubted the calculations of productivity made in the decade before that had restored Victorian businessmen to their reputation for competence. By the mere statement of the "assumptions" said to underlie the neoclassical calculation by the earlier economists he raises doubts in the minds of historians and economists. After a survey of the debate from Landes to 1982 in lucid prose, he starts off to "explain" the calculations to be criticized (86): "it is assumed [note the features of style borrowed from the language of mathematics] that the economic unit is a profit maximizer, subject to a linear homogeneous production function and operating in perfectly competitive product and factor markets. Given these limiting assumptions, the marginal productivity theory of distribution equates marginal products of factor rewards. It follows by Euler's theorem . . ." etc., etc.

To most of his readers in the *Economic History Review* he might as well have written "it is assumed that the *blub-blub* is a *blub* maximizer, *blub-blub blub-blub-blub* and *blub* in perfectly *blub* and *blub blub*. Given these limiting assumptions, the *blub blub blub blub blub blub*. It follows by *blub blub*. . . ." The audience that can understand the argument is the audience that already understands it. The people who do not understand it, who are most readers, get only the idea that "limiting assumptions" are involved (Nicholas makes a similar move in 1985, 577). The passage takes the outward form of an explanation. But the explanation merely terrifies the onlookers, as it intends to, convincing them that the neoclassical calculation makes a lot of strange and unconvincing assumptions. (Though not to the point here, it happens that the calculation does not make any of the assumptions he mentions; it is a measure; it makes no more assumptions than a bathroom scale.) Nicholas is taking on the ethos of the Profound Thinker defending the innocents from other Profound (But Irresponsible) Thinkers.

Pathos

Parallel to ethos, the audience's attention to the speaker, is *pathos*, the speaker's attention to the audience, the effort to make the audience weep and cheer. Pathos shapes the implied reader. Consider again Landes's essay of the 1960s, so plainly "using rhetoric" (though bear in mind that "using rhetoric" is not confined to the best writers, such as Landes; rhetoric is not merely elegance). The implied reader of Landes's essay is made into an ally. The reader is part of the "our" in "It is now time to pull the threads of *our* story together and ask *our*selves why the different nations of western Europe grew and changed as they did" (1969, 326; italics added). Landes sidles up to the reader. The particular appeal to pathos by the historian Landes contrasts sharply to that by the historical economists, such as Robert Fogel or Donald McCloskey, with their vulgar and lawyerly ways. The implied reader of these Perry Masons is either an imbecile who holds the views Fogel or Mc-Closkey are demolishing or else an enthusiastic ally joining them in sneering at the imbecile. Controversy in mathematics and in history is more often muted, even when its style is sharp and bright. Only a rare historian, such as J. H. Hexter, will shape the audience in the same aggressive way as do the historical economists, such as early Fogel or McCloskey. Landes's implied reader is made sweeter.

Style

Then style. A rhetoric of stories will watch the words closely. Watch, for instance, this: a text attempting to be authoritative uses the gnomic present, as in the sentence you are reading now, or in the English translation of the Bible, or repeatedly, again, in David Landes. Landes makes it a substitute for explicit social scientific theory, a function it serves in applied sociology and in much of the economic literature on growth, too. Thus in one paragraph on page 335 (italics added): "large-scale, mechanized manufacture *requires* not only machines and buildings . . . but . . . social capital. . . . These *are* costly, because the investment required *is* lumpy. . . . The return on such investment *is* often long deferred." The last two sentences of the paragraph, by contrast, revert to the ordinary narrative past: "the burden *has tended* to grow . . . *has become* a myth."

The gnomic present claims the authority of General Truth (which is another of its names in grammar). But it sidesteps whether the truth asserted is a historical fact (that in actual fact the return on "such investment" in 1900 was by some relevant standard long deferred) or a timeless scientific metaphor (that in economics of the sort we are talking about most such returns will be long deferred), or perhaps merely a logical tautology (that the very meaning of "social capital" is taken to be investment of a generally useful sort with long-deferred returns). The one meaning in the tetrad borrows prestige and persuasiveness from the other. The usage says: "I speak as a historian, telling you historical facts about Europe, this being one; but I am also a social scientist in command of the best modeling, of which I am giving you a fine example; and if you don't like that, consider that anyway my truth is logically true by definition."

The gnomic present bulks large in Landes's argument, which is again no scandal. Landes uses the device as a substitute for economic theory. He needs some device for economic storytelling, and the device of the gnomic present holds the story together as well as would explicit economic theory. Note the tense at page 336, for example, after some *aporia* (rhetorical doubt) concerning whether it is true or not, "Where, then, the gap between leader and follower *is* not too large to begin with . . . the advantage *lies* with the latecomer. And this *is* the more so because the effort of catching up *calls* forth entrepreneurial . . . responses." (italics added). That in general and as an economic law the advantage lies with the latecomer is offered as a deductive conclusion (no regular economic theory says so, but the gnomic present does). And in truth the conclusion does follow deductively from the earlier assertions, themselves expressed in the gnomic present (for instance, page 335, "There *are* thus two kinds of related costs."; italics added).

Statistics, too, contribute to a style supporting a story. The economists and the quantitative historians use a statistic as Proof, the appeals court in storytelling, just the facts, Ma'am. Landes and other non-economists tend by contrast to use the statistics essay-style, the way quotations are used. Frequent as the statistics are by the standards of other sorts of history, in Landes' writing they nonetheless do not carry much of the argument. This may be seen in the casual way that he accounts for them, drawing freely on such questionable sources as *Mulhall's Dictionary of Statistics* (4th ed., 1909), a book of impossible wonders in fact making.

By contrast, in the writing of most historical economists the statistics are deployed monographically, the thing to be established, the output of the argument, the way the story is told, as in my use of Maddison's statistics in the last chapter. The economist Lars

Sandberg did the accounting of ring spinning in the Victorian cotton industry (1974, chaps. 2 and 3); the economists Peter Lindert and Keith Trace did the accounting of the Solvay process in the Victorian chemical industry (1971); the economist Charles K. Harley did the accounting of early industrial growth (1982). Whether they did them right is not the point here. The point is that economists favor the figure of argument making-a-set-of-accounts. Accounting is in fact the master metaphor of economics, the source of most of its quantitative bite. The metaphor alarms non-economists, puzzled by the cavalier way in which bits of number from disparate sources are flung into the calculation.

Poetics: Metaphor in Aid of Stories

A weighty matter of rhetoric is the choice of metaphors with which to tell the story: by what allegory will the narrator shape the data? In the hardest as in the softest science the choice of a metaphor reflects a worldview and the evidence to be examined. Worldview succeeds worldview. The metaphor is the message. As Stephen Jay Gould recently put it in connection with the triumph of time's arrow over time's cycle in geological theory, "Hutton and Lyell . . . were motivated as much (or more) by . . . a vision about time, as by superior knowledge of the rocks in the fields. . . . Their visions stand prior— logically, psychologically, and in the ontogeny of their thoughts— to their attempts at empirical support"(1987, Preface).

The sources of the metaphors applied to Victorian failure are various. Physiocracy among non-economists (and in the British Labour Party) takes industrial production of physical things as a part standing for the whole of output, excluding especially the much despised production of services (or "the 'production' of services," as Martin Wiener says with sneering quotation marks (1981, 157). If Victorians did better selling insurance than selling steel, as they did, the insurance is reckoned a nullity. Similarly the new "McJobs" in American service industries, such as nursing and education, are reckoned as not being real jobs, like mining coal or spinning cotton.

The verbal accounting changes the history. The distinction popular among historians and other non-economists between quantity and quality of life, to give another instance, will leave the economist cold. Income captures it all. In the economist's accounting the time to smell the roses makes people happy and costs something in opportunities forgone and is therefore also income. If British (and Japanese and German) people worked less intensely than Americans in 1900, as Gregory Clark has shown (1984), then the British (and Japanese and Germans) consumed a commodity called leisure in greater amounts than Americans did. Clark worries that social pressure on the job to take advantage of every chance to loaf may have cost more in income than the average British worker was actually willing to pay. But anyway the Americans bought their larger product with greater effort.

Having admitted to using metaphors the scientist asks then about their aptness or rightness. The anti-rhetorical frame of mind will want instead to speak of their truth or accuracy, words which apply to metaphors only metaphorically if at all. Well, says the modernist, it's a matter of positive Fact, is it not? What's the *accurate* metaphor of British growth and decline? The philosopher Nelson Goodman answers in the following way. "For nonverbal versions [of the world, such as a picture of British defeat in economic battle] and even for verbal versions without statements, truth is irrelevant. . . . The same considerations count for pictures as for the concepts or predicates of a theory: their relevance and their revelations, their force and their fit—in sum their *rightness*" (1978, 19).

A metaphor used in an economic story is not "true" in a simple way. "France is hexagonal" is neither true nor false in the way a statement in arithmetic is true or false (Austin 1975 [1962], 143–45). It is right, in a certain way of speaking, which is to say, useful for some purpose (though come to think of it one could say the same thing about statements in arithmetic). The methodology of Science that economists and other scientists believe they use gives no way to evaluate the rightness of metaphors. The assertion of likeness, so important in biology and physics, involves standards of likeness that can only be human and cultural. How similar *is* the smooth pea to the wrinkled, the planetary orbit to an ellipse, Latin 101 to a hog pen? These are questions about our use of language, constrained by the universe sitting out there, to be sure, but matters of human decisions about human usefulness.

Not seeing one's own human metaphors in storytelling while sneering at those of others is funny, as in the more adolescent flourishes of the new historical economists. One of them began a paper in 1970 concerning "Britain's Loss from Foreign Industrialization" with a sneer at the very idea of metaphor: "It is pardonable to use an occasional metaphorical flourish to elevate the commonplaces and simplify the complexities of economic history. The danger, however, is that the flourish will become an obstruction rather than an aid to thought" (141). The notion is that metaphors are merely ornamental, or perhaps merely aids to the slow-witted. The author proceeds to other pieces of literary self-consciousness: "The difficulty is that these metaphors [namely, those used by the less technically up-to-date Duncan Burn, Phyllis Deane, and W. A. Cole] have attached to them no clear literal meaning, or at best none that does justice to their connotations" (141). And so forth throughout. It does not occur to him that all language—and certainly the elaborate language of supply and demand "curves" that he then deploys with much claiming of Scientific ethos—is irreducibly metaphorical. He later curls his lip in a dependent clause at the very idea, "*if* we must use metaphors" (McCloskey 1970, 152). Yes, my lad, we must. The critic and writer C. S. Lewis, followed by others, observed long ago that "the meaning in any given composition is in inverse ratio to the author's belief in his own literalness" (1962 [1939], 27).

Yet some metaphors are better, as we have seen. The students of metaphor are not saying that any version does as good a job as any other. The goodness of a metaphor, though, is not its merely propositional truth (whatever that might mean) but its aptness or rightness. Walt Rostow's famous metaphor of a "take-off" into self-sustained economic growth or Paul Samuelson's of consumers as calculating machines succeed or fail as ways of talking, our ways. The metaphor of leadership in economic growth, as was argued, fails because it veers off the subject, which is how well the economies do for their citizens, and directs attention to national vanity. The metaphor of winning replaces the metaphor of running well.

Inventio

Rhetoric concerns *inventio,* too, the finding of arguments. Rhetoric does not concern what one personally likes, in the way one likes chocolate ice cream. It concerns which arguments one is compelled by the conversation to take seriously. In the present case the main instance is: assessing British failure depends on taking comparison seriously. The assumption of failure involves comparisons left unmade. One cannot decide whether the British experience favors or disfavors capitalism by staring fixedly at Britain.

Historians such as Wiener (1981, 6–7) and Landes and economists such as McCloskey and Lazonick recognize the need to argue by comparison. If someone says that Britain failed compared to other countries he must have particular comparisons in mind. Landes and Wiener look to the German Empire; McCloskey and Lazonick to the United States.

Elbaum and Lazonick are only the latest Americans to emphasize that a notion of comparative failure must rest on comparisons across countries (1986, 2). Ironically, Elbaum and Lazonick themselves have been caught in their own failure to compare, by Gary Saxonhouse and Gavin Wright (1984, 1987; see Lazonick 1987; Elbaum and Lazonick 1986 does not mention the critics). Britain's "inflexible nineteenth century institutional legacy of atomistic economic organization" (Elbaum and Lazonick 1986, 15; compare p. 2) seems to have been as characteristic of Japanese cotton textiles as of British. But the Japanese cotton textile industry was flexible enough to seize the world market after 1918. Something has gone wrong with the notion that "atomistic economic organization" is to blame for British failure. What has gone wrong is ignoring the relevant device of rhetorical invention: comparison. Historians focused on Britain itself are liable to miss the rhetorical point, gathering elaborate evidence of failure that is not comparative and therefore unpersuasive. A paper by Donald Coleman and Christine MacLeod (1986) provides an instance of the historical side. They collect evidence about British events without looking outwards. Stephen Nicholas provides an instance on the economic side. Nicholas recalculates productivity by allowing for his guesses about monopoly and economies of scale, and finds the amended productivity growth small in Britain from 1870 to 1914 (1985, 580). Unfortunately it does not occur to him that the point is necessarily comparative, and so he does not then subject the American or German statistics to similar tortures. The mistake is embarrassing because America and Germany were growing much faster. The allowance for their economies of scale would therefore turn back to spoil his argument about Britain.

The historian will say, "Though I have not compared, I have collected facts." The master metaphor in history—surprisingly unimportant in economics—is A True Account of Events, Based on Primary Sources. The metaphor of "collecting facts from the archives" tends to crowd out more apt and more rhetorical descriptions of the historian's business (Megill and McCloskey 1987). No historian who has faced the archival opulence of the nineteenth century can claim that he writes down everything he finds in the archives. Similarly, no economist who has faced the theoretical opulence of twentieth century economics can claim that he merely follows the logic he finds on the blackboard. If the Facts and Logic were enough to settle the matter with ease then it would long since have been settled. That is to say, if the facts and logic were as simple to state and to interpret as the rhetoric of the disputants suggests, then only malice and passion could explain why the others do not agree with Me or Thee (and sometimes I wonder about Thee).

We cannot leave it at that. To do so leaves the question to be settled by irrelevancies—by one's political fancies, chiefly, un-argued in the style of a preference for chocolate ice cream; and personal favor when politics provides no guide. Half the rhetorical tetrad is not enough. In the debate on Victorian failure the levels of asserted "fact" from most global to most individual are:

Capitalism is terrible.

Britain failed in the age of capitalism.

British ironmasters failed from 1870 to 1914.

Profitable opportunities X, Y, and Z in iron were ignored.

Such-and-such a measure of profit in X, Y, and Z is less than another.

British businessmen had thus-and-such mental or emotional deficiencies.

None strictly implies the other. Yet they are properly connected in rhetoric, it being more plausible that entrepreneurs in iron and steel failed if they appear to have ignored profitable opportunities. The rhetoric needs to be made explicit.

Consider for example the rhetoric surrounding the proposition at the fourth level down, that profitable opportunities were ig-nored. The optimists wish to connect it with the next lower proposition, that such-and-such a profit falls short of some other. The main criticisms of this optimist move have been that (1) it "uses neoclassical theory" (Coleman and MacLeod 1986, 598; Nicholas 1982, 85), and (2) that the measures refer to the "short run."

Neither is correct. The history here has gotten tangled up in a battle about the status of economic theory. The black beast of neo-classical theory is actually a small and closed set of mathematical economists. They do indeed "assume" strange behavior and then proceed to strange conclusions. But working economists do not "assume" all manner of perfection in people and markets, the "possession of the requisite information on costs and markets, knowledge of the available techniques" (as Coleman and Mac-Leod put it, 598). The factual inquiry aims precisely to test how good this or that "assumption" is (cf. McCloskey 1973, chaps. 1 and 2). To understand what the historical economists are doing one must abandon the Euclidean image of axiom and proof. Serious economists do not assume a can opener. They feel around in the historical drawer until they find it.

To mention a couple of cases important in Victorian Britain, the calculations of the profitability of East Midlands iron ore, say, and of the Solvay process in chemicals are merely second guesses. That is, the historian, not the historical actor, brings the "requisite information on cost and markets" to the calculation. The calculation sees whether or not the businessmen in question knew roughly what they were doing. The so-called neoclassical assumption in the simplest calculation says merely that businessmen wish to pay no more than what a thing is worth and are forced by competition to pay no less, within rough bounds. And more commonly the economists do not assume it even in this innocuous form; they test it.

If from the second guessing the businessmen prove to have been reasonably sensible in their choices then one concludes—not assumes—that they knew what they were doing (or else that they did not know what they were doing but were lucky, which appears to have been the case of American mechanical engineers in the nineteenth century: their traditions of hard driving suited the accidents of technical development). The calculation emphatically does not assume that they knew what they were doing—to make such an assumption would hardly be productive, since it is the question at issue.

The rhetoric of economics and of history, in short, goes beyond mere "style" in the ornamental sense of the word favored since the seventeenth century. It embodies how historians and economists argue. Calling the choices of metaphor, story line, and the like "mere style" is like calling the mathematics in physics or economics "mere formalism." Usually it is not. It makes the argument, which is all we have down here below the circle of the moon.

5   The Scholar's Story

*A*n example of economic storytelling is the work of Alexander Gerschenkron (1904–76), an unusual economist and historian exhibiting the tension between the two ways of telling stories. Born in Russia, educated in Austria, for long a professor of economics at Harvard, Distinguished Fellow of the American Economic Association and honored by his peers in other ways, he combined the humanistic learning of the German-speaking *Gymnasium* with the quantitative enthusiasms of American social science in the 1950s. He wrote on the mathematical theory of index numbers and on the literary theory of translation; with equal passion he read Greek poetry and listened to the Boston Celtics.

A person's life is an argument, though often unintended—we think less of Marx for his neglect of Jenny and his ignorance of physical work; and we think less of the modernist heroes of economics now for their frank appeals to selfishness, exhibited in their lives. Gerschenkron shaped much of his life to better values. Although addicted to a sly and not always amusing gamesmanship in his dealings with students and colleagues, he stood the bigger tests. In the year of tested values, 1968, for example, this private man spoke publicly against nihilism at Harvard, and when later the Soviet tanks rolled into Prague he spoke against international participation in a conference at Leningrad. Neither cause was successful: Harvard acceded to nihilism and the International Economic History Association met in Leningrad. Yet Gerschenkron persisted in persuasion.

His main scientific contribution was a "theory of relative back-wardness" (collected in Gerschenkron 1962d), which gave an account of the differing ways that European countries industrial-ized. He argued that a country like Russia, backward relative to Britain when it embarked on industrialization, did not go through the same stages. It leapt over them, using the centralized state as a substitute for the missing prerequisites of economic growth. Growth was force-fed in Russia, and to a lesser extent in Germany, with consequences for the character of the places. Russia grew with giant enterprises instead of small firms, centralized control instead of competitive markets, an overbearing military-industrial complex instead of peace-loving capitalists.

The first point in a rhetorical criticism of the story is that Gerschenkron attempts, like any scholar, to make us look at the story through a particular grid. We cannot look at Gerschenkron's theory innocently, as a thing in itself. We place a grid over it, our own or his, measuring it along the lattices of the grid.

The usual grid is a folk philosophy of science. Historians and especially economists share a grid framed by modernism, with its forlorn ambition to predict and control. Gerschenkron might be said in this lingo to have offered a "hypothesis," itself properly part of a "hypothetico-deductive system," which can be "falsified" by "empirical testing" against "observable implications."

His own words sometimes echoed these popular misunder-standings of scientific method, telling a modernist story of his scholarly career. Thus near the beginning of "Economic Back-wardness in Historical Perspective" (1952, at age 48 [reprinted in 1962d, 6, to which reference is made here], italics added): "histor-ical research consists essentially in application to *empirical material* of various *sets of empirically derived hypothetical gener-alizations* and in *testing the closeness of the resulting fit,* in the hope that in this way certain *uniformities,* certain typical situa-tions, and certain *typical relationships among individual factors* in these situations can be ascertained." And elsewhere he would say repeatedly that the concept of relative backwardness ("concept" and "process" were favorite placeholders in Gerschenkron's prose) is "an operationally usable concept" (1962c [1962d, 354]). The words did not in Gerschenkron's practice carry the freight they usually do in economics. They did not impel him, for example, to throw away evidence on the grounds of alleged epistemological infirmity (he used both statistics and novels as sources for economic history; he used the absence of accounting terms in the Russian language of the eighteenth century to indicate the absence of commercial attitudes (1968, 449; 1970, 81). Though he detested the ruthless politics of the professorial chair that so shamed the scholarship of Europe, he did not pretend that he had no political arguments to make.

Above all, the vocabulary of social Science in the 1950s did not in the end ensnare Gerschenkron in social engineering. He rejected the notion that society was predictable. Social engineering requires prediction in detail. Gerschenkron looked to the past for wisdom, the delphic warnings that the past can give. He did not look to it for a blueprint of the future. Prediction and control, the promise of modernism, seemed to him narrow and impractical.

During the 1950s Gerschenkron outgrew a narrowing method, as many have. The great German classicist, Ulrich von Wilamowitz-Moellendorff, wrote of his own fascination with method:

Philology had [in 1870] the highest opinion of itself, because it taught method, and was the only perfect way of teaching it. Method, *via ac ratio*, was the watchword. It seemed the magic art, which opened all closed doors; it was all important, knowledge was a secondary consideration. . . . Gradually the unity of science [i.e. *Wissenschaft* = inquiry] has dawned on me. . . . Let each do what he can, . . . and not despise what he himself cannot do. (1930 [1928], 115)

The grid of folk philosophy and its Methods attributes a magic art to science.

The folk philosophy is not entirely useless. Its demarcations go some way towards classifying scholarship: scientific/non-scientific, objective/subjective, positive/normative, observable/non-observable, justification/discovery. But they do not go very far.

They cannot show science on the ground and at the bench, and they make a poor start at telling a scholar's story. An observer of science using them cannot see for instance why scientists disagree, since every scientist claims stoutly to operate on the good side of each demarcation—scientific, objective, positive, observable, and justificatory. The grid therefore worsens disagreements. It leaves the scientist to conclude that a disagreement must signal incompetence, some "unscientific" deviation in the opposition, which leaves him permanently angry at the incompetence of his colleagues. The grid of folk philosophy is itself unscientific, a bad description, and a bad moral theory of scholarship, with bad outcomes.

More often Gerschenkron himself invited the use of another grid, the practical philosophy of the scholar, an older scholarly ethic than the modernism of the mid-twentieth century. He held an elaborate and attractive theory of scholarship, exhibiting Continental values. The life's story represented in his work was that of The Scholar, an Immanuel Kant or a Jacob Grimm pondering over books by the late night's lamp. In a way that contrasts with British and some American traditions he practiced, as he affirmed often, "a program of research," less a method than a plan of life. His range as a scholar—at ease with mathematics, history, statistics, and a dozen languages—was subordinated to the program. The program was to yield not sharp or mechanical "tests of the theory," in modernist style, suitable to prediction and control, but mature judgments. The judgments would satisfy, as he frequently put it, "a sense of reasoned adequacy."

The phrase is not without mystery, but he did not intend the reasoning to be kept mysterious. The modernist asserts without looking at the history of science that only her method, *via ac ratio,* yields clear and distinct ideas. But the range of the *ratio* is too narrow, though clear and distinct within it. It resembles the method of the drunk who looks for his keys under the lamppost because the light is better there. The extreme explicitness of modernist reasoning under the lamppost is accompanied by extreme vagueness outside its range. Gerschenkron admitted all parts of the rhetorical tetrad.

Some matters of scholarship would need to remain tacit, but Gerschenkron had no patience with the unfootnoted *argumentum ex cathedra*, even from eminent scholars. Repeatedly he advocated and exhibited explicitness in argument. For instance, in his review in 1953 of Franco Venturi's *Il Populismo russo* (1968, 455), though congratulating Venturi for a "mature understanding," he complains that "one cannot but wish that the author had decided to share his thinking more fully with his readers." In a similar vein he warmly praised his student Albert Fishlow for "the statistical appendixes in which the author offers a full insight into his laboratory and without which no real appreciation of the importance of the study and of the validity of its interpretative results is possible" (1965, viii).

The scholarly ethos of care is prominently commended in Gerschenkron's reviews and in his footnote polemics. Carefulness in the European scholarly tradition has two parts, avoidance of error in detail and modesty in the putting forward of conclusions. We stop believing someone who makes little errors ("Bad spelling, bad reasoning") or who draws conclusions hastily ("How can he say such a thing?"). Gerschenkron here does not inhabit the world of modern economics, in which theory is said to provide a check on facts and in which a blackboard exercise is said to have "policy implications." Most particularly he detested theories of history that could in their rigidity supply bridges across evidential voids— Marxism most notably—and favored theories such as Arnold Toynbee's pattern of challenge and response that provided merely a way to shape the facts into a story. In this he was a modern professional historian, whose discipline is not economic or historical theory but the shaping of stories constrained by fact.

But neither the folk's philosophy of science nor the scholar's credo of virtue is much of a grid for measuring Gerschenkron. A better grid is rhetoric. A successful scholar and scientist above all engages in argument, and Gerschenkron lived a life of argument.

Gerschenkron's style of writing was the most obviously "rhe-

plaining *for us.*" In the sentence leading up to the assertion of how things are (as distinct from how they seem) he insists on the shaping eye of the observer, who "sees" a "pattern," a morphology "temporarily seen." And the paragraph following returns to how we *see* the matter: "The more backward a country, the more barren *appears* its pre-industrial landscape. . . . This then is . . . my *picture* of European industrialization" (104; italics added).

Gerschenkron drew also on the doctrines of British empiricism to attack other theories, but again with Kantian supplementation. The trouble with stage theories, he says, is that "they are not very consistent with crude empiricism, and are damaged seriously when confronted with the relevant facts as we know them" (101). He appeals here to what "we," the scientific community, know; and the vocabulary of "consistent with . . . empiricism" and "confronted with the relevant facts," as fragments of modernist dogma. Yet he attaches "not very" to "consistent" and "crude" to "empiricism," distancing himself from a modernism that would forget Kant. Gerschenkron was of course an empirical worker, as any applied economist or historian must be, but a sophisticated one, who understood that scientists do not merely tally up the world's noumena.

Gerschenkron's theory, then, is by his own description "a way of looking" at the world. The metaphor of "substitution" is useful because it is "a construct that . . . helps to *conceive* Europe as a graduated unit" (108; italics added). Note that the virtue claimed is conversational. Talking this way will be helpful to the historical conversation. He speaks frequently of the theory as a classification or typology, by which he means the classification of botanical species (96), with Russia the red butterfly at one end and Britain the blue one at the other. He is hostile to mathematical or logical metaphors to describe growth. Rostow's and other theories of prerequisites are described as "beautiful exercises in logic" (101; cf. 100, middle) which "have been defeated by history."

Gerschenkron's hypothesis about European industrialization is best described by dropping the language of "hypothesis" and using instead that of storytelling. The Bulgarian experience, for example, "rejects" the hypothesis, because Bulgaria's rate of industrial growth "was obviously far below what one should expect in view of the country's degree of backwardness" (126; cf. 1962d, 232). He notes that Bulgaria frittered away its governmental entrepreneurship on military adventures. In the "failures" of the story one's attention is drawn to illuminating facts. In the peroration of *Europe in the Russian Mirror* he specifically rejects the language of hypothesis testing even while using it:

For in trying to set up interpretative models [*read "stories"*] historians do not deal in universal propositions which can never be verified and can only be refuted [*a direct attack on modernist dogma*]. We deal in particular or existential propositions. It is the very nature of an historical hypothesis [*back to modernism: read "plot"*] to constitute a set of expectations which yields enlightenment . . . within a spatially and temporally limited zone. To determine the delimitations of that zone does not mean at all a refutation of a hypothesis [*if "hypothesis" is not understood in its modernist sense*], but on the contrary its reinforcement as a tool of historical understanding. (1970, 130)

The last sentence makes no sense if relative backwardness is a "hypothesis" like the inverse square law. If planets were attracted to each other inversely in proportion to the *cube* of the distance between them, that would be that. There would be no sense in which such a contrary finding "would not necessarily detract from my approach" (130). Relative backwardness, however, is not a scientific hypothesis in the folk philosopher's sense, but a device for telling a story, like the notion of the frontier in American history or the notion of the bourgeois revolutions of the late eighteenth century or the notion of progress in biological evolution or the notion of wrinkling through cooling in the geology of mountains. Relative backwardness can be proven wrong (as the scientific notions just mentioned mainly have been) if it violates the sense of reasoned adequacy.

By now I do not have to argue in detail that storytelling is not unscientific. Plate tectonics is a story, not a universal hypothesis like the inverse square law or the Schrödinger equation. Better yet, and more conformable with Gerschenkron's delight in botanical analogies, the theory of evolution is a story. Determining the delimitations of evolution does not mean at all "refuting the hypothesis." Anti-evolutionists think they refute evolution by taking seriously the falsificationist claims of folk philosophy. Scientists who mix amateur philosophy of science with incompetent anthropology of religion can expect no mercy from the Arkansas legislature. Not admitting that science itself uses techniques of storytelling is a strategic mistake. As a "hypothesis" (*Oxford English Dictionary*, 1933, definition 3) evolution is a failure because it is in modernist terms "meaningless." But by the standard of reasoned adequacy it is of course a spectacular and continuing success.

The difference between a modernist "hypothesis" and this way of telling a story has been discussed by Gerschenkron's colleague and friend, Albert Hirschman, without reference to Gerschenkron though in a similar spirit. Hirschman, another product of an elite Continental education, for long a professor at the Institute for Advanced Study at Princeton and an economic advisor to the democracies of Latin America, is even more explicit than Gerschenkron was about the literary character of social thinking. He has brought a self-conscious use of language to economics. An essay of 1970 entitled "The Search for Paradigms as a Hindrance to Understanding"—the title captures what irritated Gerschenkron about Marx and Rostow—complained that solely metaphorical thinking has made "Latin American societies seem somehow less complex and their 'laws of movement' more intelligible, their medium-term future more predictable," than societies north of the border (1979 [1970], 170f)]. He commended instead a storytelling mode:

This view of large-scale social change as a unique, nonrepeatable, and *ex ante* highly improbable complex of events is obviously damaging to the aspirations of anyone who would explain and predict these events through "laws of change." . . . There is no denying that such "laws" or paradigms can have considerable utility. They are . . . indispensable devices for achieving a beginning of understanding after the event has happened. That is much, but that is all. The architect of social change can never have a reliable blueprint. Not only is each house he builds different from any other that was built before, but it also necessarily uses new construction materials and even experiments with untested principles of stress and structure. (179)

The story in other words is a form of knowledge no less dignified for science than is the metaphor. Projecting metaphors into the future without the discipline of storytelling is dangerous. As Gerschenkron said, the beautiful exercises in logic are often enough defeated by history.

A rhetorical reading of Gerschenkron does not reveal him as a non-scientist, a mere word spinner. He shaped in his work a story of his own life, one of care and precision and attention to the words themselves. Master scientists are master rhetoricians, word spinners in no dishonorable sense, or else they do not win the argument. Gerschenkron's science was model building but also storytelling, using all of the rhetorical tetrad. And so in this instance again: Science is rhetoric, all the way down.

6   Metaphor Against the Story: Chaos and Counterfactuals

*B*ut all is not well. Some stories are good, some bad, as an adult needs hardly to be told. Their goodness or badness can be tested against the other parts of the rhetorical tetrad, against the facts, the logics, and the metaphors.

Facts of course constrain a story. The fish in the fisherman's story was either a lake bass or a sunfish, and that's that. The empiricist tradition since Bacon has put great emphasis on facts testing stories. No one could object, though it would be miraculous if there was anything new to say about the empiricist tradition. What is valuable in the tradition can be preserved to do its good work even if one thinks that scientific argument involves more still. The philosophically inclined need not at this point commence kicking stones and pounding tables to show that facts are facts and therefore all we need. Thinking of science as also involving stories and metaphors does not require skepticism about facts. The facts are there, killing the story or giving it life.

The story is made by people, the facts are made by God; but of course we need both to make sense. It is like fishing. We humans make the lures to catch the fish in the lake, but the fish are there by God's command, "really" there. We can believe trustingly that the fish are there even when our backs are turned, yet still admit that the design of the lures is a human job. Or we can believe skeptically that the fish are after all themselves fish by human construction (is a guppy a fish?), yet admit that the world's best lure trailed through a lake without something we call fish would not catch any. So facts criticize stories.

Logic, too, criticizes stories, of course. The rationalist tradition since Descartes has put great emphasis on the internal consistency of stories. Again no one objects. The exact meaning of "logical" constraints on stories is elusive, though perhaps the rule that two contradictory events cannot take place simultaneously is an example, equivalent to A and not-A being mutually exclusive; or perhaps the sequence of time should be put down as logic, in which the future cannot affect the past.

The other criticism of stories, and the point here, arises from the last of the tetrad, metaphors. The criticism goes both ways. Metaphors criticize stories and stories criticize metaphors. A metaphor of modern economic growth—as an airplane taking off, for example—can conflict with a story—of varied saving rates in the "great spurt," for example, depending on the previous history of backwardness. The conflict between a metaphor and a story about the economy fits under the rhetorical theory of commonplaces. Commonplaces are the arguments ready to hand about which we converse in science and ordinary life. The psychologist Michael Billig gives in this connection the example of proverbs, "Many hands make light work" as against "Too many cooks spoil the soup" (1989, 298). The two contradict each other. Is it light work or too many cooks? The ordinary deliberations of life, and of science, are like this, and the contradictions are nothing pathological. The fruitful contradiction among figures of speech is itself a commonplace of argument.

Metaphors sometimes contradict stories, and sometimes not so fruitfully. Sharon Kingsland writes about the history of population biology that "the use of models to construct plausible scenarios . . . is in its ahistorical character opposed to the way of thinking familiar to most ecologists. The difficulty of trying to reconcile these two ways of thinking has been the source of much controversy" (1985, 5). We talk about the causes of events, such as the Great Depression or the American Civil War. Economists will talk in metaphors; historians will talk in stories. But the two speak against one another. The very idea of cause in a story can be left in doubt.

A recent book by the economist and historian Robert Fogel, *Without Consent or Contract: The Rise and Fall of American Slavery* (1989), argues that there was nothing inevitable about Lincoln's election and the resulting secession. Like many historians before him he emphasizes the precarious balance of American politics in the 1850s, which could have been turned one way or the other by minor events. In the late 1850s:

The Republican party was not wrecked by the panic of 1857 and by 1860 it had lured most of the former Know-Nothings into its ranks. However, neither outcome was inevitable. . . . It is doubtful that party leaders could have continued to suppress the nativist impulses of so many of its members if immigration had returned to the 1854 rate. . . . If the party would have conceded these demands, some of the Germans and the more conservative Whigs would have been alienated. Only relatively small defections were needed to deny power to the anti-slavery coalition in 1860. (385–86)

And during the fateful month of May 1856 in bloody Kansas:

However, a sheriff who had proprietory interests in a rival town not far from Lawrence, and who was an impulsive extremist, took unauthorized command of the posse. The mob that he led burned the hotel that served as the headquarters for the New England Emigrant Aid Society. . . . Two days later, in retaliation for the "sack of Lawrence," John Brown and his sons killed "five helpless and unprepared pro-slavery settlers." . . . As the posse moved toward Lawrence, Senator Charles Sumner (R, MA) delivered a searing indictment . . . of leading Democratic members of the Senate, including Stephen A. Douglas (D, IL) and Andrew P. Butler (D, SC). Butler was absent from the chamber during Sumner's speech but Preston S. Brooks, a relative and a member of the House from South Carolina, brooded over the insults to his aged kinsmen and to his state. . . . Brooks entered the Senate chamber after it adjourned on May 22 and delivered a series of blows to Sumner's head and shoulders with his cane. (379)

Fogel identifies other turning points, too. He is trying to show that the end of slavery was by no means determined by massive and unstoppable forces, such as its alleged unprofitability or its alleged inconsistency with industry. "The overarching role of contingent circumstances in [the] ultimate victory [of the antislavery movement] needs to be emphasized. There never was a moment between 1854 and 1860 in which the triumph of the antislavery coalition was assured" (322).

James McPherson's recent history of the same era provides military examples. "The third critical point came in the summer and fall of 1863 when Gettysburg, Vicksburg, and Chattanooga turned the tide toward ultimate northern victory" (1988, 858). Vicksburg was settled by many things—one is put in mind of the much-abused term "over-determination"—but among them was a disagreement before the siege between the Confederate generals Joe Johnston and John C. Pemberton.

Johnston urged Pemberton to unite his troops with Johnston's 6,000 survivors north of Jackson [Mississippi], where with expected reinforcements they would be strong enough to attack Grant. . . . Pemberton disagreed. He had orders to hold Vicksburg and he intended to do so. . . . Before the two southern generals could agree on a plan, the Yankees made the matter moot by slicing up Pemberton's mobile force on May 16 at Champion's Hill. (630)

At Gettysburg one of numerous turning points was the desperate defense of Little Round Top on July 2 by Colonel Joshua L. Chamberlain of the 20th Maine. Chamberlain (who not incidentally was in civilian life a professor of rhetoric) ordered his men, ammunition exhausted, to attack with bayonets the massing Confederates down the hill. "The two Round Tops dominated the south end of Cemetery Ridge. If the rebels had gotten artillery up there, they could have enfiladed the Union left. . . . Shocked by the audacity of this bayonet assault, the Alabamians surrendered by scores to the jubilant boys from Maine" (659).

In the conclusion to his book McPherson writes, "Northern victory and southern defeat in the war cannot be understood apart from the contingency that hung over every campaign, every battle, every election, every decision during the war. This phenomenon of contingency can best be presented in a narrative format" (858). Precisely. Fogel and McPherson are telling the usual story: For want of a nail, the shoe was lost; for want of a shoe, the horse was lost; . . . for want of the battle, the kingdom was lost, and all for the want of a horseshoe nail.

Little events can have big consequences in some parts of the history. The parts are described by models that are nonlinear in the events and whose consequences feed on themselves. That is, a little event put into one of the equations yields a large consequence, which is then fed back as input. "Nothing succeeds like success" is such a model, and certainly applies to the decade 1856–65 in the United States.

The point is not that great oaks from little acorns grow. They do, as did Christianity and the Industrial Revolution, and the right acorn is impossible to see before the event. Any one of numberless acorns may be chosen by chance. Chance of this conventional sort is similarly difficult to narrate. But at least after the acorn is chosen it grows smoothly from acorn to sprout to sapling to tree, shaped by the great forces of its environment. The point here is rather that in some modeled worlds an acorn produces by itself a great tree in an instant. Such a world is instable. The models need not be complicated. As students of "chaos theory" have pointed out, simple models can generate astonishingly complicated patterns in which the slightest perturbation can yield an entirely different history. Confederate success depended on recognition by Great Britain, which depended on . . . Confederate success. It depended on human wills at Lawrence, Kansas or Little Round Top.

What of it? The problem is that in such a world the idea of story-telling is cast into doubt. In the opinion of two careful students, American history 1856–65 was in such a precarious state that even small events could have a big effect. The rogue sheriff and the bold professor of rhetoric "changed history," as we say. But in that case *any* of an unbounded set of little people and little events could be brought into the story. Unknown to history, a certain John Jones in Kansas, who alone had the moral authority to stop the sheriff, failed to arrive in the posse (he had a cold and was in bed). Likewise unknown to history, a political general named Robert Smith in 1861 had assigned Chamberlain to the 20th Maine quite by accident—Chamberlain should have been put in the 21st, not the 20th, but it was late at night when Smith did the job, and the orders had to go out by the next morning, leaving no time to check them.

In some counterfactual world the Civil War and its outcome might have been governed by big, simple, linear metaphors—slavery might have been steadily less profitable despite southern sentiments, the North might have been destined to win despite southern generalship. The success of Christianity, likewise, depended on the Roman Empire, and the Industrial Revolution on the freedoms of northwestern Europe. But if, as Fogel and McPherson and many historians before them have persuasively argued, the correct models for 1856–65 are models of nonlinear feedback then the story becomes unmanageable, untellable. It is a paradox.

The paradoxes that can arise from a story linked with a metaphor become most evident in the notion of a "counterfactual." Counterfactuals are the what-ifs, the thought experiments, the alternatives to actual history. They imagine what would have happened to any army, family, or economy if, contrary to fact, something in the army, family, or economy had changed. What if Representative Preston Brooks in 1856 had kept his temper and stayed his cane? What if Chamberlain in 1863 had not charged from Little Round Top? If Cleopatra's nose had been a half inch longer would the battle of Actium have been fought? If railroads had not been invented would American national income have grown much slower than it did?

The philosophical (and grammatical) literature speaks of counterfactuals as "contrary-to-fact conditionals." The notion has been used most self-consciously in historical economics. For example: "If railroads had not been invented the national income of the United States would have been at most a few percentage points lower." But counterfactuals are implied in many other parts of economics, such as macroeconomics: "If a rule of money growth at 2 percent a year were adopted then the rate of inflation would fall"; or industrial organization: "If the instant camera industry had 100 manufacturers then it would be a competitive industry."

The rhetorical problem that counterfactuals raise, and part of the reason they have attracted the attention of philosophers, can be seen in the last example. You want to compare the present monopoly of instant cameras—Kodak lost a suit some time ago about its patents on instant cameras and Polaroid since then has made and sold them all—with (nearly) perfect competition. You might want to do so in order to measure the cost of monopoly and to advise a judge in court. You want to know what is the significance of the monopoly, and such knowledge requires a counterfactual.

Now of course if somehow the instant camera industry were to have 100 sellers then each seller would be small relative to the whole demand or supply. Speaking technically, the elasticity of the demand curves facing any one seller would be on the order of 100 times the elasticity of total demand. Such calculations are the heart of applied economics. If the cigarette tax were raised what would happen to the price of cigarettes? If the money supply were increased what would happen to the general level of prices? If foreign doctors could practice freely in the United States what would happen to the cost of American medical care?

Such questions involve looking into a world having, say, an instant camera industry with 100 sellers rather than one. Such a world would not be ours. How then is the counterfactual to be imagined? By what allegory combining metaphor and story? And do the metaphor and story coexist with ease?

The rhetorical problems which can afflict counterfactuals are two: vagueness and absurdity. The vagueness arises when the metaphor used to extrapolate into the not-world is vague. The metaphor is the model. The not-world could arrive at 100 companies selling instant cameras in many different ways. For example, one could imagine getting 100 Polaroid companies by fragmenting edict now, in the style of the breakup of American Telephone and Telegraph Company. The advantages of greater competition would have to be set against the disadvantages. A breakup now would change the patent law in the future, since no one would expect the breakup of Polaroid to be the last breakup. A patent law that did not allow Polaroid to take advantage of its past cleverness in tying up the technology would change the economy for good or ill. A world in which patents were granted and then abrogated is different from the present world. To imagine it one needs a non-vague model of what would happen to inventive activity.

Alternatively one might imagine subsidies in the 1940s that would have resulted originally in 100 alternative technologies for instant cameras (in fact only two were ever developed commercially, Polaroid's and then Kodak's). Such a counterfactual would have its own costs, again by changing the expectations of inventors. A counterfactual requires a metaphor broad enough to extrapolate confidently into the not-world.

Vagueness, in other words, is solved by explicitness in metaphors. Once made explicit the metaphors can be tested for their aptness. Since the 1960s historical economists have made extensive use of such extrapolations into the not-world, riding a model out into the darkness (McClelland 1975). In the most famous use of counterfactuals that same Robert Fogel (1964) calculated what the transport system of the United States in 1890 would have looked like without the railroads. He argued that evaluating the "indispensability" of the iron horse entailed calculating what American life would have been like without it. Some historians balked at the counterfactual saying that it was "'as if' history, quasi-history, fictitious history—that is not really history at all . . . , a figment" (Redlich 1970 [1968], 95f). But economists find the notion natural, and philosophers accept it as routine.

The philosophers note that all of the following are nearly equivalent (see Goodman 1965, 44):

SCIENTIFIC LAW: *All inflations arise from monetary growth.*

CAUSAL ASSERTION: *Money growth alone causes inflation.*

FACTUAL CONDITIONAL: *Since inflation has changed, money growth has changed.*

DISPOSITIONAL STATEMENT: *Inflation is controllable with money growth.*

PARALLEL WORLDS: *In a world identical to ours (or sufficiently similar) except that money growth differed, inflation would be different.*

COUNTERFACTUAL: *If money growth were to be held at zero, then inflation would be zero as well.*

The philosophy of counterfactuals revolves around the translation of one of these into another. Non-philosophers seldom recognize that the translations are possible. Historians for example flee in terror from the counterfactual, as contrary to the rhetoric of Fact in their discipline, and cling stoutly to their causal statements. Economists have the opposite philosophical neurosis, clinging to counterfactuals—in their rhetoric, Theory, the metaphors that nourish economics—and fleeing causal statements, which they regard, strangely, as unscientific. Both believe that the thing itself can be avoided by avoiding its name.

Fogel's calculation stirred great controversy, but was robust to criticism (1979). He was interested in long-term growth, and therefore did not posit a sudden closure of the railroads in 1890. A sudden closure would clearly have driven national income down sharply. (Mental experiments of the sudden-closure type are what lie behind claims that railroads or airlines or agriculture or garbage collection are "essential.") Fogel imagined instead what the American economy would have looked like without access to railroads right from the beginning, forced from the 1830s onward to rely on substitutes like roads or canals, or manage with less transport. Such an economy would have made better roads and would have dug more canals. It would have located production and consumption closer together and both closer to natural waterways. It would have had a larger St. Louis and a smaller Denver.

Fogel did not specify every feature of the "true" counterfactual world. He did not for example suppose that the internal combustion engine would have been perfected earlier, as it probably would have in a railroadless world. He was trying to show that the railroad was not so important, and therefore biased the case against himself, allowing the counterfactual world to adjust only in a few ways: for example, Denver in his world is no smaller. The result was a calculable *upper bound* on the value of railroads—an upper bound because had the world been allowed to adjust as it actually would have, the hurt from not letting it have the railroad would have been smaller. The upper bound was in 1890 about 5 percent of national income, only two years of economic growth. The greatest invention of the nineteenth century accounted for only a small part of economic growth, at most.

Fogel was merely applying in a bold way the usual method of economics. The usual method is the poetics of economics, imagining an explicit economic model, M, with parameters, P, and initial conditions or outside variables, I, and the resulting values of the outcomes, R. The counterfactual then imagines a change in some element of the model. The simplest is a variation in I, where I might be a tax rate in a model of cigarette consumption or the number of firms in a naive model of instant camera pricing. Fogel removed from the initial conditions one of the technologies of transportation. In similar fashion a 500-equation model of the American economy allows economists to look into alternative worlds. What would happen to American prosperity if the price of oil rose? What would be the effect on the poor of a lower tax on capital gains? (The main test of Fogel's work was in fact a multi-equation model of the Midwest and West in the late nineteenth century constructed by Jeffrey Williamson [1974].)

The counterfactual is the first of two officially scientific ways that economists explore the world (a third, controlled experiment, is uncommon). The second is curve fitting, the comparative method, comparing differing true stories as they exist in the world. It asks how *in fact* the results have varied in response to differing initial conditions. The counterfactual, or simulation with a metaphor, asks how the results *would* vary. The counterfactual is in the conditional mood ("If the demand for transport in Illinois in the 1850s can be represented by a curve . . . "). The curve fitting is in the indicative ("Once upon a time there were Illinois counties that had the railroad and others that did not"). The counterfactual infers R from data on P and from reflection on M and I. The curve fitting infers parameters P from data on initial conditions I and results R and from reflection on the model M.

But in solving the vagueness of a counterfactual by positing an explicit, metaphorical model the economist runs against the other rhetorical problem with counterfactuals: absurdity in the storytelling.

Consider again the counterfactual of a 100-firm industry selling instant cameras. In fact the implied story may violate the very model being used. The problem is that the initial conditions that would lead to a 100-firm industry may be absurd. The counterfactual assertion "If the instant camera industry were perfectly competitive then the price would be lower than it is now" sounds routine. But it can have the character of the proverbial absurdity "If my grandmother had wheels she'd be a tram." The metaphor or model may be true—wheeled grandmothers may indeed be trams—but the counterfactuals may be impossible. The counterfactual may contradict the very model used; or it may contradict some wider model of how things work. Such as: grandmothers do not develop wheels; 100-firm industries do not invent and produce instant cameras.

It is possible to argue on such grounds that *all* counterfactuals are absurd. One might argue, as did Leibnitz, that a world that did not invent the railroad would strictly speaking have to be a world different from our own world right back to the Big Bang. Such a world might be one in which seas were boiling hot or pigs had wings, with different problems of transportation. The wider theory violated by any counterfactual is that the world hangs tightly together. As John Stuart Mill remarked in attacking counterfactual comparisons of free trade and protection, "Two nations which agreed in everything except their commercial policy would agree also in that" (1872, 572).

The Norwegian political scientist Jon Elster, in a penetrating discussion of the role of counterfactuals in economic argument (1978), posed the Basic Paradox of Counterfactuals. The less vague the theory, the more likely is a counterfactual using the theory to become absurd. If Fogel had developed a theory of invention to draw a less vague picture of road transport he would have faced the problem that the very theory would have predicted the invention of railroad. It had better. Railroads, after all, *were* invented. As Elster put it, "If he attempted to strengthen his conclusion . . . he would be sawing off the branch he is sitting on. In this kind of exercise it is often the case that more is less and that ignorance is strength" (206). The counterfactual must be, as Elster says, "capable of insertion into the real past." That is, the model must fit the story. But the more explicit the metaphor the more difficult it is to insert into the actual story of the past.

A mix of metaphor and story is an allegory, a narrative of "one coherent set of circumstances which signify a second order of correlated meanings" (Abrams 1981, 6). *The Pilgrim's Progress* is based on correlated metaphors such as a voyage to the Heavenly City = spiritual progress; and Christian = all men who would be saved. Yet it is not a merely timeless model but a story, too, in which Christian attains the City and loses his burden of sin. Any rich account of a real economy is going to be allegorical, requiring its stories and metaphors to coexist. The point is that they coexist uneasily.

Metaphor and story are not merely alternate ways of explaining; in a conversation of allegory, in which both must function, they can contradict each other. As the critic Northrop Frye noted in this connection, the symbol in modern literature, such as Melville's white whale or Samuelson's utility function, is a metaphor that stops short of full (naive) allegory. The symbol "is in a paradoxical and ironic relation to both narrative and meaning [to storytelling and metaphor making, in other words]. As a unit of meaning [that is, as a metaphor], it arrests the narrative; as a unit of narrative, it perplexes the meaning" (1957, 92).

The Basic Paradox illuminates a long controversy in economics about the simplicity of models. One group of economists favors simple models because they are more understandable; another group favors complex models because they are more complete. Both may be wrong. A simpler model is harder to believe in counterfactual experiments because it is not rich. But because it is not rich it is more likely to be insertable into the past—that is, it is less likely to result in absurd contradictions of what we already know in a storytelling way (that railroads were in fact invented, for example). By contrast, a 500-equation model of the American economy will more tightly constrain the story into which it is inserted than the 10-equation model. The selection of stories and metaphors is subject, like most things, to scarcity.

Synchronic, metaphoric models, if pushed, produce history contrary to fact; diachronic narratives, if pushed, contradict synchronic models we all know to be true. That is the nub of the issue. When a metaphor is used too boldly in telling a history it becomes ensnared in logical contradictions, such as those surrounding counterfactuals. If a model of an economy imagines what would have happened without the industrial revolution, then the contradiction is that an economy of the British sort did in fact experience an industrial revolution. Oh, oh. A world in which the Britain of 1780 did not yield up an industrial revolution would have been a different one before 1780, too. The model wants to imagine a different future without imagining a different past. It wants to eat the cake and have the ingredients, too. It contradicts the actual story of how Britain came to 1780 and beyond.

Likewise, when a mere story attempts to predict something by extrapolation into the future it contradicts some persuasive model. The story of business cycles can organize the past, but it contradicts itself when offered as a prediction of the future. All manner of stage theories of business cycles have this difficulty. If the stories of past business cycles could predict the future there would be no surprises, and by that fact no business cycles. Any model of business cycles must talk of people predicting badly: of bankers thinking that the boom is going to continue one month longer than it does, of auto makers investing in a big, new plant just before their sales drop. But if business cycles are unpredictable to the actors they are unpredictable to the drama critics, too. The extrapolated story contradicts a model.

Whatever difficulties a story faces in the light of a model, or a model in light of a story, economists use both. Like other human beings they use the phrases "just like this" and "once upon a time" routinely for their work. Economists are concerned both to explain and to understand. (They are concerned also, of course, to confront and to deduce: they use facts and logic, too.) Economists, that is, are allegorists. They have the same problem as the religious allegorists, such as John Bunyan the Puritan. If Christian in *The Pilgrim's Progress* is a model of fallible humanity then the ending is not credible, since no such man would obtain salvation. But if the story holds then the metaphor is wrong. Only a miracle of grace can save a sinner, and save the allegory of *The Pilgrim's Progress.* Only a miracle of intellectual compromise can fit the static model of maximization into the story of capitalist success.

Stories criticize metaphors and metaphors criticize stories. A story told through a nonlinear metaphor will break down into absurd detail. A counterfactual metaphor carried too far will absurdly violate the story of the past. But these are not knockdown arguments, merely doubts that the allegory of self-interest in economics can always bring its metaphor and its stories together. We make the stories and metaphors and are therefore unable to appeal to God's certainty in judging which one is best or how they should be combined. We must talk about them, trying one against the other in human conversation.

7 The Poetics and Economics of Magic

hen the metaphors do battle with the story, the result is nonsense, nonsense that can hurt when people believe it. People do. People especially believe in allegories, such as the combined metaphors and stories of economics, because an allegory in its completeness protects the illusion of prediction and control. The chemistry of snake oil is allegorical.

Around 1600 in England it was reported that "among the common people he is not adjudged any scholar at all, unless he can tell men's horoscopes, cast out devils, or hath some skill in soothsaying" (Thomas 1971, 227). Nowadays the press and public commonly treat the economist as a soothsayer (albeit a dubious one), to the point of believing that economics aims mainly at forecasting. The economist sometimes obliges, bemused by the physics-as-philosophy promise of prediction and control.

But the forecasting of human events—which is *not* the main activity of economics—has always been magical. In human affairs there is prediction but no profitable prediction, and therefore no perfectly reliable control. "The unscrawled fores the future casts," sings Wallace Stevens of impending death, is "damned hoobla-hoobla-hoobla-how" ("Notes Towards a Supreme Fiction: It Must Be Abstract, II," in Stevens 1972; Stevens, who read Latin well, puns the nonce-plural of fore-, as in *fore*casting, with Latin *fore* = *futurus esse* = "to be about to be," from which "the about-to-bes" = the future; and perhaps also Latin *fores* = the double doors in the poet's bedroom through which the moonlight scrawls. Harold Bloom draws out the erotic reference in the deliberate variation of hoobla-*how*—that is, *how* can a man of 63 bring back the life of Venus's dove, hoobla-hooing in the day?—but does not comment on the magic [Bloom 1976, 180–82]).

Forecasting the future seems at first more scientific and grown-up than the mere casting of spells, which commands carpets to fly or Daddy to drop dead. But forecasting the future and manipulating it are identically magical. The desire to forecast the future and the desire to change it are two sides of the same desire. The one forecasts the future from the flights of birds or the entrails of chickens, and is armed by the forecast to prevent evil. The other, less prestigious, knows already the future evil and arms itself with magic spells and amulets to prevent it.

It is superstitious to think that profitable forecasts about human action are easily obtainable. That is why economics, contrary to the common sneer, is not mere magic and hoobla-hoo. Economics itself says that forecasts, like many other desirable things, are scarce. It cannot be easy to know which great empire will fall or when the market will turn. "Doctor Friedman, what's going to happen to interest rates next year?" Hoobla-hoo. Some economists allow themselves to be paid cash to answer such questions, but they know they can't. Their very science says so.

The subject, then, is the economics of magic—not sleight of hand but real magic. Real magic claims to have solved scarcity. It leaps over the constraints of the world. If you desire a ride to Baghdad, here is a magic carpet; if you desire your enemy dead, here is a magic doll; if you desire unlimited riches, here is a forecast of interest rates. As the expressive jargon of economics puts it, magic leaps outside our "production possibilities." The "fiat" in a spell is the desire to get outside what is ordinarily possible. The magic of course begins with desire. Stevens again:

> But the priest desires. The philosopher desires.
> And not to have is the beginning of desire.
> To have what is not is its ancient cycle.

It is desire at the end of winter, when
It observes the effortless weather turning blue.

("Notes: Abstract, II")

Stevens points to the desire motivating both childish magic and adult arts and sciences, a desire which notes the "effortless" turning of seasons, and dreams therefore of similar power for itself, "pure power," the achieving without effort. An economist would call the desire a "utility function" or, less fancily, "tastes." People have a taste for going to Baghdad free of charge or have a taste for avoiding the bad luck from breaking a mirror (the term is "apotropaic" magic, averting magic). Fear of the future motivates economic advising. The hiring of economists by politicians and businesspeople otherwise hardnosed is apotropaic.

The grown-up way to satisfy the desire to avoid evil or achieve riches is to work within the world's limitations and satisfy it. Robinson Crusoe did not spend time casting spells (though he mourned a while), but stripped the wreck and built a stockade, reinventing the arts and sciences and retraining his desires. Children desire that avoiding evil or achieving riches were not so hard, a desire that is father to the thought. Children think that if they wish hard enough it will be so: "Let Daddy *die*." In his old classic on the sociology of magic, Marcel Mauss noted that "between a wish and its fulfillment there is, in magic, no gap" (1972 [1902–3], 63). A small child believes in the omnipotence of thought, as Freud put it, because he has not yet distinguished his private dreams from the collective dreams we name reality. Adults who cannot make such distinctions are said to be mentally ill.

In *Ancient Egyptian Magic* Bob Brier describes the pharaoh before a sea battle sinking toy models of enemy ships in his bathtub (1980, 51). Real magic, as distinct from the parlor trick, depends often on such a metonymy, taking a thing associated with X as *being* X. It re-presents what the magician wishes to happen. Actually, the pharaoh reminds an economist of advisors representing an economy with a model, then sinking the deficit in the bathtub.

An important magical power of words is naming. Metonymic ("other-name") magic, like the pharaoh's toy boats or the voodoo priest's dolls, reduces the thing to an object, or more conveniently to a word, and then works. Knowing the name of the man to be cursed puts him in the magician's power. "The deep tradition of efficacious words" in poetry and magic, notes the critic Hugh Kenner, "stems from an authority of naming" (1987, 16–17). Joyce's *Dubliners* was unprintable not because it used the word "bloody" but because it named actual pubs in the town, the names "frozen in the eerie finality of type," and doubly dangerous (28). Giving each American soldier a nameplate has a deeper purpose than providing introductions for the lonely crowd. In Vietnam one night a young white lieutenant faced alone a room of black enlisted men, properly nameplated, like him. Noticing that he had no business there, he edged towards the door. One of the nameplated soldiers blocked the way: "You're in trouble sir." The lieutenant gathered his nerve, braced, flipped his lapel to show his own plate, and snarled as he pushed out the door, "You remember my name, son, because I'm sure as hell going to remember yours." The nameplate worked its magic.

The power of naming illustrates the drift of the signifier towards the signified. We symbol-using animals like to name things. After a while we get to thinking that having their names is as good as having the things themselves. British people learn to name the flora of their pleasant land down to each wild flower on the verge, giving them a mastery foreign to Americans. The Russian poet and critic Andrey Bely wrote that "The process of naming . . . is a process of invocation. Every word is a charm. By charming a given phenomenon I am in essence subjugating it. . . . For living speech itself is unbroken magic. . . . The word ignites the gloom surrounding me with the light of victory" (1985 [1909], 94f.).

But the victories through words and names, of course, are cheap. This is the economic problem with magic. If mere saying is enough and if the saying is not somehow restricted, then evil eyes proliferate. Thomas M. Greene, a professor of English and comparative literature at Yale, a student of Renaissance literature (and not entirely incidentally a passionate baseball fan), has articulated recently a theory of poetry which has parallels to economics (1989). The difficulty for the symbol-using animal is to use symbols without the "pressure of desire," Greene says, which allows the symbols to become a riot of magical, desire-granting charms. Bloom quotes Santayana, an influence on Wallace Stevens in "Notes towards a Supreme Fiction," to similar effect. Santayana defines poetry as being "religion [read magic] without practical efficacy and without metaphysical illusions" (Bloom 1976, 175). Or still better, poetry says so: it is, as Greene argues, perfectly aware that the age of miracles is past.

Economics also says that desires cannot be granted easily and that magic is without practical efficacy. A functionalist and sociological argument would be that a society filled with evil eyes could not function, and therefore would not exist. Magic-haunted societies in fact are often paralyzed by conflict, as Salem, Massachusetts was in the 1690s, which played with magic under children's rules. A society that is going to come to terms with the reality principle must somehow limit the omnipotence of thought.

More economistically one could argue that people will not put a high value on what is cheap. Magic must be more expensive than merely snapping one's fingers or else it will not be accounted powerful. To deal with uncertainty we need magic, and especially we need it when poor. The winners of the state lottery are mostly poor and naive. Again the magic cannot be too cheap. A valuable magical spell is believed, and therefore one way to get it believed is to make it expensive, boldly asserting its value. ESSL Corp (P. O. Box 66054, Los Angeles, CA 90066) sells the most expensive of six programs available from various companies to guess the next numbers of the lottery. The program sells not for its cost of production (a few dollars) or for its value in use (nothing) but for the persuasively substantial price of $59.95. Psychoanalysts require that the patient pay a lot, because otherwise the therapy will not work. The patient has to make a sacrifice to get well.

In other words—and this is the essential point—magic has to be expensive. The economic idea is called "rent-seeking." Magic promises something for nothing. It is like the government and like working for the government. We clever moderns know that magic does not work. If magic is to survive (this is a third functionalist argument) it must be made expensive or else people would complain that they snapped their fingers but still got sick. The rhetoric of magic demands that the magic be difficult to perform or else its failure to work will be too evident. Magic promises profit, the same way an economic forecast does. Therefore the business of magic will attract entry, at length driving down its profit. The argument is biological: ecological niches do not lie around unexploited. At length the costs of making the last bit of magic will equal its value in free rides to Baghdad or in daddies conveniently disposed of.

The character of magic fits the argument. The standard theory, that magic is the primitive man's science, is useful but not nuanced (although see Maddison 1982, chap. 3). As Keith Thomas remarks, the theory "does not of course make clear why magical rituals should take one form rather than another" (1971, 648). By contrast:

Magic is often practical. It is businesslike, not therapeutic or ornamental: it expects to work. It is therefore humorless. The rhetorical form is that of a speech in court, with exordium, narratio, refutatio, and conviction. By contrast, nothing follows immediately from a religious ceremony or a poetry reading or a proper economic analysis. People just go home. "It is small wonder that the sorcerer's claim to produce practical results should have so often proved more attractive than stern clerical insistence that all must be left to God's inscrutable mercies" (264). From a witch's sabbath all manner of evil follows at once.

Magic is often arrogant. No business here of "Thy will be done." The god or spirit is to leap to it and is to be punished if he does not. The fiat in a spell does not pray to God; it summons the powers. "Deer's Cry" (St. Patrick, attributed, c. A.D. 440) proceeds for some fifty lines of praise for God, looking like a hymn—a lyrical assertion of a faith suitably humble—revealing its magic only by repetition. But abruptly it gets to the magical point, proclaiming, "I *summon* to-day all these *powers*" (italics added), and then lists them in detail (among them the important powers "against spells of women and smiths and wizards").

Magic is often secret. Mauss argues that "religious rites are performed openly, in full public view, [but] magical rites are carried out in secret. . . . And even if the magician has to work in public he makes an attempt to dissemble, . . . [to] hide behind simulated or real ecstasies" (1972 [1902–3], 23). One can doubt Mauss's assurance that magical and religious ceremony are sharply different, yet agree that secrecy is common for the magical type. The secrecy makes for scarcity, no less than a secret recipe for baking bread or a secret method for casting iron thin enough for pots.

Magic is often exclusive. "Nobody can become a magician at will; there are qualities which distinguish a magician from the layman" (27). Again the economics works to raise the price. The list of candidates for magical powers must be restricted to make it expensive. As Socrates says in his elitist way, "not everyone is an artisan of names, but only he who keeps in view the name which belongs by nature to each particular thing" (Plato, *Cratylus* 390E). The expert can see into the mind of God, being "a master of name giving" (389D). The candidate for magician must be unusual in some way. Smiths, barbers, shepherds, foreigners, infidels, primitives, and other special, lonely people can become magicians (Mauss 1972 [1902–3], 28ff.), meaning that one man's tribe is another's league of sorcerers. The Jews were thus steadily suspect of magic, and the Lapps could sell bags of wind to European sailors (32). Specialness, not rarity, is the key—for women were commonly magical (because excluded from religion and from science), and there are plenty of them. Keith Thomas speaks of the advantage Catholic priests had over Protestant ministers in appropriating magic in the sixteenth and seventeenth centuries: "precisely because the Church had its own magic . . . it frowned on that of others. . . . Set apart by his learning, his unique ritual power, and his official virginity, the priest was admirably qualified to be a key figure in the practice of popular magic" (1971, 274). A magician learns the language of the spirits, at large cost. He knows the words the gods speak (Mauss 1972 [1902–3], 38f; *Cratylus*, 391E; contrast 401A; and the gods loving a joke, 406C). The magician undergoes initiation. Any man can call spirits from the vasty deep, but only for a magician will they come when he does call for them.

Magic is often nontransferable: "[A] person who has bought a charm cannot dispose of it at will outside the contract" (43). The nontransferability of charms and curses is the more revealing because it contradicts another feature of magic, that charms and curses are *done,* as Thomas Greene puts it, irrevocable, rattling down the generations (thus the curse on the house of Pelops in the *Oresteia*). Magic is a speech act, but more like the speech act of marrying a couple than the speech act of promising to repay a loan. A marriage cannot be sold secondhand; a promise to repay can. A secondhand marriage ceremony would be a cheapened act, which is the point.

Magic is often particular and local. Certain days are efficacious, certain difficult circumstances must be achieved, and so forth (45f.). "If the Hindu magicians are to be believed, some of their rites could be practiced successfully only once every forty-five years" (46). Naturally: if magic could be done on any day, in any place, it would not have the scarcity that protects its claim of efficacy. There would be too much of it around, selling cheaply.

Above all, magic is often elaborate. It is notoriously so, hooblahoo, an image of mysterious wisdom won by toil. The rites can last hours or days or weeks. Magic is repetitious, covering every possibility—or else it does not work, since tiny failures to follow the prescription protect the magician from responsibility. "It is natural for a magician to take refuge behind questions of procedure and technicalities, to protect himself in case of failure in magical prowess" (50); cf. Thomas (1971, 641).

Magical ceremonies are usually more elaborate than religious ceremonies. The scarcity in religion is accomplished by a restricted priesthood and, especially, by the limited efficacy of the prayer, corresponding with the fiat in a spell. The Christian sects with less elaborate preparation for their priests expect less from prayer. The extreme cases are Amish priests chosen by biblical lot or Quakers with no priests at all. The sects that think that prayer works cheaply, every time, are regarded by mainstream religions as magical—for example, the cults of saints in the South of Italy or pentecostal sects in the United States.

The bargain with the gods in charms, spells, and religious sacrifices is a curious part of this, since it is usually small and cheap. People do not actually sacrifice much, except the time of the magician. Cheap entrails are all the god actually gets in blood sacrifice (Levy 1989). The rest is eaten by the humans. Thus in a Navaho chant, from a ceremony lasting many days, "I have made your sacrifice / *I have prepared a smoke for you*" (from The Night Chant, excerpted in Rothenberg 1985, 84). One would expect there to be a rule of equal scarcity in operation here. Cheap sacrifices would use elaborate ceremony by a restricted class of magicians or priests, to make the total costly. On the other hand, expensive sacrifices (human sacrifices especially) would be cheap and quick, contrary to what one might otherwise expect in view of the gravity of the matter. The sacrifice of Polyxena on the tomb of Achilles, "the shedding of human blood upon a grave, / where custom calls for cattle" (Euripides, *Hecuba,* line 262), the climax of the play, was short in the text and unelaborate in form (lines 520–80; compare Euripides, *Iphigenia in Aulis,* lines 1540–80).

Magic, then, is childish. Childishly it gives way to the pressure of desire. Scarcity is wished away.

But economics knows that scarcity cannot really, truly be wished away. The scarcity must show somewhere and shows in most features of magic. The supposed profit arising from the evaded scarcity gets absorbed. Economics says: At the margin the hoobla-hoo must absorb the profit from being able to take the ma-

gician to Baghdad on a carpet, if he could only get the damned
thing running.

Now poetry, Thomas Greene argues, is something different from
magic. We speak of the "magic" of poetry, but only in a manner of
speaking, hyperbole by way of careless praise. Poems commonly
allude to the forms of magic, but no one thinks they actually
achieve its substance. For all the shared rhetoric—repetition, in-
cantation, evocation—poems are not spells.

In fact, Greene argues that poetry is a way of getting beyond the
childish omnipotence of thought. Poems look like spells, but un-
dercut the fiat with intrusions of voice, doubts that it will work,
hints of the poet's personality, and other post-magical sensibilities.
Sappho pretends in "Prayer to Aphrodite" (1971, 144–45) to accomplish the same thing as the Egyptian love spell, but is notably
less businesslike, more personal, less repetitive, more revealing.
The poem claims to be a love charm, but is in fact a lyric poem. It
tells, irrelevantly for the magic, that "you, Blessed One, smiling
with your immortal face, asked what happened to me." It is pa-
thetic, not arrogant: "do not crush my heart"; "come here, if ever
in the past, hearing my cries of love from afar"; "I was begging you
to come"; "my mad heart"; "my crushing cares." Likewise, Theocritus II, "The Spell," inserts the magic in a narrative worthy of
Browning, filled with irony and self-expression. Poems have many
voices (if only the poet's in addition to the narrator's), but a spell
has only one [James Fairhall made this point to me]. The reader—
and of course it is a reader, not an audience of the shaman's patients or the local anthropologist—is made to reflect on the
poem's pseudomagic.

In a poem, says Greene, "the emergent self is acculturated; it
learns the limits of its own power" (1989, 131); "the inchoate wish
is *schooled:* it is taught to speak and it is taught to accept limitation"
(142). Like a child's game, it is "an elementary lesson in resigna-

tion" (131). "Poems tend to be pseudo-rituals which teach the subject to settle for the absence of magical power (131). Stevens:

> From this the poem springs: that we live in a place
> That is not our own and, much more, not ourselves
> And hard it is in spite of blazoned days.

("Notes: Abstract, IV")

The commonplace of classical criticism—that art and in particular poetry imitates reality—is wrong. Poetry does not imitate reality; it imitates speech acts, especially magical ones: curses, invocations, apostrophes, praise, prayer. Every poet knows it.

The awareness of its own lack of effectiveness makes poetry grown-up and post-magical. Poetry recognizes that the words are not the things themselves. It is adult, not expecting to reproduce by mere human words the effortless magic of blue-turning spring. The reader of a book in "The House Was Quiet and the World Was Calm" "leaned above the page / Wanted to lean, wanted most to be / The scholar to whom his book is true." But Stevens is here to tell you that after all it is only wanting, not achieving; that the book is true merely to the scholar, not to the gods.

In view of how grim it is to be adult and economic and aware of scarcity it is not perhaps surprising to find in poetry, as Greene does, a ubiquitous "nostalgia for magic." Poetry sometimes looks back on a time of omnipotent thought:

> The poem refreshes life so that we share,
> For a moment the first idea . . .
> The poem, through candor, brings back a power again
> That gives a candid kind to everything.

("Notes: Abstract, III")

But only "for a moment," a "kind." Candid, gleaming white, it claims to be, / But still it's hoobla-hoo. / Nostalgia might lament the truth, / But after all it's true.

Economics as a science, like poetry, is a force of acculturation. It says: you can't get that. The churches of the sixteenth and seventeenth centuries, writes Thomas (1971, 278), put "strong emphasis upon the virtues of hard work and application," and "helped create a frame of mind which spurned the cheap solutions offered by magic, not just because they were wicked, but because they were too easy. Man was to earn his bread by the sweat of his brow." Like poetry, and unlike magic, economics in the century after Defoe dwelt on scarcity. It came to tell that all good things must be scarce in equilibrium, all magical opportunities used up. It tells us we must work by the sweat of our brows to achieve our desires. It tells us that we cannot be rich by snapping our fingers. And it tells us that individual morality does not assure civic morality. Such hard messages would have been perhaps too hard for earlier and less settled times.

Economics is the science of the post-magical age. Far from being "unscientific" or hoobla-hoo, it is deeply anti-magical. It keeps telling us that we cannot do it, that magic will not help. After magic, Greene argues, poetry is scattered, dissociative, disjunctive, many voiced (compare Bloom 1976, 168, describing Stevens as "the most advanced rhetorician in modern poetry and in his major phase the most disjunctive"). Irony and self-consciousness would fit any page of Keynes.

Economics, like poetry, however, exhibits sometimes the nostalgia for magic. There's the danger. Economics can go wrong and betray its post-magical sophistication by surrendering to what Greene calls the temptation of magic. If poetry surrenders we are perhaps not seriously damaged—although the poetry then stops performing its maturing function and can even rouse men to magical beliefs in, say, the white man's burden or some corner of a foreign field that is forever England. Such notions are mischievous enough. But an economics that is nostalgic for magic is radically dangerous.

Now of course words are in fact efficacious in economics, because markets live on the lips of men and women. Every economist knows this. Money is not a thing, it is an agreement. Corporations are not corporeal. Exchange is a conversation of bids and asks.

The economy depends today on the promises made yesterday in view of the expectations about tomorrow. We can in fact (and in word) create prosperity by declaring it to be just around the corner. One is tempted to conclude that economies, and economics, are "mere" matters of words, that announcing a five-year plan or a new economic policy is the same thing as achieving it, that words after all do have the magical power to make us safe and happy.

Grown-ups must resist the temptation. Grown-up economics is not voodoo but poetry. Or, to take other models of maturity, it is history, not myth; politics, not invective; philosophy, not dogma. A correct economics—which is to say, most of the rich conversation of economics since Adam Smith—is historical and philosophical, a virtual psychoanalysis of the economy, adjusting our desires to the reality principle. On this score Marxian and bourgeois economics can be similarly childish in giving in to temptation. A Marxian economist of an old-fashioned sort trumpeting the predictive power of Marxism makes the same childish error as does a badly educated mainstream economist thinking that the future of grain prices is predictable. A grown-up epigram would be: The point is to know history, not to change it. The best economic scientists, of whatever school, have never believed in profitable casting of the fores.

The useful category for criticizing modernist culture, in other words, is not science/non-science but magic/non-magic à la Greene. It was customary in modernist circles in the 1930s to identify the enemies of modernism with Nazism. But the truth is that the Nazis drew much of their power from a modernist science grown magical. The buildings and displays of Auschwitz put one in mind not of tarot cards and crystal balls but of modernist laboratories and industrial processes gone mad in an attempt to lay down the future. Likewise, when the modern historical sciences yield to the temptation of myth—the myth of national destiny, for example, or the myth of social engineering—they become silly and magical and dangerous. Proper, non-magical science is here to tell us what we cannot do without cost. It resists making the scientists into wizards. It will not sell the snake oil. The danger comes from the modern sentimentalist armed with a myth of science gloriously magical.

8   The American Question: If You're So Smart Why Ain't You Rich?

*U*nhappily, economics sometimes forgets its scientific duty and begins to promise magical stories, reversals of fortune to be had merely by paying attention to the local economist. The magic of physical engineering in our world has long nourished a wish for social engineering. The economist is supposed to provide it, by the magic of expertise.

Americans say they don't hold much with experts. As Harry Truman said, "An expert is someone who doesn't want to learn anything new, because then he wouldn't be an expert." Europeans admit a need for expertise to keep their class struggle going, to which the American response is a Bronx cheer. Though Nicholas Murray Butler, the president of Columbia University long ago, made the university an American refuge for experts, he said that they know more and more about less and less. By way of contrast the European next to Nicholas Murray in the roll of remarks, Samuel Butler the Younger, had little respect for pretension in general but plenty for the pretension of experts: "The public do not know enough to be experts, yet know enough to decide between them." And having decided the public follows their magical advice.

You don't say. The rhetoric of the New World abounds with deflations: "Look who's talking"; "Where do you get off?" "Who d'you think *you* are, Bub?" And from Maine to California the capitalistic, American democrat relishes that most American of sneers, that American Question: "If you're so smart why ain't you rich?"

Well, why ain't you? The American scholar suffers taunts unimaginable in Germany or France, for not meeting a payroll, for not coming down from the ivory tower, for not getting wet behind the ears of his smarty egg head. Come to think of it, though, if he's so gosh darn smart why *hasn't* he gotten rich?

The question cuts deeper than most intellectuals and experts care to admit. The test of riches is a perfectly fair one if the expertise claims to deliver actual riches, in gold or in glory. At a minimum the American Question should constrain expertise about gold, and the counterstory can therefore begin with economics. It goes further, though. The American Question embarrasses anyone claiming magical and profitable expertise who cannot show a profit, the historian second-guessing generals or the critic propounding a formula for art. He who is so smart claims a Faustian knowledge, "Whose deepness doth entice such forward wits / To practice more than heavenly power permits."

Begin with economics. Take it as an axiom of human behavior that people pick up $500 bills left on the sidewalk. The Axiom of Modest Greed involves no close calculation of advantage or large willingness to take a risk. The average person sees a quarter and sidles over to it (by experiment it has been found that Manhattanites will stoop for a quarter); he sees a $500 bill and jumps for it. The Axiom is not controversial. All economists subscribe to it, whether or not they "believe in the market" (as the shorthand test for ideology goes), and so should you.

Yet it has a distressing outcome, a dismal commonplace of adult life, a sad little Five-Hundred-Dollar-Bill Theorem:

> If the Axiom of Modest Greed applies, then today there exists no sidewalk in the neighborhood of your house on which a $500 bill remains.

Proof: By contradiction, if there had been a $500 bill lying there at time $T - N$, then according to the axiom someone would have picked it up before T, before today.

From this advanced scientific reasoning it is a short step to common sense. If a man offers advice on how to find a $500 bill on the sidewalk, for which he asks merely a nominal fee, the prudent adult declines the offer. If there really were a $500 bill lying there the confidence man would pick it up himself.

Such common sense is so obvious that confidence games must clothe themselves in a false rhetoric of self-interest. In the Pigeon Drop the victim (that is, the pigeon) is persuaded to part with his bank account by way of earnest money for a share in a bundle of money "found" on the sidewalk. He must be persuaded that the con men are asking for the earnest money only as self-interested protection against the pigeon himself absconding with the bundle. (After the con men have disappeared with his bank account he finds out that the bundle entrusted to his care is paper stacked between two $10 bills). Even pigeons don't believe that someone will present them with $500 out of the goodness of his heart.

The leading case is the scheme to get rich quick. A letter arrives announcing itself as "The World's Greatest Secret! Now you can learn how to receive 50,000 crisp $5 bills in the next 90 days. . . . A personal note from the originator of the plan," Edward L. Green. His surprising kindness is affirmed by Carl Winslow of Tulsa: "This is the only realistic money-making offer I've ever received. I participated because this plan truly makes sense!"

Common sense replies that the plan truly does not make sense, not any sense at all. Though the plan uses the rhetoric of mutual interest—believe me, fella, this deal's good for you and me both—it does not turn the rhetoric on itself. If Mr. Green had the secret of receiving 50,000 crisp $5 bills he would clue you in only if your one crisp $5 bill was good for the chain and good for Edward L. Green. But you have no reason beyond Mr. Green's assurances to think you are early in the chain. If you are not you send out money and get nothing in return. A child will subscribe to a chain letter—or a guaranteed investment in Civil War figurines or a set of presidential commemorative coins suitable for collectors—and expect to win; an adult will not. No one with experience of life believes Publisher's Clearing House when it writes "*Ms. Z. Smithh*, you have just won $250,000." The adult does not expect fortune to come unbidded and asks prudently "Why are they telling me this?" Prudence is suspicious of an offer equivalent to picking up a $500 bill. Except to the flocks of optimistic Americans who invest daily in chain letters and prize-winning magazine subscriptions, all this goes without saying.

Therefore the Bargains and Hot Tips and Special Deals For You Alone offered by over-friendly men with clammy handshakes at dog tracks and used-car lots do not tempt the prudent adult. Yet similar offers made outside a Damon Runyon setting seem plausible to respectable if greedy folk. The high-class pigeons come flocking to the con, eager to believe that Mr. Expert is about to give them free advice on how to make a million.

Economists, for example, are routinely asked at cocktail parties what is going to happen to the interest rate or the price of housing or the price of corn. People think that asking an economist about the future is like asking the doctor at the party about that chest pain. You get an expert to do his job free. Take corn. Any agricultural economist in the Midwest spends much of his airtime delivering expert opinion on what will happen next month to its price. Surely he must know, this expert, if anyone does. It would be poor news to be told that after all no one does know, or can.

An economist who claims to know what is going to happen to the price of corn, however, is claiming to know how to pick up $500. With a little borrowing on the equity of his home or his reputation for sobriety he can proceed to pick up $500 thousand, then $500 million, then more. Nothing to it. If an agricultural economist could predict the price of corn better than the futures market he would be rich.

Yet he does not put his money where his mouth is. He is not rich. It follows by strict implication that he is not so smart.

It may be objected that the profitmaking is risky and that professors of economics are cautious. Therefore they do not put their money where their mouths are, even though their mouths are working fine. The objection has the problem that the bet on the price of corn can be hedged, which is insurance. It is no bet. Someone who can outsmart the market on average even a little can make a lot of money simply, at no risk. No wonder: the opportunity to buy corn low and sell high, like the right to run a TV station in the 1960s or to import Toyotas in the 1980s, is like finding a $500 bill any time you want.

It may be objected that the profitmaking is complicated and that professors of economics are elaborately trained experts in the complexities. Therefore the $500 bill is not available to just anyone, only to them. The wizards earn merely what they are worth, the normal return to years of studying wizardry. This objection, too, has problems. The first is that the wizards are telling us about the future price of corn or bonds or housing at cocktail parties and in the newspaper, free. Why are they handing over to John Doe their just rewards for going to wizard school?

The second problem is that the wizardry claimed is systematic, formulaic, and, when you come right down to it, pretty simple. It involves the fitting of a few straight lines to scatters of points. Take a course in economic statistics, the promise goes, and become able to predict the future in profitable ways. The promise is hard to believe, because it sounds a lot like The World's Greatest Secret. Ordinary secrets and routine advice do in fact flow from economics, and doubtless economists earn their keep. Unlimited wealth, however, cannot be expected to flow from a book or even from many years of concentrated study in economics. Compared to unlimited wealth, many years of study is like the trivial cost of reaching down to pick up a $500 bill. If someone knows a scholarly formula for predicting the price of corn it would already have been exploited.

The same grim truth from the American Question applies to the stock market. Because the stock market is obviously a matter of expectations, about which we all know something, and because it is crowded with experts in handsome wool suits, the truth is hard to swallow. Heh, *Barron's* and "Wall Street Week" wouldn't kid me, would they? Surely all those analysts and pundits and technical elves know *something*.

No, no, unhappily, they surely do not. They truly do not make sense; not any sense at all. The reason they do not is the American Question and the Five-Hundred-Dollar-Bill Theorem: there exists no sidewalk in your neighborhood with $500 of stock market profits lying on it. If a stockbroker were so smart he would not be making his riches by selling stock tips to widows and orphans. In the style of the chain letter, the tipster divulges inside information for his gain and your loss. The rhetorical pose of stockbrokers and racetrack tipsters to be offering prudent advice is contradicted by their circumstances, a contradiction catalogued in rhetoric as the "circumstantial ad hominem." That is to say, "Being so smart, why don't you do it yourself, if it's such good advice?"

"A tout," said Damon Runyon (1958 [1933], 19), who knew the score on the economics of prediction, "is a guy who goes around a race track giving out tips on the races, if he can find anybody who will listen to his tips, especially suckers, and a tout is nearly always broke. If he is not broke, he is by no means a tout, but a handicapper, and is respected by one and all." Runyon in truth was a sucker for tips himself, and lost so regularly and embarrassingly that he would buy a two-dollar ticket on every horse, to be able to exhibit a winner (Clark 1978, 197).

We know the force of the American Question and the Five-Hundred-Dollar-Bill Theorem as well as we know anything. If we know that the sun will rise tomorrow and that prime numbers are odd we know that people who were so smart would be rich and that sidewalks which were so filled with $500 bills would be cleared. Therefore a prediction about stocks—as distinct from mere current information about the market, a mere statement of the going odds, a mere consensus of public opinion, reflected in the price—is on average worthless.

It has been easy therefore to assemble statistical evidence that the Five-Hundred-Dollar-Bill Theorem is true about Wall Street:

stock markets everywhere do in fact jiggle about in unpredictable ways. The evidence is by now overwhelming. In 1933 Alfred Cowles, one of the founders of modern statistical economics, posed the question in a title, "Can Stock Market Forecasters Forecast?" He answered, "It is doubtful." Cowles himself had abandoned a forecasting business in 1931, ashamed of his failure to foresee the Great Crash. Burton Malkiel's *A Random Walk Down Wall Street* (1985) gives an accessible summary of the research since Cowles, such as P. H. Cootner, ed., *The Random Character of Stock Prices* (1964). The forecastability of stock prices continues to be at best doubtful.

It may be objected that sophisticated people do in fact buy stock market advice. An economist (and only an economist) would conclude that something of value had been bought. A reply has been suggested by James Burk, a sociologist and former stockbroker, who found that the advice-giving industry sprang from legal decisions early in the century (1988). The courts began to decide that the trustee of a pension fund or of a child's inheritance could be held liable for bad investing if he did not take advice. The effect would have been the same had the courts decided that prudent men should consult Ouija boards or the flights of birds. It was so at Rome: a consul who ignored the advice of the college of augurs was liable to prosecution after retirement. America decided through its judges that an industry giving advice on the stock market should come into existence, whether or not it was worthless. It did, and was. (Europe is not similarly blessed with an advice industry, because the law is different.) The industry can go out of existence the same way. The judge who first asks the American Question and rules a stockbroker liable for his unsuccessful advice will save many a widow and orphan from investment counseling.

It may be objected that after all a great deal of money is made in the stock market. But a great deal is also made at the track in Miami. Grandfather Stueland was offered Radio Corporation of America stock in the early 1920s and regretted later that he had invested in Stueland Electric instead. Some people did buy RCA: they must have known. But that some people win at the stock-broker or at the $100 window at Hialeah racetrack in lucky Miami does not mean that they were justified in their true belief. They could have won by luck rather than by a justifying technique. People win at slot machines, too, but cannot tell how, because they use no justifiable, inscribable, bookable technique. And even if some people *do* know they will win (God appears to them in a dream and tells them, maybe; or they have genuine inside knowledge), there is no way for the common pigeon to know what these alleged experts know. Why would they be telling you, Bub?

It may be objected at last that the economist or other seer in the stock or bond or housing market does not have access to the big loans to make big money. Yet consortiums do have access to the big loans, and if the wisdom comes simply from being an economist it ought to be simple to assemble a consortium of economists. A consortium of famous economists at Stanford and the University of Chicago in the early 1970s believed that interest rates, which were then at shocking, unprecedented highs (6, 6.5, my Lord, even 7.5 percent), just had to come down. The price of bonds, in other words, just had to go up. A good time to buy bonds. The economists complained at lunch that their bankers would not loan them money to exploit this Sure Thing, The World's Greatest Secret. But in the event, sadly, the bankers were right. Interest rates did not fall; they rose. The consortium of economists, relying on its collective expertise, lost its collective shirt.

The routine is the usual one. I myself have lost a shirt or two on real estate deals bound to succeed and on a consortium of economists speculating in the foreign exchanges. From John Maynard Keynes (who lost money regularly before breakfast, but had a Cambridge College backing him up) and Irving Fisher (who reduced Yale's endowment to half Harvard's by touting stocks in 1928) down to the latest scheme of some economist to make money from mathematical models of gold speculation, economists have not earned the confidence of bankers. As it was put by Paul

Samuelson, a student of these matters (1986 [1982], 541), "It's a mugs game for a dentist—or an associate professor of econometrics—to think that he and the telephone can have an edge over those who count the cocoa pods in Africa and follow the minute-by-minute arrival of new information."

The best known counterexample among economists is said to be the late Otto Eckstein, a fine economist with much common sense who extended the large-scale statistical model of the economy into commercial use. He built Data Resources, Inc. into a company with revenues in 1984 of $84 million. But Data Resources did not use its own predictions of prices and interest rates to speculate. It sold them to others, mainly to companies who wanted a myth of knowledge to comfort them in the world's uncertainty and to answer wrathful stockholders: "We took the best advice." If Data Resources had believed its own predictions to the extent of speculating on them, and was correct in its belief, then it could have become fabulously richer than it was. To say that Otto Eckstein or Paul Samuelson or other honest purveyors of economic tips became in fact a little bit rich does not answer the American Question. Eckstein and Samuelson (and Louis Rukeyser of Wall Street and Hot Horse Herbie of Broadway) became rich by *selling* advice, in the form of models and statistical equations and other charming talk, not by using it.

Cato the Elder reported of the haruspices, who examined livers in Rome with an expertise approaching the econometric, that they could not but laugh on meeting one another. Economists know lots of similar gags about their inability to predict profitably: forecasting is very difficult, especially if it is about the future; an economist is an expert who can tell you tomorrow why the thing he predicted yesterday didn't happen today; the best I can hope in a forecast is to be intelligently wrong or fortunately right.

One must not get carried away. Nobody doubts that a well-informed economist can tell you a thing or two about the future, mainly from knowing the present well. As the economist Robert Solow remarked about the predictions from Data Resources

(1982), "every month it provides an orderly description of the data, organized in such a way that one's attention is called to events that seem to conform with a reasonable person's understanding of the economy." The American Question casts no doubt on predictions that offer little or no profit. A prediction makes no profit if it is a commonplace or if does not offer a way to buy low and sell high. Predicting that the national income will not fall to zero next year is no more profitable than predicting that the sun will rise tomorrow.

Other people view economists as social weather forecasters. Economists are not so happy with the analogy, since they know they are not so smart. Weather forecasters and price forecasters could both earn a lot of money on a good forecast if they could keep it secret. In fact you will do better predicting a freeze in South Florida by watching the futures price of orange juice than by listening to the National Weather Service. Unsurprisingly, the growers and dealers have hired meteorologists to make predictions that are better than those of the Service.

Come to mention it, though, economists don't do much of a job as public forecasters. Victor Zarnowitz, the leading scholar in the field, makes only modest claims for the most promising method. A recent study by Zarnowitz and Geoffrey Moore (1982) showed that "leading indicators," invented by Moore and now reported monthly in the press, can indeed predict business cycle peaks— but with leads, alas, ranging from one to nineteen months. "The economists are generally right in their predictions," Sidney Webb said once, "but generally a good deal out in their dates." Predicting the end of prosperity as coming somewhere in the next nineteen months is a little better than saying that if it's August then Jamaica has fair chance after a while of getting a hurricane. Yet it is not so smart that the economic forecaster could retire to Jamaica. It is not good enough to be profitable; and if it were, it would be discounted already.

There are other ways of getting to the same doubt that economists can predict. For one thing, unlike humans, hurricanes are not listening. Humans react to economic predictions in ways that dampen or magnify the predictions. It would be as though the hurricane presently north of Jamaica reacted to a forecast that tomorrow it was going to move further away by saying "Hmm: I'd better turn around and go to Jamaica instead." This is the point made by the conservative economists who suggest that people have "rational expectations." One does not have to accept every part of such a theory to believe the more modest Theorem proposed here. It suggests modestly that people are not so stupid that they are easy to surprise. If they are not easy to surprise, then the economy is not easy to manipulate, and its would-be manipulators are not rich or powerful.

Further and more deeply the equations of fluid dynamics applicable to the weather do not include an equation that rules out cheap but profitable predictions. Economic models do. A person who was smart enough to know the solutions to the economic equations would be rich, unless profitable solutions were already anticipated and discounted by the model. But according to the Five-Hundred-Dollar-Bill Theorem they would already be discounted. If the alleged model is a widely available piece of information or if its essence were embodied in a widely held judgment, it would be useless for making anyone rich. Wise in retrospect, maybe; rich in prospect, no.

The American Question and the Five-Hundred-Dollar-Bill Theorem radically limit what economists and calculators can know about the future. No economist watches the TV program "Wall Street Week" without a vague sense that he is betraying his science. He should be pleased. His science proves its robustness by asserting confidently that the science cannot profitably predict; indeed, that no science of humankind can profitably predict, even the science of stockbrokers. The economic theorem is so powerful that it applies to economists.

The postmodern economist is modest about profitworthy detail, the detail from which she could buy low and sell high. She must be modest especially about the proud claim of economics in the 1960s, the claim to fine tune the economy, making detailed adjustments to money and taxes in order to offset a depression just around the corner. As economists and other expert knights of Camelot realize now after much tragedy sprung from hubris, if an economist could see around the corner she would be rich. Fine tuning violates the Theorem: a fine tuner would see dozens of $500 bills lying around her neighborhood. The knowledge that would make fine tuning possible would make the economists who have it fabulously wealthy. The economists go on relating impossibly detailed scenarios into the microphones of television reporters, but in their hearts they know they are wrong.

The American Question requires intellectual modesty in the economic expert, if he does not want people to laugh on meeting him. Hubris will need divine protection. Xenophon reported Socrates saying: "Those who intend to manage [*oikesein*] houses or cities well are in need of divination. For the craft of carpenter . . . or economics [*oikonomikon*] . . . may be learned . . . ; but the greatest of these matters the gods reserve to themselves. . . . If anyone supposes that these [divinations] are not beyond reason, and nothing in them beyond our judgment, he is himself beyond reason" (Xenophon, I.1.7). Socrates could turn to the oracles for divine supplementation of a craft. We have lost today the favor of the gods, and books on economic technique will not assuage our woe.

9   The Limits of Criticism

*I*f an economist were so smart, then, she would be rich. But there is more. The more leads back to the ancient and sensible doubt that critics can do as much in the way of art as artists can. The American Question mocks the hubris of the critic, whether the critic is a humanist or a scientist, a pundit or a policy-maker.

A crucial point is that the critic's coin of profit need not be monetary. Political power is there on the sidewalk, too, waiting to be picked up if there is something wrong with the 5,000-vote Theorem—that politicians and their advisors who think they see 5,000 votes sitting there waiting to be picked up are mistaken. But of course the Theorem is right. There does not exist a simple way, to be written down in a book, for getting 5,000 votes. The political scientists cannot predict elections in ways that would allow them to manipulate the outcome, doing better than the political artists they study.

Notice the clause of profitability. The political scientists can make predictions all right ("A declared revolutionary socialist will not soon be elected to the House of Representatives from Orange County"). But they cannot make valuable predictions ("Expenditure of $200,000 on ten-second spots on Channels 2, 7, and 9 during the three weeks before the election will assure the election of Jones to the House"). If two empires fight to the death a great empire will fall. The valuable and impossibly difficult prediction specifies which one.

This is not to say that $200,000 spent on television advertisements never won an election, or that after the election a political scientist could not interpret the events as a victory for money and television. And once it was a bright idea. After the advertisements won in the 5th Congressional District, however, it would become routine in the 4th and in the 6th and at length in the Nth. If it were so easy the 500-dollar or the 5,000-vote opportunity would be picked up. The supernormal profits, as economists put it, would be dissipated. The expected return from political advice, allowing for its uncertainty, should be approximately zero.

If a critic of elections is so smart then she should be able to sell the analysis. Isocrates the Sophist turned back the boast of the socratics that (unlike the sophists) they did not charge for their Truth. If your Truth is so valuable, why does it not meet a market test? A study of Political Action Committees that predicts elections on the basis of expenditure by the Committees should be sellable at least to the Committees. If not, perhaps it is not valuable advice. It may be good history, giving a sensible account of votes in the past, but it is apparently not good advice on how to add votes in the future. At the margin, as economists like to say, you get what you pay for. The American Question and the Five-Hundred-Dollar-Bill Theorem constrain all forward-looking arguments in the human sciences.

The payment need not be monetary, if money is not what the seer desires. Prestige in the local saloon would be cheaply available if the American Question did not also cast doubt on predictions of sporting events. But it does. The lineaments of the sporting future apparent to the average guy will be reflected in the sporting odds. Only fresh details give profits above average measured in money or prestige. Fresh details are hard to come by. Information, like steel and haircuts, is costly to produce.

The American Question can be asked of all predictions of trend, in journalism, sociology, political science, commercial art, and elsewhere. Some people can predict clothing fashions, for example, but not by a write-downable method. They may have a true belief, but in its justification it becomes false. If it can be made routine and written down it is no longer valuably true. Successful fashion designers have a private trick for which they are paid large sums and about which they are not anyway going to blab. If hem lengths followed the stock market (until recently of course they led it), then cheap fortunes could be made by exploiting the fact, and the fact would be exploited away. But cheap fortunes are oxymoronic.

As the man said about predictions on the stock market, it is doubtful that any prediction of tastes is possible. Predicting human tastes tends towards the oxymoronic, too. The claim that advertisers can predict and therefore manipulate tastes is good advertising for advertising, but otherwise doubtful. When Vance Packard wrote *The Hidden Persuaders,* which made frightening claims about the power of advertising, his friends in advertising were delighted. J. K. Galbraith likewise has done for Madison Avenue what it could not have done for itself, persuading influential people that advertisers have the power to make people buy their stuff. If tastes could be manipulated as easily as the critics of advertising say then the advertisers would be rich. It is not too surprising that a recent study at the University of Iowa has found that television advertising campaigns have less than their claimed power to change minds (Tellis 1988).

All manner of provision for the future is limited by the American Question. The legal rule of first possession, as in mining or inventing, for example, gives title to the coal seam or the patent to whoever gets there first, giving an incentive to waste resources in races such as the race between Kodak and Polaroid. The society would be better off if the outcome were properly anticipated by the sovereign power auctioning the entitlement off to the highest bidder. But as the legal economist David Haddock notes, "where new knowledge is at issue, finding appropriate solutions becomes more complex. In such situations, one cannot define an entitlement because one cannot imagine what one has not imagined" (1986, 789).

What is thrown into doubt by the American Question is a claim to systematic, justified, cheaply acquired, write-downable knowledge about profitable opportunities. The "profit," note again, is to be broadly construed. A small group of mathematicians has been complaining since early in the century that certain much-discussed mathematical objects cannot actually be constructed, even in principle. The late Errett Bishop, a leader of these "constructivists," used the American Question. A real least upper bound is supposed to exist for *every* bounded sequence (such as the bound that the sequence .9, .99, .999, .9999, .99999, . . . has at 1.0; but for *every* bounded sequence, however strange). The notion is used routinely in un-constructive, "formalist" analysis (which is most of modern mathematics). Bishop pointed out, however, that the bound would require for its construction, were it ever attempted, a systematic, write-downable "method M," applicable to all such sequences, even strange ones. But anyone so smart as to come up with method M would be mathematically rich: "Of course," wrote Bishop, "such a method M does not exist, and nobody expects that one will ever be found. Such a method would solve most of the famous unsolved problems in mathematics" (1985, 7). Like the ability to forecast interest rates or manipulate elections, method M is a five-hundred-dollar-bill machine, intellectually speaking.

The force of the American Question depends on the sums involved. A tiny edge on average over the stock market can make such a seer wealthy beyond the dreams of avarice. The sums extend beyond the normal return to normal education or normal effort. No one would deny that normal knowledge is worth its hire. So is special knowledge, when you can get it. But the special knowledge that the stockbroker or the economist or the tipster claims is not in fact special. It is easy to acquire, and therefore has no protection from entry, and therefore can earn no special return. Being able to read racing forms or study *Barron's* with care or run statistical fits on corn prices does not make one especially smart. Therefore, except by luck, one cannot get especially rich.

The American Question mocks the claims of predictors, social engineers, and critics of the social arts. The predictor who could get it usefully right would be a god incarnate, a diviner.

The reason is not that humans are too complicated or too changeable or too free. The humanistic criticisms of social science may be true but they are not telling; they are easy to make and easy to answer. The scientist answers, "Give us the money and we will finish the job." If humans are "ultimately" free considered as individuals, they still can be predicted on average and in the mass. And if human masses are complex they still can be predicted with another million dollars and another model. So long as humans are to be viewed as molecules bouncing against each other the problem is merely to get the mathematics right. It is said that predicting human beings is bound to be more complicated than predicting planets or pigeons, but that is not true. It depends on what you are trying to predict. The daily temperature variation of a human is easier to predict than the twitching of the sixty-seventh feather from the pigeon's tail. It is a matter of how ambitious the prediction is. The "simple" problem of space flight, "merely" an application of Newton's laws, requires days of computation at high speed if the ambition is to put a rocket precisely *there* on Mars. For a given ambition the complexity is only a matter of computer time.

The American Question puts more fundamental limits on what we humans can say about ourselves. It puts a limit on mechanical models of human behavior. It does not make the mechanical models useless for interesting history or routine prediction; it just makes them useless for gaining an edge about the future. If people were as predictable as naive behaviorism alleges, for instance, the psychologists would be rich and the personnel managers all-powerful. The field of industrial and managerial psychology was erected in the 1930s on just such a putative Secret, but led to miracles only on 34th Street (Waring, forthcoming). To recur to economics, the various "solutions" of bargaining problems have this flaw: that if the economist knew the solution, then so would the players, which would make the solution valueless. The computer that could predict the next move of a competitor would sell for a lot of money. If computers are cheap, no one can get rich by using them to outsmart others.

Likewise there are limits on the teachability of skills. It is paradoxical to claim that a Ph.D. qualifies one to teach "entrepreneurship," or even "excellence." The present content of the American business school, with its burden of mechanical technique, undervalues the stories and moralities that make a business culture. In pure form the successful person of business is either a lucky fool or a godlike genius. It is hard to tell the difference. I have a friend who is a businessman with spectacular recent successes, earning enormous amounts for his company, a big one. Not being a fool in any sense he looks with foreboding on what will happen to his reputation for genius when the coin turns up tails, as with 50-50 probability it will. Perhaps he understates his genius, for there *is* a genius about the entrepreneur, by which the pursuit of his own interest promotes a good social end which was no part of his intention.

It can be argued that capitalism depends for its progressiveness on such geniuses. It is observationally equivalent to say that it depends on large numbers of fools, mucking about in garages and board rooms, some of whom will be lucky (Nye 1989). A colleague in the English Department at the University of Iowa, Donald Marshall, put it this way in a note to me: "what motivates economic activity is the delusion that we can guess the future, and expertise is deployed, unbeknownst to itself, to protect us from discovering that in fact we can't do so, a discovery that would lead us to despair and paralysis. The joke is that . . . capitalism's advantage is that it maximizes the number of people who have this delusion." The clerkly treason against capitalism is contemptible, since capitalism supports the clerks. Yet there are enough rich and lucky fools to give point to the clerk's report: If you're so rich why aren't you smart?

Take publishing. Experts cannot use routine methods to improve on the tacit knowledge of a publisher. This is not an excuse for a publisher to ignore formal methods such as computerized inventory systems. It says merely that formal methods will not earn abnormally high profits for long. The formality makes them easy to copy. Going to business school is not a way to acquire immense wealth, because it is too easy to get in. The $500 bills get snapped up. The tacit and informal character of what is left for human decisions is why the publishers get paid for taking the blame. No artificial intelligence could have predicted the success of Hofstadter's *Gödel, Escher, Bach;* no central planner that of *Animal Farm.* In fact the publishers themselves did not predict it. Entrepreneurs seek and sometimes find, given proper license to stumble. One of the many American publishers who turned down *Animal Farm* explained that they weren't doing animal stories that year.

The humanities cannot be taught by machine, either. Gary Walton, an economist and former dean of a business school, has written a book called *Beyond Winning* about "philosopher coaches," such as Woody Hayes in football or John Wooden in basketball. He is aware that if coaching could be learned from a book the woods would be full of Woodys and Woodens. If coaching were mechanical in its effects on the athletes then East Germany would never lose an Olympic contest. The ability to teach exceptional performance is itself an exceptional performance. What can be said about the athletic case is what can be said about the scholarly case: that a great coach or a great scholar teaches not by instructing the students in a bookable technique but by exhibiting a way of life, which not all can follow.

The limit on calculability and sayability applies to language and rhetoric itself. If anyone could get what they wished by shouting, for example, then everyone would shout, as at a cocktail party, arriving by the end hoarse but without having gotten what they wished. H. P. Grice affixed an economic tag to the trumping of speech conventions, "exploitation." As Stephen Levinson put the point in his book *Pragmatics,*

There is a fundamental way in which a full account of the communicative power of language can never be reduced to a set of conventions for the use of language. The reason is that wherever some convention or expectation about the use of language arises, there will also therewith arise the possibility of the non-conventional *exploitation* of that convention or expectation. It follows that a purely conventional or rule-based account of natural language usage can never be complete (1983, 112; italics added)

A rhetorical analysis has this limit, that it can tell wisely and well how a speech has gone in the past, but cannot be expected to provide The World's Greatest Secret for the future. It can show how Cicero in *Pro Archia* exploited tricolon, how Descartes exploited rhetoric to attack rhetoric itself, or how Jane Austen in *Northanger Abbey* exploited an irony that was always intended, covert, finite, and stable. But rhetoric cannot be finished and formulaic, or else anyone could be a Cicero, Descartes, or Austen. The chimera of a once-finished formula for language must be left to Fregean philosophy or to magic.

In the opening lines of *Faust*, before the Doctor has turned in vexation to magic, he laments that "I see that we can know nothing! / It nearly breaks my heart." He immediately amends this sweeping skepticism, for the American Question does not imply literally that we can know nothing but merely, as he then complains on behalf of his fellow men, that he can know nothing *to better Mankind*, as he puts it. On further reflection he comes to the nub: his studies, damn them, have taught him nothing that betters *Herr Dr. Faust*, this very example of Mankind. "And *I* have neither property nor money, / Nor honor and glory in the world: / No dog should go on living so." There lies the tragedy, at the impossibility of predictions profitable to Faust himself. He seeks The World's Greatest Secret for personal profit; which in due course he obtains, though not for free on the sidewalk, and then gets his fill of property and money.

Lacking the Devil's bargain, science cannot predict itself. The paradox shows up in economics because economics so plainly must apply to itself, if it's so smart. But the paradox applies to any foreknowledge of new knowledge. The impossibility of self-prediction has become a commonplace in philosophy. You do not know today what you will decide tomorrow, unless you have already decided it, in which case it is not tomorrow but today that you decide it.

"Prescience" is an oxymoron, like cheap fortunes: pre-science, knowing before one knows. Prescience is required for central planning of science. The philosophers Karl Popper and Alasdair MacIntyre among others have pointed out that knowing the future of science requires knowing the science of the future. It is not to be done. MacIntyre notes that the unpredictability of mathematical innovation is a rigorous case, resting on theorems concerning the incompleteness of arithmetic and the incalculability of certain expressions, proven by Gödel and Church in the 1930s. And "if the future of mathematics is unpredictable, so is a great deal else" (MacIntyre 1981, 90). If someone claims to know what method or lack of method would yield good science, why isn't he scientifically rich?

The other arts are similarly constrained. Some critics in the eighteenth century believed they had methods for assuring excellence in drama or painting. Nowadays no one would claim to have a formulaic, bookable method for constructing excellent paintings, except as a postmodern joke. The method would solve painting, in the sense that tic-tac-toe has been solved. This is not to say that rules of perspective or color harmonies cannot be constructed and applied. They can, the way a poet can check for agreement with the meter she has chosen or a dancer can check his fifth position. It says only that there is at present no routine, book-readable method for achieving artistic riches. The unusually profitable opportunities have been picked up, leaving only the routine returns to routine ability.

Each bit of the accumulated routine was once someone's personal and profitable trick. The genius has more tricks than the rest of us, which become tomorrow's routines. The first Florentine businessman to use double-entry bookkeeping gained a control over his materials similar in value to the first Athenian sculptor to use the slouch of standing bodies. In this age of iron, however, no one earns $500 from the mere idea of double entries or contrapposto. And the point is that any present day is an age of iron, because gold is picked up as soon as it appears.

The distinction between routine predictions and startling and profitable divination is analogous to the distinction between routine cooking and the profitable Art of three-star cookery. In his peculiar little dialogue, the *Ion,* Plato/Socrates lampoons Ion the performing Artist who imagines he *knows* something. It is significant that to mock Ion's claim to knowledge Socrates uses the example of divining. Allan Bloom once remarked of the passage:

> If divining is to be considered an art, it is strange in that it must profess to know the intentions of the gods; as an art, it would, in a sense, seem to presuppose that the free, elusive gods are shackled down by the bonds of intelligible necessity. Divining partakes of the rational dignity of the arts while supposing a world ruled by divine beings who are beyond the grasp of the arts. (1970, 57)

As Plato and the American Question would say, the claim of divining to be an art, Greek *techne,* mere bookable craft, is absurd.

Plato therefore wished to cage poetry, the god-possession that flatters men to think they know more than does the honest artisan, a technician in every sense. The followers of Plato down to the age of technique are enamored of knowledge as *techne,* a craft written down in books. They propose to cast books lacking such craft into the flames, as poetry and pretense, mere sophistry and illusion. The trouble is that their version of the fully rational life, the bookable final rules for language games, requires non-routine prediction. And in human affairs a prediction beyond what earns routine returns is impossible, except by entrepreneurs, idiot savants, *auteurs,* and other prodigies of tacit knowledge. The notion that bookable knowledge can guide the world through its difficult moments, like the notion that central planning can guide an economy, is self-contradictory. If the philosopher kings and central planners were so smart they would be rich.

As indeed they are, for a reason other than their ability to predict. They live in a world every hopeful that procedure, mechanism, calculation, bureaucracy, MBA degrees, and other social *techne* will keep us warm and safe. It will not, as the American

Question reminds us so sharply, though the world is willing to pay for the illusion.

This is not to say that the project of getting knowledge about the economy or about poems and paintings is worthless. Inside the margin, as economists say, it is worthful. The world runs on little else. Everyone needs to know how to write with an alphabet, though it took a Phoenician genius to think it up and make his fortune. No one afterwards, though, can expect to make a fortune by knowing the ABCs.

An economist looking at the business world is like a critic looking at the art world. Economists and other human scientists can reflect intelligently on present conditions and can tell useful stories about the past. These produce wisdom, which permits broad, conditional "predictions." Some are obvious; some require an economist; but none is a machine for achieving fame or riches.

The economist says: if a government puts a tax on property the people whose property is made more valuable by good schools will in fact pay for the schools. Or again: if voluntary restrictions on Japanese automobile imports are retained then the Japanese manufacturers will benefit by about $1,000 per car and the American auto buyers will pay about $160,000 per year for each job saved in Detroit. Though useful as wisdom, and justifying the economist's role as critical theorist, neither of these predictions is bankable.

The argument is merely that at the margin, where supernormal profits and reputations for genius are being made, the observer's knowledge is not the same as the doer's, the critic is no improvement as artist over the artist, the model of the future is no substitute for the entrepreneur's god-possessed hunch. The critics become ridiculous only when they confuse speaking well about the past with doing well in the future. Critics of art and literature stopped being ridiculous this way a long time ago. It would be good if critics of society would join them in their modest sophistication.

To become an effective manager or college dean the consistent modernist must unlearn his modernism—the notion that Procedure will tell all. If it were easy to organize "correctly," then people would do it, which is what is wrong with the journalistic notion that it is easy for business to choose the Swedish Way or the Japanese Way or whatever Way is currently on their minds. The hubris of social engineering is the same as the hubris of facile social criticism.

No one is justly subject to the American Question who retains a proper modesty about what observation and recording and story-telling can do. We can observe the history of economies or the history of painting, and in retrospect tell a story about how security of commercial property or the analysis of vanishing points made for good things. An expert such as an economist is an expert on the past, and about the future that can be known without divine and profitable possession. Human scientists and critics of human arts, in other words, write history, not prophecy.

*H*arry Truman had it about right. The expert as expert, a bookish sort consulting what is already known, cannot by his nature learn anything new, because then he wouldn't be an expert. He would be an entrepreneur, a statesman, or an Artist with a capital A. The expert critic can make these non-expert entrepreneurs more wise, perhaps, by telling them about the past. But he must settle for low wages. Smartness of the expert's sort cannot proceed to riches.

Economics teaches this. What it teaches is the limit on social engineering. It teaches that we can be wise and good but not fore-sighted in detail. Economics has something to teach the humanities, if they happen to think they know the future of art. It has a lot to teach experts, if they believe in magic.

10   Keeping the Company of Economists

It is now sixteen or seventeen years since I saw the
Queen of France, then the Dauphiness, at Versailles. . . .
Little did I dream that I should have lived to see disasters
fallen upon her in a nation of gallant men. . . . I thought ten
thousand swords must have leaped from their scabbards
to avenge even a look that threatened her with insult.
But the age of chivalry is gone. That of sophisters,
economists, and calculators, has succeeded; and the glory
of Europe is extinguished for ever.

Edmund Burke, *Reflections on the Revolution*
in France, Everyman ed., p. 73.

*T*he experts claim that their stories are "positive, not normative," "is" instead of "ought," the way things are as against how they should be. The claim is at the center of modernism. But stories carry an ethical burden. Concealing the ethical burden under a cloak of science is the master move of expertise, the secret ingredient of the snake oil.

Adam Smith was a professor of moral philosophy. John Stuart Mill was a moral and political philosopher. Since then the stories of the worldly philosophers have seemed to drift away from ethics. But the subject of economics is ethical, which makes a claim to sidestep ethics worrisome. We do not worry over much if an astrophysicist refuses to think ethically about his stories. We should if an economist refuses.

The literary critic Kurt Heinzelman has placed this "divorcing [of] philosophy from economics" in the emblematic year of 1871, when John Stuart Mill issued his last edition of *Principles of Political Economy* and William Stanley Jevons, the new scientist of economics, published *The Theory of Political Economics* (Heinzelman 1980, 85–87). By 1900 the *Dictionary of Political*

Economy could formulate the business of economics in a way that few economists would now dispute:

> The relation of morals to economics is often misunderstood. Political economy is, properly speaking, a science rather than an art. [Note the English use of "science."] It aims in the first instance at the explanation of a certain class of facts. . . . The special knowledge of economic facts possessed by the economist may enable him to give valuable advice on economic questions, but this, strictly speaking, is not his business. His business is to explain, not to exhort. It is therefore beside the mark to speak of economists, as such, preaching a low morality or rejecting morality altogether. (Montague 1900)

The economist was to be seen as a man of business, not a preacher. He sold Gradgrind facts, not the mere preaching of morality. In 1900 the word "preach" already sneered, as teenagers now sneer at their parents' preaching. The *Dictionary* claims too that the economic facts are science rather than art. By 1900 the specialization of "science" in English to mean "lab-coated and quantitative" was accomplished already. The peculiarly English definition made it easy for Jevons and other English-speaking economists this century past to suppose that a science could have nothing to do with morality.

It would be a strange economics, of course, that did not treat at least the pursuit of happiness, and therefore the morality of getting more. Economics has a branch called "welfare economics" into which moral questions have been diverted since the 1920s. The graduate schools teach that the sole moral judgment an economist should make is the least controversial one: if every person is made better off by some change, the change (being "Pareto optimal") should take place. Even philosophers like John Rawls have adopted the notion of Pareto optimality, trying in the economist's manner to pull a decently detailed moral theory out of a hat. Welfare economics has shown recently some stirrings of more complex moral life, as in the works of the economist and philosopher Amartya Sen. But mainly welfare economics is Victorian utilitarianism stuffed and mounted and fitted with marble eyes.

The demise of moral reasoning in the late nineteenth century and early twentieth century would not come as news to Wayne Booth of the University of Chicago, the very model of a modern major professor, who wrote in 1988 a book called *The Company We Keep: An Ethics of Fiction*. He begins by noting how thoroughly since modernism the students of literature have segregated off the moral questions. "There is no such thing as a moral or an immoral book," said Oscar Wilde. "Books are well written or badly written. That is all." As was his talent, Wilde spoke only a little before his time. Biologists, historians, economists, even the theologians of the age subscribed at last to this bit of modernist amorality. There is no such thing as a moral or an immoral economy. Economies are efficient or inefficient. That is all. In this life "we want nothing but Facts, sir; nothing but Facts!"

Booth's book gives a reply. It suggests to an economist that the "ethical criticism" it propounds can reach beyond literature. Booth himself takes ethical criticism as far as the Ajax Kitchen Cleanser jingle. It can be taken all the way to economics and its unconscious use of ethics-laden stories. Tzvetan Todorov put the matter so: "literature . . . is a discourse oriented towards—let us not be intimidated by the ponderous words—truth and morality. . . . If we have managed to lose sight of that essential dimension of literature, it is because we began by reducing truth to verification and morality to moralism" (1987 [1984], 164). For "literature" read "economics."

The easiest point is that economists have ethics, perforce. Booth remarks that "even those critics [he could have said economists] who work hard to purge themselves of all but the most abstract formal interests turn out to have an ethical program in mind" (1988, 7). All right: ideology motivates economists, despite their protestations of ideological innocence.

The big point, however, is not ideology and its inability to see itself. We know that already. The big point is that economic stories, as Booth argues in detail for novelists, have an ethical burden: "We all live a great proportion of our lives in a surrender to stories. . . . Even the statisticians and accountants must *in fact* conduct their daily business largely in stories: the reports they give to superiors; the accounts they deliver to tax lawyers; the anecdotes and parables they hear." (Booth 1988, 14, italics his). "All of us spontaneously make narratives out of just about every bit of information that comes our way" (162). "It is impossible to shut our eyes and retreat to a story-free world" (236). If we enter into it we "embrace the patterns of desire of any narrative" (285).

Start the ethical criticism of economics, then, with Booth's central question about the corruptions of literature (11): "What kind of company are we keeping as we read or listen?" As our mothers told us, keeping bad or good company is bad for us or good. Though he can hardly be faulted for not reflecting on academic life in other books, Wayne Booth does not in *The Company We Keep* examine the reading and listening to science and scholarship (as against literature), and the company therefore that teachers and scholars keep.

The levels at which we are asked to be a kind of person by economic writing need to be distinguished.

First, the scientific paper in economics has an implied reader it shares with other self-consciously scientific productions of the culture. The implied reader has some features that are unattractive: he is cold-blooded, desiccated, uninvolved. The case of Isaac Newton and his invention, the scientific paper, is the model (Bazerman 1988, chap. 4).

Along with high-minded precepts about the production of science the scientific paper encourages the low-minded notion that other moral questions are "just matters of opinion." The scientific paper in economics treats ethical matters of income distribution, for example, as unarguable, like one's preference for chocolate ice cream. The question that remains of course, is, "How do we think about our judgments, once we decide that our goal is to *think* about them and not simply to assert them?" (Booth 1988, 59). The values asserted by the scientific paper in economics and elsewhere are certainly not all bad. But it is worth remarking sharply that they are not all good, either, even though scientific.

The second point about the people we are asked to be in the reading of economic texts is more particularly economic. The economist asks the reader to take on certain ethical positions for the sake of the economistic argument. Most of us don't like the implied reader of economic stories: "Am I willing to be the kind of person that this storyteller is asking me to be?" (33). About the coldly calculating *homo economicus*, no, say we: "A levelling, rancorous, rational sort of mind / That never looked out of the eye of a saint / Or out of a drunkard's eye." And yet the cold calculation had better be done, by someone, or else we will bomb civilians at night for no gain or choose manned space flight over unmanned. The person you are asked to be in a modern economic argument is not entirely attractive, but is not a character that society can do without. He is usefully realistic about constraints and choices, though a little unreflective.

On utilitarian grounds, in other words, the economist is necessary. In policy questions the ethical position that economics recommends is that of the social engineer, who provides plans indifferently for full employment or extermination camps. The social engineer will protest that he would have nothing to do with extermination camps. But then he must ask where he draws the line, an ethical deliberation that economists are reluctant to undertake.

Third, as Booth says, "artists often imitate the roles they create. The writer is moved, in reality, toward the virtues or vices imagined for the sake of the work itself" (108). The same is true of academics, perhaps more so. Historians of the medieval papacy or students of comparative politics adopt their subjects' methods, at least in spirit. It is not irrelevant that Henry Kissinger's first book was on Metternich. Anthropologists have begun to wonder recently about the effects their people have on them. About time.

For economics the analysis of the ethical effects of the roles they

create is simple, and partly true. Some economists imitate the role
of *ipse homo economicus* they have created (compare Klamer
1983). Anyone who has administered economists will report that
a third or so of them behave in selfish ways, justifying their behavior when challenged by smirking reference to the economic model
of man. "If I serve on the search committee I want a more than an
average raise next year." "Jim, you're kidding: I can't hitch salary
to routine service in such a mechanical way. We're in this together." "Ha! Don't talk to me about togetherness. You believe in
economics, don't you?" Historians and doubtless professors of literature have their own occupational diseases, but cheeky
selfishness is not one of them. It's not done in their circles; it is in
economics, because of the market stories the economists tell. For
the same reason it would be impossible to get a group of modern
economists in academic life or the government to vote themselves
strictly equal salary increases, so deeply do they believe in the ethics of competition. The egalitarian solution regularly occurs in
university departments of history, some of which in fact vote on
salaries.

The ethical effect of paying close attention to economic behavior, to repeat, is not entirely bad. Economists suggest sometimes
that the splendid rationality they study is worthy of imitation. Economics provides the rudiments of ethical thinking for a bourgeois
age: accumulate; think ahead; be methodical if it suits the task; be
as honest as is the local custom; above all, do not feel socially inferior to an impulsive aristocracy—their day is done. The point is
that the ethical thinking of the bourgeoisie is not worthless (an
economist would make reflexively the joke that after all it has sold
well). Most of those who sneer at it are the beneficiaries of its virtues, which, "during its rule of scarce one hundred [now near 250]
years has created more massive and more colossal forces than have
all preceding generations together." And since Marx and Engels
penned these lines in their *Manifesto* the real income per head of
Americans has increased by a factor of ten and of late comers to
capitalism by more. Viewed socially, the economic man is no pest.

Even viewed from a strictly individual point of view the merchant's virtues, though not those of Achilles or Jesus, are not ethical zeroes. In his wretched play at the dawn of bourgeois power (1731), George Lillo has his priggish ideal of the London merchant, Thorowgood, assert that "as the name of merchant never degrades the gentleman, so by no means does it exclude him" (1952 [1731], 294). Lillo lays it on thick. In the same scene Thorowgood on exiting instructs his assistant to "look carefully over the files to see whether there are any tradesmen's bills unpaid." One can smile from an aristocratic height at the goody-goody leanings of bourgeois ethics. But after all, in seriousness, is it not a matter of ethics to pay one's tailor? What kind of person accepts the wares of tradesmen and then refuses to give something in return? No merchant he.

The honesty of a society of merchants in fact goes beyond what would be strictly self-interested in a society of rats, as one can see in that much-maligned model of the mercantile society, the small Midwestern city. A reputation for fair dealing is necessary for a roofer whose trade is limited to a city of 50,000. One bad roof and he is ruined. A professor at the University of Iowa refused to tell at a cocktail part the name of a roofer in Iowa City who had at first done a bad job (he redid the job free, at his own instigation) because the roofer would be finished in town if his name got out. The professor's behavior itself shows that ethical habits of selfish origin can harden into ethical convictions, the way a child grows from fear of punishment towards servicing an internal master. A rat would have told the name of the roofer, to improve the story. After all, the professor's own reputation in business was not at stake.

The economist who relishes the telling of a story of greed is advocating it, whatever he may say about "is" and "ought." Certainly since the beginning of modern economics the economist has urged us to look on the good side of greed. Again: The morality of the almighty dollar is not the worst of moralities. Dr. Johnson said, "There are few ways in which a man can be more innocently employed than in getting money." "The more one thinks of this, [said

Strahan] the juster it will appear" (Boswell 1949 [1791], 532; 27 March 1775). So it has appeared in the long conversation after 1775. The economists have been arguing since the eighteenth century that the ancient and aristocratic distaste for acquisitiveness is naive ethically. It is naive because it fails to see that greed prospers in a market economy only by satisfying the ultimate consumers.

Donald Trump offends. But for all the jealous criticism he has provoked he is not a thief. He did not get his billions from aristocratic cattle raids, acclaimed in bardic glory. He made, as he put it, deals. All of them voluntary. He did not use a .38 or a broadsword to get people to agree. He bought the Commodore Hotel low and sold it high because Penn Central, Hyatt Hotels, and the New York City Board of Estimate—and behind them the voters and hotel guests—put the old place at a low value and the new place, trumped up, at a high value. Trump earned a suitably fat profit for seeing that a hotel in a low-value use could be moved into a high-value use. An omniscient central planner would have ordered the same move. Market capitalism can be seen as the most altruistic of systems, each capitalist working to help, for pay. Trump does well by doing good.

And yet there is an ethical problem in the theory and practice of economics. The problem is deeper than the mere distaste for calculation of selfishness or greed. Booth argues persuasively that a good author is a good friend, the good friend being "a kind of company that is not only pleasant or profitable, in some immediate way, but also good for me, good for its own sake. . . . Hours spent with this best kind of friend are seen as the way life should be lived. . . . My true friend is one who [quoting Aristotle] 'has the same relations with me that he has with himself'" (1988, 146–47).

The model of economics conserves on this sort of friendship, trying to get along on as little of its as possible. Economics was once described as the science of conserving love. The notion is that love is scarce, and that consequently we had better try to get along without it, organizing our affairs to take advantage of the abundant selfishness instead. The argument is economic to the core. As Adam Smith said famously, "It is not from the benevolence of the butcher, the brewer, or the baker, that we expect our dinner, but from their regard to their own interest" (1976 [1776], 16).

Smith did not overlook love—on the contrary, he wrote what he himself thought was his best book on *The Theory of Moral Sentiments*. Yet he never worked out the connection between his theory of love and his theory of selfishness. The problem is that conserving on love, treating it as terrifically scarce, and not expecting it, may be a bad way to encourage its growth. That is the modern social democratic position against market capitalism—that market capitalism discourages love (massive government bureaucracies, say the social democrats, encourage it).

The novelists did better in thinking about love and selfishness. It has long been realized that not economists but novelists first gave prominence to commercial selfishness. Novelists, poets, and playwrights, not primarily social theorists, were the first to portray the bourgeoisie. Smith's *Wealth of Nations* was just described as a "theory of selfishness." That is the reading that a modern economist gives the book, projecting back onto the father the sins of the children. In truth the book itself does not support such a reading very well. Smith never describes a project of rational selfishness without noting the emotional and moral obstacles to achieving it. Foreign trade free of tariffs, for example, is recommended by more than "police" (that is to say, policy, expediency, the achieving of high incomes). Most fundamentally, free trade accords with natural rights.

Notably, the idea of *homo economicus* comes late to economics, towards the end of the nineteenth century, by way of an analogy with physical molecules. Yet it comes early to the English novel, full blown in Defoe circa 1720, or prominent later in, say, Austen's comedies of calculation circa 1800 or Dickens' satires of acquisitiveness circa 1840.

Homo economicus is a facer of choices, a spurner of options known in the trade as "opportunity costs." The notion of opportunity cost, central to modern economics, does not become clear to economists until the Austrian economists of the 1870s. Yet it has ever been a commonplace of poets, two roads diverging in a yellow wood, and I, being one traveler, able to take only one. The road not taken is the opportunity cost. So is Achilles' road of fighting not taken to sulk in his tent or Satan's road of serving in Heav'n not taken to reign in Hell.

Look at Robinson Crusoe selecting what to load on his first raft trip from the wreck:

It was in vain to sit still and wish for what was not to be had, and this Extremity rouz'd my Application. . . . Hope of furnishing my self with Necessaries, encourag'd me to go beyond what I should have been able to have done upon another Occasion. My raft was now strong enough to bear any reasonable Weight; my next Care was what to load it with. . . . Having considered well what I most wanted, I first got three of the Seamen's Chests . . . and lowered them down. . . . The first of these I filled with Provision, *viz*. Bread, Rice, three Dutch Cheeses. . . . This put me upon rummaging for Clothes, . . . but [I] took no more than I wanted for present use, for I had other things which my Eye was more upon, as first Tools to work with on Shore, and it was after long searching that I found out the Carpenter's Chest, . . . much more valuable than a Ship Loading of Gold. . . . My next Care was for some Ammunition and Arms. (1975 [1719], 41–42)

This is a commercial man having to make choices under conditions of "scarcity" (another notion articulated late in economics, well after the novelists had shown it working in their stories). The raft is not of infinite size; at any moment the weather may turn and sink the wreck; this may be Crusoe's only trip. He cannot have everything, and so must make choices. He takes only the clothing he "wanted for present use," because there were "other things which my eye was more upon." That is, he chose to have fewer clothes and more carpenter's tools. He could not in the circumstances have both. He faced a road of many clothes or a diverging one of many tools and had to choose between them. He later "resolv'd to set all other Things apart [the opportunity costs], 'till I got every Thing out of the Ship that I could get" (44).

Each time Crusoe or any *homo economicus* faces a choice he draws up a balance sheet in his head—Crusoe speaks in the passage just cited of calling "a Council, that is to say, in my Thoughts, whether I should take back the Raft," but more commonly he uses commercial metaphors, especially those of accounting (most particularly on pp. 53–54). This is the rational way to proceed—understanding the word "rational" to mean merely the sensible adjustment of what you can do to what you want. So the rational person is a calculator, like Crusoe, making rough and ready choices about what to put next on the boat. After the second storm destroys the wreck, "I . . . recover'd my self with this satisfactory Reflection, *viz.* That I had lost no time, nor abated no Diligence to get everything out of her that could be useful to me" (47).

The details of the style throughout the book contribute to the force of scarcity—a contrast to the stories of shipwrecks in the *Odyssey* or the *Aeneid,* over which hover intervening gods willing to perform miracles of abundance. The miracles in Crusoe's world are naturalistic, reflecting always Adam's Curse in a way we have come to call "realistic." Defoe's story is filled with realistic disappointments, signalled often by an ominous "but." "There had been some Barly and Wheat together" on the wreck, *"but,* to my great Disappointment, I found afterwards that the Rats had eaten or spoil'd it all" (41). The wreck had "a great Roll of Sheet Lead: *But* this last was so heavy, I could not hoise [sic] it up to get it over the Ship's Side" (45). He takes a kid from a she-goat, and "hopes to have bred it up tame, *but* it would not eat, so I was forc'd to kill it and eat it myself" (50). He endeavored to breed some young wild pigeons, *"but* when they grew older they flew all away" (62). "May 4. I went a fishing, *but* caught not one Fish that I durst eat of" (68). "I searched for a *Cassava* root, . . . *but* I could find none" (79). He spent three days bringing grapes to his cave, *"But,* before I got thither, the Grapes were spoil'd" (80). The "but" is realistic, unsentimental, aware of life's scarcity. It is the economist's favorite conjunction.

Crusoe makes choices between goods, a workaday choice, not

between good and evil. The absurdity is not making a choice, like Burridan's ass, starving because he could not choose between two equally delicious piles of hay. *Homo economicus* may or may not be bad company for us, but literary artists, not the worldly philosophers, are responsible for getting us acquainted.

*I*f economists tell stories and exercise an ethical sense when telling them, then they had better have as many stories as possible. This is a principled justification of pluralism, an argument for not keeping all one's eggs in a single narrative basket. If you are accustomed to thinking in Platonic terms within which knowledge consists mainly of propositions like the irrationality of the square root of two, provable now and forever, then monism looks attractive. There's One Truth out there, isn't there? If you are by contrast accustomed to thinking in Aristotelian terms within which knowledge consists of judgments like the desirability of democracy, uncertain even when agreed to after much discussion by people of good will, then monism in the tales we tell looks foolish, as it is.

"Powerful narrative," writes Booth, "provides our best criticism of other powerful narratives" (1988, 237). Maybe. Powerful metaphors do the job, too. But there is no doubt that the mutual criticism of the rhetorical tetrad is what's called for. The application to economics is straightforward. A variety in economic narratives is good for the soul. Marxist narrative provides a criticism of the bourgeois "neoclassical" narrative, and vice versa. "The serious ethical disasters produced by narratives occur when people sink themselves into an unrelieved hot bath of one kind of narrative" (237). Dogmatic Marxists, dogmatic neoclassicals, dogmatic Austrian economists, dogmatic institutionalists, who have put the other's writings on an index of forbidden books, are ethically dangerous, all of them. They are true believers, or, rather, believers in Truth. The best lack all conviction, while the worst / Are full of passionate intensity.

The Boothian pluralism of stories, then, speaks to economics. Albert Jonsen and Stephen Toulmin have recently noted the failures of "principled dogmatism," the one-story world, as an approach to morality—"legalism without equity, and moralism without charity" (1988, 342). Economics is a spur to such dogmatism, attempting to reduce ethical questions to a system of axioms. The stories of economists could better be used casuistically, as Jonsen and Toulmin would urge. The case-by-case method is quite opposed to modernism, and was attacked by Pascal in his *Provincial Letters* of 1656–57 on modernist grounds (Jonsen and Toulmin 1988, chap. 12). It does not seek universal principles to be applied by social engineers. It seeks an ethical conversation in which principles of less-than-universal applicability are discovered.

The best economists do exactly this. Ronald Coase, for example, is a British-educated economist for a long time on the faculty of the Law School of the University of Chicago. His approach to economics is casuistic, looking for the stories and metaphors and facts and logics that fit the case at hand, and avoiding the unreasonable obsession with one of them alone. His most famous article, "The Problem of Social Cost" (1988 [1960]), is exactly casuistic. It has therefore been misunderstood by modernist economists, who see in it a "theorem" for their social engineering. The theorem, as it happens, is due to Adam Smith, some years in advance of Coase (namely, that exchange free of trammels works well; Coase's point was the opposite, that in a world of trammels the particular trammels need to be examined one by one to decide about things like air pollution and property rights). A style of ethical storytelling that insists that cases matter as much as principles is foreign to most of modern economics.

The application of an ethics of fiction to economics, though, can hardly fail to teach also in the other direction. Students of literature can learn a thing or two about ethics from economists, and not only the ethical points already sketched—that bourgeois values have their value and that we must be grown-ups and face scarcity when after all it exists. The additional lesson in ethics that literary people can take from economics—economics of any sort, and indeed from social science of any sort—is that action is social. Booth takes ethical matters to be one-on-one affairs. An economist listening to the stories told by Adam Smith, David Ricardo, Knut Wicksell, John Maynard Keynes, or Paul Samuelson cannot narrow the ethical question down to me and thee. The economist has too lively an appreciation of the we. An economically consequential book—from *Atlas Shrugged* to *The General Theory of Employment, Interest and Money*—can have its consequences in wholly unintended ways on the individual reader (which Booth emphasizes) and in wholly unintended ways on people beyond the reader (which he does not). For example, *Atlas Shrugged* can inadvertently sustain a country-club Republicanism far removed from the romance of the novel. *The General Theory* can help create an atmosphere of democratic interventionism that results in a permanent underclass of welfare recipients serviced by well-paid bureaucrats.

In other words, the economist looks for moral consequences beyond the dyad of author and reader. A book can have obviously good ethical effects on individuals, encouraging them to save (to take the standard Keynesian example), yet the saving can have bad effects in the society at large. We recognize the pursuit of profit as an ethical failing in an individual—relative to Pauline perfection, at least—yet at the social level it can lead to good.

The classic definition of economics was given by Alfred Marshall in 1890 on the first page of his *Principles of Economics*—"a study of mankind in the ordinary business of life." To this the literary critic Northrop Frye would answer, "The fundamental job of the imagination in ordinary life . . . is to produce, out of the society we have to live in, a vision of the society we want to live in" (1964, 140). Economists preach ethics unaware, but have limited their imagination in the telling of ethical stories.

Economics seems to be ready to turn back to some ethical thinking. Many economists have realized the utilitarian hat does not have a rabbit inside. Economics requires ethical thinking in detail, and ethical thinking requires stories, the imagination exercised through time. A proper *homo economicus* recognizes that he is *homo narrans*, a teller of stories and a conveyer of character, and therefore, as Booth points out, *homo iudicans*. When he catches on he'll make better company to keep.

11 The Common Weal and
and Economic Stories

*T*he worldly philosophers change the world with their stories and metaphors. There's work for the econo-literary critic in showing how the rhetoric matters to policy and in distinguishing the good stories of policy from the bad. (Robert Boynton, among other things a politico-literary critic, has done so for the Senate Agriculture Committee [1987].)

The stories in economics are numerous beyond count. The moral outrage that fuels some of them is surprising in so desiccated a science. Since its beginnings economics has reserved its second greatest indignation for monopolists (its first greatest is for clumsy governments). When most economists think of American doctors, for example, they think of monopoly. On the face of it the analogy does not look persuasive. After all, there are hundreds of thousands of doctors, not one, so in no literal sense does the medical profession constitute one seller. Medicine talks about itself in noncommercial terms, as a disinterested science and a sacrificing profession. The economists see it differently, largely because of the story they tell (see McCloskey 1985b, 345). Once upon a time (namely, until the 1930s) medical doctors in the United States earned roughly the same as lawyers or middle management. Then, beginning about 1910 and concluding by about World War II, through their state boards of medical examiners and the corruption of state legislatures, the doctors seized control of the supply of health care, closing medical schools, forbidding foreign doctors to immigrate, and preventing nurses, pharmacists, and others from practicing medicine, at just the time that medicine began to cure more people than it killed. The result was an astonishing increase in the relative income of American doctors (not matched in places like Britain or Italy where the doctors did not succeed in blockading entry), who now earn three times what comparable professionals earn, happily ever after. The economist views the behavior of the American Medical Association as union power more effective than that of plumbers and electricians, concealed behind a myth of self-sacrifice and a facade of ethical purpose. The economic story results in shockingly harsh ethical judgments about the American doctor. A bus driver, says the economist, holds the lives of more people in his hands; a lawyer works longer hours; a professor studies more. But the doctor exploits the most tax shelters, putting medical care out of the reach of the poor.

Economists have developed over the past twenty years or so a similar story about regulation, which, like the medical story, they teach to their students as gospel (291). What is notable is the change in attitude. Economists once retold the Progressive story, assuming without irony that regulators would be able to defy politics for the good of the community. Prohibition, the city manager movement, and especially the regulation of monopoly were all favorites of American economists in the first two decades of the century. The Progressive program was of course put into practice by the New Deal and by the Great Society programs of the 1960s. But since those Progressive times the economists have changed their story.

In the new story, the Interstate Commerce Commission, for example, is said to have been taken over by the very railroads it was supposed to regulate shortly after its formation in 1887 (and later by the big trucking firms). The hero of the Progressive story, a selfless regulator protecting the little man from big business, has for two decades raised increasingly derisive laughter in the halls of economics departments. The economist asks with a smirk: "Do you really expect United Van Lines to sit idly by while the ICC guts its profit?" The moral authority of one regulatory commission after another has been undermined in the eyes of economists by the new story line (lately, for example, the Securities and Exchange Commission, by Phillips and Zecher 1981). The results show in deregulation, an example of the power of ideas as against vested interests. Ideas, not dollars, conquered the regulatory agencies. Many of the agencies were in fact infiltrated by economists educated at universities like Chicago and UCLA, which had long been telling the anti-regulatory tale. The economist's story has become the law.

The story of monopoly, to take a related example, was told for a long time in economics as a story of "structure, conduct, and performance." That is, monopoly was viewed as rain, some of which must fall upon each society. Markets came with "structures" of one seller or two sellers or many sellers, causeless and natural. The job of the economist was to provide umbrellas for the victims of the bad performance. Until the 1970s every course in "industrial organization" (the field of economics that studies monopoly and competition) outside the University of Chicago and a few other places told this tale: monopoly just happens and the economist just stops it. Since the 1970s a new and richer story of monopoly has been told, of how a monopoly comes to be a monopoly, and what therefore is to be done about each separate history. The new theories are casuistical, argued case by case under principles that cannot be applied as invariant rules. If a monopoly of computers arises from one of many potential competitors, for example, it may not be desirable to regulate it, since the disciplining threat of new entry remains.

The analogous case is slum clearance, a long-standing policy of enlightened nations. Slums are bad relative to ideal communities, of course, just as a monopoly is bad relative to an ideal industry. The instinct of the social engineer is therefore to clear the slums and break up the monopoly. But the result has commonly been the concentration of the poor into housing projects worse than the original slums, and the concentration of political pressure into regulatory commissions more monopolistic than the monopolies.

The causes of slums reassert themselves in the Robert Taylor Homes along the Dan Ryan Expressway in Chicago, since the housing was not itself a cause. So too in the regulation of monopoly: when monopoly is caused by the exercise of political power, as it often is, putting politics in charge of the industry is not going to help. The political economy asserts itself in the golden rule, that those who have the gold, rule.

The stories of economics matter to all manner of economic policy. Consider the story of helping poor countries, whose minimal plot is: Once the poor countries were poor, then the rich countries helped them, and now they too are rich. Peter Bauer, an Austrian-British economist who has long criticized the ruling metaphors in this story, has now the satisfaction of seeing his grimmest prediction come true (1984). As he feared some decades ago the advice of economists has on balance hurt the poor countries of the world, hurting more as the quarrel over equality between "The North" and "The South" has intensified. Most of the followers have moved along the track, but notably slower than the leaders.

It is not surprising that an economics taking itself to be value-free social engineering should do a poor job in advising poor countries. Economics around 1950 gave up social philosophy and social history to become a blackboard subject. The poor countries provided convenient laboratories to try out what was discovered on the blackboard. The governments of Western Europe proved wary of the snake oil, but other governments, and intergovernmental governments, lined up at the wagon to buy.

The result was a devaluation by intellectuals of voluntary exchange. After all, what is so fine about voluntary exchange if crushing it can produce the wealth of nations? And why should historical and philosophical doubts that the wealth arises from planning be entertained if a sweet diagram can prove that planning works? The planning and government programs worked badly, on the whole, as is suggested by the unraveling of Eastern Europe and the stagnation of South Asia and the long night of Africa. The postwar experiment with planning was a treason of the clerks, arising from their religion, an irrational belief in their ability to predict and control.

The metaphor of the "Third World" itself was born (as Bauer has noted) with foreign aid and anti-communism shortly after the war. It asks a question of equity. Is it fair that the First World has all the riches? By the mere act of speaking of equity versus efficiency the economists import into the argument, as though it was uncontroversial, a utilitarian ethic. The audience is invited to think of tradeoffs between the one and the other. As the economists would say, mathproudly, $U = U$ (Efficiency, Equity), in which Efficiency is the size of national income and Equity is measured by the distribution of income. This is not "wrong"; it is simply one metaphor among many, some more apt for particular uses than others. If economists think of equity in such terms, for example, they will not ask how the Efficiency was achieved (by executing people jailed in football stadiums, say) or whether Equity entails stealing from innocents (by executing people who buy low and sell high).

The North is meant to feel guilty that by the grace of God it gets more than the South. Bauer has treated at length (1984, chap. 5) the use of the notion of "our" guilt as a justification for compulsory charity. Clergymen and upper middle class intellectuals delight in the transformation of *mea culpa* into *nostra culpa,* prejudging in a word the weighty question of whether charity should be individual or social.

Bauer notes similarly the danger in the related metaphor of "nation building," a handsome neoclassical building in which political prisoners scream in the basement. The figure of a building treats people as "lifeless bricks, to be moved by some master builder" (5). Nation building is not merely a metaphor, mere ornamental rhetoric, but a political argument put into a word. The "nation" is to be "built" by the government, indeed by the present set of colonels and chieftains in charge of the building project.

The very word "development" is a metaphor, of course, limiting our thinking at the same time it makes thinking possible. "Economic growth" sounds better than "economic change," and "change" better than "losing existing jobs," but they are translatable one into the other, suggesting different policies. Economists are not usually conscious of the difference the words make. A self-conscious metaphor has a different effect from an unself-conscious one. The economist and social thinker Mancur Olson has used comparisons among one-man boats, eight-man boats, and multi-oared galleys to illuminate the wealth of nations (Olson 1987). He uses the figure openly and self-consciously, and therefore the effect is merely communicative and ornamental. An explicit metaphor does not bite.

The word "problem," likewise, answers an economic question before one thinks to ask it. Many reputable economists argue for example that the balance-of-payments "problem" is not a problem at all, in the sense of something requiring that "we" find "a solution." No one would worry about the balance of payments if the statistics on it were not collected—which is not something that can be said about some other problems facing an economic community, such as poverty or inflation. Yet many people are exercised about The Problem and propose desperate remedies. The statistics led the British government during the 1950s and early 1960s to a policy of "stop-go," with lurching booms and governmentally-induced busts, damaging the British economy for the long run.

The nineteenth century invented the talk of a "social *problem*," an "economic *problem*," and the like, problems which finally the Great Geometer in London or Washington is to solve with compass and straightedge. The economic historian Max Hartwell speaks often of the rhetoric of British parliamentary inquiries in the nineteenth century as defining problems where no one had seen them before. It is not always done with mirrors, of course; this or that condition worthy of correction does exist. But in any case it is done with words. Someone who has persuaded you to speak of inequality of income as a problem has accomplished the most difficult part of her task.

In particular, the array of metaphors taken from sport are crucial to the solving of problems. Sporting metaphors present themselves as innocuous ornaments and are especially popular among Americans, who, goodhearted as they are, favor the happy notion that in a conflict no one really gets hurt (Europeans will use metaphors of war and conquest in similar cases). The ideal is team play, joining together to score a goal against the foreigner or in a more mellow way to "achieve a personal goal." Whenever we hear that "we" should do such and such the signal has been raised: watch for the team metaphor in action.

The best that human frailty is likely to achieve along this line is a book on *The Zero-Sum Solution: Building a World-Class American Economy* (1985) by Lester Thurow, an economist and dean of the business school at the Massachusetts Institute of Technology. It is an intelligent work from which much can be learned. The book illustrates how much economists agree and how much their agreement depends on their shared devotion to quantitative thinking, the metaphor of a set of accounts.

The trouble lies in its metaphors in aid of storytelling. The book treats income and wealth throughout as being extracted like football yardage from non-Americans, especially Japanese and other Asian non-Americans. "To play a competitive game is not to be a winner—every competitive game has its losers—it is only to be given a chance to win. . . . Free market battles can be lost as well as won, and the United States is losing them on world markets" (59). One chapter is entitled "Constructing an Efficient Team." Thurow talks repeatedly about America "competing" and "beating" the rest of the world with a "world-class economy." At one point he complains that more people do not adopt his favored metaphor, which he calls "reality": "For a society which loves team sports . . . it is surprising that Americans won't recognize the same reality in the far more important international economic game" (107).

In more aggressive moods Thurow trades his football helmet for a flak jacket: "American firms will occasionally be defeated at home and will not have compensating foreign victories" (105). Foreign trade is viewed as the economic equivalent of war. Unsurprisingly, British journalists in the late nineteenth century spoke in identically bellicose terms about the American "threat" and the German "menace." And in part, with due allowance for contingency, the competition for first place on the metaphorical battlefield of commerce led most gratifyingly to the literal battlefields of the Somme and Verdun.

Three metaphors govern Thurow's story: this metaphor of the "international zero-sum game"; a metaphor of the domestic "problem" that damages performance in the game; and a metaphor of "we" who face the problem. We have a domestic *problem* of productivity that leads to a *loss* in the international *game*. Thurow has spent a long time interpreting the world with these linked metaphors (he has written other books using them, as have many journalists: Thurow is unusual only in being a good economist using such rhetoric). It is America's job to "compete on world markets" (48), not to make itself wise and competent; what "counts" in Japanese economic performance are its export industries (49), not its wretchedly inefficient agriculture and retailing.

The subject, though, is the exchange of goods and services, Japanese automobiles for American timber, German steel tubes for Soviet natural gas. The game metaphor does not seem apt. If exchange is a game it resembles one in which everyone wins, like aerobic dancing. Trade in this view is *not* zero sum. It is positive sum. There are social, overall, mutual gains from trade. How does an economist know? Because the trade was voluntary. That's Adam Smith's metaphor.

To be sure, viewed from the factory floor the trade with Japan (or for that matter with Massachusetts or with the town over the hill) *is* zero sum, which gives Thurow's metaphor an air of common sense. To a businessperson "fighting" Japanese competition in making automobiles, her loss is indeed Toyota's gain. (Thurow does not view California's competition against Massachusetts with the same alarm. When you think of it, this is strange. If the object is to preserve jobs in Massachusetts, then assembly plants in California or Tennessee are the main competition, the main taker of jobs, to use the non-economist's way of saying it. Why pick on foreigners?)

The game-playing metaphor looks at only one side of the trade, the selling side. As Adam Smith remarked famously, "Consumption is the sole end and purpose of all production; and the interest of the producer ought to be attended to, only so far as it may be necessary for promoting that of the consumer" (1976 [1776], 179). Economists claim to see around and underneath the economy. They claim to do the accounts from the social point of view. Underneath it all (again: the economist's favorite metaphor) Jim Beam of Iowa trades with Tatsuro Saki of Tokyo. A Toyota sold to the United States pays for 2,000 tons of soybeans bought by Japan. The mainstream economist's metaphor of mutual trade differs from that of the anti-economic economists, such as Friedrich List, the German theorist of the *Zollverein*, or Henry Carey, the American theorist of protection in the nineteenth century, or Lester Thurow.

"The heart of America's competitiveness problem is to be found in low productivity growth. . . . [Well-wishers of America] would have to advocate some form of industrial policy to cure the competitiveness problem" (100–01). Problems have solutions, called "policies," which "we must adopt." It is not hard to guess who the Solver is: I'm from the Government, and I'm here to solve your problem. The confidence in the ideas of economists and planners is hardly justified by experience. Do economists really know enough that planning for research and development, in imitation of the Japanese, should be handed over to a MITI-ish organization? Thurow speaks repeatedly of "social organization": we can do better by conscious planning, says he, and of course we know the group of experts who should do the planning.

Thurow's metaphor gets its appeal from the story into which it fits. The story is the one imposed on late Victorian Britain: in the sunset of hegemony, Britain basked complacently while others hustled. American intellectuals are worried that something similar is about to happen to them. The same reply can be made: American income after all will continue to grow whether or not America continues to have the literal lead in income. (In any case, American growth has been slower than that of most countries for most of its history: like Britain, it started rich.)

And why would one wish American hegemony to be fastened on the world forever? Is it God's plan that the United States of America should ever after be Top Nation? Why should we wish relative poverty in perpetuity on our Chinese and Latin American friends? Is this what economic ethics leads us to? It is a finding of economic history that trade among rich nations is better for the rich nations than trade with poor countries (McCloskey 1981, chap. 9). In any case, one would think that the proper audience for policy would be a citizen of the world, not merely an American. What does it matter to me if my relatively wealthy neighbor in Virginia chooses to read too few good books? Shouldn't I care more about the appalling poverty of people in Bangladesh?

The answer is not obvious one way or the other. The claims of community have to be taken seriously. The appropriateness of a strictly nationalist rhetoric for policy, however, is seldom questioned. What is the ethically relevant community? Some years ago at the Institute for Advanced Study at Princeton the political scientist Joseph Carens gave a luncheon talk about his research on American immigration policy. The audience expected him to say that concerning illegal immigration We Have a Problem—namely, how to prevent it without adopting too obviously barbarous measures—because that was the line among megalopolitan intellectuals, raised to believe that trade unions and progressiveness are one. Instead he argued that Mexicans who come to America to better themselves, even if they hurt some workers with American passports, have equal claim to our ethical concern as people born north of the Rio Grande. To the audience at Princeton it was a startling idea, that the egalitarian ethic should extend to the wretchedly poor across the border. The shock in those liberal halls of intellectual power was palpable. People were embarrassed that someone had spoken against nationalism in ethics. It was evident that stories and metaphors about immigration, which spoke of good unions undermined by foreign scabs, were largely unexamined.

Talk of America's problem with foreign competition entails a bitter nationalism. The nationalistic, game-playing (and war-mongering) stories can fit with any sort of economics. Linked with socialism, they become national socialism, the better to protect the fatherland, or socialism in one country, the better to protect the motherland. Linked with laissez faire, they become imperialism, the better to protect United Fruit. As Smith said in 1776, "A great empire has been established for the sole purpose of raising up a nation of customers who should be obliged to buy from the shops of our different producers" (Bk. IV, chap. viii; Cannan, 2:180). None of these can be the intent of Thurow and the anti-immigrationists and the other enthusiasts for protection and industrial planning. All the more reason to examine soberly their metaphors and stories.

The Productivity Problem in recent American history is not a figment. Considering their incomes, Americans are for instance alarmingly badly educated (for which we professors, incidentally, need to take some blame). Maybe such embarrassment is to be expected out of the great experiment of getting along without an aristocracy. Tocqueville thought so, and he was often right. But in any case productivity has nothing to do with international competitiveness and the balance of payments. As your local economist will be glad to make clear, the pattern of trade depends on comparative advantage, not absolute advantage. That Michael Jordan can do everything with a basketball does not suggest a policy of having the rest of his team sit down. That some country—say, the fabled America of yore, "dominant" in world manufacturing—can do both agriculture and manufacturing better than anyone else does not suggest a policy of making it do everything and import nothing. The overall level of productivity has no effect on America's trade balance. None. And the trade balance is not a measure of excellence. None. The two having nothing to do with each other. We could achieve an enormous and positive trade balance tomorrow with no pursuit of excellence by forbidding imports. Americans want to trade with Tatsuro, and it makes them better off to do so: that is all.

The idea is not to "compete," whatever that might mean in thrillingly collective policies, but to become skilled and hardworking and therefore rich. Why *foreign* trade should be especially important to the matter is obscure, though speaking against the outlanders is a common topic. The American economy, it happens, has been largely self-sufficient since its beginning, which is no surprise, since it stretches over half a continent. Lester Thurow pooh-poohs as not wealth-producing the "taking in of one's own washing," that is, trading with ourselves. But that is what Americans mainly do and always have done, with good results, thank you very much. The "lost jobs," to repeat, are mainly lost to *domestic* competition.

Like the failed war on poverty and the soon-to-fail war on drugs and the other attempts to arouse "us" to face "our" problems, the national challenge to engage in sporting and more bellicose competition with foreigners is snake oil. If it frightens Americans into investing more in bridges and education maybe it will do some good, by inadvertence. But the danger is using inapt and uncriticized stories and metaphors to rouse us from our slumber. The apter metaphors of economics say this: We do not need to be Number One in order to be happy and prosperous; we do not need to crush the Japanese to keep our self-respect.

So the ethics and policy of economic stories comes round to snake oil again. Eric Hoffer, the San Francisco dock worker and sage, asserted in one of his last books that "The harm done by self-appointed experts in human affairs is usually a product of a priori logic. . . . the logic of events may draw from man's actions consequences which a priori logic cannot foresee" (1979, 26, 28). The distinction Hoffer had in mind is not between logic in the strict sense and events in the strict sense. He was no symbolic logician or runner of controlled experiments. He meant the distinction between metaphors and stories. The *a priori* logic is the extrapolated metaphor, such as the Third World or America's economic game. What we need from our experts is less pretended omniscience and more real wisdom, wisdom to tell the stories testing metaphors and to frame the metaphors that test the stories.

Reunifying some pieces of the conversation of humankind is best tried with hard cases. Economics is a hard case, wrapped in its prideful self-image as Social Physics. The neighbors of economics hate its arrogance, as the neighbors of physics do. If even economics can be shown to be fictional and poetical and historical its story will become better. Its experts will stop terrorizing the neighborhood and stop peddling snake oil. Technically speaking the economist's story will become, as it should, a useful comedy—comprising words of wit, amused tolerance for human folly, stock characters colliding at last in the third act, and, most characteristic of the genre, a universe in equilibrium and a happy ending.

"Now, Herbie," I say, "I do not doubt your information, because I know you will not give out information unless it is well founded. But," I say, "I seldom stand for a tip, and as for betting fifty for you, you know I will not bet fifty even for myself if somebody guarantees me a winner. So I thank you, Herbie, just the same," I say, "but I must do without your tip," and with this I start walking away.

"Now," Herbie says, "wait a minute. A story goes with it," he says.

Well, of course this is a different matter entirely.

Damon Runyon, "A Story Goes with It," *A Treasury of Damon Runyon* (NY: Modern Library, 1958), 152

Works Cited

Abrams, M. H. 1981. *A Glossary of Literary Terms.* 4th ed. NY: Holt, Rinehart and Winston.

Adams, Henry. 1931 [1906]. *The Education of Henry Adams.* NY: Modern Library.

Allen, Robert C. 1979. International Competition in Iron and Steel, 1850–1913. *Journal of Economic History* 39 (December): 911–37.

Austen, Jane. 1965. [1818]. *Persuasion.* NY: Houghton Mifflin.

Austin, J. L. 1975 [1962]. *How to Do Things with Words.* Cambridge, Mass.: Harvard University Press.

Bauer, Peter. 1984. *Reality and Rhetoric: Studies in the Economics of Development.* Cambridge, Mass.: Harvard University Press.

Bazerman, Charles. 1987. Codifying the Social Scientific Style: The APA *Publication Manual* as Behaviorist Rhetoric. In *The Rhetoric of the Human Sciences,* 125–44. *See* Nelson, Megill, and McCloskey, eds., 1987.

———. 1988. *Shaping Written Knowledge: The Genre and the Activity of the Experimental Article in Science.* Madison: University of Wisconsin Press, in the series The Rhetoric of the Human Sciences.

Bely, Andrey. 1985 [1909]. The Magic of Words. In *Selected Essays of Andrey Bely,* 93–104. Translated by S. Cassedy. Berkeley and Los Angeles: University of California Press.

Billig, Michael. 1989. Psychology, Rhetoric, and Cognition. *History of the Human Sciences* 2 (October): 289–307.

Bishop, Errett. 1985. *Constructive Analysis.* Berlin and NY: Springer-Verlag.

Black, Max. 1962. *Models and Metaphors.* Ithaca: Cornell University Press.

Bloom, Allan. 1970. An Interpretation of Plato's *Ion. Interpretation* 1 (Summer): 43–62. Reprinted in Thomas Pangle, ed., *Roots of Political*

Philosophy: Ten Forgotten Socratic Dialogues, 371–95. Ithaca: Cornell University Press, 1987.

Bloom, Harold. 1976. *Wallace Stevens: The Poems of Our Climate.* Ithaca: Cornell University Press.

Booth, Wayne C. 1974. *Modern Dogma and the Rhetoric of Assent.* Chicago: University of Chicago Press.

————. 1988. *The Company We Keep: An Ethics of Fiction.* Berkeley and Los Angeles: University of California Press.

Boswell, James. 1949 [1791]. *The Life of Samuel Johnson, LL. D.* Everyman's Library, in two vols. Vol. 1. London: Dent.

Boynton, G. R. 1987. Telling a Good Story: Models of Argument, Models of Understanding in the Senate Agriculture Committee. In Joseph W. Wenzel, ed., *Argument and Critical Practices,* 429–38. Annandale, VA: Speech Communication Association.

Bridbury, A. R. 1975. *Economic Growth: England in the Later Middle Ages.* Brighton: Harvester.

Brier, Bob. 1980. *Ancient Egyptian Magic.* NY: Morrow.

Brooks, Peter. 1985. *Reading for the Plot: Design and Intention in Narrative.* NY: Vintage.

Bruner, Jerome. 1986. *Actual Minds, Possible Worlds.* Cambridge, Mass.: Harvard University Press.

Bruns, Gerald L. 1984. The Problem of Figuration in Antiquity. In G. Shapiro and A. Sica, eds., *Hermeneutics: Questions and Prospects,* 147–64. Amherst: University of Massachusetts Press.

Burk, James. 1988. *Values in the Marketplace: The American Stock Market under Federal Security Law.* Berlin and NY: W. de Gruyter.

Burnham, T. H., and G. O. Hoskins. 1943. *Iron and Steel in Britain, 1870–1930.* London: Allen and Unwin.

Campbell, John Angus. 1987. Charles Darwin: Rhetorician of Science. In *The Rhetoric of the Human Sciences,* 69–86. *See* Nelson, Megill, and McCloskey, eds., 1987.

Carlston, Donal E. 1987. Turning Psychology on Itself: The Rhetoric of Psychology and the Psychology of Rhetoric. In *The Rhetoric of the Human Sciences,* 145–62. *See* Nelson, Megill, and McCloskey, eds., 1987.

Carus-Wilson, E. M. 1954 [1941]. An Industrial Revolution of the Thirteenth Century. *Economic History Review* 2d ser. 11 (1): 39–60. Reprinted in E. M. Carus-Wilson, ed., *Essays in Economic History,* vol. 1, 41–60. London: Edward Arnold.

Clark, Gregory. 1984. Authority and Efficiency: The Labor Market and the Managerial Revolution of the Late Nineteenth Century. *Journal of Economic History* 44 (December): 1069–83.

Clark, Tom. 1978. *The World of Damon Runyon.* NY: Harper and Row.

Coase, R. H. 1988. *The Firm, the Market and the Law.* Chicago: University of Chicago Press.

Cole, Arthur H. 1953 [1946]. An approach to the Study of Entrepreneurship. *Journal of Economic History* 6 (Supplement): 1–15. Reprinted in F. C. Lane and J. C. Riemersma, eds., *Enterprise and Secular Change: Readings in Economic History,* 181–95. Homewood, Ill.: Irwin.

Coleman, D. C. 1977. *The Economy of England 1450–1750.* Oxford: Oxford University Press.

Coleman, Donald, and Christine MacLeod. 1986. Attitudes to New Techniques: British Businessmen, 1800–1950. *Economic History Review* 2d ser. 39 (November): 588–611.

Collins, Harry. 1985. *Changing Order: Replication and Induction in Scientific Practice.* London and Beverly Hills: Sage.

Cootner, P. H., ed. 1964. *The Random Character of Stock Prices.* Cambridge, Mass.: MIT Press.

Cowles, Alfred. 1933. Can Stock Market Forecasters Forecast? *Econometrica* 1 (July): 309–24.

Crafts, N. F. R. 1977. Industrial Revolution in England and France: Some Thoughts on the Question "Why was England First?" *Economic History Review* 2d ser. 30 (August): 429–41.

————. 1984. *Economic Growth During the British Industrial Revolution.* Oxford: Oxford University Press.

Cunningham, J. V. 1976. *The Collected Essays of J. V. Cunningham.* Chicago: The Swallow Press.

Davis, Philip J., and Reuben Hersh. 1987. Rhetoric and Mathematics. In *The Rhetoric of the Human Sciences,* 53–68. *See* Nelson, Megill, and McCloskey, eds., 1987.

Defoe, Daniel. 1975 [1719]. *Robinson Crusoe.* Edited by Michael Shinagel. Norton Critical Edition. NY: Norton.

Elbaum, Bernard, and William Lazonick, eds. 1986. *The Decline of the British Economy.* NY: Oxford University Press.

Elster, Jon. 1978. *Logic and Society: Contradictions and Possible Worlds.* NY: Wiley.

Euripides. *Hecuba.* Translated by W. Arrowsmith. In *Euripides III: Four Tragedies.* Chicago: University of Chicago Press, 1958.

————. *Iphigenia in Aulis.* Translated by W. Bynner. In *Euripides IV: Four Tragedies.* Chicago: University of Chicago Press, 1958.

Fenoaltea, S. n.d. *Italian Industrial Production, 1861–1913: A Statistical Reconstruction.* Cambridge: Cambridge University Press. Forthcoming.

Fogel, Robert W. 1964. *Railroads and American Economic Growth: Essays in Econometric History.* Baltimore: Johns Hopkins University Press.

———. 1979. Notes on the Social Saving Controversy. *Journal of Economic History* 39 (March): 1–54.

———. 1989. *Without Consent or Contract: The Rise and Fall of American Slavery.* NY: Norton.

Frye, Northrop. 1957. *An Anatomy of Criticism.* NY: Athenaeum.

———. 1964. *The Educated Imagination.* Bloomington: Indiana University Press.

Fussell, Paul. 1979. *Poetic Meter and Poetic Form.* Rev. ed. NY: Random House.

Galison, Peter. 1987. *How Experiments End.* Chicago: University of Chicago Press.

Geertz, Clifford. 1988. *Works and Lives: The Anthropologist as Author.* Stanford: Stanford University Press.

Gergen, Kenneth J., and Mary M. Gergen. 1986. Narrative Form and the Construction of Psychological Science. In T. R. Sarbin, ed., *Narrative Psychology: The Storied Nature of Human Conduct,* 22–44. NY: Praeger.

Gerschenkron, Alexander. 1952. Economic Backwardness in Historical Perspective. Reprinted in *Economic Backwardness,* 5–30. *See* Gerschenkron 1962d.

———. 1962a. On The Concept of Continuity in History. Reprinted in *Continuity,* 11–39. *See* Gerschenkron 1968.

———. 1962b. The Typology of Industrial Development as a Tool of Analysis. Reprinted in *Continuity,* 77–97. *See* Gerschenkron 1968.

———. 1962c. The Approach to European Industrialization: A postscript. In *Economic Backwardness,* 353–66. *See* Gerschenkron 1962d.

———. 1962d. *Economic Backwardness in Historical Perspective: A Book of Essays.* Cambridge, Mass.: Harvard University Press.

———. 1965. Foreword. In Albert Fishlow, *American Railroads and the Transformation of the Ante-Bellum Economy.* Cambridge, Mass.: Harvard University Press.

———. 1968. *Continuity in History and Other Essays.* Cambridge, Mass.: Harvard University Press.

———. 1970. *Europe in the Russian Mirror: Four Lectures on Economic History.* Cambridge: Cambridge University Press.

———. 1977. *An Economic Spurt That Failed: Four Lectures in Austrian History.* Princeton: Princeton University Press.

Gibson, Walker. 1980 [1950]. Authors, Speakers, and Mock Readers. *College English* 11 (February). Reprinted in Jane P. Tompkins, ed., *Reader-Response Criticism,* 1–6. Baltimore: Johns Hopkins University Press.

Goodman, Nelson. 1965. *Fact, Fiction and Forecast.* 2d ed. Indianapolis: Bobbs-Merrill.

_____. 1978. *Ways of Worldmaking.* Indianapolis: Hackett.

Gould, Stephen Jay. 1987. *Time's Arrow, Time's Cycle: Myth and Metaphor in the Discovery of Geological Time.* Cambridge, Mass.: Harvard University Press.

_____. 1989. *Wonderful Life: The Burgess Shale and the Nature of History.* NY: Norton.

Greene, Thomas M. 1989. The Poetics of Discovery: A Reading of Donne's Elegy 19. *Yale Journal of Criticism* 2(2):129–43.

Haddock, David D. 1986. First Possession versus Optimal Timing: Limiting the Dissipation of Economic Value. *Washington University Law Quarterly* 64 (Fall): 775–92.

Harley, C. K. 1982. British Industrialization before 1841: Evidence of Slower Growth during the Industrial Revolution. *Journal of Economic History* 42 (June): 267–90.

Hartwell, R. M. 1967 [1965]. The Causes of the Industrial Revolution: An Essay in Methodology. *Economic History Review* 2d ser. 18 (August): 164–82. Reprinted in R. M. Hartwell, ed., *The Causes of the Industrial Revolution in England,* 53–80. London: Methuen.

Heinzelman, Kurt. 1980. *The Economics of the Imagination.* Amherst: University of Massachusetts Press.

Hexter, J. H. 1986. The Problem of Historical Knowledge. Washington University, St. Louis. Typescript.

Higgs, Robert. 1987. *Crisis and Leviathan: Critical Episodes in the Growth of American Government.* NY: Oxford University Press.

Hirschman, Albert O. 1970. The Search for Paradigms as a Hindrance to Understanding. *World Politics* 22 (March). Reprinted in P. Rabinow and W. M. Sullivan, eds., *Interpretive Social Science: A Reader,* 163–79. Berkeley and Los Angeles: University of California Press, 1979.

Hoffer, Eric. 1979. *Before the Sabbath.* NY: Harper and Row.

Iser, Wolfgang. 1980. The Interaction between Text and Reader. In Susan R. Suleiman and Inge Crosman, eds., *The Reader in the Text: Essays on Audience and Interpretation,* 106–19. Princeton: Princeton University Press, 1980.

Jonsen, Albert R., and Stephen Toulmin. 1988. *The Abuse of Casuistry: A*

History of Moral Reasoning. Berkeley and Los Angeles: University of California Press.

Keegan, John. 1978 [1976]. *The Face of Battle.* Harmondsworth, Middlesex: Penguin.

Kennedy, George A. 1984. *New Testament Interpretation through Rhetorical Criticism.* Chapel Hill: University of North Carolina Press.

Kennedy, William P. 1982. Economic Growth and Structural Change in the United Kingdom, 1870–1914. *Journal of Economic History* 42 (March): 105–14.

Kenner, Hugh. 1987. *Magic and Spells (About Curses, Charms and Riddles).* Bennington Chapbooks in Literature, Ben Belitt Lectureship Series. Bennington, VT.

Kingsland, Sharon E. 1985. *Modeling Nature: Episodes in the History of Population Ecology.* Chicago: University of Chicago Press.

Klamer, Arjo. 1983. *Conversations with Economists: New Classical Economists and Opponents Speak Out on the Current Controversy in Macroeconomics.* Totowa, NJ: Rowman and Allanheld.

———. 1987a. As If Economists and Their Subjects Were Rational. In *Rhetoric of the Human Sciences,* 163–83. *See* Nelson, Megill, and McCloskey, eds., 1987.

———. 1987b. The Advent of Modernism in Economics. University of Iowa. Typescript.

Klamer, Arjo, Donald N. McCloskey, Robert M. Solow, eds. 1988. *The Consequences of Economic Rhetoric.* NY: Cambridge University Press.

Korner, S. 1967. Continuity. In *The Encyclopedia of Philosophy.* NY: Macmillan and Free Press.

Landau, Misia. 1987. Paradise Lost: The Theme of Terrestiality in Human Evolution. In *The Rhetoric of the Human Sciences,* 111–24. *See* Nelson, Megill, and McCloskey, eds., 1987.

Landes, David. 1969. *The Unbound Prometheus: Technological Change and Industrial Development in Western Europe from 1750 to the Present.* Cambridge: Cambridge University Press. (Reprinting with additions his book-length essay Technological Change and Development in Western Europe, 1750–1914 in *The Cambridge Economic History of Europe,* Vol. 6. Cambridge: Cambridge University Press, 1965.)

Lavoie, Don. 1985. *Rivalry and Central Planning: The Socialist Calculation Debate Reconsidered.* Cambridge: Cambridge University Press.

Lazonick, William. 1987. Stubborn Mules: Some Comments. *Economic History Review* 2d ser. 40 (February): 80–86.

Levinson, Stephen C. 1983. *Pragmatics*. Cambridge: Cambridge University Press.

Levy, David. 1989. *The Economic Ideas of Ordinary People*. Department of Economics, George Mason University. Book manuscript.

Lewis, C. S. 1962 [1939]. Buspels and Flansferes: A Semantic Nightmare. In his *Rehabilitations and Other Essays*. Reprinted in Max Black, ed., *The Importance of Language*. Englewood Cliffs, NJ: Prentice-Hall.

Lillo, George. 1952 [1731]. The London Merchant. In Ricardo Quintana ed., *Eighteenth-Century Plays*. NY: Modern Library.

Lindert, Peter H., and Keith Trace. 1971. Yardsticks for Victorian Entrepreneurs. In Donald N. McCloskey, ed., *Essays on a Mature Economy: Britain after 1840*, 239–74. London: Methuen.

McClelland, Peter D. 1975. *Causal Explanation and Model Building in History, Economics, and the New Economic History*. Ithaca: Cornell University Press.

McCloskey, D. N. 1970. Britain's Loss from Foreign Industrialization: A Provisional Estimate. *Explorations in Economic History* 8 (Winter): 141–52.

————. 1971. [with Lars G. Sandberg] From Damnation to Redemption: Judgments on the Victorian Entrepreneur. *Explorations in Economic History* 9 (Fall): 89–108.

————. 1973. *Economic Maturity and Entrepreneurial Decline: British Iron and Steel, 1870–1913*. Cambridge, Mass.: Harvard University Press.

————. 1979. No It Did Not: A Reply to Craft's Comment on "Did Victorian Britain Fail?" *Economic History Review* 2d ser. 32 (Nov): 538–41.

————. 1981. *Enterprise and Trade in Victorian Britain: Essays in Historical Economics*. London: Allen and Unwin.

————. 1985a. *The Rhetoric of Economics*. Madison: University of Wisconsin Press, in the series The Rhetoric of the Human Sciences.

————. 1985b. *The Applied Theory of Price*. NY: Macmillan.

McGrath, Francis C. 1986. *The Sensible Spirit: Walter Pater and the Modernist Paradigm*. Tampa: University of South Florida Press.

MacIntyre, Alasdair. 1981. *After Virtue*. Notre Dame, Ind.: University of Notre Dame Press.

McKeon, Richard. 1987. *Rhetoric: Essays in Invention and Discovery*. Woodbridge, Conn.: The Ox Bow Press.

McPherson, James M. 1988. *The Battle Cry of Freedom*. NY: Oxford University Press.

Maddison, Angus. 1989. *The World Economy in the Twentieth Century.* Paris: Development Centre of the Organization for Economic Co-operation and Development.

Madison, G. B. 1982. *Understanding: A Phenomenological-Pragmatic Analysis.* Westport, Conn.: Greenwood Press.

Malkiel, Burton. 1985. *A Random Walk Down Wall Street.* 4th ed. NY: Norton.

Mantoux, Paul. 1961 [1928]. *The Industrial Revolution in the Eighteenth Century.* NY: 1961.

Marshall, Alfred. 1890. *Principles of Economics.* London: Macmillan.

Martin, Wallace. 1986. *Recent Theories of Narrative.* Ithaca: Cornell University Press.

Mauss, Marcel. 1972 [1902–03]. *A General Theory of Magic.* NY: Norton.

Medawar, Peter. 1964. Is the Scientific Paper Fraudulent? *Saturday Review.* 1 August, 42–43.

Megill, Allan, and D. N. McCloskey. 1987. The Rhetoric of History. In *The Rhetoric of the Human Sciences,* 221–38. *See* Nelson, Megill, and McCloskey, eds., 1987.

Mill, John Stuart. 1872. *A System of Logic.* 8th ed. London: Longmans.

Mokyr, Joel, ed. 1985. *The Economics of the Industrial Revolution.* Totowa, NJ: Rowman and Allanheld.

Montague, F. C. 1900. Morality. In R. H. Palgrave, ed., *Dictionary of Political Economy.* London: Macmillan.

Moore, Ruth. 1985 [1966]. *Niels Bohr.* Cambridge: MIT Press.

Mulkay, Michael. 1985. *The Word and the World: Explorations in the Form of Sociological Analysis.* Winchester, Mass.: Allen and Unwin.

Nash, Christopher, and Martin Warner, eds. 1989. *Narrative in Culture.* London: Routledge.

Nef, J. U. 1932. *The Rise of the British Coal Industry.* 2 vols. London: Routledge.

Nelson, John, Allan Megill, and D. N. McCloskey, eds. 1987. *The Rhetoric of the Human Sciences: Language and Argument in Scholarship and Public Affairs.* Madison: University of Wisconsin Press, in the series The Rhetoric of the Human Sciences.

Nicholas, Stephen. 1982. Total Factor Productivity Growth and the Revision of Post-1870 British Economic History. *Economic History Review* 2d ser. 35 (February): 83–98.

———. 1985. British Economic Performance and Total Factor Productivity Growth, 1870–1940. *Economic History Review* 2d ser. 38 (November): 576–82.

Nye, John. 1989. Lucky Fools. Department of Economics, Washington University, St. Louis. Typescript.

Olson, Mancur. 1963. *The Economics of Wartime Shortage: A History of British Food Supply in the Napoleonic War and in World Wars I and II*. Durham: Duke University Press.

————. 1987. Diseconomies of Scale and Development. *Cato Journal* 7 (Spring/Summer): 77–98.

Oxford. 1933. *The Oxford English Dictionary*, vol. 9, S–Soldo. Oxford: Clarendon Press.

————. 1982. *A Supplement to the Oxford English Dictionary*, vol. 3, O–Scz. Oxford: Clarendon Press.

————. 1989. *The Oxford English Dictionary*. 2d ed. Vol. 14, Rob–Sequyle. Oxford: Clarendon Press.

Payne, Peter. 1978. Industrial Leadership and Management in Great Britain. In P. Mathias and M. M. Postan, eds., *The Cambridge Economic History of Europe*, vol. 7, pt. 1, 180–230. Cambridge: Cambridge University Press.

Perelman, Chaim. 1982. *The Realm of Rhetoric*. Notre Dame, Ind.: University of Notre Dame Press.

Perelman, Chaim, and L. Olbrechts-Tyteca. 1969 [1958]. *The New Rhetoric: A Treatise on Argumentation*. Translated by J. Wilkinson and P. Weaver. Notre Dame, Ind.: University of Notre Dame Press.

Phillips, Susan M., and J. Richard Zecher. 1981. *The SEC and the Public Interest*. Cambridge, Mass.: MIT Press.

Plato. *Cratylus*. Translated by H. N. Fowler. Loeb Series. London and NY: Heinemann and Putnam, 1926.

Prince, Gerald. 1973. *A Grammar of Stories*. The Hague and Paris: Mouton.

Propp, Vladímir. 1968. [1928]. *Morphology of the Folktale*. 2d ed. Translated by L. Scott and L. A. Wagner. American Folklore Society. Austin: University of Texas Press.

Rabinowitz, Peter J. 1980 [1968]. "What's Hecuba to Us?" The Audience's Experience of Literary Borrowing. In Susan R. Suleiman and Inge Crosman, eds., *The Reader in the Text: Essays on Audience and Interpretation*, 241–63. Princeton: Princeton University Press.

Redlich, Fritz. 1970 [1968]. Potentialities and Pitfalls in Economic History. *Explorations in Entrepreneurial History* 2d ser. 6 (1): 93–108. Reprinted in R. L. Andreano, ed., *The New Economic History*. NY: Wiley.

Rosaldo, Renato. 1987. Where Objectivity Lies: The Rhetoric of Anthropology. In *The Rhetoric of the Human Sciences*, 87–110. *See* Nelson, Megill, and McCloskey, eds., 1987.

Rosenblatt, Louise M. 1978. *The Reader, the Text, the Poem: The Transactional Theory of the Literary Work*. Carbondale: Southern Illinois University Press.

Rostow, W. W. 1960. *The Stages of Economic Growth*. Cambridge: Cambridge University Press.

Rothenberg, Jerome, ed. 1985. *Technicians of the Sacred*. Berkeley and Los Angeles: University of California Press.

Runyon, Damon. 1958 [1933]. Money From Home. In *A Treasury of Damon Runyon*, 18–32. NY: Modern Library.

Ruthven, K. K. 1979. *Critical Assumptions*. Cambridge: Cambridge University Press.

St. Patrick (attributed). 1947 [c. 440]. Deer's Cry. In Kathleen Hoagland, ed., *1000 Years of Irish Poetry*, 12–14. NY: Devon-Adair.

Samuelson, Paul A. 1986 [1982]. Paul Cootner's Reconciliation of Economic Law with Chance. Reprinted in K. Crowley, ed., *The Collected Scientific Papers of Paul A. Samuelson*, vol. 5, 537–51. Cambridge, Mass.: MIT Press.

Sandberg, Lars G. 1974. *Lancashire in Decline: A Study in Entrepreneurship, Technology, and International Trade*. Columbus: Ohio State University Press.

Santayana, George. 1986 [1943–53]. *Persons and Places*. Vol. 1 of the Works of George Santayana. Cambridge, Mass.: MIT Press.

Sappho. Prayer to Aphrodite. In C. A. Trypanis, ed., *The Penguin Book of Greek Verse*, 144–45. London: Penguin, 1971.

Saussure, F. de. 1983 [1916]. *Course in General Linguistics*. Translated by Roy Harris. London: Duckworth.

Saxonhouse, Gary R., and Gavin Wright. 1984. New Evidence on the Stubborn English Mule and the Cotton Industry, 1878–1920. *Economic History Review* 2d ser. 37 (November): 507–20.

———. 1987. Stubborn Mules and Vertical Integration: The Disappearing Constraint? *Economic History Review* 2d ser. 40 (November): 87–94.

Scholes, Robert, and Robert Kellogg. 1966. *The Nature of Narrative*. London and NY: Oxford University Press.

Schultz, Theodore. 1988. Are University Scholars and Scientists Free Agents? *Southern Humanities Review*. 22 (Summer): 251–60.

Sellar, W. C., and R. J. Yeatman. 1931. *1066 and All That*. NY: Dutton.

Smith, Adam. 1976 [1776]. *An Inquiry into the Nature and Causes of the*

Wealth of Nations. Edited by E. Cannan. Chicago: University of Chicago Press.

Solow, Robert. 1982. Does Economics Make Progress? American Academy of Arts and Sciences, 10 May. Typescript.

Spaziani, Eugene, R. D. Watson, Mark P. Mattson, and Z.-F. Chen. 1989. Ecdysteroid Biosynthesis in the Crustacean Y-Organ and Control by an Eyestalk Neuropeptide. *Journal of Experimental Zoology* 252 (1989): 271–82.

Stevens, Wallace. 1972. *The Palm at the End of the Mind: Selected Poems and a Play.* Edited by Holly Stevens. NY: Vintage.

Tellis, Gerard J. 1988. Advertising Exposure, Loyalty and Brand Purchase: A Two-Stage Model of Choice. *Journal of Marketing Research* 15 (May): 134–144.

Theocritus. II. The Spell. In *The Greek Bucolic Poets,* 24–39. Translated by J. M. Edmonds. London and NY: Heinemann and Putnam, 1923.

Thomas, Keith. 1971. *Religion and the Decline of Magic.* NY: Scribner's.

Thurow, Lester. 1985. *The Zero-Sum Solution: Building a World-Class American Economy.* NY: Simon and Schuster.

Todorov, Tzvetan. 1973/75 [1970]. *The Fantastic: A Structural Approach to a Literary Genre.* Translated by R. Howard. Ithaca: Cornell University Press.

———. 1977 [1971]. *The Poetics of Prose.* Translated by R. Howard. Ithaca: Cornell University Press.

———. 1980 [1975]. Reading as Construction. In R. Suleiman and Inge Crosman, eds., *The Reader in the Text: Essays on Audience and Interpretation,* 67–82. Princeton: Princeton University Press.

———. 1987 (1984). *Literature and Its Theorists: A Personal View of Twentieth-Century Criticism.* Translated by C. Porter. Ithaca: Cornell University Press.

Vickers, Brian. 1988. *In Defense of Rhetoric.* Oxford: Clarendon Press.

Waring, Stephen. n.d. *Beyond Taylorism: An Intellectual History of Business Management since 1946.* Chapel Hill: University of North Carolina Press, forthcoming.

Weinberg, Steven. 1983. Beautiful Theories. Revision of the Second Annual Gordon Mills Lecture on Science and the Humanities, University of Texas, 5 April. Typescript.

Weintraub, E. Roy. 1991. *Stabilizing Dynamics: Constructing Economic Knowledge.* Cambridge: Cambridge University Press.

White, Hayden. 1973. *Metahistory: The Historical Imagination in Nineteenth-Century Europe.* Baltimore: Johns Hopkins University Press.

_____. 1981. The Value of Narrativity in the Representation of Reality. In W. J. T. Mitchell, ed., *On Narrative*, 1–24. Chicago: University of Chicago Press.

Wiener, Martin. 1981. *English Culture and the Decline of the Industrial Spirit, 1850–1980*. Cambridge: Cambridge University Press.

Wilamowitz-Moellendorff, Ulrich von. 1930 [1928]. *My Recollections, 1848–1914*. Translated by G. C. Richards. London: Chatto & Windus.

Williamson, Jeffrey G. 1974. *Late Nineteenth-Century American Development: A General Equilibrium History*. Cambridge: Cambridge University Press.

Woolf, Virginia. 1953 [1925]. *The Common Reader, First Series*. NY and London: Harcourt Brace Jovanovich.

Xenophon. *Memorabilia and Oeconomicus*. Translated by E. C. Marchant. Loeb Series. London and Cambridge: Heinemann and Harvard, 1923.

Zarnowitz, Victor, and Geoffrey Moore. 1982. Sequential Signals of Recession and Recovery. *Journal of Business* 55 (January): 57–85.

Index

Accounting, 4, 15, 62, 64, 72, 145
Adams, Henry, 18
Allegory, 12, 31, 63, 89, 94, 96–97
Allen, Robert, 50
American economic failure, 4, 43, 63, 156–61
American question, 4, 98, 111–34
Augustine, St., 37
Austen, Jane, 32, 143
Austin, J. L., 64
Austrian economics, 9, 11, 27, 144, 146
Authority, appeals to, 9, 59, 61, 100, 151

Backwardness, theory of relative, 71
Bauer, Peter, 153–54
Bazerman, Charles, 8, 30, 138
Bishop, Errett, 126
Black, Max, 12
Bloom, Allan, 98, 108, 132
Bohr, Niels, 22, 34
Booth, Wayne, 5–6, 8, 12, 38, 52, 135–49
Boynton, Robert, 150
Bridbury, A. R., 17
British economic decline, 4, 9, 40–54, 57–69, 155, 158
Brooks, Peter, 14, 50
Bruner, Jerome, 8
Bruns, Gerald, 37
Burke, Edmund, 135
Burn, Duncan, 40
Burnham, T. H., 54

Campbell, John Angus, 8
Cato the Elder, 119
Chaos theory, 87
Chicago school economics, 9, 147, 152
Cleese, John, 4
Coase, Ronald, 30, 147
Cole, Arthur, 52
Coleman, Donald, 17, 67–68
Collins, Harry, 8
Cootner, P. H., 117
Counterfactual, 12, 57–58, 88–96; basic paradox of, 94
Cowles, Alfred, 117
Crafts, Nicholas, 17, 21, 51
Crusoe, Robinson, 99, 108, 144–46
Cunningham, J. V., 33

Darwin, Charles, 12
Defoe, Daniel, 99, 108, 143–46
Descartes, René, 5, 84, 130
Doctors, 150–51

Eckstein, Otto, 119
Elbaum, Bernard, 41, 45, 49–50, 66–67
Elster, Jon, 94
Entrepreneur, 54, 62, 68, 76, 80, 128–29, 132–34
Expert: economic, 3–5, 9, 36, 114–15, 118–19, 122, 134–35, 158, 161–62; noneconomic, 103–4, 111–12, 127–29

177

Fenoaltea, Stefano, 22
Fishlow, Albert, 74
Five-Hundred-Dollar-Bill Theorem, 112, 116, 121, 124
Fogel, Robert, 60, 85, 87–88, 90–92, 94
Frye, Northrop, 33, 55, 94, 148
Fussell, Paul, 56

Galbraith, J. K., 125
Galison, Peter, 8
Geertz, Clifford, 52
Gergen, Kenneth, 8
Gergen, Mary, 8
Gerschenkron, Alexander, 19, 20–22, 70–82
Gibson, Walker, 38
Goodman, Nelson, 64
Gould, Stephen Jay, 36, 63
Greene, Thomas, 100–101, 104, 106–9

Haddock, David, 125
Harberger, A. C., 27, 30
Harley, C. K., 17, 62
Hartwell, Max, 18, 155
Heinzelman, Kurt, 136
Hexter, J. H., 14, 61
Hirschman, Albert, 81
Hoffer, Eric, 161

Imlah, Albert, 54
Immigration, 159
Industrial Revolution, 87–88, 95
Institutionalist economics, 52, 146
Iser, Wolfgang, 35

Jevons, W. S., 136
Johnson, Samuel, 141
Jonsen, Albert R., 147

Kant, Immanuel, 76, 79
Keane, Alderman Thomas, 15
Keegan, John, 33
Kennedy, George A., 8
Kennedy, Senator Theodore, 15
Kennedy, William, 57–58

Keynes, J. M., 36, 40, 118
Kingsland, Sharon, 84
Klamer, Arjo, 5, 8, 35, 140

Landau, Misia, 8
Landes, David, 17, 40–43, 45, 52–54, 59–62, 66
Lazonick, William, 40–41, 49–50, 66–67
Levinson, Stephen, 129
Levy, David, 105
Lewis, C. S., 65
Lillo, George, 141
Lindert, Peter, 62
Literary methods of economic criticism: allegory, 12, 31, 63, 89, 94, 96–97; authorial audience, 38–39; authority, appeals to, 9, 59, 61, 100, 151; ethos, 57–60, 65, 74–75; fantasy, 30; gnomic present, 61; hermeneutic circle, 45; indirect speech, 32; marvellous, pure theory as, 30; narrative audience, 38–39; pathos, 60; picaresque, 27; realism, 83; sense of an ending, 27; style, 59, 61, 69, 74; style indirect libre, 32. *See also* Literature as method of science; Metaphor; Tetrad, rhetorical
Literature as method of science, 1, 4, 8, 30–33, 39, 55, 63, 81–84, 107
Lombardi, Vince, 43, 49

McClelland, Peter D., 90
McGrath, Francis, 5
MacIntyre, Alasdair, 131
McKeon, Richard, 8
MacLeod, Christine, 67–68
McPherson, James, 86–88
Maddison, Angus, 46–48
Madison, G. B., 102
Magic, 3–4, 72, 97–110
Malkiel, Burton, 117
Marshall, Alfred, 19, 27, 148. *See also* Neoclassical economics
Marshall, Donald, 128
Martin, Wallace, 33

Marxist economic history, 17, 50, 52, 54, 74, 76, 140
Marxist economics, 9, 20, 109, 146
Marx, Karl, 27, 70, 76, 81, 140
Mathematical arguments, 8–9, 50, 55, 59, 61, 126, 131; in economics, 19–21, 23, 28, 37, 59, 68–69, 79, 154
Mauss, Marcel, 99, 103–4
Medawar, Peter, 30
Mendel, Gregor, 11–12
Merton, Robert, 53
Metaphors: accounting, 63; economic development, 154–55; models as, 1, 4, 10–12, 23, 34; as part of tetrad, 6, 39, 69, 146; poetic, 1–2, 10–13, 28–29; sporting, 41–46, 156–58; stories conflicting with, 4, 36, 79, 81, 84, 88–90, 93–97; truth of, 64–65, 83, 154
Mill, John Stuart, 94, 135
Models, economic, 15, 23, 76, 82, 87, 90, 92–96
Modernism, 5–8, 64, 70–73, 79–81, 109
Mokyr, Joel, 17, 21
Motivism, 52
Mulkay, Michael, 32

Nash, Christopher, 14
Neoclassical economics, 9, 19–20, 50, 53, 59–60, 68–69, 146
Newton, Isaac, 30
Nicholas, Stephen, 59–60, 67–68
North, Douglass, 51

Olson, Mancur, 42, 155

Packard, Vance, 125
Parker, William, 77
Payne, Peter, 51
Perelman, Chaim, 8
Plato, 4–5, 103–4, 132, 146
Polaroid, 90, 125
Popper, Karl, 131
Positive vs. normative economics, 72–73, 135, 153

Positivism. See Modernism
Prediction and control, as ideal of modernism, 12, 71–73, 97, 109, 154
Prince, Gerald, 25–26
Propp, Vladímir, 24–25

Rabinowitz, Peter, 38
Rawls, John, 136
Reeves, Clara, 30
Regulation, 151–52
Ricardo, David, 15, 25
Rosaldo, Renato, 52
Rosenblatt, Louise, 29–30
Rostow, Walt, 17, 21, 65, 76, 81
Rukeyser, Louis, 119
Runyon, Damon, 114, 116, 163
Russell, Bertrand, 6
Ruthven, K. K., 31

Samuelson, Paul, 38, 66, 94, 119
Sandberg, Lars, 50, 62
Santayana, George, 6
Sappho, 106
Saussure, Ferdinand de, 24
Saxonhouse, Gary, 66
Schultz, Theodore, 13
Science: definition in English, 1, 7–8, 136; folk philosophy of, 71–72, 80
Smith, Adam, 135, 143, 158, 160
Snake oil, 3, 9, 36, 97, 110, 135, 153, 161–62
Social engineering, 3, 40, 72, 97, 109, 111, 126, 134, 139, 147, 152–53
Sociology of science, 52, 54
Socrates, 103, 122
Solow, Robert, 120
Stevens, Wallace, 97–99, 101, 107–8
Style of writing, 59, 61, 69, 74
Supple, Barry, 51

Tetrad, rhetorical, 1–2, 4–6, 24, 39, 61, 68, 74, 82–84, 146
Theocritus, 106
Thomas, Keith, 97, 102–4
Thurow, Lester, 156–58, 160

Todorov, Tzvetan, 25, 30–31, 35, 137
Toulmin, Stephen, 147
Toynbee, Arnold, 74
Trace, Keith, 62
Treason of the clerks, 128, 153
Truman, Harry, 111, 134
Trump, Donald, 142
Tugan-Baranovskii, M. I., 75
Two Cultures, 7, 55

Vickers, Brian, 8

Walton, Gary, 129
Warner, Martin, 14

Weinberg, Steven, 29
White, Hayden, 27, 32
Wiener, Martin, 40–41, 45, 49, 51–52, 63, 66
Wilamowitz-Moellendorff, Ulrich von, 72
Wilde, Oscar, 137
Woolf, Virginia, 35
Wright, Gavin, 66

Xenophon, 122

Zarnowitz, Victor, 120

Praise for *Her Best-Kept Secret*

"Glaser makes a persuasive case that A.A., which enjoys a monopoly in nearly every recovery sphere, is structurally and functionally unsuited to many women."

—*The New York Times Book Review*

"Glaser has written an engaging account of women and drink, citing fascinating studies about modern stressors . . . and evidence that some problem drinkers can learn moderation. . . . Bound to stir controversy."

—*People*

"Glaser approaches [her topic] with investigative rigor and thoughtful analysis."

—*Boston Globe*

"Did you ever consider that [a girlfriend] might be standing at the edge of a liquor cliff? If you didn't, *Her Best-Kept Secret: Why Women Drink—And How They Can Regain Control* is bound to make you reconsider."

—*Atlanta Journal-Constitution*

"In a heartfelt and tender examination of the issue, [Glaser] looks not just at the problems unique to women, but at the ways in which methods of recovery may be tailored to the fairer sex to maximize their effectiveness."

—*Daily Mail*

"[I]nsightful and provocative . . . this quick read is full of encouraging and informative advice, and it's sure to ignite renewed discussion about one-size-fits-all treatment options."

—*Publishers Weekly*

"An important addition to feminist literature that calls upon women to reject a spurious equality 'whose consequences in broken families, broken hearts, and broken futures are all too real' and face up to the problem of alcohol dependency before it takes over their lives."

—*Kirkus Reviews*

"With humor, thoughtfulness, and skillful research, Glaser paints a picture of mature female drinking today. You'll see yourself or your friends on almost every page."

—Parents.com

"A well-researched look into the differences between how men and women drink, what their motivations are for drinking, and how they should cope with drinking problems."

—Jezebel.com

"That so many American women stand at the edge of a liquid cliff is a surprising and scary problem that Gabrielle Glaser illuminates powerfully. For those who have a loved one standing there, you will find hope here."

—Sheryl WuDunn, Pulitzer Prize–winning coauthor of the national bestseller *Half the Sky*

"*Her Best-Kept Secret* reveals the existence of an epidemic with profound implications for women and their loved ones. This compassionate yet authoritative book explains why millions of ordinary women are turning to alcohol to handle the strains of daily life—and what they can do about it."

—Hilda Hutcherson, MD, bestselling author of *What Your Mother Never Told You About S-e-x*

Also by Gabrielle Glaser

The Nose: A Profile of Sex, Beauty, and Survival

Strangers to the Tribe: Portraits of Interfaith Marriage

Her Best-Kept Secret

WHY WOMEN DRINK—AND HOW THEY
CAN REGAIN CONTROL

GABRIELLE GLASER

Simon & Schuster Paperbacks
New York   London   Toronto   Sydney   New Delhi

In memory of Nana and Poppy,
wholly immoderate in courage, affection, and fun

Simon & Schuster Paperbacks
A Division of Simon & Schuster, Inc.
1230 Avenue of the Americas
New York, NY 10020

First Simon & Schuster paperback edition July 2014

SIMON & SCHUSTER PAPERBACKS and colophon are registered trademarks of
Simon & Schuster, Inc.

For information about special discounts for bulk purchases,
please contact Simon & Schuster Special Sales at 1-866-506-1949 or
business@simonandschuster.com.

The Simon & Schuster Speakers Bureau can bring authors to your live event.
For more information or to book an event contact the Simon & Schuster Speakers
Bureau at 1-866-248-3049 or visit our website at www.simonspeakers.com.

Permissions for photographs appear on page 231.

Designed by Aline C. Pace

Manufactured in the United States of America

10 9 8 7 6 5 4 3 2 1

The Library of Congress has cataloged the hardcover edition as follows:

Glaser, Gabrielle.
    Her best-kept secret : why women drink—and how they can regain control /
Gabrielle Glaser. — First Simon & Schuster hardcover edition.
        pages cm
    Includes bibliographical references.
1. Women—Alcohol use—United States. 2. Women alcoholics—Rehabilitation—
United States. I. Title.
    HV5137.G56 2013
    362.292082'0973—dc23
                                                    2013001088

ISBN 978-1-4391-8438-7
ISBN 978-1-4391-8439-4 (pbk)
ISBN 978-1-4391-8440-0 (ebook)

Contents

Prologue   1

1. Lush   17

2. We Are Women, Hear Us Pour   27

3. I Have to See a Man about a Dog   57

4. One Day at a Time: A.A. and Women   81

5. Rehab Nation   99

6. The Thirteenth Step   121

7. Twenty-First-Century Treatment   147

Conclusion   181

Acknowledgments   185

Notes   191

Index   233

Prologue

My name is Gabrielle, and I'm not an alcoholic.

In the field of women who write about alcohol, that makes me unusual. Much of the memorable writing on this subject comes from women who have suffered from their abuse of alcohol—with broken marriages, ugly custody battles, and repeated DUIs. These addiction chronicles trace the now-familiar path from debauchery to redemption with lively anecdotes about waking up in the beds of men whose names the author can't or doesn't want to remember.

This is not one of those books.

I'm a journalist who has written about the overlapping universes of women, health, and culture for two decades. A few years ago, I started noticing signs that women were drinking more—a lot more. I saw it in the consumption of young

women who seemed determined to keep up with the boys and continued on through the stumbles of early adulthood. Women well into the responsible years of family and career were boozing it up—my friends; my neighbors; even, on occasion, me.

As I began to explore the overlapping universes of women and alcohol, I wanted to understand what I was noticing all around me: from glossy ads to my own refrigerator; from social networking to television. I have lived in a lot of places, moving from the East to the West and back again, and the trend was evident wherever I looked.

When my oldest daughter entered kindergarten in the mid-1990s, wine wasn't a part of obligatory school functions in the New York suburbs where I lived with my family. But a few years later, when my second daughter entered school, a couple of mothers joked about bringing their flasks to Pasta Night. *Flasks?* I wondered, at the time. Wasn't that, like, from *Gunsmoke?*

In 2001, I had a third child, and even without looking hard I could see that something had significantly shifted. It was a few months after 9/11, and loving friends dropped off dinner, flowers, and baby clothes. Everybody seemed happy for a break in the terrible news. (Nine people in my small town had been killed in the towers.) But several women—editors, advertising executives, marketing consultants—delivered unusual presents. I got wine—lots of it—in binary wine carriers that reminded me of double strollers. "You'll be needing this!" was the general message. Two people told me: "One for you, one to share." It was an anxious time, but even so it struck me as odd. Why would I drink a bottle of wine by myself? I was nursing, for God's sake. I chalked it up to my surroundings, where, in the

middle of memorial services and anthrax scares, stress was at a peak. If you weren't drinking at that time, you had to have a pretty damn good excuse. Still, wine as a baby gift?

In 2002, my husband and I got jobs at a newspaper in Oregon, where I have roots stretching back 150 years. Almost as soon as we were settled in Portland, I noticed women even in that relaxed city bending their elbows with the same enthusiasm as stressed-out New Yorkers. It was against company rules to drink on the job, but women I interviewed routinely paired their lunches with beers and wine flights. After work, I occasionally joined some female colleagues who met at a cozy wood-paneled bar across the street. They were regulars, and the bartenders usually had their drinks poured the minute they took off their coats. I always left after one glass of wine—my kids were young, and I wanted to get home to make dinner. My coworkers stayed, usually for another couple of rounds, then drove home on the rainy roads. It wasn't as if I was sipping herbal tea at night myself: I usually had a small juice glass of wine while I was cooking, and another small one during dinner. But evenings at the bar used to make me a little worried. Those women sort of . . . tied one on. What if someone got into an accident, and I hadn't said anything?

I realized that it wasn't just the pressure of meeting deadlines. Women drank if they worked; women drank if they didn't work. They even drank at the parent meetings for the laid-back environmental middle school. There was no need for flasks there—half the time, gatherings were in wine bars.

Women drank in my sister's elegant suburb, before dinner, during dinner, instead of dinner. They drank just as much in my hipster neighborhood on the other side of the river, too. One Sunday night as I was doing the dishes, I saw a woman

with an ancient yellow Lab pause on the parking strip outside next to the recycling bin, out for the next morning's pickup. She glanced around furtively, then shifted her backpack around to her chest. She slid first one giant empty green bottle into the plastic box, and then another. She did this as noiselessly as one might move a sleeping baby from the car seat to the crib, so as not to disturb. At first I thought maybe she had just forgotten to take out her own bin, but those big merlot bottles were there every Monday morning for the next six years.

It became clear that this wasn't just in New York and Portland. My survey was decidedly unscientific, but wide ranging. Women drank in Seattle, they drank in Chicago, they drank in San Francisco. They just . . . drank.

●　　●　　●

As I began to think about this book, I realized that drink was more of a subtext in my own life than I had understood. As a child, it was a thrill for me to stride into rural Oregon bars and pool halls with my granddad, a handsome French Canadian with deep-set blue eyes, the nose of a hawk, and smooth broad cheekbones that looked like they'd been chiseled from marble. Poppy managed a jukebox and pinball-machine operation his brother-in-law owned, and when we would walk into a place—nobody cared much about minors not being allowed—people sat up and took notice. The bars made me feel like I was visiting Jeannie in her bottle. The wall, incandescent with green gin, topaz whiskey, and gleaming vodka, looked to me like a library of giant jewels. The cocktail waitresses always gave me Shirley Temples loaded with maraschino cherries, plastic monkeys dangling from the side of the tall glass.

Poppy had come to the United States as a teenager, in the midst of Prohibition, and his knowledge of the Canadian border's back roads came in handy during that long dry spell. Only after he died did I understand what he had meant when he joked that he had been in the "thirst" business.

My parents weren't teetotalers, but they were hardly big tipplers, either. Drinks were for special occasions: my dad liked Black Russians, but only in restaurants, and once on vacation my mom ordered a Blue Hawaii. When I was in high school in the early 1980s, somebody would pass around a bottle of MD 20/20, or draw a crowd with a case of contraband Rainier someone had begged an older brother to buy. The beer was invariably warm, and invariably bad, and I could never understand what the fuss was about.

In college, I got really drunk a single time, on a bottle of Cracklin' Rose. It was the fall of 1982, and as freshmen we envisioned the need for some sort of terrific mass relief after our first set of midterms. We organized an evening with a purpose, something we called The Get Drunk and Fall Down Party. I finished most of my bottle and spent many hours that night trying to calm my spinning bed. I was eighteen and stupid, but I learned a fast lesson. For two years after, I worked hard and rarely drank.

But then I went to study in France. The girls who lived across the hall in my squat concrete dorm always kept their door open, Gallic insouciance on constant display. They sat cross-legged on the floor and smoked cigarettes, tapping away at their typewriters and occasionally pouring Bordeaux from the collection of half-drunk bottles on their desks. The boys had brown bottles of Kronenbourg 1664 in a small refrigerator in the hallway, and the students shared drinks like American

students stuck their hands in bowls of air-popped popcorn. Not once did I hear the slurred squawks and boozy bellows so common on my campus six thousand miles away.

On weekends, I lived with a couple outside Paris who were friends of my parents. Guy, my host, made a delightful show of presenting his wife, Arlette, and me with beautiful pink Kirs, and he was even more theatrical about the wine he had chosen to accompany the meal. Usually we drank a bottle among the three of us; sometimes more. We did the same thing at Paris restaurants on Saturdays. They were never drunk, and neither was I. Moderation is easy if that's what everyone does.

Ever since, I have enjoyed wine most nights in pretty much the same way, except when I've been sick or pregnant. My husband and I drink wine with dinner, finish perhaps two-thirds of the bottle, and put it away for the next night. In the summer, or when we have guests, sometimes we drink cocktails.

But a few years ago, I began to notice distressing articles—"Moderate Drinking Poses Breast Cancer Risk"—or questionnaires in women's magazines asking "Are you an alcoholic?" No matter how low my score, I still felt the slightest bit unsettled: Was there something I was missing? Did I like drinking too much, look forward to it too much, enjoy what felt like a wintergreen Certs coat my veins about a half hour after I'd had my small glass? Did liking it mean I had some sort of a problem? Nonsense, I'd think: I don't get drunk, I never black out, I've never dreamed of hiding my consumption. And besides, the French and the Italians drink much, much more, more regularly, and they're not alcoholics. But wait, said the news crawl of worries that advances through my brain daily. What if they are? The logical counterargument

responds: Don't be such a prig! Moderate drinkers outlive everybody, and even heavy drinkers outlive teetotalers. I almost never have more than two of those little glasses a night.

Except a few years ago, when I was leaving my job and extended family in Oregon. I was trying to find a house in suburban New Jersey over the Internet, sell one I'd hoped never to leave, and had frequent long-distance quarrels with my husband, who was commuting between Portland and his great new job in New York. My parents were sad. My sister and I snapped at each other. My teenagers were angry and tense; my youngest daughter, then six, was bewildered. Whenever I stopped to see my parents-in-law, who had moved from Boston to a retirement community near us, I felt an anvil of guilt.

And that is how, during a rainy Pacific Northwest winter, I found myself anticipating my nightly wine.

On my last day of work, I made sure I waited to cry until I got to my car with a box of my belongings: yellowed clippings, a vase, my photographs. I followed the Willamette River eastward, finally sobbing as I crossed my favorite red bridge. Mount Hood glowed pink in the eastern sky. I drove past my quirky gym, which was also a video store that carried independent films; past a guy on a unicycle; past the tapas bar we could walk to; past the giant old-growth fir trees. I could feel a headache, the kind I get from crying, crawling up my skull.

Until that moment, drinking to steady my nerves hadn't really ever occurred to me—and certainly not when I was by myself. I might feel a little looser after drinking, but I always stopped. I despised the sensation of losing control.

That night (and several that followed), I found myself hating it a lot less than usual. Here is what I told myself: I knew

the small juice glasses I used for wine held five ounces, be-cause long ago I measured them, just like the posters on the back of my doctor's door advised. So that one-third of a bottle isn't actually your "one glass." My glasses were what Ameri-can guidelines consider a "serving," and I never filled it to the top—only sots would do such a thing. So my ordinary two glasses weren't even two servings. Besides, I was supposed to drink a glass of red wine every night. My dad's cardiologist told me so himself, as my dad recovered from triple-bypass surgery. Okay, so I preferred white. It had to have some help-ful effect, too.

I got home, pulled open the refrigerator, and opened my favorite wine, a sauvignon blanc from New Zealand. The girls were watching TV and didn't have much interest in talking to me anyway. I started cooking and dialed my husband in New York. I poured, drank, poured some more. The girls and I ate dinner, during which I poured some more. We cleaned up. I eyed the bottle on the counter, alarmed. It was two-thirds gone. And five days later, I realized I had polished off two other bottles. Alone.

One afternoon, after leaving my house several times so that unexpected prospective buyers might roam it freely, my heartbeat felt like a car alarm. I was on deadline with a free-lance magazine piece, but the day was spent. I looked anx-iously at the clock. It was 4:45, too early to drink. I took the dog for a walk, and suddenly felt my face flush hot. What was I thinking? What about wine at five o'clock would make that day better? What was it about wine—too much of it, at least—that was making anything better?

So to test myself, I stopped for a couple of weeks. No drinking, no buying. In the grape-producing western states,

the vegetable-museum supermarkets have aisles of wine, stacked high, with helpful aproned stewards there to pluck out just the right bottle to go with your salmon, your roast chicken, your barbecued lamb. Proud winery representatives stand behind makeshift bars with tiny plastic tasting cups, inquiring if you'd like to try some. *Why, thank you, I would.* Safeway gives out free cloth wine totes whenever you buy six bottles. You can even buy wine at the gas station, not that you would. But you could. It's everywhere. I hadn't even noticed—until I looked.

I passed my little test, but I also gained an understanding. I saw how easily, how swiftly, how imperceptibly you could slip into a habit. Since then, I keep a strict internal log: no more than two drinks on any night, a few nights a week with none. I can't say I feel better, or notice even the slightest difference on the nights I don't drink—or the mornings after.

Even so, this usually bumps my tally to more than seven drinks a week (though not by much), and by U.S. standards that makes me a "heavy drinker." This strikes me as odd, since the government guidelines for "safe" female drinking in Australia, Denmark, Canada, Holland, and New Zealand roughly double that of the United States. In the wine-producing countries of Italy, France, and Spain, recommendations for moderate daily limits are even higher.

In August 2008, just as the economy was tanking, my family and I moved to New Jersey. Everything looked pretty bleak, and again I noticed women joking about how much they were imbibing. When I stopped at a liquor store for some Spanish wine to pair with paella one hot day, my eye was drawn to the opposite side of the store, where women in microscopic miniskirts presided over a display of dry ice. They were promoting

a new drink called "Sparkling Nuvo," a clear pink concoction made of vodka, sparkling white wine, and passion fruit juice. "It's like vodka and champagne!" said a young woman as she stroked her long hair. I was decidedly not the demographic they were after, and no one noticed when I took a whiff of the viscous stuff. It looked and smelled like Benadryl.

As I glanced down the rows of booze past the women, though, I recognized that I had missed a dramatic cultural shift. In the years I'd been in Oregon, I hadn't set foot in a liquor store because my alcohol of choice—wine—is sold on every corner there. In New Jersey, it's usually only available in specialty outlets. And much of the merchandise I saw was perched in what could only be described as the Lady Aisle. I wandered past complete mysteries: watermelon-flavored vodka, vanilla-flavored vodka (wouldn't that just be called vanilla?), even pink tequila. There were odd foil pouches of pre-mixed cocktails that boasted how they took the "guesswork" out of mixing drinks. Capri Sun for moms!

The week I saw the Sparkling Nuvo, I made a trip to my town's recycling depot. We had finally finished unpacking, and I wanted to get rid of the boxes I had shoved into the backseat of my car. Once I found the place, behind a high chain-link fence, I noticed a long line of luxury metallic SUVs with female drivers. One after the other, they parked next to the truck for metal and glass and jumped out of their seats. Like the merlot drinker in Portland, these women had a singular mission: to deposit their shameful proof and leave as quickly as possible. Expert multitaskers, these women did not speak on their iPhones—the violent crash of the bottles, crunching into the iron maws of the trucks, would have been a dead give-away. Their arms, ropey from years of yoga or miles on the

elliptical trainer—"Best shape of her life!"—reached for the bags that are the totems of upper-middle-class life: silver ones from Nordstrom, white ones from Williams-Sonoma, plain ones from Whole Foods. Out poured the bottles, the bottles, the bottles. The bottles they intend to start just sipping from, but end up finishing before their husbands get home.

"Here every week," said John, who mans the depot on Wednesdays. He folded his three middle fingers into his palm, and extended his pinkie and his thumb. He cocked his head back and pointed his thumb toward his open mouth, as if it were the neck of a bottle. He smiled, and shook his head.

On a sunny July Sunday in 2009, a thirty-six-year-old Long Island mother named Diane Schuler killed her daughter, her three nieces, herself, and three men in an oncoming car when she careened the wrong way up a New York highway.

At first, sympathy swirled around Schuler, who reminded women of themselves. She had juggled a marriage, two kids, and a job—in her case, as an executive at Cablevision. The Taconic Parkway, the road where she crashed, is notorious for accidents, and initial reports focused on the possibility that a medical condition had disoriented her. But when the toxicology report from her mangled body revealed that she had a blood alcohol level at twice the legal limit, as well as trace THC, the psychoactive ingredient in marijuana, compassion turned to contempt. "How Could She?" demanded the *New York Post*. Her widower insisted, even years later, that his wife couldn't have had a secret drinking problem—despite the fact that ten shots of vodka were in her bloodstream at death. "She was a great mother," he has said.

Great mothers, of course, can't have hidden drinking problems.

Women who drink face more scrutiny than men. But the most vitriol is reserved for mothers who drink too much.

Several weeks after the Taconic tragedy, news of a second accident, also caused by a drunken mother, blared across New York tabloids. This time, a Bronx woman, blitzed on cognac, flipped her carful of girls while speeding on the Henry Hudson Parkway. Eleven-year-old Leandra Rosado, a friend of her daughter's, died after she was thrown from the car, and outrage about the incident was so palpable that New York legislators swiftly made driving while drunk with a child in the car a felony. In the nine months that followed, police made 514 arrests under the new law. And while 63 percent of drunken drivers were men, it was the women who stirred the most outrage—and the most news coverage.

A handful of mug shots of the men appeared in local and metropolitan papers, but inebriated women invariably warranted bigger headlines: "Boozed-Up Mom Charged" and "Drunk Mom Behind Wheel." Online commenters dished predictable invective: "Disgusting excuse for a mother!" "Feed her to the wolves!" "Poor white trash!" They have been shamed, then forgotten. Written off. Barflies.

There is another realm of women drinkers—those who fear they drink too much but haven't yet suffered serious consequences. They don't intend to cross that line, but sometimes there are scary signs: drunken e-mails, wholly forgotten until morning; angry words blurted when the salve of wine morphs into a serum for ugly truths.

Online, in posts to perfect lady-strangers, the women confess. They unburden themselves to other worried drinkers who find that their own jobs and cooking and homework and college applications and clothes left in the dryer—for the love

of *God,* can't somebody, anybody, please match the *socks* in this house?—are all a little easier to cope with after they pour themselves a nice glass of chardonnay, or zinfandel, but probably chardonnay. They have the sneaking suspicion that the one glass that slid into two and then three and, oh, what the hell, now four, is a bad sign.

They try many things. They try not buying alcohol. They try drinking only on weekends. They try drinking pomegranate juice with seltzer. They try putting ginger tea over ice. They try sucking Jolly Ranchers. They pick up the cigarettes they last smoked in college. They love, love, love the days they wake up clearheaded. They read at night, they watch TV at night, they are sometimes more, sometimes less, interested in sex. But then something happens: a snide comment at work; the check for camp that goes missing in the backpack vortex; a nasty driver in the supermarket parking lot. A trigger, one of the many that drip, drip, drip like water seeping from a leaky roof, and the cork comes off. The glass gets poured. Down the hatch.

But let's be clear: The trigger is usually quite simple. It is evening itself.

The worry festers. Do I have a problem? Am I some sort of lush?

• • •

Today's excess imbibing is only the latest sharp swing in America's complex relationship with alcohol. I wondered how, exactly, did our cultural icons go from the saloon destroyer Carry Nation to the Cosmopolitan-sipping Carrie Bradshaw in just a couple of generations? How had we gotten

from abstinence crusades to Girls Gone Wild and, for women a few years older, furtive trips to the dump?

Over the two and a half years I spent talking to women for this book, I found only a few who were willing to reveal themselves. Some cited the writer Stefanie Wilder-Taylor, who had created an identity for herself as a drinking mom in such books as *Sippy Cups Are Not for Chardonnay*. In 2009, though, Wilder-Taylor, the mother of three young daughters, announced on her blog that she drank too much and needed some help stopping. She cofounded an online group for women struggling with alcohol, the Booze-Free Brigade, that has grown to fifteen hundred members.

Yet because female excess drinking is a shame to be hidden at all costs, the drinking stays hidden, revealing itself at jewelry parties where Heather or Denise stay a little too close to the wine, a little too far away from the earrings. In today's confessional world, where even e-vites seem to demand elaborate explanations for why guests can't make it to a birthday party, the women worry. In my small town, the wine store owners, like hairdressers, hear everything. One told me that she has a customer who always asks for the store's fancy gift bags, as if somehow sheathing the same bottles of cheap pinot grigio she buys will help repackage the truth. Another woman comes in once a week to get several liters of inexpensive cabernet—"for cooking," she says, as she races to the back of the store, then plunks down exact change. "Must be making a lot of coq au vin," the store owner says.

American women afflicted with some form of embarrassing excess or painful deficiency have a lot of modern help. If you have an "overactive bladder," there are a handful of drugs about which you may "ask your doctor," and if you're

depressed, you might take anything from Abilify to Zoloft. There are whole industries of fat-busters: appetite suppressants, fat-absorption inhibitors, experimental doses of human growth hormone. You can buy special prepackaged diets; memberships in Weight Watchers, Jenny Craig, and gyms. You can announce that you are "off carbs," without so much as raising an eyebrow. You can get liposuction; you can get lap band surgery or a gastric bypass. Since two out of three Americans are overweight, the subject is open game. When Oprah wheeled a wagon carrying sixty-seven pounds of fat onto her set in 1988, she launched a national conversation.

But rare is the woman who can openly declare that she's having trouble cutting back on booze. In this book, I distinguish between proven fact and conjecture, what is national habit, what is solid science, and what is rooted in our attitude toward alcohol. I also take a hard look at our country's traditional remedy for drinking problems, Alcoholics Anonymous, and how an increasing number of women are questioning its effectiveness and safety. Why are women drinking more than in previous eras, and what does it mean? Alcohol is a socially acceptable, legal way to muscle through the postfeminist, breadwinning, or stay-at-home life women lead. It's a drug women can respectably use in public and in private, even if it carries with it the risk of taking them under. It pops up in the headlines when a suburban mom kills seven others, including the kids she loves, but that's a gory headline. The real story is a silent, utterly bourgeois, and hiding-in-plain sight problem: How a lot of American women are hanging right over a cliff.

1 *Lush*

Solid statistics on women's drinking habits are hard to come by. In part, that's because all measures of potentially illicit behavior—sex, drugs, alcohol—are subject to the inherent inaccuracies of self-reporting. ("How many drinks a week?" "I don't know, Doc—maybe three or four.") There's also the historic indifference of the mostly male research community to focusing on gender differences in the science of disease. In recent years, however, a critical mass of credible studies have emerged that quantify the anecdotal evidence I had glimpsed in Portland and New York.

The findings are incontrovertible. By every quantitative measure, women are drinking more. They're being charged more often with drunk driving, they're more frequently measured with high concentrations of alcohol in their bloodstreams

at the scene of car accidents, and they're more often treated in emergency rooms for being dangerously intoxicated. In the past decade, record numbers of women have sought treatment for alcohol abuse. And, in perhaps the most undeniable statistic of all, they are the consumers whose purchases are fueling steady growth in the sales of wine. Meanwhile, men's drinking, arrests for drunk driving, and alcohol purchases are flat, or even falling.

Contrary to the impression fostered by reality shows and *Gossip Girl*, young women alone are not responsible for these statistics. There are plenty of girls going wild on the nation's college campuses, but there is an even more striking trend of women in their thirties, forties, and fifties who are getting through their days of work, and nights with teething toddlers, trying teenagers, or sick parents, by hitting the bottle.

The risky habits of young women are well documented in articles, graphic memoirs, and cautionary TV specials. But their stories are more than just sad tales, or the school nurse's hyperbole: They are a serious public health concern. A national analysis of hospitalizations for alcohol overdose found that the rate of young females age eighteen to twenty-four jumped 50 percent between 1999 and 2008. In the same period, the rate for young men rose only 8 percent. The most alarming statistic was the sharp rise in the number of young women who turned up at hospitals having OD'd on both drugs and alcohol: That number more than doubled. Among young men, it stayed the same.

These data are part of a broader cultural shift in which drinking by women is seen as a proud rite of passage—or, at least, nothing to hide. I once shared a train ride with a loquacious college student who told me she was "practicing drink-

ing" in advance of her planned spring break in Mexico. "It was my mom's idea, after I got sick over Christmas break from mixing rum with beer," she explained. "She doesn't want me making a fool of myself in Cabo, so we're working on getting my tolerance up."

Nothing like a little mother-daughter bonding—especially when gals with hollow legs get such respect. In 2011, students at Rutgers University chose *Jersey Shore*'s Snooki as a guest speaker on campus. The reality TV star—whose on-camera antics included blackout falls, an arrest for drunken and disorderly conduct, and the admission that she had often gotten so intoxicated she had woken up in garbage cans—was paid thirty-two thousand dollars for her talk. That was two thousand dollars more than writer Toni Morrison received for giving the school's commencement address six weeks later. Who needs guidance from a Nobel Prize winner when you can get advice like Snooki's? "Study hard," she told the crowd, "but party harder."

Middle-aged women aren't pounding shots or slurping tequila out of each other's belly buttons, but they, too, are drinking more than at any time in recent history. Their habits are different from those of their younger sisters. Their beverage of choice, after all, is wine, and their venue is less likely to be public.

In fact, the middle-class female predilection for wine seems like it's just a jolly hobby for time-stretched mothers. There are T-shirts with a spilled wineglass and the shorthand plea, "Not so loud, I had book club last night." Nearly 650,000 women follow "Moms Who Need Wine" on Facebook, and another 131,000 women are fans of the group called "OMG, I So Need a Glass of Wine or I'm Gonna Sell

My Kids." And the wine-swilling mom pops up as a cultural trope, from the highbrow to the mass market. In Jonathan Franzen's *Freedom,* Patty Berglund shuffles out for the morning papers every day with the "Chardonnay Splotch," the ruddy face of heavy drinkers. Nic, the driven doctor played by Annette Bening in *The Kids Are All Right,* downs her red wine a little too eagerly for her partner's taste. "You know what, Jules? I like my wine! Okay? So fucking sue me!" In the film *Smashed,* Kate, the fresh-faced first-grade teacher, wets her bed, throws up in front of her students, and drunkenly steals wine from a convenience store before she sobers up and leaves her drinking-buddy husband. Courteney Cox's *Cougar Town* character pours her daily red wine into giant vessels she calls Big Joe, Big Carl, and Big Lou. When Big Joe breaks, she holds a memorial service for its shards, tearfully recalling, "He was always there for me when I needed him." And drinking wine is so linked to the women of *Real Housewives* shows that three of the women it made famous—Bethenny Frankel, Ramona Singer, and Teresa Giudice—introduced their own brands.

In 2010, Gallup pollsters reported that nearly two-thirds of all American women drank regularly, a higher percentage than any other time in twenty-five years. Like many other studies around the world, Gallup found that drinking habits correlated directly with socioeconomic status. The more educated and well off a woman is, the more likely she is to imbibe. Catholics, atheists, agnostics, and those who identified themselves as non-Christians were also far more likely to drink than churchgoing Protestants.

White women are more likely to drink than women of other racial backgrounds, but that is changing, too. An anal-

ysis of the drinking habits of eighty-five thousand Americans between the early 1990s and the early 2000s found that the percentage of women who classified themselves as regular drinkers rose across the board. The number of white women drinkers increased 24 percent; Hispanics, 33 percent; and black women, 42 percent. (American Indian women were not included in this study. Because of the isolation of many Native American communities and the devastating role alcohol often plays in them, researchers typically study tribal alcohol use separately. Asian women were also not included; of all ethnic groups, they drink the least, perhaps because of a genetic intolerance that creates an uncomfortable flushing of the face and chest.)

Women are the wine industry's most enthusiastic customers. Despite the recession (or perhaps because of it), wine consumption in the U.S. continued to grow between the years 2009 and 2012, according to wine industry analysts.

Not all that wine is being decorously sipped. In 2012, the Centers for Disease Control and Prevention released a study that found 13 percent of American women binge drink regularly, about half the rate of men. Researchers define binge drinking as more than four drinks in two hours for women, and five drinks in two hours for men. We often hear about binge-drinking youths, but adult women aren't far behind: The CDC found that while more college-age women binge drink, the frequency of binge drinking among women ages forty-five and older is about the same as it is for younger females, about once a week. The average number of drinks downed per binge is six.

No surprise, then, that the number of women arrested for drunk driving rose nearly 30 percent in the nine years between

1998 and 2007. In California alone, between 1994 and 2009, that number doubled, going from 10.6 percent of all drivers to 21.2 percent. Women over forty had among the highest rates of arrest.

There is evidence that alcohol dependence among women is also rising precipitously. Two large national surveys of drinking habits, conducted in 1991 and 1992, and again in 2001 and 2002, found that women born between 1954 and 1963 had an 80 percent greater chance of developing dependence on alcohol than women who were born between 1944 and 1953. For men of those generations, the rate stayed flat.

The topic of women and alcohol is a relatively new one in academic research, with only a handful of experts around the country. Sharon Wilsnack, a distinguished professor of clinical neuroscience at the University of North Dakota School of Medicine and Health Sciences, became one of its pioneers as a graduate student at Harvard in the early 1970s. Though she has published hundreds of academic papers about women and alcohol, she is perhaps best known for the longitudinal studies of women's drinking she began conducting with her husband, sociologist Richard Wilsnack, in the early 1980s. Since then, the Wilsnacks have directed and analyzed in-depth, face-to-face interviews about drinking habits with more than eleven hundred women ages twenty-one to sixty-nine.

In the most recent evaluations of the study completed in 2002, Wilsnack noticed a startling shift: a substantial increase in the number and ways in which women reported intoxication. While the stigma of female drunkenness has faded since the first study in the early 1980s, Wilsnack is struck by the openness with which women today describe their drinking habits. She wasn't at all surprised by the frank talk of my train

partner, since she hears similar anecdotes at the lectures she gives on college campuses.

"There is a pattern of intentional drinking, with a whole plan behind it," she says. "Drinking on an empty stomach; predrinking before going to a party or a bar; learning to do straight shots. They are very aware of their drinking, and how to manipulate it for maximum effect."

Wilsnack was struck by another new finding. In the early 1980s, one in ten women answered yes to the question: "Are you concerned about your drinking?" In 2002, it was one in five.

That corresponds with what Rick Grucza, an epidemiologist at Washington University in St. Louis, found in his research on the generational shift of female alcohol dependence. Because it's unlikely that anyone could accurately remember how much they drank the previous decade, Grucza compared how people in the same age groups responded to questions about their consumption in two national surveys, the first conducted in 1991–1992, and then ten years later. What he found among women was especially striking. When Grucza and his colleagues compared the two surveys, they saw a flattening in consumption among younger and older men. The opposite was true for women. "More women were drinking, and among those women, more women were becoming dependent," Grucza told me.

Grucza is a young guy, in his midforties, with a salt-and-pepper goatee and a wry midwestern wit. He also partakes—"I enjoy it," he told me—and steers clear of moralizing. He is careful not to place a value judgment on the behavioral narrowing of the gender gap. For Grucza, the issue is how alcohol disproportionately harms women.

Women of childbearing age are incessantly warned that alcohol poses a danger to the developing fetus, but nobody talks much about why women in general are more vulnerable to alcohol's toxic effects, too. They absorb more alcohol into their bloodstream than men because they have a higher percentage of body fat, and a lower percentage of water. Fat cells retain alcohol, but water dilutes it, so women drinking the same amount as men their size and weight become intoxicated more quickly than the men. Males also have more of the enzyme alcohol dehydrogenase that breaks down alcohol before it enters the bloodstream. This may be one reason alcohol-related liver and brain damage appears more quickly in heavy-drinking women than men. Alcohol-dependent women have death rates 50 to 100 percent higher than those of alcohol-dependent men, including those from suicide, liver cirrhosis, and alcohol-related accidents.

Increasingly, inebriated women get behind the wheel and careen into inanimate objects and other drivers. The tabloid photos of smashed starlets crashing their cars reflect a lot more than just celebrity culture: They're part of a gruesome wider trend. In California, the number of young women responsible for alcohol-related accidents jumped 116 percent between 1998 and 2007. It rose as well among young men, but only by 39 percent. While the number of U.S. drunk-driving deaths fell between 2001 and 2010, from 12,233 to 9,694, the number of female drivers responsible for them rose by 15 percent.

One way to measure the changes in women's drinking habits is in the frequency with which they seek help. Between 1992 and 2007, the number of middle-aged women who checked into rehab nearly tripled. That's especially telling: Disappearing for a month or more is difficult for any-

one, but it's especially tricky for women who have children at home.

•   •   •

When it comes to alcohol treatment, there's growing evidence that women are different as well. The antidote most commonly recommended to problem drinkers in America—Alcoholics Anonymous—is particularly ill-suited to women. A.A.'s twelve-step approach instructs drinkers to surrender their egos to a higher power, but it doesn't take a gender-studies expert to know that women who drink too much aren't necessarily suffering from an excess of hubris. The A.A. approach, developed by men, for men, in the 1930s, is widely endorsed by our medical and judicial systems and used by the vast majority of all treatment facilities in this country. No doubt it has helped many people to a saner life. But an increasing number of Americans, from addictions researchers to ex-A.A. group leaders disturbed by some of the group's practices, are challenging its toehold in U.S. society. They are frustrated with the fact that many doctors, educators, and the general public remain unaware of (or insist on ignoring) the numerous scientific advances in the treatment of alcohol disorders.

Just as middle-aged women's drinking has been overlooked, so, too, has the success of recent evidence-based treatments, methods whose efficacy has been determined by rigorous scientific studies. A.A., a faith-based group whose philandering, LSD-tripping cofounder, Bill Wilson, has achieved the status of a demigod, remains embedded in public minds as the best approach.

This tension over how to treat women who abuse alco-

hol is a new phenomenon, but the figure of boozy broads has deep roots in American history. In fact, the notion of the woman as the sober member of the household, the teetotaling mom, is relatively recent. Women who traveled from England on the *Mayflower* downed beer just like the male passengers, and women who trudged along on the Oregon Trail nipped from their whiskey jugs alongside the menfolk. How could they not? There was no safe drinking water, and when food supplies got low, alcohol had to fill in for calories' sake alone. Over time, however, women became leaders of the temperance movement, and by the early twentieth century, female imbibers fell into two categories. For one group of women, drinking was an act of rebellion, and a powerful declaration of modernity. For another, it was a shameful sin, a weakness to be hidden.

None of this thinking, now a century old but still deeply embedded in popular culture, takes into account what we now know about science, gender differences in the brain, and our peculiar history with alcohol itself. Nor does it presume to imagine the enormous ways in which our society has changed—particularly for women, who after all drink for reasons unimaginable to their colonial sisters.

2 *We Are Women, Hear Us Pour*

> She was depressed. She was anxious. Because she was depressed and because she was anxious she drank too much. This was called medicating herself. Alcohol has its own well-known defects as a medication for depression but no one has ever suggested—ask any doctor—that it is not the most effective anti-anxiety agent yet known.
>
> —Joan Didion, *Blue Nights*

The numbers seem clear enough. Women are drinking more. But data can only tell us so much. To understand *why* women are imbibing so frequently, we need to visit a place that is far less susceptible to quantitative assessment: the psyche of American women. Researchers believe that the predisposition toward alcohol abuse is a mix of factors, including learned behavior, genes, and psychology. My conversations around the country with women of varied ages, races, religions, and political outlooks returned again and again to a single theme. Drinking, they suggested, was a poorly chosen but understandable way to cope with the stresses of modern life.

Women are twice as likely to suffer from anxiety and depression as men, and they are more likely than men to treat

their symptoms with alcohol, according to numerous studies. Other risk factors include a history of sexual abuse and bulimia, both of which also affect more women than men.

Alcohol ultimately depresses the working of the central nervous system, and heavy drinking compounds mood disorders, but initially, it delivers a quick cure for an ordinary day's blues. That's what makes it feel like an effective answer to life's rough patches, whether they're caused by financial worries, sleep problems during menopause, the illness of a parent, or sending the youngest kid off to college. It also helps stanch regretful ruminations. Many professional women I met had become mothers late in life and taken a hiatus from their careers, only to discover that motherhood wasn't quite as thrilling as they anticipated. They drank to cope with the boredom. The guilt. And above all, the jangling nerves.

Until recently, nobody even thought to look at how differently alcohol (and other mood-altering drugs) affected men's and women's brains. Some emerging neuroscience yields clues. In 2012, Yale researchers using advanced imaging equipment found that the areas of the brain associated with craving were activated by different cues in men and women. Stress was the predominant trigger in cocaine-dependent women, while visual cues, such as photos of the drug, stimulated cravings in the brains of cocaine-dependent men.

In a study she conducted as a graduate student at Harvard in the 1970s, Sharon Wilsnack discovered that alcohol generated different moods in men and women. Men reported feeling increasingly aggressive and powerful as they drank, while women said they felt calmer, less inhibited, and more easygoing.

These glimpses into alcohol's effects on women dovetail with much of my own reporting: I found women who functioned at a high level in high-pressure jobs, then came home and downed a bottle of wine while they made dinner. They'd hide the empty and open a second to share with their husbands, making it look as though they were just getting started. I met mothers who poured Baileys into their steel coffee cups as they drove their kids to elementary school, and more than a few who filled Poland Spring bottles with vodka and took them on their commutes.

If this sort of drinking sounds like a bourgeois problem, that's because largely it is. Alcohol problems aren't restricted to middle- and upper-middle-class women, but many of the enormous cultural shifts in our country have had an outsize impact on them.

The first change was an increased acceptance of female drinking: In the years after World War II, the growing American middle class turned cocktail hour into evening sacrament. In the proliferating suburbs, it was testament to civility. Men wanted to unwind after a hard day at the office and long commutes; women, too, craved some adult conversation after a long day of housework and childrearing. The kids trotted off to their rooms and the parents kicked back with martinis, manhattans, and mai tais. Like their bosses, career women often tippled themselves—and not just at the end of the day.

The late postwar era wasn't the first period in American history in which it was acceptable for women to imbibe (not by a long shot), but demure drinking had a powerful model at the highest level. Jacqueline Kennedy, an icon for modern new women, was educated, urbane, and sophisticated. Her style

was a marked departure from the dour Bess Truman and the grandmotherly Mamie Eisenhower. She was a new American woman, inspiring tastes in fashion, art, food—and alcohol.

On Valentine's Day 1962, Jacqueline Kennedy guided television viewers through an hourlong tour of the White House, explaining architectural details and restored paintings. The tour was remarkable for a number of reasons, particularly because it was the first prime-time documentary directed specifically toward a female audience—many of whom were deeply anxious to get a glimpse into the life of this intriguing woman who, like them, was a young wife and mother.

When they saw the elegant place settings in the White House dining room, American women seized on a small piece of Kennedy glamour they could own for themselves. The camera panned across the gold-embossed official plates, and then lingered for a few seconds on the four adjacent crystal glasses. Mrs. Kennedy praised their graceful simplicity, mentioning offhandedly that they had come from a factory in West Virginia. This might seem like a minor detail, but fifty-six million Americans—three-quarters of all TV viewers—were watching. So much of the First Lady's life—her designer gowns, her summers on Cape Cod, her multilingual refinement—was out of reach. But anybody could buy her crystal, and the glass factory in Morgantown, West Virginia, struggled to keep up with the deluge of requests for its product. It would be years before they could fill all the orders.

The appetite for news of the Kennedys' style was insatiable. Even amid the anxiety of the Cold War and the Cuban missile crisis, the White House seemed determined to enjoy itself. When Letitia Baldrige, Mrs. Kennedy's social secretary, ordered the installation of a bar in the State Dining Room,

early press reports were critical. But visitors soon adjusted to the elegance of the butlers who mixed drinks, circulated trays of champagne, and poured bourbon, scotch, and vodka. Under the Eisenhower administration, guests had to wait for an hour before dinner started with nothing stronger than fruit punch. By the time dinner rolled around, Baldrige later recalled, guests were in a lousy mood. The Kennedys' visitors strolled to the table in much higher spirits.

The glamorous first couple didn't invent cocktail parties, of course, but they were certainly part of the modern national Zeitgeist. Like all things in our free-market society, it was reinforced by innovative consumer goods, especially for women. Through the early 1960s, you couldn't open a magazine without seeing ads for cocktail dresses, cocktail aprons, cocktail rings.

But there were far more substantive changes afoot. Rick Grucza, the Washington University epidemiologist who has studied female drinking habits, correlates the rise in women's alcohol consumption to the increase in female college attendance. "Clearly there were many changes in the cultural environment for women born in the forties, fifties, and sixties compared to women born earlier," Grucza says. "They were freer to engage in a range of behaviors that were culturally or practically off-limits—and that includes excessive drinking."

Between 1940 and 1960, the number of women who had attended college, even for a year or two, rose sharply. Away from the watchful eyes of parents or spouses, women drank freely at mixers and fraternity parties, and continued the pattern as young wives. By 1963, Gallup pollsters found that 63 percent of all Americans were drinkers, a 15 percent increase from 1958. That survey doesn't show gender differences, but

it's hard to imagine that the influx of college girls and Camelot didn't have something to do with the uptick.

By the mid-1970s, Gallup divided respondents by gender and age groups, and in 1977, the number of women who said they drank at least occasionally was up to 65 percent. The 1970s marked a high period for drinking in the United States after many states lowered their drinking age to eighteen. (Most had set the age at twenty-one after the repeal of Prohibition, but during the Vietnam War, many protesters argued about the absurdity of drafting eighteen-year-olds into army service when they couldn't yet buy beer. Highway fatalities skyrocketed, and by the early 1980s, the drinking age went back up to twenty-one.)

At the end of the 1970s, nearly half of all women were in the workforce, and the number of women graduating from college was nearing that of men. Many of these women began demanding a place in male-dominated careers like law, business, and journalism. They felt pressure to prove they were men's equals in the boardroom and at the bar. Grucza calls this voyage to a new world "immigrating."

These modern new women transformed American society in many ways. But modern American society would also transform them. Women's access to a wider world brought them greater achievements, greater equality, higher salaries, and more power. They also had a lot more of something once reserved mainly for men: stress. Luckily, there was a ladylike remedy for that modern affliction. Women didn't know it yet, but it would come in an ancient form: wine.

The migration of women into previously male bastions couldn't have arrived at a more opportune moment for the California wine industry.

In the decades after Prohibition's repeal, the state's wine producers had struggled to build a market for their product. Americans ate meat and potatoes, and like their Anglo-Saxon forebears, had a hankering for beer, or spirits that had been disguised with sweet mixers to mask the taste. They also consumed oceans of the sugary soda pop that had gained popularity during the country's dry spell: Coca-Cola, Dr Pepper, ginger ale, and 7Up, which had debuted originally as an antacid. Wine was the drink of the poor—for immigrants and skid-row drunks—or the well-traveled upper classes. For the rest of the country, exposure was limited to sips of the stuff during religious ceremonies: Catholics took syrupy wine at Communion, and Jews drank Manischewitz at the Sabbath table.

Not long after World War II, in a desperate attempt to introduce their product to Americans, vintners turned to Lucille Ball as a pitch woman. An ad in *Life* magazine shows Lucy with a frozen expression somewhere between a wince and a pained smile, clutching a highball full of California Burgundy over giant ice cubes. "Lucille Ball agrees!" Lucy helped move a lot of products, from cigarettes to face cream, but even she couldn't convince consumers to buy wine. The ad had a brief career.

Harvey Posert, one of the industry's first marketers, says Americans were deeply skeptical of wine as a routine refreshment. The Memphis-born, Yale-educated Posert came to San Francisco as vice president and western manager of the Edelman public relations agency after stints as a newspaperman and as a counterintelligence officer in the U.S. Army. When he was hired by the wine industry, he decided to conduct some research.

"Before we could get wine into people's houses, we had to get them to taste it," he says. "That wasn't so easy." In the mid-1960s, American moms were mixing up pitchers of Tang and Kool-Aid for their kids. Flavors of more adult refreshment weren't far off: This was the era of the Piña Colada, the White Russian, and the Pink Squirrel—Cool Whip cocktails! Posert hired ten representatives around the country to serve as informal wine ambassadors (my term, not his). He dispatched them to ski clubs, gourmet clubs, hiking clubs—anything that might reflect a desire for new experiences—and had his minions conduct wine tastings.

I met Posert a couple of times, and on this occasion we were in his airy, modern home in St. Helena, the epicenter of the California wine universe. Posert, now in his eighties, remains a Southern gentleman. He had poured me a flute of sparkling wine and a bourbon for himself—Posert discovered he is a "nontaster," unable to distinguish all but the bluntest of flavors—and we sat on the couch to chat before heading out for dinner.

The first several wine tastings, he recalled, were far from encouraging. Conveying the complexity of wine was going to take some work. The barriers seemed fundamental: Americans didn't like the taste. Red wine seemed "too strong." White wine seemed "sour." The hiking, cooking, and skiing tasters lacked even a language to describe what they disliked.

Still, the wine makers kept trying. "We used to joke that if we could just get a bottle of sherry into the kitchen, we'd be off," Posert says.

To the extent it was drunk at all, wine was a man's realm. Sommeliers were men, wine makers were men, wine merchants were men. In restaurants, wine lists (and the corks)

were presented to men. Even ads were almost wholly masculine: Ludwig Stossel tottered around in lederhosen for Italian Swiss Colony wine, and Paul Masson promised not to serve wine before its time. Meanwhile, there was no guesswork to a gin and tonic.

Change arrived slowly, but got a boost from popular culture—especially from Julia Child's successful cooking show, *The French Chef*. As she lopped off fish heads and julienned carrots, she sipped wine liberally, and told Americans they could, too. Like wine growers, she, too, was from California, and she would become an important asset.

The Golden State itself embodied a new American style, the test kitchen for everything cool and interesting. Tourists flocked to the south to catch some of the Beach Boys' surfer vibe, and to visit Disneyland.

In the north, wine maker Robert Mondavi was creating a draw of his own with the 1966 opening of his majestic, Spanish-mission-style winery in Oakville. Designed by California architect Cliff May, the winery, bounded by the green Mayacama Mountains and shrouded with Pacific fog in the morning, was as distant from a modern amusement park as Europe itself. Mondavi envisioned a lifestyle—one he hoped Americans would adopt—based on the very old-world appreciation of wine, food, art, and music. He teamed with great chefs, including Child and Alice Waters, who had opened Chez Panisse in nearby Berkeley, and set upon producing wines he thought could compete with the great wines of Europe.

To make all this a commercial success, wine makers needed new customers, and they knew exactly who they were: American housewives. A pamphlet the wine industry circulated to grocers and liquor stores enlisted the merchants as allies in

reaching her: "Wine is still new to Americans!" the undated copy reads. "*You* probably know at a glance what a wine bottle contains, but thousands of Americans might think it's syrup or salad oil. . . . That's why vendors need to 'Flag Customers Down' and explain why they want it."

Though three-quarters of wine buyers were male, the pamphlet said, the trend was changing. "Wine is used mostly in the home — on the dinner table and for entertaining. . . . The person who does the shopping for most of the home-used items is logically the one to do the wine buying. That person is the housewife."

It advised: "Before a housewife can be expected to buy a bottle of wine she must be given information concerning the use of that wine and a reason to use it. For example, 'Please your dinner guests — serve them this red table wine' tells her why she wants it."

In California, where laws allowed the sale of wine in supermarkets, Mondavi's marketing team hired housewives to stand at in-store tasting booths, offering other shoppers sips from bottles that would pair perfectly with what they planned to make for dinner. The saleswomen, often middle-aged, were friendly and reassuring. To young women especially, they helped make wine seem approachable.

Those young women would become an essential element in the astounding growth of wine sales. As the chief buyers of the growing middle class, with a new washing machine, dryer, and dishwasher, they had a lot of extra time on their hands — and a proliferating number of magazines to tell them how to fill it.

While Posert is a lively narrator, press clippings from those days give an even fuller picture of the campaign to get

wine into America's kitchens. The University of California at Davis library has a vast collection of wine history, and its affable wine librarian, Axel Borg, directed me toward some remarkable evidence. In the early 1960s, food magazines carried a few timid mentions of serving wine to dinner guests, and there were odd suggestions here or there about the new craze in California: wine-tasting parties! Thumbing through a late-1960s *Ladies' Home Journal,* I saw an odd notation—a note about a "wine survey" the magazine had conducted in 1967. Borg dug up a reference, and a few weeks later, a copy of the study arrived in the mail.

The report, called "Wine and Women: A Ladies' Home Journal Reader Reaction Bureau Report," looked about as official as something I might have typed in junior high, but the information it contained was an intriguing snapshot.

The magazine's interviewers had fanned out into ten cities, identifying a hundred women who said they drank wine at least once a month, and were confident enough around it to serve it to guests. The majority were in their thirties and forties, had graduated from or attended college, did not work outside the home, and had high-earning professional husbands. "The results of this study may be used to gain understanding of the attitudes behind the buying and serving of wines, with an eye to future sales," the report said.

The interviewers asked about the types of wine the women liked, what they believed about wine drinkers, and wine's importance. Overwhelmingly, the women found wine drinkers educated, cultured, successful people, and said they thought wine added "class." "It's nicer to serve than highballs," one woman wrote.

It's hard to say what the results of the report actually meant,

and even Posert can't recall who might have commissioned it. But it was clear the industry was seeking early adopters, a term coined in 1962 that meant the initial customers of a company or product. These people, marketers believed, would go on to spread the word about a product as a trendsetter.

Many of the questions involved the women's willingness to attend, or throw, a wine-tasting party, and where they might get the training to do it.

It didn't take long for women to get comfortable. By the early 1970s, wine was ubiquitous. Magazines from *Vogue* to *Family Circle* covered the new fad, with tips on what to drink daily, and what to serve to your guests. Bridal magazines gave instructions on choosing the proper glasses for a registry, the right wines for the wedding reception, and which to have at home. For the uninitiated, there were directives: "Do You Know How to Order Wine in a Restaurant?" bellowed a headline in *Travel + Leisure*.

Wine was glamorous and hip, and it could also take the edge off. The Anti-Tension Diet in the February 1977 issue of *McCall's* gave wine a starring role. "Daily use of wine is recommended," it read. "A small amount of wine taken with meals is relaxing and promotes digestion, and table wines have another plus—since they're made from grapes, they're high in potassium."

In the 1970s, sixty-two million newspapers were sold in the United States every day, and publishers were expanding their feature sections in an attempt to reach a broader range of advertisers. Naturally, this included food and dining, a perfect outlet for the wine industry. It lavished its product on newspaper food writers, who were mostly women, when it hosted conferences on California cuisine. As food writers began to

replace sloppy joe recipes with instructions for quiche and fondue, marketers believed they could help demystify wine, too. Advice from a trusted local voice felt like getting kitchen help from an aunt.

The marketing strategy soon branched beyond just house-wives. Airlines offered California wines on flights to San Francisco and Los Angeles, exposing neophytes to their first sips of Golden State glamour. In buttoned-down Washington, D.C., California senators and congressmen held evening wine-tasting parties that drew hundreds of thirsty interns, who in turn began buying wine themselves. More than two hundred colleges staged tastings, and industry representatives intro-duced wine at more than forty-five hundred women's groups, from grandmotherly garden societies to political clubs.

"Anything to get people to taste it, to familiarize them-selves," Posert says. "We thought of as many ways as we could."

For Margrit Biever, who would become Mondavi's second wife, selling wine seemed like second nature. The Swiss-born Biever had arrived in Napa as a young army wife with three children. Bored at home once her children were in school, she took a job at the winery in 1967, leading crowds through tast-ing rooms with her considerable charm. A student of art, a lover of music, an accomplished, effortless chef and gardener, fluent in seven languages, Biever embodied the lifestyle Mon-davi had both envisioned and hoped to project with his prod-uct. The two fell in love, marrying in 1980.

At lunch recently in St. Helena, Biever Mondavi entered the restaurant in a pink sweater and red patent leather peep toes. She sat back in a booth across from me, addressing one acquaintance in Spanish, another in Japanese, and brushed her chic blond bob back from her face as she daintily dipped her

sushi into soy sauce. As a child, she says, she attended La Scala twice a year, and learned to enjoy wine from her father's cherished wine cellar. "My father gave my brother, sister, and me an appreciation of which Beaujolais or Fendant paired well with what," she recalls. "He told us great stories about the wines, the regions they came from, even the vintages. Wine was something special, and I knew it could be in America, too."

Her arrival at Mondavi would help cement the transformation. "What a wonderful time those days were!" she says. "It was so exciting, helping explain the wine, the tastes, how to pair it. It was helping open another world, and it was wonderful!" Once, as the winery neared closing time, a group of hippies arrived in a beat-up van. "Everyone was a little leery of them—you know, their beards, their long hair," she says. "Napa Valley in the early 1970s was still a very traditional place." Biever led the group through the tasting rooms, offering sips from reserve bottles as her colleagues grumbled. An hour later, her group bought eight hundred dollars' worth of wine—the equivalent of forty-two hundred dollars today. "Wine is life," she says. "Passion! Beauty! Joy! Fun!"

By the late 1970s, California wines were earning respect outside the U.S., even winning two blind taste tests at a Paris competition. They helped put traditional little Napa on the map for good: In just one decade, Americans had doubled their wine consumption, from 267 million gallons in 1970 to 480 million in 1980.

Behind the scenes, California's wine makers were unintentionally tweaking their product in ways that made it even more appealing to women. European wine making was ruled by a strict code of tradition and *terroir*, the French term for the

special characteristics that the geography, geology, and climate of a certain place bestow upon certain crops. Americans, starting almost from scratch after Prohibition, felt free to experiment with how best to turn their grapes into a likable product. At the University of California at Davis, wine makers tried a variety of techniques, using different oak barrels and fermentation processes that could influence flavor. Though wine making was predominantly male, in the changing social climate of California, it had attracted bright young women.

One was a young scientist named Zelma Long, the second woman to be awarded a master's in enology and viticulture from Davis. In 1970, she landed a job as one of the country's first female wine makers at Mondavi's winery. Long, who was reared in the small town of The Dalles, Oregon, had started her career as a dietitian, but quickly grew bored with the restrictive regimens she felt she had to recommend for her diabetic and hypertensive patients. Long had grown up in a Swedish American household on simple, hearty food she recalls as subtly delicious. She was drawn to Davis, an innovator in the evolving field of sensory science—how humans responded to the appearance, flavors, and aromas of food, drink, and other substances, including tobacco. (As Americans consumed more packaged and canned foods, by then easily transportable on the expanding interstate highway system, manufacturers needed researchers to investigate the best ways to preserve flavor and consistency.)

When Long arrived at Mondavi, she almost couldn't believe her luck. She was immersed in—indeed, part of—the transformation of the American table even as it was occurring.

One of the wines Long began to experiment with was

chardonnay, which had gone from virtually no plantings of the grape in the mid-1960s to overnight popularity.

Taste tests from the early California whites were universally negative—they were too dry and thin for American taste buds, accustomed, as they were, to sugary drinks. Chardonnay, a thick-skinned grape originating in eastern France, had shown promise as one that adapted easily to many climates, and it thrived in Napa. By using a process called malolactic fermentation, wine makers can reduce tartness and turn the natural green fruit into soft, buttery flavors.

Long was among a handful of vintners who helped perfect a golden, velvety chardonnay that American women liked immediately. "For people who were new to wine, it had a rich, satiny, smooth texture. On top of that, it had these vanilla, apple, spicy scents that were already familiar, like apple pie," says Long, who has become an admired wine maker and business owner. She now works as a consultant with wineries around the globe. "It was just an easy wine, and people liked it." Chardonnay also sounded fancy, even feminine. It was easy to say, easy to drink, and had fewer astringent tannins than, say, the cabernet sauvignons the region was also developing.

Sales of chardonnay skyrocketed, and women emerged as its top consumers. In the 1980s, it became the thinking woman's drink, especially for those who were born in the early part of the baby boom. As that group of women matured, they drove consumer markets with their tastes. They wore shoulder pads and business suits, and they drank chardonnay. It seemed thoughtful, intelligent, serious, and markedly different from the heavy cocktails of their parents' generation. Press reports began to emphasize how healthy wine's effects were (and in moderation, they can be). For a brief period, until ad-

vertising rules restricted the use of the vague word "light" in promoting lower-calorie foods, white wine was also touted as an alcoholic diet drink, especially if you mixed it with ice and seltzer. That claim proved difficult to substantiate: absent dilution, and depending on its alcohol content, white wine has about five fewer calories per ounce than red. That would give a small glass of white wine about 100 calories; a small glass of red, 120. But for many years, women associated white wine with dietary restraint.

It is impossible to gauge precisely how much women buyers helped boost the early sales. The wine industry only began analyzing the gender of its consumers in the mid-1990s, and by then, women made up the majority of its buyers.

It is certainly in their kitchens. Today, women buy nearly two-thirds of the 784 million gallons of the wine sold in this country, and they drink 70 percent of what they buy.

•   •   •

The wine industry's efforts to market its product to women came at a pivotal moment in America's ever-changing gender roles. By the 1980s, the struggle for women's rights had brought some remarkable strides. An Arizona rancher took her place beside eight elderly men on the nation's Supreme Court. One of the nation's political parties chose a woman as its vice presidential candidate. Sally Ride circled the earth. Women were graduating from college with degrees in math, science, and engineering in unprecedented numbers.

They didn't need to go to frat parties to drink, since they lived alongside boys in college dorms across the country. The beer bongs were always within reach, along with treacly Tia

Maria and wine coolers. That kind of drinking was just kid stuff: nothing serious. It continued on through first jobs, when the women would cluster with colleagues at happy hour for free food and cheap drinks. Even if the women woke up most mornings in a fitful self-loathing start, there were *possibilities*. As the president of my university told young women when Ride was launched into space, orbit was our destiny!

For a decade or more, their lives were on track: a solid career, a steady marriage, children. They could do it all—manage their jobs *and* immerse themselves in their children. They would bake birthday cakes from scratch; they would go to every swim meet. They would be there, period. No Carnation Instant Breakfast mothering for them.

But somehow, something changed. Those same young women, so full of determination, found themselves scaling back their dreams: for running the English Department, for winning a Pulitzer, for becoming CEO. Aspirations somehow dropped to the bottom of the grocery bags that used to be plastic bottles. The women haven't even made good on their intention to compost.

When they are honest about it—and it is hard to be, because sometimes it's too painful to look—the women realize they are doing the same chores as their mothers. They scale back at work, or maybe even take off a few years, and before long, the women find themselves isolated, responsible not only for care of the children but for most details of their lives: trips to the doctor when the baby has croup; combing through tangled braids on the lookout for lice; making appointments with the orthodontist. They didn't plan it that way, but that's how it happened. Resentment creeps up, imperceptibly, not

the least of which stems from the fact that the closet full of size-six clothes don't fit a size-eight body. They haven't had more than social drinks in years—all that time pregnant or nursing, no way. But then they remember how it made them feel. The fun of it. What would be wrong with a little wine now and then?

And so the drink becomes the release valve, for so many things. For Memorial Day. For the Fourth of July. For Halloween—especially Halloween, when women gather with other moms for "trick-or-drinking." And summer, when they are all at the beach, and the beers come out at noon. Giggle, giggle. Mommy's right here!

The drinks kept coming, especially when parents got sick, when teenagers got testy, when promotions were handed to younger, prettier women who tweet. If the women had had hold of the torch, they might be ready to pass it. But expectations exceeded reality, and they never held on to it.

Psychologist Bruce Alexander, a Canadian addiction expert, believes the unrelenting pressures of our modern capitalist society have created the emotional, psychological, and spiritual dislocation that triggers alcohol abuse. Modern society distances people from their extended families and propels a desire for an increasing number of goods—particularly technological ones—that in the end isolate them even more. Lacking the intimate ties necessary for humans to live happily, a growing number of people around the world turn to chemical crutches. Alexander is also a student of history, which he used to link to his work as an addiction psychologist. The more he examined history, the more Alexander became convinced that the breathtaking pace of modern economic and social change

has left an emotional, physical, and spiritual void so profound that it triggers excess drinking.

The richer societies get, Alexander argues, the more their addiction problems multiply—and so far, our responses to treating them have been only nominally successful. A century ago, society blamed addiction on a person's weak moral character. In the 1940s and '50s, this belief was replaced by the idea that addiction was "brain disease," and it was one that seeped into the public consciousness. Alexander doesn't reject the idea that some people may have biological and psychological vulnerabilities that predispose them toward chemical dependence. But, he argues, addiction is also an adaptation to the pressures and fragmentation of modern life—and above all, a social problem, not an individual one.

Alexander's views are a compelling explanation of why twenty-first-century women have emerged as such heavy drinkers. Our fractured modern society subjects everyone to immense pressures, but it spawns competition that is particularly grueling near the top of social hierarchies—especially those in affluent communities. Absent the support of an extended family and a long-standing community, these deracinated American women—Grucza's immigrants to male culture—suffer without a spiritual safety net. Regardless of their professional achievements, they still do the lion's share of domestic chores in the United States. A quick fix for the frustration that this can engender is just a bottle away.

Consider the time, long ago, before mothers were assigned snacks for children famished by forty-minute soccer games. Saturdays weren't vaporized by long-distance drives to "travel" soccer (or lacrosse, or hockey), since sports were school functions and practice was after school. Perhaps more

important, women lived near their own parents, sisters, brothers, in-laws, or cousins, whom the school secretary recognized as next of kin. There was no need to fill out multipage forms detailing one's relationship to emergency contacts, with slots for their cell, work, and home phone numbers. Everyone knew everyone, and if children were sick, someone could come pick them up. A few generations ago, homework assignments rarely required (or would have prompted) parental help, with rushed trips to Staples for foam boards.

While women surely have fretted forever about aging, they were resigned to the inevitable wrinkles in the end. Today, aging can feel a lot like a decision. Forget Botox: Magazine ads make us wonder about Radiesse, Juvederm, the length of our eyelashes. Middle-aged starlets tweet photos of themselves in bikinis; blond sixty-something celebrities boast of their renewed libido, thanks to HGH, the human growth hormone. This is all just background chatter in the bête noire of middle- and upper-middle-class anxiety: college applications. What if a son doesn't bring up his critical reading score in the SAT? What if a daughter only gets into her "safety" school? What if the hired school getter-inner is steering you all wrong? Did you read this blog? Did you read that book? Does your kid have enough work experience? Any work experience? There is nothing wrong with state schools.

Is there?

•　　•　　•

It is easy to see these luxury anxieties as unseemly complaints by people who enjoy substantial benefits from our consumer society. But my experiences—and reporting—show there is

a profound disquiet playing out in the work and home lives of these women, in the vise between their families and their hopes. For the six years we lived in Portland, Oregon, my kids played with neighborhood kids, climbing trees and riding their bikes to the corner store for Popsicles. Across the country, in the New Jersey suburb where I live now, freedom is much more limited. In the densely populated East, competition for the brass ring of college is greater. And time—free time—is the first casualty. Sociologist Annette Lareau describes this phenomenon as "concerted cultivation" by upper-middle-class parents. The effects on kids are documented in the poignant film *Race to Nowhere*, which features the parents of a thirteen-year-old girl who killed herself after she got a bad math grade. We see it in Richard Louv's powerful book lamenting housebound children, *Last Child in the Woods*.

The impact of this self-induced stress on mothers is palpable. A few years ago, Valerie Ramey, an economics professor at the University of California's San Diego campus, found herself spending an increasing amount of her nonworking, alleged free time engaged in child-related activities. Being a quantitative sort, she immediately wondered: How common is this?

It was a natural question for Ramey, an economist whose specialty, among other topics, is how Americans use their time. I met her on a drizzly fall day, rare in San Diego, for a long afternoon. She is small and athletic, with a trim build, long, thick blond hair she inherited from her Swedish ancestors, and a gentle, youthful face. Ramey, now in her early fifties, grew up in the Panama Canal Zone, where her father worked as an electrician. She graduated summa cum laude with a double major from the University of Arizona, and got her Ph.D.

at Stanford University. Her midwestern parents instilled in Ramey a love of books, adventure, and the abiding sense that American society was a meritocracy in which hard work was rewarded.

And so Ramey worked hard. She married a fellow economist, Garey Ramey, in her midtwenties, and had her first child, Sean, a few years later. The couple bought their first house, in a working-class San Diego neighborhood, where most of their neighbors were immigrant families.

When Sean approached middle school, the family moved to a more affluent neighborhood near campus, where schools offered more opportunities. But perhaps the biggest difference in their new location was the daytime milieu: Most of the mothers were home during the day. As the Rameys' two children made friends, she met their mothers. The new neighbors fretted openly about how good grades were no longer sufficient in securing a bright future. It was essential, the women told Ramey, that kids be involved in a range of activities in order to earn a spot at the country's top schools.

As an academic, Ramey was well aware of the increasing selectivity of American universities, but the anxious talk made her snap into action. She enrolled her daughter in Brownies and softball. She baked cookies, gave rides, arranged rides. She insisted that her extroverted, mechanically minded son join the water polo team, even though he had despised the other sports she had suggested he try—Pop Warner football, baseball, soccer. After school, father and son drove to and from practice, while Ramey and her daughter would race to softball and Brownies. Garey and Sean would have much preferred to spend more time at their favorite activities together—making airplane and ship models, or playing strategic board games—

but Ramey kept urging her son to keep up with sports. Sports, sports, sports.

Meanwhile, Ramey's daughter developed a passion for horseback riding. The stables were far, and the riding commitment was a minimum of six hours a week. After all her talk about the importance of being well rounded, Ramey didn't feel like she was in a position to discourage this new athletic interest.

But one day, after a particularly hectic workweek, Ramey found herself in a stall next to her daughter. Her back ached from hauling the heavy saddle out of the trunk, and as she bent to pitch hay and manure she found herself flat-out furious. What the hell was she doing heaving horse manure when she could be home poring over cookbooks—*her* passion? Reading a novel? Dancing? "My husband had asked me, 'Why are you doing all this stuff?' I said, 'Because you have to!' His response was, 'Says who?'"

The baking and the driving, though, were precisely what many of her new neighbors were doing. Many had graduate degrees and had reached enviable status in their fields, particularly law and business. Unlike Ramey, though, many had left their jobs, their tailored clothing, and their access to high-speed copiers because they needed more time to drive their kids to art class and swim meets. "I couldn't understand why anyone would make such a decision," she said. At first, she assumed the answer was simple economics: that the male overwhelmingly outearned the woman, or had huge demands on his schedule.

The Rameys were not in that position. While comfortable, their lifestyle was far from lavish. And the family often bickered—over who did what, whose turn it was do the dishes or

clean the pool—a direct result of the lack of time. Her son, especially, complained about his grueling water polo schedule. Her daughter asked if she could stop playing softball. Ramey did not back down. Kids had to play sports! Everyone said it! "What is happening?" she asked out loud one evening as she poured herself a second glass of zinfandel. "What am I doing?"

"I'll tell you what you're doing," her husband said gently. "I know you're competitive, but these other mothers are competing to see who is spoiling their children the most. You're always saying that you don't want spoiled, entitled kids." He took a deep breath. "Is this one you really want to win?"

She came, she says, to her senses—and pulled back. "Make your own choices," she told her kids.

Ramey saw changes in her family immediately. Her son became involved in their neighborhood Catholic church (which was only a block from home and required no driving), where he led a youth group and became involved with literacy programs for immigrant families. "He was relieved to do what he wanted, not what I thought was a good idea for his college application," Ramey says. (He is now a graduate student at Stanford.) Her daughter, an animal lover, transferred her passion for horses to the local shelter, and used her skills as a photographer to help shoot pictures of creatures that needed homes. Rather than squander hours on the freeway, she spent time developing her own photographs in a makeshift studio she made with her dad. (She is now a student at the University of California at Berkeley.)

Valerie, too, was relieved, turning more to the activities that she found relaxing: cooking, dancing, reading. (She enjoys wine, but never steps beyond what she calls the "law of dimin-

ishing returns"—where pleasure is replaced by a hangover, or the inability to grade papers at night.) As her son moved through his high school years, students around him kept an exhausting pace. Was this nonstop enrichment, abetted by mothers who had quit their jobs or cut back their work hours, a fad that affected only their San Diego zip code? Together, Valerie and Garey, an economic theorist at UCSD, decided to investigate.

By studying Bureau of Labor Statistics data from 1965 to 2007, the Rameys discovered a national trend: For all the upper-middle-class frenzy about the never-ending workday, the researchers found that the amount of time dedicated to child care increased dramatically in the past fifteen years, even as the number of children in households dropped. The Rameys' analysis revealed another detail: Parents reported that their child-care demands increased as their kids grew older.

On average, college-educated women in 2007 spent twenty-two hours per week on child care, an increase of nine hours more than women in the mid-1990s; women without college educations had an increase of five hours, from eleven to sixteen. Meanwhile, college-educated fathers increased the time they spent with their kids to ten hours from four, while fathers without a college degree logged a four-hour increase, up to eight from four hours in the 1990s. Overwhelmingly, the time-use category with the biggest upswing was "chauffeuring."

What could account for this huge shift? The government sample hadn't changed over the years, and the time jump wasn't attributable to a rise in income. Crime, which prompts parents to keep closer tabs on their kids, had dropped from its all-time high in the early 1990s. Workplace flexibility hadn't increased. Nor had the mothers suddenly developed an over-

whelming desire for late-afternoon driving. In fact, on the enjoyment scale, women ranked this kind of "child care" below cooking, cleaning, and folding laundry. The hours have more than a social and emotional impact: They come at an economic cost, too. The Rameys calculated that they account for more than $300 billion of forgone wages a year.

"We were so puzzled," Ramey says. "Why were women with master's degrees quitting their jobs to drive their kids around? Why would they have made that decision?" The Rameys concluded that the women in their neighborhood were part of a national trend, and that the increased scarcity of college slots has heightened rivalry among parents, taking the form of more hours spent on college preparatory activities. "In other words, the rise in child-care time resulted from a 'rug rat race' for admission to good colleges," they wrote.

To test their hypothesis, the Rameys compared child-care data in the United States and Canada, since the countries share many social trends. In Canada, however, college admissions are less competitive. In addition, most cities and towns have free community centers where kids play hockey and basketball or swim; buses, not parents, transport children there from school. The Rameys found that the amount of time parents spent on child care in Canada remained the same during the past two decades.

Ramey does not see the American trend reversing itself anytime soon. "I think a lot of women feel they are really making the best decision for their children," she says.

But what about their own lives? Do these mothers feel fulfilled by the successes of their children—or resentful of their own sacrifices? Evidence suggests that the pattern is helping to produce a generation of very unhappy women. According

to a 2009 study released by two Wharton School economists, data from the government's General Social Survey revealed that women rated their own happiness at the lowest level in thirty-five years. Each year, the survey includes a representative sample of fifteen hundred men and women of all ages, races, marital status, and educational and income levels, for a total of fifty thousand people so far.

Regardless of whether they work or stay home, are single or married, have graduate degrees or high-school diplomas, women rated feeling bleak about the state of their lives. And overall, mothers had the gloomiest outlooks of anybody.

By comparison, men responded to the same survey with downright giddiness compared to women.

The study's authors, economists Betsey Stevenson and Justin Wolfers, suggested that men might feel less of a burden because they no longer carry the sole financial responsibility for the household. They now work less and relax more. With divorce now commonplace, men are free to leave unhappy marriages. (So are women, but more than two-thirds of mothers are awarded sole or primary custody after a divorce.)

Women, on the other hand, feel the loss of social and family cohesion their mothers enjoyed more acutely. They also report more anxiety than previous generations: In the 1970s, women were at once more optimistic about the future and had lower expectations for what they might achieve. Today, they rate a low level of perceived success both as mothers and as professionals. And, as the Rameys demonstrated, women dislike how they spend their leisure time.

There are a number of theories for why women report such unhappiness. Perhaps earning a higher income has led to greater financial pressures—a bigger mortgage, or unaffordable

private school tuitions. Or maybe women are judging their lives against a new frame of reference. Today, a woman who is dismayed at being passed over for company vice president might report more dissatisfaction than her predecessors, who compared themselves to fellow homemakers. Despite their increased opportunities, many women feel they still haven't measured up. "Or," Stevenson and Wolfers conclude, "women may simply find the complexity and increased pressure in their modern lives to have come at the cost of happiness."

For many women, the unfulfilling, stressful tasks of running a household, mixed with the regret of lost opportunities and the loneliness of social isolation, add up to a 750-milliliter reason to drink. Of course, women don't just turn to wine, or even just alcohol. The leading character on the Showtime drama *Nurse Jackie* hoards, pops, and snorts pain pills. They don't smell, and they're easy to hide. Unlike alcohol, though, they are hard to get: They require prescriptions, pharmacies, and the complicated underworld of shady pain-management doctors who don't ask questions.

Wine is far easier. It's civilizing. It's *good* for us. We're supposed to drink it, right? What's wrong with a group of gals enjoying their chardonnay? The problem, of course, arises when the drinking becomes something more than a festive night out, when women begin downing their wine urgently, on empty stomachs. These women are not sipping a glass or two with dinner to relax. They are building their days around drinking time. Which for some begins as soon as the youngest child gets on the bus.

3 *I Have to See a Man about a Dog*

In the ebb and flow (but mostly flow) of booze in America, liberal drinking among women is nothing new. The Pilgrims packed more beer than water on the *Mayflower,* landing in Plymouth when supplies got low. Alcohol was essential for hydration, and during lean times, calories. It disinfected wounds and eased pains from childbirth to abscessed teeth. No one ate mashed potatoes at the first Thanksgiving, but there were seconds and thirds of beer, brandy, rum, and gin.

In colonial America, booze making was women's work. In addition to the usual domestic chores of cleaning, sewing, and cooking, colonial women prepared the alcoholic drinks their families drank at breakfast, lunch, and dinner. They used fermented apples to make cider, rotting peaches to make brandy, and a drink called "perry" from pears. They made wine out of

celery and onions and brewed beer out of pumpkin and spruce. They made wassail. They concocted a drink called "flip": a pint of beer mixed with sugar and molasses, topped off with a shot of rum and heated with a red-hot poker. Even babies drank home brew in tin or pewter "nursers," bottle-shaped vessels with crude spouts.

By the early 1700s, northern colonies were distilling their own rum with sugar from the Caribbean, and it became the most popular beverage in the taverns central to colonial life. Taverns welcomed both men and women, and were orderly meeting places to discuss politics and conduct business, read the newspaper, and exchange local gossip. But the main draw was drink, especially rum. Everybody partook—even the Puritans. We often dismiss negative attitudes toward alcohol as "puritanical," but in fact it was drunkenness, not drinking, the Puritan preachers condemned. On frigid Sunday mornings, Puritan worshipers filed into the pubs built adjacent to their churches so they could warm their hands by the tavern's fire— and their bellies with rum—before services.

By the mid-1700s, rum consumption was beginning to present some social problems. The settlers were accustomed to downing big mugs of low-alcohol cider and beer, and treated rum as if it were just the same. But it had five times the alcohol content, and drunkenness grew to be so common that the colonists developed more than two hundred expressions to describe various states of inebriation. Ben Franklin published a list of them in an article called "The Drinker's Dictionary."

To be sure, there weren't a lot of nonalcoholic choices. Milk was available only during calving season, and required proximity to farms. Water lacked flavor, especially to taste

buds accustomed to more exciting refreshment. It was also dangerous. Wells were easily contaminated by human or animal waste, and settlers living near the seashore, as most did, had to cope with brackish water that flowed into their streams during storms. Tea and coffee were luxuries for the wealthy alone.

It's fair to say that booze played a part in fueling the American Revolution. Paul Revere nipped rum during his midnight ride. Jefferson drank three or four glasses of wine a night. John Adams started every morning with a tankard of hard cider, and George Washington set up a Mount Vernon whiskey distillery in the waning days of his presidency.

Like everybody else, women drank plenty, too.

As it turns out, Martha Washington was more than just the first First Lady: She was also a Founding Mixologist. In a collection of recipes she gave to her granddaughter as a wedding gift, she lists instructions for sausage, stews, and puddings. But she really gets serious with her recommendations for boozy drinks. Rum punches, berry wines, meads, and liqueurs were crucial for any great party, Martha wrote. She also issued some practical advice: Birch wine could prevent kidney stones, poppy seeds soaked in spirits could relieve a hangover, and regular doses of an herbal cordial called aqua mirabilis was good for fighting the blues: "It disperseth melancholly & causeth cheerfulness."

But this one makes me laugh out loud every time I read it:

Capon Ale

Take an old capon with yellow leggs. Pu(ll) him and crush ye bones but keep ye scin whol(e) & then take an ounce of

carraway seeds and an ounce of anny seeds and two ounces of har(ts) horne and one handful of rosemary tops, a piece or two of mace and a leamon pill. sow all these into ye bellie of your capon and chop him into a hot mash, or hot water, and put him into two gallons of strong ale when it is working. . . . This ale is good for any who are in a consumption & it is restorative for any other weakness.

Nobody took much note of women's drinking in the eighteenth century, unless they really overdid it. Betsy Ross's sister was expelled from her Friends meetinghouse for "excessive use of strong drink." During the Revolutionary War, General Henry Knox got regular updates from the Connecticut landlord who was renting his home to Knox's young wife, Lucy. She and her army-wife roommate treated the place like it was a frat house. The landlord complained that the women had smashed his crockery, and emptied his cellar of twenty-five gallons of rum.

Liquor did have its critics, and one of the most outspoken was Benjamin Rush, a doctor who signed the Declaration of Independence. Rush wrote a pamphlet about the effects of alcohol in which he suggested that wine and beer could be beneficial in moderation, but that distilled spirits resulted only in poor mental and physical consequences.

From a public health standpoint, Rush was a pioneer in understanding, and communicating, the impact of prolonged excess. Tucked into his treatise was an argument that abstinence was the only cure for compulsive drinking. Educators and clergy embraced his message, but Americans didn't. The four decades after the Revolutionary War were tumultuous years of high national debt, inflation, unemployment, expan-

sion, and immigration—and the country relied on copious amounts of booze to get through it.

In his investigation of early American drinking, historian W. J. Rorabaugh estimated that between the 1790s and the 1830s, every man, woman, and child over the age of fifteen consumed about six and a half gallons of pure alcohol a year, a level not reached before or since. Drinking crossed gender, class, and racial boundaries. Whites introduced American Indians to alcohol, to devastating effect. And though booze was largely off-limits to enslaved Africans, plantation owners shared their supplies on holidays.

In the early years of the republic, the burgeoning East was blotto: Buffalo, transformed by the completion of the Erie Canal in 1825, had a saloon for every eighty-four men, women, and children. New York State had a distillery for every fourteen hundred residents.

On the vast and expanding frontier, stills for barley, corn, and rye marked every property. Western farm, lumber, and mining towns were packed with saloons, which had become central to the lonely and uncertain life of the migrants who ventured there. "Bread is considered the staff of life," wrote a thirteen-year-old Missouri girl who arrived in a Colorado mining town in the 1860s. "Whisky the life itself."

I thought about one of my own great-great-grandmothers, whose name I could not have invented even for purposes of this book. Martha Ann Drinkard traveled from Missouri to Oregon in 1865, walking—while pregnant—from a hardscrabble present into a frighteningly uncertain future with four children in tow. Pioneers on the Oregon Trail packed between five and ten gallons of whiskey onto their wagons for medicinal use (and calories). Martha's prairie schooner is the centerpiece of a

small pioneer museum in Brownsville, Oregon, that outlived any journal in which she may have recorded her thoughts.

But many women on the trail wrote of hitting the bottle from time to time. What else could quell the rootless uncertainty, the longing of homesickness? How else to cope with the grief of burying children or spouses who dropped dead of cholera the same day they got sick? Drink was adaptation, and it is as clear as the names of landmarks where I grew up: Whiskey Creek, Whiskey Lake, Whiskey Butte. Those are just some gulches, rivers, and runs named after the liquor in my home state. From Tennessee to Alaska, there are nearly five hundred more.

●　　●　　●

In the early years of the country, men outnumbered women by a significant margin. While women were considered the "weaker sex," their skills as midwives and seamstresses were essential, and therefore valued, in the new society. They lacked economic, political, and legal rights, but in the colonial era women were nevertheless important figures in the chief unit of the colonial economy: the family. The work required to sustain it demanded that all members step in wherever they were needed, whether it was driving a plow horse or delivering livestock. Though it didn't exclude love, colonial marriage was a business partnership first.

As the economy of the East and Midwest shifted from agriculture to manufacturing in the first part of the nineteenth century, the white, nonimmigrant women who lived there found themselves with a dwindling realm of influence. Males, as wage earners or business owners, became families' sole

breadwinners. New social values restricted women to house-keeping, childrearing, and religious education, with no role in their financial futures. A new generation of women were now isolated in their homes.

The economic shift was accompanied by a religious revival called the Second Great Awakening. Starting in the 1820s, Protestant preachers fanned throughout the growing frontier seeking converts. They emphasized personal salvation and the pressing need to clean up the country's social ills in preparation for the return of Christ. Nearly all of the denominations denounced slavery, prostitution, and gambling. But most saved their most powerful vitriol for the evils of alcohol. The rapidly growing Methodist, Baptist, and Congregationalist churches demanded congregants give up alcohol before they could join. (This was made possible by the expansion of public filtering systems, which had eased the replacement of booze with clean drinking water.)

The stark message of the religious revival—hell's fires for the wicked, the promise of heaven for the virtuous—struck an especially sharp chord with middle-class women, who were struggling to articulate their roles in the new social order. Technological advances were building a new country, but the prevailing ideology made clear that it would fall to women to civilize it.

Mass communications helped show them how. Unlike the friendly wine-drinking tips in 1970s publications, nineteenth-century women's magazines were loaded with morality lessons. They stressed the dangerous nature of the competitive industrial world, and instructed readers to create an ethical haven at home. Architects of these new "separate spheres" argued that women could demonstrate their virtuousness by accepting these strict divisions of labor.

The most popular guidance came in a magazine called *Godey's Lady's Book,* which ran a mix of poems, articles, editorials, and serialized novels, often written by women. It had a circulation of 150,000 in the 1840s, but its readership was far higher than that. Women who couldn't afford the cost of a subscription joined clubs in order to share the magazine and discuss its contents. Its editor, Sarah Hale, an antislavery novelist, poet, and author of the nursery rhyme "Mary Had a Little Lamb," had an Oprah-like influence on her middle-class readers in matters of taste, etiquette, and opinion.

Hale used her forty-year reign at *Godey's* to rally support for her favorite causes, and her efforts were remarkably fruitful. The publication of a treatise on women's education generated the founding of a dozen girls' schools and colleges. She campaigned five presidents for the proclamation of Thanksgiving as a national holiday, finally succeeding with Lincoln. When she serialized T. S. Arthur's antialcohol novel, *Ten Nights in a Bar-Room and What I Saw There,* she effectively ensured that the topic would, in today's terms, go viral.

The book describes the downfall of a small town after the opening of its first tavern. None of its characters is immune from alcohol's destruction, regardless of whether they drink it. Readers responded to Arthur's sensationalistic narrative as if it were gospel, and the book became a bestseller. The tales of the weak-willed drunks and their hapless families grew even more popular when the book was developed into a play that ran in small towns for another half century.

Meanwhile, a group of six ex-drinkers had formed what they called the Washingtonian Total Abstinence Society. The group gathered to recount their drunken exploits, salvation through faith and abstinence, and the belief the meetings

themselves could help keep them sober. The tales of down-and-out drunkenness had wide appeal as cautionary tales, and attracted crowds of men and women, northerners and southerners, laborers and educated elite.

The lurid popular fiction and stirring testimony helped galvanize a movement of middle-class women, who responded as if it were a national imperative. They crafted an absolutist message: All drinking, any drinking, could bring with it only disaster. In 1874, a group launched the Woman's Christian Temperance Union in Cleveland, Ohio.

The WCTU, which required that members be white, Protestant women born in North America, quickly spread East, where the group faced an enormous challenge: millions of new immigrants who were arriving from central and southern Europe, and whose cultures and faiths gave them a very different relationship with alcohol. Overwhelmingly Roman Catholic, Jewish, or Greek Orthodox, they drank moderately, regularly, and, shockingly, even as part of their religious celebrations.

The WCTU hoped to demonstrate the wisdom of abstinence by education and example, but it was up against some powerful traditions—centuries of moderate drinking that were accepted and tolerated by women, and encouraged even by religious leaders.

The mission, of course, was about much more than booze. The women leading the antialcohol crusade had roots in rural America and were deeply suspicious of cities, which now teemed with baffling customs. From Denver and Milwaukee to Newark and St. Louis, German-born brewers established industrial breweries that produced rivers of urban beer. German immigrant communities re-created their traditional beer

gardens, which entire families attended—even on Sundays. In New York, Boston, and Philadelphia, Jewish, Italian, and Greek women not only drank wine at the dinner table, they also served small amounts to their kids.

Still more shocking, many of these new female arrivals left their homes every day for long hours in garment and textile factories. The WTCU disapproved, failing to note that the women were motivated by poverty—not a lack of education about the importance of domestic virtue. To combat this great ignorance, the group set up shop on Ellis Island, so they could indoctrinate women in the righteous ways of their new land as soon as their papers were processed.

If the WCTU failed to impress immigrant mothers, the group had a second chance through their children. The group dispatched its deputies—young teachers—into schools. Under pressure from dry lobbyists, Congress had mandated that a quarter of all health and hygiene lessons include temperance education, and the approved texts left no room for doubt. In one, a boy drops dead a few hours after he takes a nip from a flask; another described how alcohol burst blood vessels. One warned how booze transformed the robust muscles of the heart into pure fat, "sometimes so soft that a finger could be pushed through its walls."

Young schoolmarms—by the late nineteenth century teaching was an almost all-female profession—were also instructed to persuade students to sign pledges of total abstinence, or T.A. (from this derived the term "teetotaler"). Imagine the confusion of immigrant children, learning by day of alcohol's deathly properties, yet watching their parents sip beer at night.

To members of the WCTU, alcohol was the common thread in all social ills, from poverty, prostitution, and domestic violence to urban overcrowding—even women in the workplace. (If men didn't drink, the argument went, their wives wouldn't need to work.) A ban on the manufacture and sale of alcohol was the only possible solution.

Without the vote, temperance leaders could never achieve it. So they forged an alliance with early suffragists. Two of the most prominent, Elizabeth Cady Stanton and Susan B. Anthony, had joined the temperance movement early, and it was through their involvement in the antialcohol campaign that they helped gain credibility for the women's vote. It was an awkward partnership. To many middle-class Americans, the suffragists, absent temperance, seemed radical and unladylike. But the WCTU, with its symbol of purity—a tidy white ribbon—was an acceptable cause into which women could channel their ambitions.

By the early 1900s, temperance groups had branches in every state, and had adopted increasingly aggressive tactics. Activists, mostly women, surrounded saloons to sing hymns, hoping their prayers would convert the men inside. (Saloon owners often responded by "baptizing" the women with buckets of beer tossed their way.) The reformers made unannounced "shaming" visits to the homes of women they suspected of making "too free use" of alcohol. And some were masters of publicity. Carry Nation, a manic middle-aged Kentuckian, traversed the Southeast with an axe, smashing whiskey barrels and barrooms in what she called divinely inspired "hatchetations." She said her activism stemmed from her first marriage to an abusive heavy drinker whom she blamed for their daughter's poor health. Arrested for

vandalism more than thirty times, she paid for her jail fines with speaking fees and the sale of souvenir hatchets. Part vaudeville, all mad, Nation inveighed against "Demon Rum," describing herself as a "bulldog running along the feet of Jesus, barking at what He doesn't like."

I wanted to get beyond the hyperbole of the reformers, and found the work of Madelon Powers, a lively professor at the University of New Orleans who has devoted most of her career to the study of urban working-class customs.

On a frigid December day, Powers was visiting New York from Louisiana and we met at her hotel in the Lower East Side. We planned to take a neighborhood walking tour in which Powers would point out former saloons and speakeasies, but the wind was bitter, so we got into my car instead. At lunch, we ducked into McSorley's Ale House, which has been in operation since the 1850s and still has a layer of sawdust on the floor. Before Prohibition, saloon keepers coated their floors every morning with a fresh layer of sawdust or wood chips, which absorbed spilled beer and urine, was easy to sweep, and masked the stink of the combined fluids.

Over hearty chicken soup and the roar of some firefighters celebrating behind us, Powers described her decades of research into business records, letters, music, photographs, and diaries. The saloon, she says, was the central feature in the lives of the urban working class: a meeting place, a reminder of the old country, and a crucial spot for the organizing of both unions and social clubs. Perhaps most important, in pre-Prohibition industrial America, the saloon was where much of the urban labor force ate their midday meals. For the cost of a nickel beer, they received a hot lunch. Amid the slog of factory work, the lunches refreshed and revived. "It drove the

reformers crazy, because they lured female customers, too," she says.

Powers recounts the story of a Mrs. Mooney, an Irish laundress in New York who was outraged when a young coworker collapsed from exhaustion. It's "them rotten cold lunches you girls eat," Mrs. Mooney declared, and marched the women to a nearby saloon for a hot lunch. "Six beers with the trimmins!" Mrs. Mooney ordered, to the shock of one young colleague, Dorothy Richardson. "I, who never before could endure the sight or smell of beer, found myself draining my 'schooner' as eagerly as Mrs. Mooney herself," Richardson said later. "I instantly determined never again to blame a working man or woman for dining in a saloon in preference to the more godly and respectable dairy-lunch room."

Mrs. Mooney and Miss Richardson were by no means the exception. Powers found that a great number of respectable female drinkers frequented saloons through the discreet "ladies' entrance," commonly placed in the side or rear of the building. This allowed them to avoid public scrutiny; to bypass such indelicate barroom features as urinal troughs, positioned right beneath the bar; and to have easy access to the "take-out" counter where many women (or their children) came for large buckets of beer called "growlers." Seldom, Powers says, were they prostitutes.

But the image of ordinary women enjoying drinks in the saloon—or their take-out beer buckets on their roofs, porches, and courtyards—is mostly lost to history. "Theirs," she says, "wasn't the story the country cared about."

Instead, she says, the nation worked itself into a frenzy over lunchtime beer. Certainly, alcohol sometimes resulted in domestic violence, and of course some men drank their wages

away. But many such stories were exaggerated for political effect, and sensational tales like Arthur's *Ten Nights* were told — and retold—with evangelical zeal. Alcohol consumption had declined considerably since it was at its peak in the 1820s, aided not only by clean drinking water but also by America's other emerging beverage, coffee. By the late nineteenth century, its mass-scale production in South America had made it affordable, and the invention of the percolator simplified preparation.

•   •   •

By the early 1900s, several states and many counties prohibited the sale and consumption of alcohol. The stated goal, in part, was to prove how "truly American" their populations were. The WCTU, together with the efforts of the Anti-Saloon League, which formed as a lobbying group, were also buoyed by anti-German sentiment in the years leading up to World War I. Rejecting the beer made by German immigrants, suspected of being loyal to the Kaiser, could help demonstrate one's patriotism.

Abstaining from alcohol didn't mean middle-class women refused all mood-altering substances: They were principal users of opiates, which were available over the counter and by mail order. In 1897, the Sears, Roebuck catalogue offered a kit with a syringe, two needles, two vials of heroin, and a handy carrying case for $1.50.

They also made Lydia Pinkham a wealthy woman. Pinkham marketed an herbal tonic for ailments from cramps to menopause. Pinkham was a temperance supporter, but 20 percent

of her herbal tonic was alcohol. She said it was used as a "preservative."

Not even all temperance reformers were actually "dry." Many Victorian-era women, including reformers, indulged in dainty drinking rituals of their own. It was hardly even *drinking* to sip sherry or Madeira with guests, or enjoy a cool gin and tonic after a tiring day shopping. In any case, ladies knew their limits. And if they didn't, women's magazines instructed the untutored just how much liquor to pour to achieve "gaiety" but avoid getting sloshed. It was unchecked *male* drinking—the kind that took place without female supervision—that had to be stopped.

In 1919, after decades of vandalized saloons and public protests, the antialcohol forces triumphed, pushing through a constitutional amendment banning the manufacture, distribution, and sale of beer, wine, and spirits in all forty-eight states.

●　　●　　●

Women enthusiastically joined the millions of Americans who flouted the new law, which took effect in January 1920. Many of those who did were among the small but growing number of women who had stepped into the male world—of universities, employment, even the battlefield. And once they arrived, they had no intention of returning to the narrow world of their mothers. Twenty-one thousand American women had served as nurses during World War I, exposed to fear, death—and gallons of French wine. Tens of thousands more had attended college. Fewer than 10 percent of Americans sought higher education in 1920, but if they did, they found a near-equal ratio

of male and female students. It was so common for women to join the booze-fueled socializing there that it inspired a popular joke: "She doesn't drink / She doesn't pet / She hasn't been to college yet."

Many young women also worked before they married. They took jobs in offices and department stores; in publishing, real estate, and hospitals. By the end of the decade the workforce was almost a quarter female, up from 15 percent in 1890. Women had the vote, some made their own money, and they often lived on their own in small apartments or girls' dorms. Vacuum cleaners, electric washers, and plug-in irons had eased the drudgery of housework. Even preparing food was easier: There were cold cuts from the deli, canned vegetables, and ready-sliced bread from the corner store.

All this gave young women something their forebears could never have imagined: leisure time. Untethered to a family, these new women helped fuel a culture that revolved around consumer goods and mass entertainment—around fun. They wore short dresses, tossing their restrictive corsets and knee-length bloomers for step-in panties. They bobbed their hair, smoked cigarettes, swore, painted their faces, and even experimented with sex. In *This Side of Paradise*, F. Scott Fitzgerald shocked readers with his portrayal of the debutante Rosalind, who declares that she has kissed dozens of men, and would probably kiss "dozens more." To Victorian sensibilities, such words were downright pornographic: Respectable girls were to kiss only the man they intended to marry.

It was this very group of people—the educated middle and upper-middle classes—that set the standards of national behavior. And among them, defiance of Prohibition quickly became the social norm. These new women were nobody's moral

guardian: They were tomboy drinking buddies. "Women who, a few years before, would have blanched at the idea that they would ever be 'under the influence of alcohol' found themselves matching the men drink for drink," wrote essayist Frederick Lewis Allen. "They, too," he wrote, enjoyed its "uproarious release."

•   •   •

By the early 1930s, it was clear the Prohibition experiment had failed. Instead of disappearing, alcohol generated enormous profits for organized crime and crooked politicians. Illicitly manufactured alcohol had blinded, paralyzed, and killed scores of Americans. Even many female reformers, dismayed at the results of the ban, threw their efforts behind repeal.

After the stock market crashed, business leaders argued that the taxing of legal alcohol sales would raise much-needed revenues. And rebooting America's breweries and distilleries (wine would come a few years later) would help put the 25 percent of unemployed Americans back to work.

On December 5, 1933, Congress voted to repeal the Eighteenth Amendment. It had the desired effect on the government's dire fiscal straits. In the first year, consumption was estimated at one gallon per person, and alcohol sales yielded $259 million in federal taxes.

But Prohibition had lasting cultural effects, especially on women. The slamming of the saloon doors gave rise to an exciting, coed culture of drinking. In countless towns and cities, speakeasies were a force for social change, mixing men and women, blacks and whites (at least in the North). It also gave rise to a new form of entertainment: jazz.

It spurred some practical changes. One was table service, since not even a prostitute could holler her order at the bar. The second, mercifully, was the powder room, since in mixed company men couldn't relieve themselves in floor troughs. Ladies Night was decades away, but it was a start.

Prohibition also changed the way Americans drank. In speakeasies, the focus was on liquor—or, as the code of the day put it, "seeing a man about a dog." Patrons drank, and drank quickly, so they could accomplish their goal before it was time to leave (or before the feds showed up). Evening cruises, popular in coastal cities, had the same effect. These "ships to nowhere" sailed into international waters, served copious amounts of alcohol, and returned their inebriated passengers to shore. Like the frat parties that would come decades later, these developments normalized public drunkenness.

Prohibition also fundamentally changed drinking habits at home. As historian Catherine Gilbert Murdock put it, the Eighteenth Amendment "let domestic drinking out of the closet." In speakeasies, the presence of women took male drinking behavior down a notch, with fewer brawls, more flirting. At home, the opposite occurred. Sipping claret in the dining room was just as illegal as guzzling bathtub gin at a bar. So even at home, drinking took on an urgency, in back rooms and damp basements. Dainty Victorian drinking rituals, so decidedly old-fashioned, belonged to the past—and stayed there.

Ironically, the temperance reformers, in demanding a national abstinence to be overseen by the moral authority of women, created instead an irresistible underground for female drinkers. And despite the passage of almost a century, it is where many women still reside: secretly, drinking to get

drunk, hiding the evidence before the authorities—their husbands, their neighbors, their kids—find out.

*　　*　　*

The reformers' image of the drinker as morally bankrupt persisted, of course, but after Prohibition ended, it attached itself mainly to women who drank. Since legislating integrity hadn't cured the nation of its habit, society had to consider other ways of looking at drinkers—at least male ones. In the nascent field of alcohol studies, there was a growing theory that liquor created a physical and psychological dependence. Men who fell prey to its powers were not so much weak as they were ill, and deserving of compassion.

This belief did not extend to women. Women who drank too much weren't just inferior—they were sideshow freaks. They were so far outside the margins, they barely merited mention even in the new medical field. By midcentury, the most notable work involving women and alcohol was a sturdy-looking book called *The Alcoholic Woman: Case Studies in the Psychodynamics of Alcoholism.*

The author, Benjamin Karpman, had an impressive résumé: He was a professor of psychiatry at Howard University College of Medicine, a member of the New York Academy of Sciences, and for decades the chief medical officer at St. Elizabeth's, a preeminent psychiatric hospital in Washington, D.C.

His 1948 book on women and alcohol established him as an authority on the subject, even though his writing merely reflected the conventional opinions of the day. Karpman laid out his jaundiced view of female drinkers in his preface, writ-

ing: "What alcoholic women seem to lack in quantity, they certainly make up in quality. . . . [A]lcoholic women are much more abnormal than alcoholic men; in common parlance, when an alcoholic woman goes on a tear, 'it is terrific.'"

In 1934, Karpman was asked to give a talk about female alcoholics to fellow psychiatrists. Though he confessed to knowing little about the subject, the address nevertheless created a considerable stir, with articles in the national press, and requests for help from desperate strangers. Karpman then decided to profile three female inpatients who drank to excess. Their stories, he wrote, were intended to represent "a *certain* type of alcoholic woman" (the italics are his). "It need not be thought, however, that *all* alcoholic women are as difficult and are as promiscuous sexually or lead a checkered sex life." He added this reassuring coda for worried husbands: "I have had under my care cases of alcoholic women who were very chaste and entirely faithful to their spouses."

But those stories didn't merit telling. Instead, it was the morally dubious pasts of his three patients that *seemed* right, since their experiences mirrored what people expected of female drinkers. Women, he said simply, were "more difficult to cure than alcoholic men partly because theirs are more complex problems and partly because it is hard to keep them in treatment."

He attributed the excess drinking of a patient named Frances to her subconscious desire for women: Liquor allowed her to "escape" when she had to endure "normal" intercourse with her husband.

Another patient, Vera, had a sadistic mother who lamented that Vera had survived the childhood illnesses that had killed

her brothers. "Why couldn't it have been you?" she would cry as she beat the girl. Karpman made no comment on the mother's cruelty, or the serial loss and violence that marked Vera's young life. Instead, he described her as a knowing, naughty nymphet. At age fourteen, he asserted, she was "seduced" by a thirty-year-old coworker of her mother's from whom she contracted gonorrhea; other sexual partners followed. (If Karpman had any judgment on a man who sought sex with a child, he withheld it.)

Vera longed to go to the movies or out for ice cream with her friends, but since her mother disapproved of such trifles, she had no way to pay for them. One day, an elderly man approached her on the school grounds, offering her a dollar for each time she would fondle him. She agreed, thinking ahead to the freedom spending money might bring her. Karpman seized on this as evidence of her depravity: Vera was a prostitute! Once, she snatched a ten-dollar bill from the old man's hands, an infraction he reported—and that landed Vera in reform school. Karpman did not question this injustice, or the motives of the pervert, whom he described as "an eccentric old man": it was Vera who was the sexual degenerate. Her drinking was added proof of it.

The third woman, Elizabeth, also had physically and emotionally abusive parents. The insecure Elizabeth sought reassurance through sex, but could only achieve orgasm through masturbation or (gasp!) oral sex. She was, he wrote, "most unattractive" and a "general flop"—divorced, childless, and suffered from a penis envy so severe she had to drink herself to numb the pain of it. But her real debauchery came in what she said was a history of forced intercourse. Karpman scoffed at this. "Rape," he wrote, "was her specialty."

Karpman evinced no sympathy for his patients, or so much as a shred of compassion for the broken childhoods, the lost siblings, the physical abuse, or the sexual violence they suffered. By the mid–twentieth century, psychoanalysts had gained wide acceptance for their theories on a wide range of behaviors, and Karpman was a nationally respected expert. Like his colleague Bruno Bettelheim, who held mothers liable for their children's autism, Karpman blamed his patients' drinking on their licentiousness and their inability to accept their roles as wives and mothers.

Colleagues revered Karpman, the author of dozens of academic studies, as an unparalleled thinker. So did the lay press, from *Time* to *Playboy,* which quoted him frequently on sexually charged topics. In an obituary, a protégé remembered him as a "dedicated champion of the dispossessed." But when it came to women who drank too much, Karpman merely added a scientific veneer to conventional wisdom—and a national anxiety about the postwar role of women.

After two decades of tumult—first with the Depression, then the war—men and women had undergone significant shifts. Women had gained economic importance within their families by producing their own goods and stepping up to fill jobs even in heavy industry, showing their ample ability to assume male roles. But once the war was over, social critics were dismayed by anything less than a return to separate spheres. That included a national obsession with where—and how—women drank.

A New York columnist described the "Bistro Berthas, Cocktail Lounge Lorettas and Barfly Beatrices" as "1947's Problem People." Such behavior, he wrote, was "sickening to people who respect womanhood and think that women's

place, while it may no longer be strictly in the home, is certainly not in the corner dive." *Newsweek* had a name for these women: "Mrs. Drunkard."

Noel Busch, a writer at *Life* magazine, issued a stern reprimand in 1947. "In the olden days lady tipplers were rare to start with, and what few there were at least tried to conceal their weakness, shut up in some attic and ignored by society. Of late, however, they have entered into the broad daylight." He blamed the trend on women's efforts to achieve parity, which had "merely gotten them more mixed up than they were in the first place." He admonished them to "go back to cooking, sweeping, and attending to their children." He was aghast that women should enter bars—which, after all, were "men's clubs—not a hospital for housewives with the fidgets." They should order wine or beer—nothing that would take the barkeep's time—and after thirty minutes, get up and go home. "Drinking in the home, of course, poses other questions—but at least does not constitute a public menace." Of the dozen or so ads the issue carried for beer and whiskey, not a single one showed a woman.

Through it all, Karpman's *Alcoholic Woman* remained riveting enough to sustain readers' interests. It went through several printings in the 1950s, was released as a mass-market paperback in 1966, and was published continuously until 1974. Karpman's voice, likewise, was that of an expert—*the* expert—on troubled female drinkers, and what was perceived as their twisted desires, for almost a quarter century.

4 One Day at a Time:
A.A. and Women

If a woman had an uncontrollable drinking problem, there were few places she could turn. By the late 1940s, Alcoholics Anonymous had taken root as the nation's most popular remedy for excess drinking. Founded by two men in the mid-1930s, A.A. was initially inhospitable to women. Early members told women who were daring—or desperate—enough to attend its meetings that female alcoholics simply didn't exist. Nice ones, anyway.

The story of A.A.'s beginnings and its cofounder Bill Wilson has been told many times, first by Wilson himself and later, often from the affectionate perspective of writers who felt they or their loved ones had benefited from the program. In barest terms, the tale is this: Wilson and a small group of men created a fellowship of laymen whose personal experi-

ences helped other sufferers triumph over a malady that resisted all other remedies. Most of the early members were upper-middle-class men like Wilson—lawyers, stockbrokers, and other professionals brought low by alcohol.

I scoured the literature for clues about the role of women. In its early days, there wasn't much, but what little I could find suggested that the group took a dim view of female talents and possibilities—and was intolerant of their flaws. Historians suggest that these attitudes should be understood in the context of the period. But as I looked at A.A.'s treatment of women in the modern era, I found numerous echoes of the past. History casts a long shadow within A.A., a group that venerates its founders and whose members can quote sections of Wilson's 1939 text, known as the Big Book, by heart.

Today, A.A.'s approach to alcoholism has come to dominate alcohol treatment in the United States. If you seek professional help, the odds are overwhelming that you will be referred to a program that is founded on the notion that problem drinkers are powerless in the face of a disease and must religiously follow twelve steps if they hope to stay sober. If you get arrested for driving while drunk, or admit to a court that alcohol was involved in a crime, there's a good chance you'll be ordered to attend A.A. meetings, sometimes by a judge who's been through the program. In the majority of the nation's rehab facilities, the twelve steps of A.A. are the foundation of treatment. Its popularity, I discovered, was more a matter of historical happenstance than scientific choice. A.A. has legions of supporters and devoted, grateful followers, and its twelve-step model for recovery has been replicated in myriad ways in American culture.

But there are many other evidence-based approaches that

researchers say are superior to the faith-based model. There is also a growing chorus of addiction experts who suggest that its key tenet—that problem drinkers are powerless over drink—might actually undermine women's efforts to get well. It is worth noting that no other industrialized country relies on this approach for treating people with alcohol problems to the extent the United States does. The commitment to twelve-step programs is as American as baseball and big-budget disaster movies. To understand how we got here, you need to journey back to the Great Depression.

In the 1930s, Bill Wilson was an unsuccessful stockbroker and a "chronic inebriate" who had drunk his way through Prohibition. Desperate to stop, he sought the help of a friend who had found sobriety through the evangelical Oxford Group. It believed that men were sinners who, through confession and God's help, could right their paths and help others.

Wilson was intrigued, but he still couldn't quit drinking, and in 1934 he checked into Manhattan's Towns Hospital for his fourth attempt at drying out. There, his doctor, William Silkworth, told him that his condition was the result of an illness—not a moral shortcoming. Over a four-day period, Silkworth gave Wilson a powerful cocktail that included the hallucinogen belladonna, sedatives, and laxatives. The hope of the treatment, seen as a last resort, was that after several days of vomiting and diarrhea, the hallucinogen could psychically jolt drunks into sobriety. Patients called the method, which had been developed by a life insurance salesman named Charles Towns, "purge and puke."

It worked for Wilson. Lying in his hospital bed, Wilson shouted out to God to reveal himself. He then reported seeing a blinding light and feeling the most serene calm he had ever

experienced. He left the hospital, joined the Oxford Group, and stopped drinking for good. In 1935, on a business trip to Akron, Ohio, Wilson contacted another Oxford Group member, a proctologist named Bob Smith.

Together, they formed Alcoholics Anonymous, based loosely on the Oxford Group philosophies, the Washingtonians' nineteenth-century group meetings, and Benjamin Rush's eighteenth-century concept that excessive drinking was a sickness. By coming together for mutual support and spirituality, alcoholics could help each other keep from drinking, one day at a time. Though they made exceptions for themselves, the founders agreed that members should be anonymous. It was as much a defense against individual self-importance and stigma as it was a protection for the group. (They reasoned that the failures of any well-known members would embarrass the organization.) While they didn't advocate abstention for everybody, Wilson and Smith were unequivocal: For problem drinkers like themselves, one drop of booze was like a match tossed into a pool of gasoline.

Wilson and Smith developed the now-famous twelve steps. At their core was a declaration of powerlessness over alcohol. Members were encouraged to admit that their thirst for booze was beyond their control. To regain their health, excessive drinkers needed to relinquish their self-centeredness and submit to a higher power. Eventually, they could regain their footing and help other drunks do the same. There was little else in the way of hope for alcoholics, and by the late 1930s the group spread to a few dozen men in the Midwest and New York, eventually attracting a handful of women.

Like many innovators, Wilson was complicated, and once he stopped drinking, his other, equally ravenous appetites be-

came apparent. He downed astonishing quantities of coffee, chain-smoked the cigarettes that would ultimately kill him, and was a compulsive womanizer. He suffered from deep depressions, which many of his friends believed were triggered by the guilt he felt about repeatedly betraying his wife, Lois. Eventually, he became an enthusiast of LSD, for both himself and other alcoholics; at the time, science was intrigued by its potential as a tool for a variety of psychiatric conditions. He took megadoses of niacin as a mood regulator, and developed a passion for conducting séances in his home in Westchester County, New York, where he claimed to receive frequent messages "from the other side."

His philandering was an open secret. In the 1960s, longtime A.A.s became so alarmed by his constant attraction to young female newcomers, they formed what they called "Founder's Watch," a group of friends delegated to steer Bill away from pretty women who caught his eye during A.A. functions. For the last fifteen years of his life, Wilson had an affair with an A.A. colleague and beautiful actress twenty-two years his junior, Helen Wynn. Unlike Lois, who was a normal drinker, downing a single cocktail before dinner every night, Wynn was a recovering alcoholic who followed the A.A. program. Though he could not know it, the early tolerance for Bill's sexual conduct would set a behavioral precedent for the organization.

As the group spread, Wilson and other early members drew up a blueprint they titled *Alcoholics Anonymous: The Story of How More Than One Hundred Men Have Recovered from Alcoholism.*

It was, in effect, a New Deal for drunks—as long as the drunks were men. Women were barely mentioned. Near the

end of the first edition of *Alcoholics Anonymous,* the unnamed author—though the book was a joint project, Wilson is said to have been its chief writer—concedes that the program could help women, too. But in the A.A. worldview, a woman's most conceivable role was as the wife of an alcoholic. In a chapter called "To Wives," the text offers women specific instructions for bolstering their husbands' precarious mental health. Never be angry, the book warns, even if you have to leave your husband temporarily. "Patience and good temper are most necessary. . . . If he gets the idea that you are a nag or a killjoy, your chance of accomplishing anything useful may be zero. . . . He will tell you he is misunderstood. This may lead to lonely evenings for you." Wilson hinted at the unpleasant consequences for wives who didn't take his advice: "He may seek someone else to console him—not always another man."

The book included a brief chapter written by the group's second female member, a divorced housewife named Florence R. The self-loathing she felt at being a filly in a stable of stallions is painfully apparent. "To my lot falls the rather doubtful distinction of being the only 'lady' alcoholic in our particular section," she wrote. "I have learned to recognize and acknowledge the underlying cause of my disease: selfishness, self-pity, and resentment." A few months later, Florence R. (later identified as Florence Rankin) resumed drinking and committed suicide.

The book made clear that men who drank too much were in the grips of a disease that gave them an uncontrollable urge. In the view of A.A. members and others, women drinkers had themselves to blame. They were widely seen as trollops, their drinking a symptom of unchecked libidos. Records from the period show the men of A.A. worried about what might hap-

pen if these femmes fatales mixed with male sufferers, sometimes with good reason. In A.A.'s early days, a former Akron mayor consummated his affair with a woman on Dr. Bob's examining table. The episode scandalized the group. "As drunks, I don't know why we should have been," Bill would later say, adding that the woman was the first they had ever dealt with. In any case, the incident left the impression that women could bring only one thing: trouble. Bill and others feared such antics would disrupt the organization entirely.

Male drinkers often had the support of intact families, even if only because their wives were financially dependent on them. But few men tolerated alcoholic women, and many of the first female A.A.s were divorced or single—and therefore posed a threat to the wives. Men developed a truism of their own: "Under every skirt there is a slip." Dalliances with women trying to get sober were sure to provoke a relapse.

To manage this potential distraction, women who did come sat opposite men in the rooms. And women were sponsored not by other alcoholics, but by the alcoholics' wives. Eventually, the group developed "closed" and "open" meetings, which anyone was welcome to attend. Women-only meetings developed, too—but those quickly generated controversy, as the women who attended were suspected of being lesbians.

There was a woman among the founders of A.A., and she played a crucial role in popularizing the group. Her name was Marty Mann, and in 1939, she was in a Connecticut sanitarium headed toward the same dismal fate as Florence R. Born into a wealthy Chicago family that counted the educator Horace Mann among its forebears, Mann was a debutante, educated at exclusive private schools. Married and divorced by twenty-five, she had joined the hard-drinking field of public relations

after her family lost its fortune in the 1929 crash. On a usual day, she'd have a few swigs and six martinis—and that was just before lunch. One night, so drunk she couldn't remember if she jumped or fell, Mann plunged from a second-story window in London, breaking multiple bones. She checked into the Connecticut hospital to dry out, but kept sneaking out for drinks. When her psychiatrist gave her the manuscript of the Big Book, she recoiled at its religious message, and put it away.

During a fit of anger weeks later, Mann picked up the book again. This time, she described feeling her rage lift and her hopelessness recede. She left the sanitarium and sought out A.A. in New York. Her blue-blood lineage may have helped persuade the male members she was respectable, but she was far from accepted. To the men, Mann recalled, she was "just some kind of a freak." Ironically, it was the wives who helped welcome her. Mann was a lesbian, and posed no romantic risks with the men.

With her skills in public relations, Mann quickly emerged as an effective messenger for the idea that alcoholics were sick and deserving of compassion and help. Wilson was the architect of the twelve-step program, but Mann planted A.A. in the public consciousness. Her prominence was striking among the all-male leadership, especially one so hostile to women.

Mann had three "slips" during her first eighteen months in the program, which underscored her fears of helplessness— and helped fuel male doubts about her participation. "Nobody thought it was possible that I, or any other woman, would ever make it," she later recalled.

It didn't stop her from reaching out to other female drinkers. She estimated that in her first year, she had tried to help at

least a hundred women, but only she and three other women showed up regularly at the new New York office. "This was a man's problem and A.A. was a man's program and this was a man's world," Mann would later say. As late as 1959, Mann noted disapprovingly, many A.A. chapters continued to refuse to admit women.

She blamed the predicament on the enduring double standard that regarded male drunkenness as acceptable on some occasions—but always deplored the same behavior in women. It's no wonder, she would say, even decades after A.A.'s founding, that women went underground with their drinking. "We hide," she said. "We do our drinking in our bedroom, at least as much as we can, until we're too drunk to know the difference and we go wandering out, and everybody does find out."

The double standard, she said, was also why getting help was so hard for women. "I knew an awful lot of women the first years I was in A.A. who couldn't make it, who didn't make it," she said. "I always felt in many cases it was because they were women—not because they were so much sicker, or because they didn't want to make it, but the odds were so stacked against them that they never really had a chance." It didn't dawn on Mann, though, that perhaps the solution that had worked for her was not appropriate for other women.

Mann did not appear to have experienced any doubts. In 1944, she established a foundation called the National Committee for Education on Alcoholism (it would later become the National Council on Alcoholism). She went public with her name, contrary to the A.A.'s rules guarding anonymity, in the hope that her regal carriage and solid upbringing could show that anybody, even women, could be afflicted with the disease of alcoholism.

• • •

Paradoxically, A.A.'s remedy for this disease was a purely spiritual approach. But since doctors could only offer such dubious cures as belladonna, A.A.'s faith-based methods filled a therapeutic vacuum. Nonetheless, its founders hungered for the medical community's stamp of approval, and an after-the-fact search for scientific proof of A.A.'s efficacy for treating alcoholism was a natural next step. Science could boost the movement, and so the research, funded in part by alcohol companies, began. Those efforts, it turned out, weren't terribly rigorous, even by standards of the day. Not surprisingly, they excluded women.

The epicenter of the nascent field of alcohol research was Yale's Center for Alcohol Studies. Its researchers founded a journal, devised Yale Plan treatment clinics, and instituted a six-week summer school of alcohol studies to educate clergy, temperance workers, probation officers, and medical professionals in the revolutionary way of viewing the problem drinker. Founded in 1942, the Yale center launched a medical movement around the concept of alcoholism as a disease. Americans had dedicated countless resources to demonize the evils of alcohol, but now came a swift reversal: The nation didn't have an alcohol problem; alcoholics did.

Mann attended the Yale summer school and began to work closely with the center's top researcher, an enigmatic biostatistician named E. M. Jellinek. Mann's skills in crafting strategic communications and Jellinek's scientific mantle were mutually beneficial: Jellinek received widespread attention for his research, while Mann's ties to the prestigious institu-

tion lent her—and A.A., apprehensive that its insistence on member abstinence would link it to old-fashioned temperance groups—credibility.

Jellinek was by all accounts a polyglot and charming colleague. His qualifications, however, were dubious, and his curriculum vitae included at least one invented degree: a 1936 doctorate in science from the University of Leipzig. Jellinek was Jewish, and by that date Jews in Hitler's Germany were barred from sitting for their doctorates.

Jellinek's scientific rigor was equally questionable. Data for one of his early studies, on the psychological and physical trajectory of alcoholism, came from questionnaires devised not by Yale researchers but by A.A.'s General Service Office (GSO) in New York. Of the 1,600 questionnaires mailed, only 158 people responded. Working together, Mann and Jellinek tossed the forty-five that were incomplete or indecipherable, and another fifteen that had come from women. Their answers diverged so far from the men's that they would have changed the findings. So the physiologist and the PR lady, keen to promote the disease theory—each for their own reasons—decided to discard them.

This left ninety-eight self-selected white men, not exactly a scientifically representative sample. From them, Jellinek published a 1946 paper that was seminal in the establishment of alcoholism as a disease. Using the answers on the questionnaires, he came up with a theory of how people succumb to alcohol, in a series of stages that closely replicated the A.A. experience. Over the next many years, it came to be illustrated by a curve in which alcoholics progressed from normal social drinking to sneaking drinks, then to increased toler-

ance, guilt, blackouts, withdrawal symptoms, and hopelessness, then finally to a low point where the drinker realizes he must reform. The chart circulated nationwide.

Jellinek continued to refine his theories in the years that followed, and as he did, he began to distance himself from much of the popular interpretations of his work. He became especially concerned about the widespread use of the word "alcoholic." As he rightly noted, everybody from social scientists to journalists and general practitioners had adopted it as the label for any kind of excess drinking—not only the distinct, well-defined behaviors that eventually led to physical dependence. The misapplication of the word could only undermine the whole disease concept, he warned in 1952: If everybody could attribute bad drunken behavior to a disease, they couldn't possibly be accountable for it.

In his 1960 book, *The Disease Concept of Alcoholism,* Jellinek described five "phases" of alcoholism he arbitrarily identified with Greek letters. "Gamma" alcoholics were those who were physically and psychologically dependent—the truly diseased.

Yet Jellinek had become uncomfortable with the growing role laymen were taking in defining the affliction—and how best to treat it. He acknowledged that his conclusions were drawn from a small number of subjects, and urged the "student of alcoholism" to "emancipate himself from accepting the exclusiveness of the picture of alcoholism as propounded by Alcoholics Anonymous." At a 1959 alcoholism conference at Columbia University, he even pleaded that "A.A. leave science alone—so that scientists might get along with the business of objective research into the problem."

But that didn't happen. With his 1960 book, the press seized upon the idea that alcoholics—"real" alcoholics—had

no choice about their drinking, sharing an inability to stop once they'd had a single sip. Jellinek wrote that "recovered alcoholics in Alcoholics Anonymous speak of 'loss of control' . . . when the ingestion of one alcoholic drink sets up a chain reaction so that they are unable to adhere to their intention 'to have one or two drinks only' but continue to ingest more and more . . . contrary to their volition."

The qualifiers—"recovered alcoholics in Alcoholics Anonymous"—were overlooked. Like the fictional ten nights in a barroom that galvanized the temperance workers, Jellinek's findings seeped into the public consciousness as scientific fact.

As someone who has written for various daily publications for more than twenty years, I can understand the impulse to emphasize the most dramatic findings under deadline pressure, but the effects can be damaging—and lasting. That's how we wound up with "crack babies," infants born to mothers who used that drug during pregnancy and who experts erroneously predicted would be severely mentally, physically, and emotionally disabled; and how autism got linked to vaccines (the so-called findings of Andrew Wakefield, the British doctor who first reported the connection in the *Lancet*, have been completely discredited). Unfortunately, though, many of these early (and, as it turns out, bogus) ideas take hold.

Jellinek's caveats went unnoticed, and by the time of his death in 1963, the fusing of public belief and science seemed complete. In his book *Alcohol: The World's Favorite Drug*, Griffith Edwards, a British alcohol researcher, described the climate this way: "The disease of alcoholism was the whole problem, and any other view was a heresy to be preached down. So deft and politically astute was the reformulation of the problem that it seems almost like a conjuring trick. A rab-

bit in the form of a disease was brought out of the hat, and alcohol vanished into thin air."

At midcentury, Americans' faith in medicine seemed boundless. Vaccines, steroids, and antibiotics vanquished deadly, painful ailments. Researchers discovered DNA; physicians performed open-heart surgery and organ transplants. And so, too, could medicine have an answer for the alcoholic.

Except for one thing: This new, medically approved program did not rely on anyone with medical training. These new helpers would be peers who had "hit bottom" themselves and, with the aid of a higher power, returned to sobriety. The cure for the hapless drinker, then, wound up being exactly where the United States had started: religion.

A.A. and Popular Culture

Marty Mann was remarkably gifted at spinning the bottle. Throughout her tenure, she met with—and by some accounts, collaborated with—reporters, broadcast executives, and Hollywood screenwriters whose work extolled the redemptive powers of A.A.

In the 1940s, newspapers and national magazines began to feature tales of male drunks saved by A.A. On radio and television shows, men poured out their emotional stories to living room audiences around the country. And in a sign of the mores of that time, those interviewed on television wore Lone Ranger masks to hide their identities.

In 1945, moviegoers turned *The Lost Weekend* into a blockbuster. The dark, edgy film, directed by Billy Wilder, was a dramatic departure from the 1930s romps of W. C.

Fields or *The Thin Man* team of Myrna Loy and William Powell, in which drinking was a comedic prop. *The Lost Weekend,* adapted from an autobiographical novel by A.A. member Charles Jackson, depicts a struggling writer who lurches through a five-day bender of shameful flashbacks and terrifying hallucinations. "He's a sick person," his girlfriend confides at a key point. "It's as though there was something wrong with his heart or his lungs. You wouldn't walk out on him if he had an attack. He needs our help."

Such compassionate language—which echoed through popular culture—went a long way in helping Americans accept that male alcoholics shared an affliction.

An orthodoxy took hold. When heavy drinkers appeared in plays, in films, and on living room television screens, the plot followed predictable lines: the drunk falls off the deep end if he or she doesn't join A.A. Singer Lillian Roth told of her descent into booze and recovery through A.A. in the worldwide best-seller, translated into twenty languages, called *I'll Cry Tomorrow.* Actress Susan Hayward earned an Oscar nomination for playing Roth in the hit movie.

By contrast, Kirsten Arneson, the alcoholic played by Lee Remick in *The Days of Wine and Roses,* rejects A.A.—and with it, all respectability. Her husband, played by Jack Lemmon, sobers up, but Kirsten doesn't, and becomes a derelict wife and mother. She even picks up strangers in bars—she prefers their company to her husband's "holier-than-thou, do-gooder Boy Scout" A.A. buddies. At the end of the film— equal parts horror movie and cautionary tale—she tells her husband, "You better give up on me."

She turns away, toward a neon bar sign glowing in the distance. Director Blake Edwards later said he had quit drinking

before shooting the film. "I was one of those lucky people who found the power to stop on my own," he told the *New York Times*. Kirsten, poor unfortunate, was hopeless. She didn't fit into A.A.—but paradoxically, she was doomed without it.

The real world was hardly more empathetic to women who drank too much. Male alcoholics were celebrated for seeking A.A.'s help, but women were castigated for needing it. A Boston newspaper used the headline "Women Drunkards, Pitiful Creatures, Get Helping Hand," to describe female members of the group.

By then, A.A. began to accept greater numbers of women, but they remained decidedly second-class citizens. In 1946, the *Grapevine*, the group's monthly newsletter, printed a front-page litany of complaints about women's behavior in A.A., amassed from groups around the country. Its author was a woman, Grace O. (She noted, writing in the third person, that she was "grateful" for the anonymity that allowed her to "stick her neck out.")

She called it "Female Frailties":

1. The percentage of women who stay with A.A. is low—too many drop out after the novelty wears off.

2. Women form emotional attachments that are too intense.

3. So many women want to run things. To boss, manage, supervise, regulate, and change things. Twenty want to decorate; one will scrub or mend what is already around.

4. Too many women don't like women.

5. Women talk too much. Women . . . worry the same dead mouse until it's unrecognizable.

6. Women shouldn't work with men, and vice versa.

7.   Sooner or later, a woman-on-the-make sallies into a group, on the prowl for phone numbers and dates.

8.   A lot of women are attention demanders. Spotlight sisters. They want to be spoon-fed, coaxed, babied, encouraged, teased, praised, and personally conducted into recovery.

9.   Few women can think in the abstract.

10. Women's feelings get hurt too often.

11. Far too many women A.A.'s cannot get along with the non-alcoholic wives of A.A. members.

These beliefs reflected an organizational opinion, as their prominent display indicated. They also revealed a deeper truth about the predicament of the woman who drank too much: It was vulgar to drink like a man, but you'd better sober up like one. Strong. Silent. Undemanding. "Spotlight sisters" who wanted to be "personally conducted into recovery" need not apply.

A.A.'s most prominent initiative for women was Al-Anon family groups. Created by Lois Wilson and Dr. Bob's spouse, Anne Smith, Al-Anon was a twelve-step program for wives of alcoholics. The organization, which would develop the theory of "codependence"—being addicted to the person with the addiction—urged women to "let go and let God." It also counseled them to provide an emotionally secure atmosphere that would solidify their husbands' sobriety. Cultural historian Lori Rotskoff suggests that this ideology—the patient, accepting wife; boys-will-be-boys husband—helped rebuild the gender roles upended by the Depression and the war. A woman's job was to maintain the family morally and emotionally; a man's was to provide financially. In the study of what came

to be called "the alcoholic marriage," social workers judged wives equally responsible for their husbands' drinking. "The wife of an alcoholic is not simply the object of mistreatment in a situation which she had no part in creating," one social worker wrote. Such women fit into four neat wifely categories: Controlling Catherines, Wavering Winnifreds, Punitive Pollys, and Suffering Susans.

Paradoxically, Al-Anon offered no such convenient excuses for husbands whose wives drank to excess. There were no Demanding Dicks, Raging Roberts, or Explosive Eds to blame.

• • •

Few people questioned how well A.A. worked—or whether there might be gender differences in the way women and men recovered. Speaking to a Canadian audience celebrating the thirtieth anniversary of the group, Mann declared that the twelve-step approach worked equally for both genders. She did not mention that she herself had recently relapsed.

"The full realization that A.A. is just as much for women, that it works just as well for women as it does for men—is a tremendously important message."

5 *Rehab Nation*

In 1970, the United States formally embraced the twelve-step approach when Congress passed the Comprehensive Alcohol Abuse and Alcoholism Prevention, Treatment, and Rehabilitation Act. The law was known as the Hughes Act for its sponsor, Iowa senator Harold Hughes, and it dedicated millions to the study, education, and treatment of alcoholism, which in 1956 had been designated an "illness" by the American Medical Association. (It stopped short of calling it a "disease.") The legislation reflected broader American enthusiasm about the possibilities of science and technology. America had won the race to space, beating the Soviet cosmonauts to the moon, and had defeated scourges from polio to smallpox. After addressing alcoholism, Congress declared war on cancer, creating fifteen cancer research centers to invent new drugs that would combat it.

The Hughes Act created a new, centralized research agency, the National Institute for Alcohol Abuse and Alcoholism (NIAAA), with authority to develop and conduct health, education, training, research, and planning programs for the prevention and treatment of alcohol abuse and alcoholism. In the years that followed, Mann's group, renamed the National Council on Alcoholism and Drug Dependence, grew fivefold. Government funding accounted for more than 75 percent of its budget.

In addition to underwriting research, the Hughes Act barred employers from discriminating against alcoholics, a seemingly simple provision that turned out to have far-reaching implications. Companies that worried about legal liability dramatically expanded their employee assistance programs, which referred employees with drug or alcohol problems to the growing number of for-profit treatment centers springing up nationwide. At the same time, major insurers recognized alcoholism as a disease and began paying for inpatient treatment at these centers, which were overwhelmingly staffed by recovering alcoholics who remained active in A.A. and used literature sold by A.A.'s publishing arm, Alcoholics Anonymous World Services, in rehab. At typical treatment centers, patients received on-site counseling combined with other therapies. Regular attendance at A.A. meetings was an essential component of a stay.

The A.A. view of alcoholism was ideally suited to the profit needs of the rehab industry: Counseling could be delivered by people whose main qualification was having recovered from "hitting bottom" through a strict adherence to the twelve steps. Instead of hiring a staff of highly paid doctors, rehab centers could rely on laymen with life experience. The

counselors established a group called the National Association of Alcohol Counselors and Trainers, in order, as one of its founders said, to "make alcoholism counselor trainers look professional." He told an interviewer: "The training we taught [our new counselors] was not based on clinical skills; it was based on a community development model with emphasis on A.A."

With insurers and companies footing the bill, rehab blossomed into the multibillion-dollar industry it is today. Consider this: In 1969, the outgoing Johnson administration had budgeted $4 million nationally for community alcohol treatment programs. Hughes, a self-declared member of A.A. who was known by his colleagues as "Mr. Addiction," said the sum would be about as effective as trying to stop the floodwaters of the Mississippi with a pebble. Hughes stepped down from the Senate after a single term, and returned to Iowa, where he became an alcohol treatment entrepreneur, founding several private centers.

In 1972, the NIAAA budget was $84.6 million; by 1975, that figure was $146 million. In 1973, there were roughly 1,800 treatment facilities. By 2009, that number had jumped to more than 13,500, nearly a third run by for-profit companies. (In 2012, the NIAAA's budget was $469 million.) Much of the alcohol research supported with federal dollars focused on the twelve-step approach.

The contrast between the research on alcohol and cancer launched by the federal government in the 1970s is illuminating. Government-supported researchers have discovered hundreds of new cancer therapies over the past four decades, and there are nearly 1,000 more biopharmaceutical cancer drugs in development. Yet there are a mere six drugs to treat alco-

hol abuse; two, Antabuse and naltrexone, had been developed long before the passage of the Hughes Act.

As more Americans entered rehab, more joined A.A. Between 1965 and 1975, A.A. membership in the United States jumped almost 130 percent, from 144,000 to 331,000. By 1968, females accounted for 22 percent of the group.

Just as they were being accepted in A.A., many American women were beginning to challenge their position and rights in society, and taking their place inside the institutions that had been dominated by men. Congress passed Title IX, and the Supreme Court guaranteed women the right to end a pregnancy. By the end of the decade, nearly half of all women were in the workforce, and for the first time, more women than men entered colleges.

Paradoxically, these advances added burdens for millions of women with families. As they entered public life and industry, women remained responsible for the majority of housework. Sociologists found that married American women in the 1960s and '70s were working an extra month of twenty-four-hour days when compared with their husbands. (Researchers tallied the total time spent by men and women on domestic chores and child care.)

Many women accepted this imbalance to maintain peace in their marriages and to fulfill their ambitions or keep their family finances afloat. Their mothers' and grandmothers' generation had managed to raise kids and keep a clean house. But as Arlie Hochschild noted in her book *The Second Shift,* these women also suffered from exhaustion, low sex drive, irritability, and some pretty serious anxiety. In national drinking surveys taken in 1967 and 1984, the number of

women in their thirties who said they were regular drinkers rose by almost 9 percent. And in that seventeen-year gap, the number of women who reported binging, being unable to stop until they were drunk, and suffering professional consequences more than doubled.

There were other dramatic social changes occurring, too: As states passed no-fault divorce laws, the divorce rate began climbing, reaching an all-time high in 1981, when more than half of all marriages dissolved.

Not surprisingly, there was a lot of public hand-wringing about the state of women—including their alcohol intake. Though American women had begun to drink more since the end of the Second World War, in the 1970s there was sudden concern about the "epidemic" of female drinking. The discovery in the 1970s and '80s that alcohol had dangerous effects on fetuses (called fetal alcohol syndrome, FAS), while legitimate and alarming, escalated concerns about women's drinking as a wider social problem. A century after the founding of the WCTU, the outcry over FAS turned attention solely on female imbibers. Suddenly, there was intense focus on women's drinking habits, regardless of whether they were pregnant. And the pressures were growing: In this brave new universe of negotiating day care and custody agreements, trying to make partner while keeping a marriage together, who had time to relax? If a woman poured herself a glass or two (or three) of the culturally sanctioned wine, she could cook dinner, fold clothes, and fall asleep. This drinking wasn't social: For many women at the breaking point, it felt like first aid.

●　　●　　●

Shortly after the Hughes Act became law, one of Sharon Wilsnack's Harvard professors asked her to contribute to his book on the human motivations for drinking. Wilsnack recalls that day more than forty years ago with fresh disbelief. As she read through the draft, she noticed a startling omission: In nearly six hundred pages of text, there was no mention of a single female subject. Mustering her courage, Wilsnack asked her professor why women had been overlooked. Sheepish, he admitted that he had had a "huge blind spot," and encouraged Wilsnack to learn more. Wilsnack headed to the Widener Library, one of the nation's best, to immerse herself in the existing scholarly literature on women and alcohol.

Over the next several months, she combed through books, academic journals, and papers. She found hundreds of thousands of studies of alcoholism, but only six of them involved female subjects. "And they were lousy, tiny studies," Wilsnack says. Many researchers, she discovered, had even omitted the effects of alcohol on female rats. "They had either not included them in the first place, or tossed them out because their fat ratios or estrus cycle screwed up the results," she says. "Researchers were treating women just like men, even if it was clear from the outset that there were huge differences."

One Harvard study piqued her curiosity. It had enlisted males at a frat party, asking them to look at pictures and describe their emotions at certain intervals after drinking. A large majority of the men described feeling "tough," and with greater inebriation reported feeling even more confident of their physical and social powers.

Wilsnack got funding to conduct a similar study, this time using men and women. She devised two parties for Harvard students with identical lighting, music, and ambience, but at

one, they were served alcohol; at the other, soft drinks. After the students were finished imbibing, researchers showed pictures and asked them to talk about their emotions. The male drinkers reported feeling more aggressive, replicating the earlier study.

It was the early 1970s—an optimistic time to be a young woman on the Harvard campus, and Wilsnack had wondered if the female drinkers might report feeling strong and capable, too. Instead, they said the opposite of what she expected: They described feeling calmer, less inhibited, and both emotionally and physically warmer than the nondrinking female subjects.

But the female alcohol drinkers reported feeling less powerful, socially and personally, than the soda-pop-drinking women. The findings took her aback. "I had some vague ideas about what I might find," Wilsnack recalls, "but that women felt less powerful when they drank—that really surprised me."

In the wider world, women were beginning to question their treatment at the hands of the largely male medical profession, particularly when it came to pregnancy, childbirth, and menopause. Not far from Wilsnack's office, the authors of *Our Bodies, Ourselves* were researching and revising the first edition of their book, which would sell 250,000 copies without any formal advertising. Alcohol and drug abuse, in part due to the Hughes Act, was also in the public consciousness, so Wilsnack's research put her in high demand with reporters, even though she was a graduate student in her early thirties with no clinical practice.

But there was still so little known about women and alcohol. Wilsnack's two published studies brought the global literature on women and alcohol to a total of fifteen papers.

Women were all but ignored by researchers studying alcohol abuse, too. By 1976, the increasingly significant NIAAA had funded 574 treatment programs; a mere 14 of them were for women. Of 384 research grants, just 16 had any relationship to women, and only five were specifically designed for studying female drinkers.

And no one even bothered to track whether women were seeking treatment for alcohol abuse. I searched government databases for female treatment admissions for some sense of the numbers in the years between 1970 and 1985, but couldn't find them anywhere. Leigh Henderson, an epidemiologist at the Substance Abuse and Mental Health Services Administration, the agency the government created in 1992, told me why. "No single national data source covers the entire period, and there are no national data prior to 1977," she wrote in an e-mail. ". . . Data on the characteristics of females in treatment who abused alcohol alone simply do not exist for that period."

In other words, nobody was even thinking to count them.

This much is clear. When women broached their worries and anxieties with family doctors (the vast majority of whom were male), they were likely to be brushed off, prescribed Valium, and labeled "troublemakers." The 1960s might have been an epoch of free love and questioning of authority, but expectations remained high for women. In sociological surveys designed to test tolerance for the shifting mores of the 1960s and '70s, Americans across all social, class, racial, and regional lines cited contempt for drunken female behavior. The antics of inebriated men, meanwhile, were viewed far less dimly.

The Hughes Act gave people with alcohol problems a place to go. And it wasn't long before the definition of who qualified for help began to broaden. "My name's Jan, and

I'm an alcoholic," came into the national lexicon as short-hand for a lifelong condition, a course from which you could never graduate. If you could recognize yourself on Jellinek's curve, then you, too, could find a place for yourself within the A.A. narrative. Whether you thought about drinking too much; whether, during a period of stress, you looked forward to an evening cocktail too much; or whether you had progressed to the point where you had a shot of whiskey in the morning to calm the shakes, there was a cure: cold turkey and group support. It would require vigilance: At any moment, a drop of alcohol could sweep aside decades of sobriety and develop into a binge. The triggers could be as innocent as a bite of Grandma's bourbon-soaked Christmas cake, or filet mignon with red wine sauce. Some argued that even pain medication after surgery—Bill W. called them "goofballs"—could set off a bender.

While the treatment centers broadcast this gospel to a much wider audience, a handful of U.S. researchers began to question whether abstinence was an appropriate approach for everyone with worrisome drinking habits. In 1976, the Rand Corporation released results of a study of more than two thousand subjects—all male—who were patients at forty-five NIAAA-funded treatment centers. The report, underwritten by NIAAA, analyzed a wide range of data about the patients, but a small passage in the findings generated a huge controversy. Researchers found that eighteen months after alcohol treatment, 24 percent of the men were abstaining, and another 22 percent were drinking moderately, reporting no associated problems. The authors concluded that it was possible for some alcohol-dependent men to return to controlled drinking.

Separately, two California researchers, Mark and Linda

Sobell, reported success with teaching alcohol-dependent subjects to drink in moderation using behavior modification. All of the Sobells' seventy subjects were male.

You would have thought the scientists had reported that a steady diet of bacon grease was good for your heart. Attacks from some researchers at Marty Mann's organization, the National Council on Alcoholism, were swift and vitriolic, and charged that the news would lead alcoholics to falsely believe they could drink safely. Prominent NCA board members tried to suppress the findings drawn from the treatment center data, and the NIAAA, which had funded the study, repudiated it. In response to the criticism, Rand researchers expanded their study to include more subjects, this time for a four-year period, with similar results—and equally fevered reactions. The second study included 922 subjects, all men. The Sobells fared little better. They were accused of fraud, ridiculed in the scientific and popular media, and ultimately moved to Canada, where they replicated their findings without causing a furor.

The root of the angry responses was obvious to many researchers, especially the late Alan Marlatt, a psychologist at the University of Washington who defended the experiments in follow-up journal articles. "We were told that we were irresponsible, that we were going to kill people, that we were in denial about what alcoholism really was," he told me. Marlatt, who died in 2011, said the findings called into question the foundations of the lucrative alcohol treatment industry. "It was all quite clear: There were interests people wanted to protect," he said.

The conflict over whether anyone identified by A.A. as an alcoholic (a self-selecting, broadly defined group) could ever drink in moderation has divided treatment experts ever since.

For proponents of twelve-step programs, the issue is doctrinal and beyond discussion. Decades before the Rand studies, the Big Book put it this way: "Physicians who are familiar with alcoholism agree there is no such thing as making a normal drinker out of an alcoholic. Science may one day accomplish this, but it hasn't done so yet."

Those who questioned this view—in the United States at least—were castigated. Marlatt, who was Canadian, was especially reviled. "Anyone who was considering the science of controlled drinking was accused of being in denial, of giving people permission to 'relapse,'" he told me. No one was *recommending* that alcoholics take up controlled drinking. The scientific findings merely reported that for some people, it was possible without advancing alcohol dependence.

●　　●　　●

At about the same time, another academic was beginning to question some of A.A.'s tenets, too. This time, however, the researcher challenged the group's suitability for herself. Sociologist Jean Kirkpatrick had joined the group as a graduate student at the University of Pennsylvania in the mid-1950s, and had stayed sober for three years. She worked through the steps, but little of the program's dogma made sense to her.

Kirkpatrick was an exemplary scholar who quickly earned the respect of her professors, as well as numerous honors and scholarships. But she was unable to internalize her accomplishments, convinced they were the result of a series of flukes. In 1958, when she became the first woman to receive one of Penn's most prestigious fellowships, her obsessive self-doubts took hold: Surely the university had made a terrible mistake.

She started drinking again, and didn't stop for another thirteen years.

Kirkpatrick came to realize that two of A.A.'s key messages—she was powerless over her drinking and must relinquish her ego in order to stop it—actually fueled her deep insecurities. As she thought about her drinking, she began to understand that her problem was an excess of humility—not a lack of it. The fundamental problem for her and other female drinkers was their lack of confidence, which society and culture reinforced. "For too long," she wrote in 1986, "programs for alcoholics have been designed by men, administered by men, dominated by men, and applied to women."

But what really rankled her was the notion of defenselessness against alcohol. Kirkpatrick felt that female problem drinkers needed a wholly different approach, and in the mid-1970s, she began a group called Women for Sobriety. She based its thirteen-step program on the writings of Ralph Waldo Emerson, her understanding of A.A., her experiences as a woman, and her knowledge of sociology. The program and its language are very much a product of the era, emphasizing self-assurance and independence, as well as reducing negative feelings a woman might have about her drinking and her perceived failures as a wife, mother, daughter, or professional. Like A.A., it promotes abstinence from alcohol. But Kirkpatrick's program encourages women to find spirituality within themselves—not from a higher power. It discourages the retelling of traumatic drinking stories, which Kirkpatrick believed only reinforced feelings of shame and worthlessness.

But her ideas were largely overlooked. Most treatment centers continued to use the same approach with men and

women, relying on the twelve steps to treat a growing female clientele. By the early 1980s, the disgrace of being a woman with a drinking problem had begun to fade. Betty Ford left the White House, announced her recovery from pill and booze addictions, and founded a California facility that hewed to the twelve steps. Soon after it opened in 1982, the Betty Ford Center, which offered separate treatment quarters for men and women, was overwhelmed with requests from female patients, including some world-famous celebrities. Elizabeth Taylor and Liza Minnelli told their fans they "needed help" before they were admitted. Drew Barrymore checked in as a teenager. Elsewhere, Ann Richards campaigned for governor of Texas and openly discussed her drinking past. During her term, she established rehabilitation programs in prisons. On one prison visit, the governor introduced herself to the inmates by saying, "My name's Ann, and I'm an alcoholic."

The success stories of famous women were splashed across the pages of glossy magazines. It all seemed so simple: You admitted you had a problem, you went to rehab, you followed the twelve steps, and you got better. Between 1968 and 1989, the number of women in A.A. rose almost 60 percent, from 22 to 35 percent of all members. If the program helped Elizabeth Taylor, with her tangled love life and fragile health, it could surely work for women battling life's ordinary stresses.

Yet some feminists joined Kirkpatrick in their skepticism about the twelve-step gospel. In 1990, *Ms.* magazine published a piece by psychologist Charlotte Kasl called "The Twelve Step Controversy," in which she challenged its message to women, and later developed a sixteen-step recovery plan of her own. But to a great extent, Kirkpatrick's dissent remains

an exception. Decades later, A.A. endures as the gold standard for recovery in America.

• • •

The nature of A.A. makes it difficult to analyze. While it conducts membership surveys every three years, A.A. keeps no records of who attends meetings. Members come and go, and are, of course, anonymous. Perhaps most important, A.A. itself is not a treatment; it is a support group. Researchers can observe A.A., but studying it scientifically poses huge challenges. Scientists like to conduct double-blind studies in which two statistically comparable groups are assembled. One receives the treatment, the other a placebo. Such an approach cannot be used for studying A.A., since participants are fully aware they are attending. Then there's the problem of measuring success. For A.A., it is abstinence, and a new way of thinking. But other approaches—such as harm reduction, which seeks to reduce or minimize the negative health and social consequences of alcohol or drug use—have different yardsticks, whether it is the ability to return to controlled drinking, or even drinking in such a way that poses no risks to others.

In the early days of A.A., Bill Wilson said he had observed a success rate of 75 percent among those who had come to A.A. and "really tried." About half of those who began attending meetings quit drinking in the first few weeks, and an additional 25 percent ultimately joined them in sobriety.

In the decades since, the sole source of data on A.A. membership has been A.A. Results are released to researchers sporadically, and one analysis of them appeared in the journal *Alcoholism Treatment Quarterly* in 2000. Researcher Don

McIntire, who had been given the data by A.A., found that only 5 percent of people who began attending A.A. meetings in 1990 were still participating a year later. This represented a significant decline from earlier surveys, which found that 25 percent of those who joined A.A. permanently stopped drinking.

Critics of A.A. immediately cited the 5 percent figure as proof of failings in the twelve-step approach. Actor Charlie Sheen even mentioned it while ranting on a radio talk show in 2011. But no less an authority than Dr. Drew Pinsky, a twelve-step proponent, admitted that Sheen "had a point" about A.A.'s success rates.

It was clear from the opening sentences of McIntire's paper that he anticipated criticism from A.A. members who view the group as the best way to address alcoholism. "The problem with the conclusions drawn from this data," McIntire wrote with homespun bluntness, "is that it does not sit well with the experience of seasoned A.A. members."

His author's note was also unusual: It listed neither his educational credentials nor a research institution, only his home address in Burbank, California.

A search turned up the telephone number instantly, and an older woman answered on the first ring. She identified herself as Carol McIntire, Don McIntire's widow. Her late husband, she said, had died in 2007 at the age of eighty-seven, an A.A. member for more than half his life. In his forties, he had sought treatment for alcoholism at Hazelden, where he forged friendships with many men who would go on to become prominent in A.A., Mrs. McIntire said.

She knew of the paper but said he hadn't talked about it much. "He kept his work to himself," she said. "That's how he was." She was aware of the controversy surrounding it, how-

ever, but said her mathematically oriented husband was clear on one thing: data. "It was black and white with him. Numbers were numbers," she said.

In this case, though, they revealed some unwelcome news. In fact, McIntire suggested structuring future studies to consider only those who completed A.A.'s ninety-day trial period, disregarding entirely the 81 percent of beginners who left before that point. (This is a little like clocking a triathlon that omits the swimming portion for athletes who hate getting wet. Of course the outcomes will be better.) If you followed McIntire's methodology, you would reach this conclusion: A.A. doesn't work for the vast majority of people who try it, but the small percentage who don't give up find it highly effective. A.A.'s most recent member survey, published in 2011, noted that 36 percent of the people attending meetings had been abstinent for more than a decade, powerful evidence that those who can stick to the program benefit from it.

Successful graduates of twelve-step programs vociferously defend their virtues, reacting to critics as if their religious beliefs had been questioned. On blogs and radio talk shows over the past decade, the debate has become confrontational, even ugly. Twitter followers snapped at Charlie Sheen; three A.A. members published their own rebuttal to McIntire's numbers. In it, they wrote: "The erroneous 10%, 5%, or less success rate myth for contemporary A.A. has proliferated without as much as a token challenge to its veracity or investigation of its origin. The topic of A.A. success or failure outcomes suffers from a great deal of anecdotal misinformation, misinterpretation, and editorializing." Somehow, the writers seem to have overlooked that the numbers came from A.A. itself.

Admirers and adherents of A.A. are quick to point out that it has saved the lives of "untold millions." To be sure, it offers a structure and a group of people who understand a drinker's frustrations and struggle. It provides a place to go, and a community that shares one's wishes for an undrunk future. It helps a person break away from drinking buddies and watering holes.

But many female problem drinkers, particularly stay-at-home mothers, drink in isolation. Meetings might help with many things, but it's hard to keep avoiding one's own kitchen. Since meetings are supposed to focus on alcohol alone, there is little tolerance of talk that veers toward sexual abuse, depression, or anxiety—proven predictors of risk for alcohol abuse among women.

To understand A.A. better, I attended about ten meetings in various parts of the country. I never spoke, and always went to open meetings that under A.A. protocol anyone can attend. Where I could, I found women's meetings in New Jersey, Manhattan, California, and Oregon. I started at the group's hub, the General Service Office on Manhattan's Upper West Side.

On Fridays, A.A.'s offices are thronged with visitors who have come for an 11 a.m. meeting in a large conference room. Afterward, they take a tour of the office, housed in a dull midcentury tower called the Interchurch Building, and visit the group's archives. Many pose for photos next to portraits of their heroes, or sitting in the couch said to be used by Wilson in the original New York office.

The first time I went, the place felt like Lourdes without the trail of canes. A group from Ireland stood reverentially before some framed documents. A woman blew into a Kleenex as she stood in front of Bill W.'s stony likeness, instructing her

son to snap a photo. "Bill W. is like . . . our godfather!" she announced. A Miami woman from the meeting wept openly as she took a seat on Wilson's couch. "Tears of *felicidad*," she called out sunnily.

On the second visit, I was with a woman I know named Joy, a paralegal and community organizer who has been a member of A.A. for almost twenty-five years. Was it typical for people to be so moved? I asked her. She smiled. "Always," she said. "A.A. saved our lives." Joy is a striking woman in her early fifties who looks at least a decade younger, with unlined bronze skin and long black hair to her waist. She is unflinching in her assessment: "Critics call the program brainwashing, and in a way, it is. But you know what? Before I got here, my brain needed to be washed." Her parents both died of alcoholism, she said, but it wasn't enough to stop her from drinking. At the worst of it, Joy told me, she would reach to her nightstand and take a swig of tequila before she even got out of bed. "That was my life," she said. "To go from that to a college graduate with responsible jobs was unthinkable."

Unlike many A.A. members, she was unguarded about its statistics. "I'd say a 5 percent success rate is probably generous," Joy said, shrugging as she contemplated the menu in the boisterous Cuban restaurant where we went for lunch. "It taught me a different way to live. I had to stop lying, admit who and what I was," she said. She speaks softly, choosing her words carefully. "Because of A.A., I don't get up every day and destroy myself in a multitude of ways. But it's not for everybody."

With many other A.A. members, I quickly learned that posing certain questions is like criticizing your in-laws' politics in the middle of Thanksgiving dinner: You just don't do it.

But this was one point no one in A.A. seemed able to explain: Why, if alcoholism is a medical problem, do alcoholics need to rely most heavily on other alcoholics? It's one thing to get support; it's another to imbue that person, namely, a sponsor, with expert status in the process of getting better.

Do cardiologists need to have blocked arteries in order to successfully treat them? I have chronic sinus disease, but I don't need friends or even physicians who suffer from it—I only need a doctor trained in the most recent science, and who enlists me as a knowledgeable partner in the management of my condition. A.A. speaks of alcoholism being a spiritual, mental, and physical disease. But for many members, turning to physicians for help with an alcohol problem is taboo.

Within A.A., many women like the idea of a sponsor who has "been there"—someone who won't judge as she hears confessions of infidelity or deceit. In part because of this, Trysh Travis, a women's studies professor at the University of Florida who examines A.A. and its offshoots, describes A.A. as an "idealized mutual aid society." Travis is the author of *Language of the Heart: A Cultural History of the Recovery Movement from Alcoholics Anonymous to Oprah Winfrey,* and is a managing editor of *Points,* a blog for the Alcohol and Drugs History Society.

"Many people revere the idea of experience as the best teacher," Travis says. "But different people bring different skills to the table. You can be a masterful teacher without credentials." While privileged society may shun this notion, Travis says, many of those who have been victimized by elite institutions take comfort in it.

Yet because so many of its members see the organization as a savior—one that, as Travis puts it, made the differ-

ence between freedom and prison, home and the street, life and death—it inspires some powerful feelings. "There is a hagiographic tendency within A.A.," she says. "And what's unfortunate is that for many of these people, their personal experience becomes a closed-mindedness." Such stridency is not unique to A.A., of course: It happens when people alter their behaviors to conform to new belief systems, whether it's feminism or veganism. "They say, 'I got a message, I was able to change my thinking in the most powerful, meaningful way, and I want to spread the good news—and if you don't like it there is something wrong with you.'"

But is it possible that some problem drinking is just that— problem drinking—and not a progressive disease? At the end of her life, Elizabeth Taylor was a once-a-week regular at a West Hollywood bar called the Abbey, where she downed tequila shots and watermelon martinis. Did that make her unrecovered? What if you struggle with drinking but don't believe you are powerless?

Mark Willenbring, a Minnesota psychiatrist who for five years served as director of treatment research at NIAAA, has spent much of his adult life trying to bring rigor to the question of how to treat problem drinkers. He chooses his words carefully, which is why I was surprised when he told me it is pointless to try to quantify the efficacy of A.A.

"You can't really study whether it works, because people who affiliate find it useful, and will therefore report that it does work [for them]. People who don't affiliate will report that it doesn't work," he says. "It's like trying to study the 'effectiveness' of yoga, prayer, or confiding in a friend. It's really the wrong question to ask."

Still, researchers do—perhaps because it is so ubiquitous. A comprehensive analysis in the *Cochrane Review*, a prestigious British journal, compared A.A. and twelve-step programs to other treatments, and found that A.A. and related programs were no more effective at reducing alcohol abuse than any other method.

In the early 1990s, an NIAAA study called Project MATCH compared twelve-step treatment with cognitive behavioral therapy, which teaches patients skills that might help avoid drinking triggers, and motivational enhancement therapy, which helps patients generate their own incentives to quit. The $30 million study found all treatments equally effective for both genders—and generated immediate criticism. Psychologist and author Stanton Peele noted that the study hadn't included a control group of untreated problem drinkers who also wanted to stop drinking. Alan Marlatt called it "poorly conceived," and said it allowed addiction specialists to project their own views onto treatment.

Many researchers remain dismayed at the expense and design of the study. In a reanalysis of the data published in 2005, researchers Robert Cutler and David Fishbain wrote that most of the patient improvements noted in the study were interpreted as the result of effective treatment—when in fact they were due mainly to the motivations of the patients themselves. And, as Willenbring pointed out, the studies were largely conducted in academic settings, where the counselors were well trained, highly monitored, and had extensive clinical supervision. In fact, he said, most treatment facilities rely heavily on lower-paid alcohol counselors, many of whom have only a high school education.

The study overlooked another important complication, especially for women with histories of sexual abuse. As more and more women entered twelve-step programs in rehab and A.A., they faced yet another difficulty as they entered coed facilities and attended mixed-gender meetings. The "sex thing," as Bill Wilson's friend Tom Powers had dubbed it, began to emerge as a national problem.

There has been little if any open discussion of sexual predation by participants in the nation's brand-name recovery movement. The group's adoption of the term "thirteenth-stepping"—the euphemism for a broad range of behavior ranging from creepy come-ons to statutory rape—implies it is a behavior to be expected. Its prevalence is an open secret.

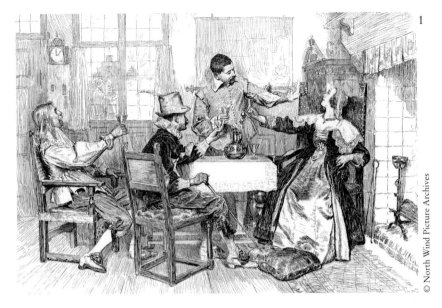

Early colonists drank beer, hard cider, and rum daily. Alcohol was safer than water, which was often contaminated with raw sewage. Here, some Dutch settlers in New Amsterdam celebrate the New Year.

The Mother of our Country liked to party. Martha Washington's collection of five hundred recipes included fifty for alcoholic drinks, and even a few hangover cures. One concoction called for plunging the meat of a raw, castrated rooster into two gallons of ale. Historians estimate adults in the eighteenth century drank about a gallon of beer a day.

3

By the late nineteenth century, much of the nation had clean drinking water, and religious reformers turned their sights on banning booze. Women were its earliest and most ardent supporters. Here, a temperance worker records the names of those entering a saloon.

4

Carry Nation believed she had divine orders to smash up bars with an axe, which she called "hatchetations." Nation described herself as "a bulldog running along at the feet of Jesus, barking at what He doesn't like." Between 1900 and 1910, she was arrested thirty times for vandalizing saloons.

5

Many young women in the Prohibition era enjoyed a radical new independence. They went to college, joined the workforce in large numbers, and dressed, danced, and drank in scandalously modern ways. They also had clever ways of hiding liquor.

Postwar imagery of women and alcohol was often at odds. California wine makers were eager to promote their product to American consumers as an everyday drink. In the late 1940s, they brought out Lucy as a pitchwoman.

In this friendly, freedom-loving land of ours... *Beer Belongs—Enjoy It!*

BEER AND ALE — AMERICA'S BEVERAGES OF MODERATION
Sponsored by the United States Brewers Foundation ... Chartered 1862

Likewise, beer producers portrayed beer as a wholesome grown-up drink that was also patriotic. Hundreds of Rockwellian images like these ran in magazines between 1945 and 1956.

At the same time, it was clear that women who drank too much would lose everything that mattered in the strict mores of postwar society. In the biopic *I'll Cry Tomorrow*, Susan Hayward portrays the drunken torment of the actress and singer Lillian Roth.

In *The Days of Wine and Roses*, Lee Remick's drinking prompts her family to cut off her access to her child.

Alcoholics Anonymous grew rapidly in the 1940s as the remedy for alcohol-ism. Marty Mann, left, was one of its first women. She used her skills as a public relations executive to help publicize its story. Here, she is with E. M. Jellinek, an alcohol researcher whose CV included fake degrees. Working closely with Jellinek, Mann helped craft the message of alcoholism as a disease that had a precise trajectory and treatment.

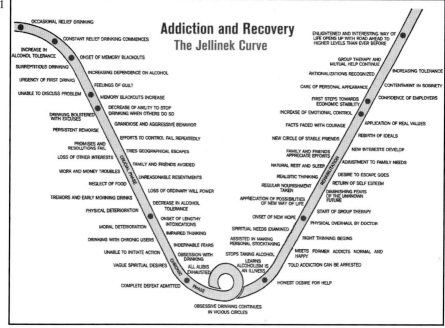

Addiction and Recovery
The Jellinek Curve

OCCASIONAL RELIEF DRINKING
CONSTANT RELIEF DRINKING COMMENCES
INCREASE IN ALCOHOL TOLERANCE
ONSET OF MEMORY BLACKOUTS
SURREPTITIOUS DRINKING
INCREASING DEPENDENCE ON ALCOHOL
URGENCY OF FIRST DRINKS
FEELINGS OF GUILT
UNABLE TO DISCUSS PROBLEM
MEMORY BLACKOUTS INCREASE
DRINKING BOLSTERED WITH EXCUSES
DECREASE OF ABILITY TO STOP DRINKING WHEN OTHERS DO SO
PERSISTENT REMORSE
GRANDIOSE AND AGGRESSIVE BEHAVIOR
PROMISES AND RESOLUTIONS FAIL
EFFORTS TO CONTROL FAIL REPEATEDLY
LOSS OF OTHER INTERESTS
TRIES GEOGRAPHICAL ESCAPES
WORK AND MONEY TROUBLES
FAMILY AND FRIENDS AVOIDED
NEGLECT OF FOOD
UNREASONABLE RESENTMENTS
TREMORS AND EARLY MORNING DRINKS
LOSS OF ORDINARY WILL POWER
PHYSICAL DETERIORATION
DECREASE IN ALCOHOL TOLERANCE
MORAL DETERIORATION
ONSET OF LENGTHY INTOXICATIONS
DRINKING WITH CHRONIC USERS
IMPAIRED THINKING
UNABLE TO INITIATE ACTION
INDEFINABLE FEARS
VAGUE SPIRITUAL DESIRES
OBSESSION WITH DRINKING
ALL ALIBIS EXHAUSTED
COMPLETE DEFEAT ADMITTED

CRITICAL PHASE

CHRONIC PHASE

OBSESSIVE DRINKING CONTINUES IN VICIOUS CIRCLES

REALISTIC THINKING
REGULAR NOURISHMENT TAKEN
APPRECIATION OF POSSIBILITIES OF NEW WAY OF LIFE
ONSET OF NEW HOPE
SPIRITUAL NEEDS EXAMINED
ASSISTED IN MAKING PERSONAL STOCKTAKING
STOPS TAKING ALCOHOL
LEARNS ALCOHOLISM IS AN ILLNESS
HONEST DESIRE FOR HELP
TOLD ADDICTION CAN BE ARRESTED
MEETS FORMER ADDICTS NORMAL AND HAPPY
RIGHT THINKING BEGINS
PHYSICAL OVERHAUL BY DOCTOR
START OF GROUP THERAPY
DIMINISHING FEARS OF THE UNKNOWN FUTURE
RETURN OF SELF ESTEEM
DESIRE TO ESCAPE GOES
ADJUSTMENT TO FAMILY NEEDS
NEW INTERESTS DEVELOP
REBIRTH OF IDEALS
APPLICATION OF REAL VALUES
CONFIDENCE OF EMPLOYERS
CONTENTMENT IN SOBRIETY
INCREASING TOLERANCE

REHABILITATION

NATURAL REST AND SLEEP
FAMILY AND FRIENDS APPRECIATE EFFORTS
NEW CIRCLE OF STABLE FRIENDS
FACTS FACED WITH COURAGE
INCREASE OF EMOTIONAL CONTROL
FIRST STEPS TOWARDS ECONOMIC STABILITY
CARE OF PERSONAL APPEARANCE
RATIONALIZATIONS RECOGNIZED
GROUP THERAPY AND MUTUAL HELP CONTINUE

ENLIGHTENED AND INTERESTING WAY OF LIFE OPENS UP WITH ROAD AHEAD TO HIGHER LEVELS THAN EVER BEFORE

Proponents of Alcoholics Anonymous cited scientific-looking studies to bol-ster the narrative that A.A. was the most effective treatment of alcoholic depen-dency. Charts named for Jellinek's work appeared in magazines and in doctor's offices, but they were based on a self-selected group of A.A. members, none of whom were women.

12

13

In the 1960s and '70s, California's laid-back culture influenced the country in music, food, surfing—and wine. Napa Valley wine growers promoted their product as part of a healthy life, and they targeted a new generation of customers: women.

In *Cougar Town*, Courteney Cox's character Jules loves her gigantic wine vessels so much, she has a memorial service for the shards of one that breaks.

Annette Bening as the on-edge doctor, Nic, in *The Kids Are All Right*. Her drinking is a source of tension in her relationship with her partner, who is constantly monitoring her consumption.

6 *The Thirteenth Step*

For years, Monica Richardson, a singer and actress in Los Angeles, spoke to no one about her early experiences in A.A. She felt she had been naive, even partly responsible for what happened. Best to move ahead. It had been a rocky period in her life. Richardson pushed the memories into the deepest recesses of her mind, to the point that they almost didn't exist. After a few years in A.A., she came to believe that she was fundamentally broken. She never bought into the group's clichés, but this passage from the Big Book made sense: "We are like men who have lost their legs; they never grow new ones."

Richardson had a wild adolescence in 1970s New York, pounding shots in bars, smoking pot, and experimenting with sex. In high school, she was hospitalized after a serious drinking binge. A social worker assigned to the case warned her:

"You'd better watch this, or you're headed for serious trouble." Using money she'd saved from a babysitting job, Richardson decided to leave the chaos of New York for Hawaii, where her father lived at the time. The calm of her new surroundings eluded her: Isolated, anxious, and lonely, she drank to excess almost every night. One evening at a party, she drank so much she stripped off her clothes and dove into the pitch-black ocean. She woke up the next morning doubled over in stomach pain, and scared as she tried to recall the night's events. The social worker's words haunted her. "Am I an alcoholic?" Richardson wondered.

Two weeks later, a man approached her as she sunbathed on a beach, and began telling her about the kinship and peace he had found through A.A. "It seemed like a message from the universe," she says. She joined him and his friends at a meeting. The tales people told of hitting rock bottom terrified her. Soon, she was convinced that she, too, was an alcoholic—and that without A.A., she would meet a hopeless end. She was eighteen years old.

It is salient to point out that today Richardson, in her midfifties, is a statuesque stunner, with huge green eyes, curly auburn hair, and a husky contralto. Perhaps this is why a half dozen men rushed forward after her first meeting and offered to guide her through recovery. One of those who approached her was a handsome, bearded man I'll call Ken. Seven years her senior, Ken wasted no time inviting her on a hike. The two hit it off, and soon Richardson was spending most days—and every night—with Ken, who worked as an addictions counselor at a methadone clinic.

Thrilled with sobriety and her new community, she devoured the Big Book, attended daily meetings, and did the first

few steps on her own. Ken was like no one she had ever met in New York: He sang folk songs as he strummed his guitar, quoted from *Siddhartha,* and massaged deep knots out of her neck with his suntanned hands. Richardson felt as if she had found a new spiritual home, and partner.

A.A. discourages sexual relationships between longtime members and newcomers. That advice is mentioned in the Twelve Traditions, the principles A.A. describes as the fellowship's common spiritual guidelines. The theory is that a person struggling to quit drinking and put his or her life back together can't make sound decisions, and that there is an inevitable imbalance between A.A. beginners and those who have been sober for years. Richardson was unaware of the rule, and Ken certainly didn't tell her. Ken had been in the program five years; Richardson, less than a month. She had not yet asked anyone to be her sponsor.

A few weeks into their relationship, the couple flew from Oahu to Maui for a weekend. Late one night at a rustic motel, geckos darting through the jalousies, Ken asked Richardson how she had come to be so sexually confident at such a young age. At the time, Richardson was working through A.A.'s fourth step, taking a "searching and fearless moral inventory" of her character defects: fears, resentments, sexual conduct, and ways in which she had harmed others. Ken urged her to share her history. "Let it all out," he said.

Richardson's accounting of herself included sexual encounters she had come to regret, including some evenings with a group of swingers. As Richardson poured out dark moments from her past, Ken withdrew his hand from Richardson's knee, his face twisted with horror. "That's disgusting," he told her, rising abruptly from the bed. "This is over."

The reproach took Richardson aback, particularly because it came from someone who preached free love and boasted about his dozens of partners. He had encouraged Richardson to continue on A.A.'s path, which counsels members to confess their most shameful secrets as a way to liberate them from the malady of excess drinking. "You are only as sick as your secrets," an A.A. slogan says. The point of working through your most toxic transgressions with another alcoholic, after all, is because the fellow drunk has "been there." The newcomer is less likely to feel judged in the company of other reforming drunks.

"You don't walk into A.A. because your life is going great," she says now. "You walk into A.A. because you are desperate. You think it will be a safe place, with people who are healthier than you. And A.A. tells you you're powerless, your thinking is flawed, you have defects, to shut up and listen," she says. "You're fuzzy-headed, you're confused, you're clearing booze from your brain. You don't know how to have relationships without alcohol, so you do what they say. They've been there. They're there to help, right? Alcoholics helping alcoholics."

But as Marty Mann had pointed out, female alcoholics face a double standard. Richardson booked a flight back to Oahu, retrieved her bike at Ken's, and sobbed as she pedaled back to her father's. She went home to New York, where she attended A.A. several times a week. She returned to Hawaii ten months later, and resumed meeting with her first A.A. group.

A few weeks from her nineteenth birthday, two men at the meeting persuaded her to have sex with them. She trusted the men, and consented. They were more than two decades older, and had been sober for many years—one would go on to be-

come a counselor at a respected Hawaiian treatment center. As she tried to live her life without alcohol, she thought that the men might have insights on the inner peace she believed she lacked. Instead, she felt used and humiliated.

Determined to put the incidents behind her forever, Richardson switched groups, and stayed in Hawaii for another seven years before leaving for Los Angeles to launch her career as a singer and actress. Despite her negative experiences in A.A., she remained wedded to the group's ideas, and the notion that she was an alcoholic.

Once in L.A., she found a women's group she liked, which helped to root her in her new city. Over the next fifteen years, she established herself as a singer, recording folk music in two albums, and studied at Groundlings and Playhouse West, two prestigious acting schools. Through her work, she met and married a television engineer, and had two sons. As a tired thirty-something working mother, Richardson found that her interest in sex plummeted, and the marriage began to falter. She and her husband sought counseling, and the therapist gently asked about her sexual past. The questions set alight some disturbing memories from her early time in A.A. and along with that, the molestations she had suffered for years at the hands of her great-aunt. In sessions with a separate therapist, Richardson learned how to channel her anger productively, and to shed guilt for experiences, like sexual abuse, over which she had had no control.

Like many victims of childhood sexual abuse, Richardson had spent much of her life feeling voiceless around people she perceived as powerful. In therapy, she began to realize why it had been so difficult for her to say no to the sexual advances of the older men she met in A.A. The relationship, she began

to see, was a familiar one. As a child, her molester, a great-aunt who lived a block away, had helped to raise Richardson and her two siblings as part of an extended family. After school, the great-aunt often babysat for the three kids, getting them ready for dinner and bathing them. She frequently took them to her own small apartment to spend the night, where Richardson shared her bed. It was understood that Richardson was never to discuss her aunt's inappropriate nighttime touching.

The episodes also set in place a dynamic that would take Richardson years to recognize as harmful. In public, her late great-aunt was a loving, protective authority figure, revered and respected in Inwood, their close-knit Manhattan neighborhood. In private, she violated intimate boundaries.

Studies show that Richardson's experiences are common. Sexual abuse, as either a child or an adult, is one of the largest risk factors for women who become problem drinkers. Some researchers have found that women who were victimized as children are three times more likely to develop alcohol or other chemical dependence problems than women who were not.

As adults, it is also common for such women to be preyed upon in twelve-step programs by those who are purporting to help them heal. Psychologist Charlotte Davis Kasl writes that the A.A. old-timer who sexually exploits a new member is replicating the twisted bond between a child and a sexually abusive relative. Lacking the power to speak up, particularly when the trusted figure tells the child she is "special," the child accepts the behavior as normal. So when an older A.A. member encourages a sexual relationship, many newcomers, already accustomed to this pattern, find it difficult to say no.

Since the group's first days in Akron, A.A. has advised

new heterosexual members to seek sponsors from among their own gender while encouraging gays to do the opposite. These are only suggestions, and A.A. makes clear that it has no authority in enforcing them

Another recommendation, also stemming from the early days, is that women should attend women-only groups. This is often not practical. While one-third of A.A.'s membership is female, the number of women-only meetings is scant: A 2010 sociology journal found that only 3 percent of the twenty thousand weekly meetings in a large metropolitan area were for women only.

Whatever precautions are being taken, they don't appear to be working. A 2003 study in the *Journal of Addictions Nursing* found that half of the women surveyed said they had experienced various forms of thirteenth stepping, from groping to pressure for dates or sexual liaisons. Four percent said they had been raped by a sponsor or fellow A.A. member.

The advances typically take place like this: At coffee after the meeting, a man is chatty and friendly, asking a newcomer if she has any questions, or needs any help with the steps. "You're not in a bar, where you're prepared for guys on the prowl," Richardson says. "You're at an A.A. meeting with people who are supposed to show you how to live in a healthier way." (I witnessed some of this behavior myself. At the meetings I attended, I always dressed dowdily—and I'm in my late forties. After a meeting in suburban New Jersey, one man followed me up the stone steps of a church, asking if I was new. I told him I was a journalist—"Just here to listen!"—but it didn't stop him from thrusting his card into my hand and inviting me to come see his new Mercedes. He offered to take me for a "ride.")

I also read the creepy diary of Sean Calahan, a Montana sex offender who used A.A. as his personal pickup joint. In April 2012, police found that Calahan, on probation for the sexual assault of a twelve-year-old girl, was violating the conditions of his parole by initiating sexual relationships with multiple members of the women in his A.A. group. In a journal entry called "Sean's Dark Side," he wrote how he preyed on A.A. members: "Will take sex where I can get it. Whoever I can trick or use. Usually women early in sobriety 'cause they are the most vunerable. They have the most insecuritys so just a few words and a little care and they fall rite in to my trap. Its not there falt but I make them think it is there falt and tell them I love them and everything will be okay."

This, too, fits a pattern, and manipulators like Calahan are likely to know it, since, as Kasl points out, women who have been sexually taken advantage of are nonetheless often afraid to leave the group. She says this replicates an earlier relationship in which abusers often warned their victims to keep silent. So they did, afraid that they might be punished. When these women are sexually exploited in A.A., they repeat the pattern, Kasl found. "Fearing relapse, rejection, or being shamed," she wrote, they "continue with the group or deny their internal wisdom. As a result they deepen the wounds inflicted by their family of origin."

Richardson believed that without A.A., she would be "struck drunk," a permanent condition from which she might never recover. In fact, she immersed herself in the group, serving as a sponsor for several women, a public information chairwoman, a group secretary and treasurer, and founder of a group for young people. For many years, she went into prisons to oversee groups for convicted felons and juvenile delinquents.

In 2009, she was elected a general service representative, or GSR, an unpaid but important position within A.A. that transmits ideas and opinions between a local group and others in A.A. Richardson's home group of mostly women seemed cozy and safe. What had happened to her in Hawaii, she believed, was isolated bad luck. It had been a confusing time — for the country, for her, and for a group trying to help some of society's most desperate people.

•   •   •

More than thirty years later, Richardson learned differently when a twenty-two-year-old woman named Gwen began attending her home meeting. The evening Gwen first spoke, her words came between sobs. When she first joined A.A., Gwen said, she had no car, no license, "really not even a life," so she walked to and from meetings. As she tiptoed into a life without alcohol, Gwen told herself to be especially on guard about the opposite sex. When men in the group asked her if she wanted a ride home, she would always just flash the small can of mace she kept in her purse and smile. "I'm fine," she would tell them. "I can go by myself."

An especially unrelenting member would not take no for an answer, pestering Gwen one night to get into his car. "No, I already told you, I'm fine walking," she said. As Gwen marched homeward, he circled the block several times, asking her to get into the car every time he passed. "I don't want you to walk," he called out. Finally, worn down, and believing he had her best interests in mind, Gwen said yes and climbed in. When they got to Gwen's driveway, the man came to the door.

The man had five years' sobriety to Gwen's few weeks, and he convinced her that she should let him spend the night. He did, and stayed for months, rent-free, insisting that it—and sex on demand—was part of Gwen's "service" to other alcoholics. With him, the man promised, Gwen would certainly stay sober. Instinctively, she knew the situation was wrong, but old-timers at her meeting told her daily that her misguided "best thinking" had landed her in A.A. When Gwen dared question the appropriateness of the relationship with her female sponsor, her sponsor asked, "Well, what's your part in it?" The term is A.A. shorthand for a fundamental tenet—that alcoholics have a "part" in all misfortunes that befall them.

As soon as the meeting was over, Richardson hurried across the room to comfort Gwen. "I'm so sorry that you've had to go through this," Richardson told her. "I was abused by some members in my early days, too. I didn't know that kind of thing still happened." Gwen looked at her, stunned. "It's not only me," she said. "This is going on everywhere!" For the next several weeks, Gwen and Richardson went to mixed meetings throughout Los Angeles. Richardson was shocked to hear incident after incident of wrongdoing: rapes, unwanted touching, harassment. She documented many young women's claims in videotaped interviews.

At home one night on her computer, Richardson typed in "thirteenth step in A.A." She found several blogs that were critical of A.A., and links to 2007 articles in *Newsweek* and the *Washington Post* that detailed the sexual and emotional abuse of young women at a cultlike A.A. group in Washington, D.C., called Midtown. Richardson was shocked by what she read. In the stories, the young women recounted how they were pressured to have sex with many A.A. members, but es-

pecially with the group leader, Michael Quinones. A woman identified as Kristen told the *Post* that her psychologist had referred her to the group at age seventeen. Soon, her sponsor instructed her to have sex with Quinones as a way to solidify her sobriety, and once Kristen became a sponsor she encouraged the women she was helping to do the same. "I pimped [them] out," she told the *Post*.

Women who belonged to the group said they were ordered off their psychiatric medication, told to stop seeing their therapists, and allowed to visit family members only in the company of other Midtown members. The allegations suggested not only a frightening level of control, but also a codified thirteenth step.

Police concluded no crime had been committed, since the young women in question were over the age of sixteen and therefore consenting adults. The young women told police that sexual relations between teenagers and older men was rampant, but were unwilling to admit they were victims themselves.

Richardson recognized that much of what had gone on at Midtown violated A.A.'s traditions, including the suggestion for same-sex sponsors and the idea that newcomers should choose sponsors, not be assigned to them.

Midtown's opposition to members taking psychiatric meds like antidepressants is not unusual. While A.A. instructs members not to "play doctor," many members take it upon themselves to counsel against ingesting any psychoactive drugs, even those prescribed by a physician.

This view is at odds with modern psychiatry. If patients stop taking antidepressants abruptly, they can experience unpleasant side effects. But they don't create dependency in the

traditional sense, since they don't induce euphoria or cause people to act inappropriately in order to obtain them.

I asked A.A.'s General Service Office how the group enforces the guidelines laid out in the Twelve Traditions and other documents. Does it, for example, ever expel a local organization like Midtown, which violated a host of A.A. standards? She replied in an e-mail: "The Traditions are not rules—they are spiritual principles that guide A.A. members in their relations with each other and with the community," wrote Mary C., public information officer at the General Service Office, A.A.'s headquarters in Manhattan. "There is no central mechanism in A.A. to 'enforce' the Traditions or any existing guidelines or, for that matter, most anything at all."

When ex-Midtown members contacted the New York office with complaints about the group's tactics, the GSO said it had no authority over local groups. A.A. is not a franchiser like McDonald's or Burger King. Each group is free to structure itself as it wishes. Reports flow from individual groups to districts, from districts to areas, and from areas to the GSO in Manhattan. Every local group elects a general service representative to represent the group at district meetings, and each area in the U.S. and Canada elects a delegate to attend an annual conference, which holds votes on "matters of importance." All of these positions are held by unpaid volunteers.

As Richardson scrolled through the *Newsweek* and *Washington Post* stories, she felt her face flush and her stomach lurch. At that point in her life, A.A. was her anchor, a nurturing family whose virtues far outweighed its flaws. She was committed to the fellowship that had served as her beacon. The group had shaped much of her adult life. Her first sponsor, a kind, loving woman, had encouraged her to develop her

talents as a performer. When she had singing gigs at nightclubs, buddies from her group showed up by the dozens.

In late 2009, Richardson reached out to a friend who had worked as a paid staff member at the GSO for a decade. He listened intently as Richardson recounted the experiences she had documented, and suggested that she meet a trustee, whom I will call Mr. X. The friend handed Richardson some documents. One was a 2001 memo from Australia's General Service Board that outlined how to halt spiritual, sexual, and financial predation within the group—including barring predators from meetings, if needed, and notifying the police. It said that older members and office holders had a "moral obligation" to help protect vulnerable members, and possibly even a legal one.

In 2002, Richardson learned, Britain's thirty-four hundred A.A. groups had adopted a "code of conduct" regarding sexual behavior, after British newspapers had reported that a number of groups were under police investigation for allegations involving predators who operated telephone help lines. They would visit the homes of callers under the guise of offering help, and then sexually assault them.

The phone lines were supposed to be staffed by members with appropriate experience and long-term sobriety. But a British A.A. memo, leaked to the press, revealed that those rules were often broken by "a small minority of men and women who operate with sick but hidden agendas." It warned that "the organization has the potential to become a breeding ground for predatory behavior."

In the leaked documents, A.A. nonalcoholic trustee Geoffrey Brown, an Anglican priest, likened the abuse within A.A. to the sexual abuse scandals roiling the Catholic Church.

"The problem with caring communities is that, by definition, they are bound to attract the kind of vulnerable person that a very small minority can prey upon. . . . It is because of this fact that such groups need constantly to be on their guard against any conduct that takes advantage of the powerless.'"

The British behavioral guidelines include instructions for members and newcomers to have third parties present during talks and home visits. They warn specifically against bullying, harassment, and discrimination, and direct groups to hold frequent meetings to discuss member conduct. The guidelines conclude: "Failure to challenge and stop inappropriate behaviour gives the offender permission to repeat the offensive behaviour and encourages others to follow suit."

Fewer than 1 percent of Britain's A.A. groups objected to the new rules.

So Richardson felt hopeful when she pored over one of the other documents her friend had given her, a confidential seven-page memo Mr. X had sent in 2007 to A.A.'s Subcommittee on Vulnerable Members. Written against the backdrop of the *Washington Post* and *Newsweek* stories and reports of pedophile priests, it detailed multiple instances of sexual abuse within A.A., and called for the group to draft clear guidelines to protect members from predators. Under no circumstances, he wrote, should the group allow its long-standing traditions of anonymous participation to cover up criminal behavior by members. "There is confusion about taking legal action against perpetrators because the victims think they will be breaking anonymity, fear retribution . . . and won't be believed."

In his letter to the subcommittee, Mr. X acknowledged that while women may also be predators, "the vast majority of

situations appear to involve men preying on underage girls." His language was blunt: "A man in A.A. who becomes sexually involved with a minor . . . is taking advantage of a child at a most vulnerable time in her life, and committing a serious crime."

He then listed several examples of sexual abuse for which he had direct evidence. They included:

- A thirty-five-year-old woman was raped at age fifteen by a member in his twenties. Her sponsor told her to "pray for him."

- A woman with long-term sobriety asked for guidance after learning that a man in A.A. had molested her daughter. Mr. X advised her to go to the police, but the woman feared breaking A.A.'s promise of anonymity to the abuser.

- Another woman said she had been tied up and raped by a man who broke into her house after meeting her in A.A. Her sponsor told her to "forgive him."

- A speaker at an A.A. convention was found having sex with the fifteen-year-old daughter of another A.A. member attending the convention.

To demonstrate the persistence of the problem, Mr. X quoted a 1993 letter published in the *Grapevine*. It was written by a woman whose fifteen-year-old daughter had been impregnated by an A.A. old-timer. "Those with maturity and leadership in A.A. have a responsibility to be very vocal about the dangers of Thirteenth Stepping. No more turning a blind eye to this problem," the woman wrote.

Richardson knew she had an ally, and immediately called Mr. X. Fueled by the scandal at the Midtown group in Wash-

ington, Mr. X's support, and her own documentation, Richardson was certain she could spur action. Members of her women's home group were outraged when they learned of the documents, and the systemic manner in which sexual abuse had flourished within A.A. "We were sick about this," she says. "I thought everyone would be."

She was mistaken.

In October 2009, more than two years after the trustee wrote his memo, A.A.'s six-member Subcommittee on Vulnerable Members responded with a one-page letter. Its sentences were lawyerly but the intent was clear. A.A. headquarters in New York would do nothing to set standards for American groups and would accept no liability for anything that went awry at A.A. meetings.

Here's the key passage: "The subcommittee members agree that the General Service Board in its position at the bottom of the A.A. service structure would not have a role in setting any behavioral policy or guideline for the A.A. groups or members in regards to protecting any vulnerable member including minors coming into A.A. The A.A. groups and A.A. service entities such as Areas and Districts are autonomous and direct and guide their own affairs. The General Service Board has no authority, legal or otherwise, to control or direct the behavior of A.A. members and groups."

Protecting members was up to local groups. "It is hoped that the areas, districts, and groups will discuss this important topic and seek ways through sponsorship, workshops and assemblies and committee meetings to raise awareness in the Fellowship and encourage the creation of as safe an environment as possible for the newcomer, minors and other members or potential members who may be vulnerable."

Richardson gathered additional evidence. In late 2009, she wrote a seven-page letter of her own, describing five additional rape cases she had learned of in recent months, and sent it to all members of A.A.'s board, as well as five paid staff members at Alcoholics Anonymous World Service. No one responded.

She approached her district chair about getting on the agenda to speak at a district meeting. "You can't just ask to do that," he told her. "You have to go to a committee meeting first and get their approval." A few weeks later, she and a friend from her home group attended the committee meeting, and asked to be put on the agenda. All voted no. "This could hurt A.A.'s name," they told her. "This is an outside issue."

That term has special meaning in the A.A. view of alcoholism, and it explains a lot about the organization's reluctance to address the issues of sexual misconduct. Its roots lie in the fate of the nineteenth-century organization, the Washingtonians. The group allowed politicians and temperance reformers who were not alcoholics to join the group, and soon it became embroiled in the country's other pressing political battle, abolition. Infighting about slavery ultimately led to the group's demise, and as Wilson began to sketch A.A.'s blueprint, he took note. In the Twelve Traditions, the group sets specific rules for refraining from all "outside issues" that are unrelated to the group's primary goal: helping others stop drinking. The group's Tenth Tradition states: "No A.A. group or member should ever, in such a way as to implicate A.A., express any opinion on outside controversial issues—particularly those of politics, alcohol reform, or sectarian religion. The Alcoholics Anonymous groups oppose no one. Concerning such matters they can express no views whatever."

This broad guideline is considered by many to include all matters apart from alcohol, including sexual relationships.

Hearing this, Richardson was incredulous. "Outside issue? We're talking about women getting groped at meetings, sexually harassed at meetings. This is not an outside issue!"

Twenty women in her group signed a letter so that as a GSR, Richardson might address the topic at an upcoming area meeting. She was granted one minute of speaking time at the day-long January 2010 meeting. "I realize that this sounds like a very small amount of time," the area chairman wrote in an e-mail.

After that meeting, two people came up to tell her they knew of rapes in their local groups.

A few weeks later, an editor of the *Grapevine* called her from New York, saying she had seen her letter. She offered to publish Richardson's tale from Hawaii—but not the newer stories of the five rapes—in the newsletter. Richardson demurred. "Why would I want to talk about something that happened in 1975 when the point was informing people that it was still happening today?" she recalls wondering.

Mr. X advised Richardson to organize a workshop on predatory behavior. She again approached her district chairman to ask if she could make an announcement about her workshop. "No," he told her. "You can't."

Richardson is a fearsome woman with a thick skin—years of acting training had taught her not to take rejection personally—and this time, she would not take no for an answer. Fed up with the many obstacles she had encountered, she spoke up anyway, asking members at the meeting if they wanted fliers to the upcoming workshop. Only twenty-five of the seventy-five people assembled held out their hands. The hostility, she recalls, was palpable.

Richardson redoubled her efforts. She investigated more cases and started a blog, *Stop13stepinaa.com*. She published a pamphlet titled "Make A.A. Safer" and handed it out at area meetings, and, buoyed by the support of Mr. X, began planning a workshop about predatory behavior. She met with women in Spanish-speaking groups, who told her horror stories of their own. They translated Richardson's materials into Spanish and distributed them widely. She approached the area and district chairs to have them post her workshop on the Los Angeles–area website calendar. They declined. So she trudged from meeting to meeting in an attempt to publicize her workshop.

She pressed on, eventually getting permission to speak for ten minutes at a larger area assembly. A handful of people voiced support, but many complained that open discussion of the matter would hurt A.A.'s reputation.

Late in the summer of 2010, Richardson heard that a Honolulu A.A. member and her daughter had been murdered by a violent Iraq veteran ordered into A.A. by a judge.

Richardson learned that the troubled veteran, Clayborne Conley, had briefly dated Kristine Cass after meeting her in A.A. Conley, once convicted of the assault and "terroristic threatening" of an ex-girlfriend, struggled with post-traumatic stress disorder. He spent ten months in a Hawaii state mental hospital, agreeing to attend A.A. as part of his conditional 2009 release. Friends in his A.A. group told a newspaper reporter that Conley was smart and funny, and had no inkling of his record. Cass, a Honolulu marketing consultant, was unaware, too, until she broke off the relationship. Then, he began calling her at all hours and showing up at her workplace, demanding to see her. On August 19, 2010, she told a friend that

she planned to seek a temporary restraining order against him. Hours later, Conley ripped apart the security bars on Cass's windows, broke into her house, and shot her, her daughter, and a neighbor's dog before killing himself.

Richardson was stunned when some fellow A.A. members dismissed the murder-suicide as something that could "happen anywhere." She finds this logic skewed. A.A. presents itself as a healing community, a fellowship in which people voluntarily help each other. What, she asks, would stop A.A. from warning members that some of those in the meetings were attending not because they desired sobriety, but because a court had ordered them there? "Why wouldn't the organization want a members' safety statement read before every meeting, just to make the fellowship aware of potential dangers?"

Her outspokenness took a toll. By the time she was ending her stint as a GSR, Richardson's A.A. friends had stopped coming to her singing engagements and her poolside karaoke parties. The more outspoken she became, the more ostracized she felt. For more than three decades, A.A. had been Richardson's foundation, providing a social circle and professional contacts.

None of the evidence that motivated Richardson seemed to matter to many others: not the trustee's letter, not Richardson's new documentation, not her position as a GSR, not the fact that A.A. groups abroad had confronted the issue and acted a decade earlier.

"I went through every channel I could possibly go through," she says. "A.A. tells you that it's an upside-down organization, where the groups have the power, but that's just not true."

• • •

Richardson left A.A. as soon as her term was finished, in early 2011, and is making a documentary about the experiences of many women in the group. Little seems to have changed since then regarding A.A.'s response to the issue of violence against women. In late 2011, I spoke to a former A.A. board member who was familiar with the internal memo and insisted on not being identified. The former trustee likened the possibility of A.A. enacting swift reform to turning a battleship on a dime. Unlike Richardson, the former trustee seemed resigned to the group's inability to act with any sense of urgency. "It's a little harsh," the former board member told me hesitantly, "but women have been getting raped since A.A. started."

Not much appears to have changed in the culture of Washington's Midtown group. Marc Fisher, the *Washington Post* writer who covered the scandal, told me he still receives calls and e-mails from family members of those ensnared in the group, desperate for help to get them out. Quinones, who was dying of cancer when the stories appeared, never responded to Fisher's requests for an interview. But some of his friends did, and told Fisher privately that what he had reported was just the "tip of the iceberg."

Ellen Dye, a Washington-area psychologist, concurred. In 2006, Dye wrote an open letter to the D.C. recovery community about how members of Midtown had abused two of her clients. Like many mental health professionals, Dye has seen A.A. achieve some notable successes. But she says the events at Midtown have given her pause. "It's still going on," she says. Some of her clients have told her that nothing has changed.

Women are hesitant to discuss sexual abuse openly, and they're even more reluctant when they've been branded as alcoholics. "Who's going to believe a drunk girl when she says she's been raped?" asks Amy Lee Coy, a Los Angeles singer and author of a book about her own recovery from alcohol abuse, *From Death Do I Part.* Coy was barely out of detox at a tony twelve-step facility in Malibu before a counselor made a pass at her. Louise, a Cleveland lawyer who left A.A. in 2007 after members of her home group made excuses for the Midtown scandal, says double standards endure. She likens it to the Penn State sex abuse case. "It's one thing when cute, innocent little boys are being raped by a nasty-looking old man, but quite another when nasty barflies are getting raped by other nasty barflies."

A.A. loyalists often scoff at those who say they've been victims of the thirteenth step. In a forum on the anti-A.A. blog *Orange Papers,* a commenter wrote: "You are responsible for who you shack up with, give money to, or move in with. You can blame A.A. or anyone else all you wish, but the responsibility lies with each individual. Even if you've drank and drugged yourself to a state of vulnerability and naive desperation, who's [sic] fault is that?"

Gwen, the young woman Richardson met in 2009, addressed that point on Richardson's weekly Internet radio show, which attracts thousands of L.A. listeners.

"What was 'my part'?" Gwen asked when speaking of the man who demanded sex as part of her "service" to other alcoholics. "My part was that I was twenty-two. My part was that I showed up at A.A. My part," she concluded, "was believing people who told me my 'best thinking' was wrong."

• • • •

Richardson and others argue that A.A. is in much the same position as the Catholic Church in the 1990s. The signs of sexual misconduct are unmistakable. Yet the leadership fears that taking action will be an admission of liability. And women remain reluctant to press charges.

Among the predominantly male leadership and rank and file of A.A., there is little appetite to deal with this issue. When I was on a tour of the General Service Office in 2010, I identified myself as a journalist at work on a book about women and alcohol. My companion, a longtime A.A. member, introduced me to some staff members, including one who had just returned from a meeting with A.A. leaders in eastern Europe. "Thirteenth stepping is a big problem over there," he said, out of the blue. My companion told me later she was "shocked" that he had volunteered the information.

When I mentioned the problem to others, I heard these defenses: "All recovery communities involve sexual abuse." "The sexual appetites of alcoholics 'go haywire' when they're newly sober and they have to get that rush from somewhere, so they seek sex." "There's no way to keep deviants out of any group." The public information officer said A.A. is simply a microcosm of society.

But like the Boy Scouts of America, the Big Brothers and Big Sisters of America, and the YMCA, Alcoholics Anonymous is a helping organization, designed to reach the vulnerable. While most of A.A.'s members are adults, like the other groups, it also aims to pair newcomers with healthy role models.

Since sexual abuse scandals in nonprofit organizations became public thirty years ago, most of the large youth groups have drafted—and enforce—tough antiabuse policies. They require criminal background checks on volunteers and prohibit one-on-one adult-youth activities. The Boy Scouts, for instance, issued guidelines about inappropriate conduct, which parents must discuss with their children as a condition of joining.

Victor Vieth, a former Minnesota prosecutor who heads the National Child Protection Training Center in Minnesota, has been involved in sexual abuse cases and prevention for twenty-five years. A.A., he told me, is a "ticking time bomb. Like the Catholic Church, like Penn State, and many other groups they have not paid attention to the warning signs," Vieth said.

Because of A.A.'s decentralized structure, though, it takes no responsibility for what happens to the vulnerable women and men who find themselves there, either by court order, an employer's demand, or their own desperate search for help. As Mary C., the GSO's public information officer, wrote in her e-mail to me: "The responsibility for creating a safe environment within the groups rests with the groups themselves and with the individual members.

"Would it be possible for the boards and office to develop some form of document related to vulnerable members?" she continued. "Yes, it is possible, if the members of the fellowship of A.A. in the U.S. and Canada, beginning at the grassroots level of the groups and working its way through the service structure, indicated that they wanted such a piece created."

In April 2012, Richardson posted an accounting of her attempts to attract the local and regional hierarchy's attention

on her blog. A writer who claimed to be her district chairman defended A.A.'s handling of her complaints. Richardson's ideas for protecting women, he wrote, would have been "impossible to enforce.

"Our primary purpose is sobriety," he wrote. "At what point do we allow people to date? At one year? Six months? . . . You can't stop people in the rooms from dating; because then you have to decide when they *can* date, and who talks to who—men have to be a year sober to talk to women?" Besides, he noted that two associates in senior positions in his district had ignored those rules themselves and had dated newcomers. "Of course," he wrote, "they aren't going to say anything."

•   •   •

It's been more than two years since Richardson left A.A. for good. She urges her callers to attend Smart Recovery, a group she admires. She has also experimented with sips of wine, even allowing herself a glass now and then. "I don't get drunk, and I certainly haven't 'relapsed,'" she says. She says she is "deprogramming" herself.

She senses a shifting mood. In 2011, Chris Rock starred as a sexual and financial predator in A.A. in the award-winning Broadway play *The MotherF**ker with the Hat*. The curator of the anti-A.A. blog the *Orange Papers* told me he gets about a million hits each month. Its posts include numerous allegations of sexual abuse within A.A.

Sometimes Richardson agonizes over the years she sacrificed to the group. "My part," she says, "was trusting people in A.A."

7 *Twenty-First-Century Treatment*

Joanna made two big decisions when she turned fifty. The first was that she was going to quit drinking. The second was that she was going to find an evidence-based treatment approach to help her do it.

The director of information technology at a large multi-state hospital system, Joanna has an MBA, travels extensively, and is an accomplished mezzo-soprano who learns operas the way others might memorize pop lyrics. For decades, alcohol was an effective tool for squashing anxiety and numbing grief. But over the years, her little issue with chardonnay developed into a big one.

At the end of her drinking career, she was downing almost two liters daily. Her tall, athletic body showed no obvious physical effects, although one time during a gallstone attack,

a sonogram revealed a slightly enlarged liver. Terrified, Joanna confessed to her doctor that she drank "a lot of wine" most nights. When her liver enzyme test came back normal, he dismissed her concerns. "You don't have a drinking problem. Your liver's fine! Don't be hard on yourself!" Joanna tolerated her liquor well, rarely appearing inebriated. Then again, she took great pains to conceal it: She threw away most of her big golden bottles, wrapping them first in newspaper and plastic before burying them in the trash can.

Her husband was not so reassuring. One well-oiled evening, Joanna got too loud at a party. "She's a drunk," he said, by way of apologizing to other guests. Joanna's drinking was a frequent source of tension in her marriage, but public humiliation was a blow.

Occasionally, she could stop—during several attempts at in-vitro fertilization, she went cold turkey for weeks, imagining herself as a mother during the shots, blood tests, and ultrasounds. Every time she got the call with the news that the embryos hadn't implanted, her disappointment was somehow tempered by the thought that at least she could drink that night.

When Joanna was in her early forties, her Polish grandmother died, leaving her distraught with grief. She saw a psychiatrist who diagnosed depression and alcohol dependence, and directed her to A.A. Joanna told the doctor that she was disinclined to find an answer to her problems in the twelve steps. Her soft-spoken Canadian mother had tried it several times without success, even staying once for a month in a punitive rehab facility that left her more depressed than ever. To Joanna, the forced attendance at A.A. for all women abusing alcohol was akin to breast cancer before lumpectomies, a limited understanding of the disease prompted the medical com-

munity to recommend double mastectomies for every woman with the diagnosis.

Her psychiatrist was unequivocal. Recovery would elude Joanna if she didn't find a sponsor and do the program. "It's the only way," she insisted. So Joanna tried several meetings. She felt most uncomfortable at all-female meetings, where many women imbued their sponsors with a kind of superhuman importance. If the women had good sponsors, they seemed to achieve the status of some sort of omnipotent Boss Mother. If the relationship had soured, the speaker sounded like nothing quite so much as a jilted lover, or an angry, betrayed friend. There seemed to be no room for nuance: Things were either wonderful or awful.

Eventually, Joanna just stopped going—both to the psychiatrist and to meetings. "If A.A. was the only alternative," she says, "I'd rather just drink."

As Joanna neared fifty her mother died, and her stoic Polish-born father, her touchstone, was diagnosed with an aggressive cancer. She tried to moderate her drinking, a wish her dad had expressed frequently. But as he neared death, Joanna turned to chardonnay for comfort. "I was drunk when he died," she says, sorrow catching in her voice.

With her consumption up to almost two giant bottles a day, Joanna knew she had to change something—just not the drinking. She took up martial arts. She stopped eating meat and fish. She quit her job of twenty years and founded a new company. Still, she felt sluggish, and in the martial arts class she struggled to concentrate. While Joanna had blamed her job for her drinking, she found herself imbibing even more once she started working from home. Sometimes she'd pour herself a big glass of wine at 2 p.m. and keep drinking all afternoon.

Most days, she woke up with a pounding head and a queasy stomach, and knew she couldn't ignore her drinking problem any longer. She knew she didn't like A.A., and she didn't think the communal approach of Women for Sobriety or other groups would be appropriate, either. So she started researching scientific literature on alcohol treatment.

When her father was sick, she had located the best oncologists for his cancer—doctors familiar with cutting-edge treatments—at a teaching hospital. She applied the same logic to her own condition. "You find someone who studies the most recent journals, someone who's not afraid of new ideas," she says. "I wanted pros."

One evening, Joanna typed the words "non-twelve-step treatment" into Google, and pulled up the website of an alcohol treatment practice in Palos Verdes, California, called Your Empowering Solutions. Its approach relied on cognitive behavioral therapy and motivational interviewing, techniques that help clients avoid triggers and understand the risks of their behavior. Immediately Joanna liked what she read: The psychologists, Mary Ellen Barnes and Ed Wilson, offered an intensive five-day, one-on-one therapy program that enlisted their clients to determine what might work best in stopping their alcohol abuse. She was also intrigued to learn that their clients were overwhelmingly women.

The pair also worked with a family medicine doctor who prescribed naltrexone, a medication that for decades has been effective in blocking alcohol cravings and is used widely in western Europe.

There was no "facility," no lengthy stay, no pottery class, no equine therapy, no lockdown. Instead, the pair helped clients design a plan for avoiding triggers, develop new inter-

ests away from drinking, and learn calming techniques that would replace the need for alcohol's quick fix. The weeklong meetings were followed by twelve or more weeks with regular phone sessions as clients returned to their "real lives."

Barnes and Wilson listed their educational and professional credentials, and conducted the treatment themselves without relying on lesser-trained counselors. Addictions counseling licensing requirements vary widely from state to state, but in many, the most basic certification requires only a high school diploma and 125 hours of addiction studies coursework.

One brisk fall morning, completely hungover, Joanna punched in the numbers on her telephone and Wilson surprised her by answering the line himself. (She was hoping she'd reach an answering service.) She blurted out some questions: What, she asked, would she *do* in their meetings? Wilson told her they would examine the emotional, social, physical, professional, and educational aspects of her life, to see what might need more attention. How did the psychologists define "success"? That, he said, was the outcome she defined for herself, whether it was abstinence, moderating her intake, or simply choosing one option and deciding on the other later. "We don't pretend it's not hard," he told her. "But we don't believe in generalizing that all alcohol abuse is the same. It's a mosaic, with a spectrum, just like any other condition. That's how it is with changing it. We help you find a mosaic that works for you. Everyone's mosaic is different."

Before she lost her nerve, before she even discussed it with her husband, Joanna wrote out a deposit check for twenty-five hundred dollars and drove straight to the post office drop box. She reserved a room at a luxurious inn near the ocean— Wilson's and Barnes's clients stay in nearby hotels after they

are done with their all-day therapy sessions—and booked a flight for mid-November. She didn't want to wait until after the holidays. She wanted to confront her drinking head-on.

•　　•　　•

The Sunday before her sessions were to start, Joanna ducked into an elegant Southern California Safeway to buy a bottle of her favorite chardonnay—possibly her last—and drove to her hotel. She guzzled it, unpacked, and went to sleep. The next morning, shaking with fear, she climbed the poured pebble steps to Barnes's and Wilson's office. "I couldn't believe I had allowed myself to get to that point," she says.

When she opened the door, Barnes's elderly dog, Shogun, loped up to greet her. Barnes, a California native with thick copper curls, a gentle voice, and a direct gaze, stands as a foil for the towering, mustachioed Wilson, who, despite forty years away from his native Pennsylvania, sometimes sounds as if he is still there. ("Water" comes out like "wooder.") Wilson sometimes uses the vernacular of his past as a steelworker and commercial fisherman. He rolls up his shirtsleeves, not bothering to conceal the giant black koi tattoo that meanders down his left forearm. When he laughs, which is often, he flashes a gold front tooth etched with a tiny star. When Joanna first noticed it, she felt herself relax. "Suddenly he seemed a lot less threatening," she says.

Joanna took a seat in a comfortable leather chair and answered some simple questions. Was her hotel okay? Did she have health, social, marital concerns? What were her hopes for a life without alcohol abuse? There were no inquiries about her childhood, or unresolved feelings about her mother. The questions

were straightforward, and focused on her vision for the present and the future—not the past. Joanna wrote out a check for the remainder of the total: $8,750 for the five days of therapy, a medical evaluation, and three months of follow-up sessions—even daily if necessary. The sessions aren't cheap, but they're a bargain by the standards of private rehab. Other clinics nearby charge upward of a thousand dollars a day for a minimum twenty-eight-day stay.

As Joanna looked through her paperwork, she noticed another unusual document requiring her signature. It said she understood that all records of her visit would be destroyed after she left. Treatment programs that accept medical insurance or local, state, or federal funding typically keep records of each patient. Under some circumstances, such records can be made available to any government agency, prospective employer, and insurance company. This fact alone makes many reluctant to seek treatment, since exposure can have devastating personal and career consequences.

•   •   •

The morning of their first meeting, Wilson drove Joanna to the office of Dr. Tim Norcross, a family medicine doctor who conducts thorough physical exams of the pair's clients. If the client is in good health (those needing detox are referred first to hospitals), he prescribes naltrexone, a drug developed in the United States in 1963 and long used in western Europe to treat alcohol and drug dependence. The World Health Organization approved the use of the drug in 1994, followed by the Food and Drug Administration in 1995 and the American Medical Association in 1996. But few Americans—either laymen or physicians—are familiar with it. It is available in

generic pill form for around a hundred dollars a month, so pharmaceutical companies don't do much to promote it.

Naltrexone works by blocking the brain's release of endorphins, chemicals that allow humans to feel pleasure during sex, after exercise, or when they take some drugs, such as alcohol. When this interaction is blocked, drinkers feel less compulsion to drink. Without a reward, there is less desire. Naltrexone also allows the brain to jump-start a normal production and release of endorphins, which helps to suppress the craving to drink. This two-pronged approach—cutting the cravings and blocking the rewards—helps people moderate their alcohol use. (Because it targets opioid receptors, not the release of endorphins, it does not affect or diminish pleasure from exercise or sex.)

Unlike disulfiram, another medicine that is often used to treat alcohol abuse, naltrexone does not make you feel sick if you drink alcohol while taking it. After publication of the first two randomized, controlled trials in 1992, dozens of studies have confirmed its efficacy in reducing frequency and severity of drinking. In 2006, the NIAAA released the results of the three-year study of nearly fourteen hundred subjects that examined which combinations of pharmaceutical treatments and behavioral therapies might best treat alcohol dependence. Subjects of the study (known by its acronym, COMBINE) were enrolled in one of nine protocols, which used different variations of drugs, placebos, behavior therapy, and what is known as medical management—supervising, educating, monitoring, and caring for a patient. Naltrexone, when combined with medical management, was found to be the most effective of all treatments.

Two other drugs, acamprosate and topiramate, have also shown limited promise for treating alcohol abuse in several

studies. The FDA approved acamprosate, used extensively in Europe, for the treatment of alcohol abuse in 2004; researchers have found that it improved rates of continuous abstinence, percent of days abstinent, and the time until the first drink. Topiramate, an anticonvulsant, has similar effects.

Dozens of studies show that naltrexone and topiramate reduce the number of drinking days among those who desire moderation, and increase the ability for others to stay abstinent. In repeated clinical trials, naltrexone has been found to reduce the percentage of heavy drinking days and the number of drinks consumed. Meta-analyses have shown that oral naltrexone is effective in preventing relapse to heavy drinking— or any drinking at all. In a study of the use of extended-release naltrexone, Yale researcher Stephanie O'Malley found that 32 percent of patients receiving extended-release naltrexone, which is delivered by injection and therefore eliminates the need for patients to take it every day, were abstinent over six months, compared with 11 percent using a placebo. That is nearly a 200 percent difference.

Only a handful of studies, published in the last five years or so, have even considered analyzing the effects of gender on the drug. But some small studies have reported that naltrexone reduces alcohol euphoria most effectively in women, as well as people carrying a variant of the OPRM1 gene, an opioid receptor gene that plays a key role in both pain perception and addiction. Different variants of the gene may help explain differences in the way humans respond to alcohol, as well as how effectively the drug binds to the opioid receptor. Researchers are hopeful that more widespread clinical testing can yield clues about which patients will respond best. For example, in 2011, Canadian researchers found that among those with

a variant of the gene, known as A118G, 87 percent were able to reduce their drinking days significantly. That compared to 49 percent of those receiving placebos, and 55 percent without the gene but who received either the drug or a placebo.

Studies involving naltrexone and gene variants have been small, using only a few hundred subjects, but researchers are optimistic that the findings can be used to help identify which people are best suited for the drug. The Canadian researchers, who studied twenty women and twenty men, wrote that they were optimistic that their findings might help in the search for personalized alcohol treatment.

Another study showed promising signs for naltrexone's use for women. In 2008, Brown University scientists examined naltrexone's effects on 180 heavy drinkers, of whom seventy-two were women. The study was notable because the subjects were not seeking treatment for their drinking—they had simply answered a research ad placed in newspapers. It was also significant because the subjects recorded their cravings, consumption, and moods after drinking on handheld devices that allowed the researchers to analyze data in real time from home—not memories recorded later, or in the clinical setting of a lab. In that study, the researchers found that naltrexone was effective in reducing the quantity of alcohol and frequency of alcohol consumption, but they noted some important differences: It significantly blunted alcohol's euphoric effects on women.

In the United States, naltrexone is generally prescribed with the goal of at least temporary abstinence, allowing patients to break their dangerous cycles of drinking before attempting moderation at a later date. In Finland, however, an American doctor named John David Sinclair uses it for heavy drinkers who plan to drink for the rest of their lives. His the-

ory is this: If you drink, prompting the brain to release endorphins, each glass of wine reinforces that behavior. But if you drink and get no endorphin release, the urge fades. With the craving blocked, problem drinkers are able to limit their consumption—not by abstaining, but by drinking a moderate amount. Using this method, Sinclair claims a success rate of 78 percent, using as a yardstick the practice of drinking within safe limits (although those vary from country to country).

Sinclair advises his patients to take the pill an hour or so before drinking. With the drug, heavy drinking will give way to normal drinking. Naltrexone itself is "lapse prevention," but the method demands compliance in order to work.

This approach is rarely embraced in the United States, since it requires little behavioral adjustment on the part of the client. And even Wilson, a fan of the drug, says it's no magical answer. But he says it helps to prepare a problem drinker for a new kind of life. "Think about it: Less drinking tends to free up time for other activities, and a lot of clients find themselves easing out of alcohol abuse the same way they fell into it."

●   ●   ●

Joanna wasn't looking for magic, though; she was looking for results. When she stepped into Tim Norcross's bright, modern office, the staff was welcoming and friendly, and even the magazines were upbeat. When she fretted about her weight, his kind nurse told her to step on the scale backward. When she worried aloud to Norcross that she had ruined her liver forever—a fear she had harbored since her mother's days in A.A.—he told her, "Let's find out, and move forward." Indeed, while most injured organs can heal, new tissue appears in the form of scars. The

liver, however, is able to replace damaged tissue with new cells. Despite her years of heavy drinking, Joanna's liver enzymes were normal. "I dodged a bullet, and I know it," she says.

Norcross prescribed a week's worth of the antianxiety medication Klonopin, as well as three months of naltrexone. Research shows that taking the drug for three to six months gives new, nondrinking behaviors time to establish themselves into patterns. Joanna returned to Barnes's and Wilson's office.

Then the three went out to lunch, to a local Tex-Mex restaurant known for its generous salads. There was no dining hall, no other patients she had to make small talk with: just Joanna and her two shrinks.

The next step in Joanna's treatment was a written test designed to evaluate her emotional maturity, a series of sentence stems that she had to complete. Such tests have been in use since the late nineteenth century as a tool to assess attitudes, beliefs, and motivation. Wilson administers one designed in the 1970s by Jane Loevinger, a developmental psychologist who taught at Washington University in St. Louis. Loevinger was a pioneer in the study of female psychology, as well as the concept of ego development. She theorized that humans advance through a series of stages that reflect growing levels of cognitive and emotional maturity, and that they make decisions based on their gradual internalization of social rules and personal experiences.

Her test, known as the Washington University Sentence Completion Test, measures nine stages, and is used as a tool in settings as varied as freshman dorms and corporate recruitment. It seeks to assess how a person's experiences and identity—their hardwired selves—shape their approach to life.

Joanna found the exercise amusing, and raced through it in about a half hour. Wilson, who has scored thousands of the tests

for medical schools, prisons, and elite branches of the military, tallied her score as an 8, a stage Loevinger described as "autonomous." Joanna's answers to the brief sentence stems, such as "A man's job . . ." and "When I'm criticized . . ." revealed a highly evolved sense of independence and self. (Loevinger found that the majority of American adults tend to settle in stage 5, which she called "self-aware." At this stage, adults have limited curiosity about the experiences of others. Their powerful motivators are guilt and concerns about what others might think.)

The test, they say, offers valuable clues for how to shape a client's treatment. Those who score at the higher end of the scale tend to be independent thinkers who are introspective and aware of their inner conflicts. They are able to tolerate, even appreciate, life's ambiguities, paradoxes, and inconsistencies and can integrate new experiences, learning, and skills into changing self-perceptions.

Those who score in the middle ranges often have fixed self-perceptions, tend to prize conformity, and function best within strict rubrics. Wilson says such people are better suited to A.A., with its clearly delineated rules and limits. Many find comfort in the repetitive axioms of A.A. ("Once an alcoholic, always an alcoholic") and its sobriety chips. Those who score higher on Loevinger's test tend to do least well with twelve-step programs. "A.A. is not for people who have a lot of questions," Wilson says.

As they continued through the week, Wilson and Barnes addressed Joanna's goals for her future, examined what prompted her drinking, and discussed ideas she might have for achieving better physical and mental health. That task seemed overwhelming, but as she wrote out her objectives, she realized that her leisure time could be productive instead of numb-

ing. Her aspirations were far from lofty: In addition to adding more exercise and eating better, she wanted to finish decorating her master bedroom, organize her belongings better, and hang pictures that had been sidelined next to the wall for years.

In the afternoons after her sessions, Joanna took long walks on the beach and listened to meditation CDs. Skeptical at first, she was surprised at how they were able to help relieve her anxiety in a way completely different from alcohol. As she returned to Pennsylvania, she felt armed with knowledge—about herself, her personal development, and the vision she had for her life.

Given Joanna's drinking history, Barnes warned her outright that she would not be a good candidate for moderation, even with naltrexone. At first, Joanna was disappointed. "You mean I really can't drink again?" she said. "You can try it," Barnes said, "but I would wait for at least a year."

Back home, Joanna took naltrexone for ninety days, stopping when she began suffering from headaches (they are among the drug's side effects). But by then, she says, she had developed a routine of work, healthy eating, voracious evening reading—when she was drinking, she was always too inebriated to remember where she had left off—and a rededication to exercise. She made a weekly schedule for yoga and jogging, and stepped up her participation in martial arts. (Since quitting drinking, she has advanced four belt colors.) Quickly, she says, she began to see the possibilities for a better life. She was also surprised to feel her desire for chardonnay fade, so much so that she didn't feel the need to remove the bottles from her pantry. "I still have some, for guests," she says. "My husband could take or leave it, and if people come over and want some, they can."

Her transition was surprisingly smooth. What she had dreaded for so long—shifting from a drinking life to a non-

drinking one—had so many pleasant side effects, she doesn't even feel tempted to slip. "I wanted to live my life without drinking the way I had been, and I was really focused on that. Drinking would only take me back a step, and I knew it." For example, fights in her marriage often centered on her drinking, but drinking, of course, was easy to blame. Without the veil of alcohol, she and her husband communicate more directly about what might be bothering them.

That is not to say that there have been no stumbling blocks. Several months into her wine-free life, the neighbors at her summer lake house invited her to an evening barbecue. At previous gatherings, Joanna drank too much, but then again, so did almost everybody else. On one hand, she didn't want to feel uncomfortable, sipping soda while everyone else got sloshed; on the other, she didn't want to have to out herself in a small community. She took a deep breath and told her neighbor the truth: She was new to not drinking, and was unsure about whether to attend. Her neighbor was silent. Finally, she said, "Then maybe it's better if you don't come."

Joanna hung up the phone and sobbed.

A few months later, when I met Joanna for the first time at her house, she was anxious about a long-planned weekend with her best friends from college. They were scheduled to gather in Chicago to eat in the newest restaurants, see an exhibit at the Art Institute, and shop. She was worried, since girls' weekends often include copious amounts of alcohol. Joanna had told them all ahead of time that she wouldn't be imbibing with them, but they encouraged her to come.

Joanna was delayed and arrived in Chicago long past the scheduled meeting time. Once she made it to the restaurant to meet her friends, she noticed they had already had a few cock-

tails each. Anxious at first, Joanna downed her seltzer with lime. Their buzzes fading, they ordered dinner—and talked deep into the night. Joanna was thrilled in the morning: She remembered everything everybody had said, and didn't have to repeat questions or cover up for her herself by saying, "Oh, yes, that's right, you told me that!"

When she travels to the Caribbean each January, she has to swallow hard when she hears the steel drums play, and sees couples downing frosty rum drinks on the beach. "It's a chain reaction, and I understand it," she says. "I hear the music, smell the saltwater, and want a drink like everybody else." In the beginning, she dreaded occasions where wine had been her crutch—the first boating excursion of the summer, for example—without a tumbler of wine. She would call Barnes. "What if someone says something?" Joanna asked. "Nobody cares about your drinking," Barnes told her, "as long as you are not interfering with theirs."

A few months ago, she and her husband went to the opera in Manhattan. It was her first without chardonnay. Joanna knew the libretto—this was *Carmen,* one of her favorites— and as she took her seat she felt her pulse quicken. The curtains rose, and the singer's notes were so pure and electric, Joanna felt as if they were entering her bloodstream. As she followed the opera, she, too, felt the gigantic emotions—jealousy, rage, passion, joy. Now, the extravagance of her enjoyment felt as amplified as the music itself.

●　　●　　●

Like Joanna, Wilson's and Barnes's clients tend to be educated and highly motivated women. Six years into their partnership,

their 240 clients report a 70 percent success rate. This means that clients say they have achieved the outcome they desire, whether it is abstaining or moderating. Of the remaining 30 percent, half drop out, and the other 15 percent continue to struggle.

Many battle with identity crises that crop up in middle age. Alcohol might seem like the culprit, but it is often more likely the symptom of a larger problem. "They might feel powerless over alcohol, but the real problem is that they feel powerless in their marriages, in their jobs, in their decisions," says Barnes. Many women had established careers before they had children, then chose to stay home. "They might have their first baby in their late thirties or early forties and decide that after all this dedication at work, they'll stay home with the baby," she says. "It's not that they don't love their babies, but they didn't count on what they were giving up. They're not getting a pat on the back for a job well done—the baby's crying. They're not getting paid. They're bored—and really anxious, and feel guilty that they are bored and anxious."

So they drink to get through it—and before they know it, fifteen years have passed. "Alcohol works," says Barnes, "until it doesn't."

Barnes and Wilson describe a recent client, a former businesswoman who left her job after the birth of her second child. As a way to keep busy, she had hosted occasional jewelry parties. The more wine drunk, the more jewelry sold. One morning after, her head pounding, she surveyed her empties—thirty-five bottles of chardonnay for twenty women—and called Barnes and Wilson for an appointment.

For many such clients, their advice (and they give it freely) is straightforward. If stay-at-home mothers complain that they're bored, they suggest finding work they find

more meaningful. If women are overwhelmed with the tasks of modern motherhood, Barnes and Wilson point out other solutions: cutting back on their kids' extracurricular activities and having them pitch in more—making their own lunches, doing their own laundry. Most emphatically, they prescribe finding alternative activities in the late afternoon or evening that have nothing to do with alcohol—volunteering at Habitat for Humanity; taking a yoga class; joining Audubon Society bird walks; going for a long stroll with the dog.

If clients feel trapped in unfulfilling marriages, the counselors are likely to suggest recalibrating the relationship. One of their most common findings is about how frequently drinking spouses are afraid to be assertive in their personal relationships, regardless of how they act professionally. Many female clients feel resentful about the sacrifices they made to raise children, and are also envious of their spouses' success. They turn to alcohol rather than make an affirmative change in their professional or personal status.

Unlike in most treatment programs, Barnes and Wilson also incorporate the client's significant other into the sessions. "Alcohol abuse doesn't occur in a vacuum," Wilson says.

They also discuss a woman's diet and exercise habits, as well as her hormone levels. As hormones fluctuate in menopause, alcohol can intensify symptoms such as hot flashes and insomnia. Drinking even moderate amounts of alcohol can raise estrogen levels, and many studies have linked it to an increased risk of breast cancer.

Many of their clients are thin, preferring to drink, rather than eat, their calories. Often, they are also dedicated exercisers, a paradox confirmed in a recent study that found that the more some people drink, the more they exercise. They point

out that alcohol cravings are often triggered by hunger, not a desire to get high. Calorie counters, concerned with staying thin, may forgo balanced meals for more booze—and then exercise to keep from gaining. Though it may seem obvious, Wilson and Barnes suggest drawing out meal plans that include plenty of protein, fruit, and vegetables.

They also emphasize the importance of learning to cope with the aftermath of an occasional drink or two. If clients drink while they are trying to abstain, they encourage them to call. "It's not, 'Oh my God, you've *relapsed*,'" Barnes says. "We point out how well they did on so many of the other days before it. You had a drink; it's not the end of the world. You didn't 'ruin your sobriety' or 'undo' anything."

She likens the concept of "relapse"—it's a term she and Wilson avoid—to a pattern that is common among dieters. "Let's say that over the course of six months, you've lost twenty-two pounds by changing your diet and exercising more," she says. "Are you back to square one if you gain five back in the month of December? Certainly not," she says. "You return to your healthy habits, and lay off the pecan pie and the Christmas cookies."

Recently, a woman who once drank two bottles of pinot grigio a day called Barnes in a panic. It had been a year since they'd spoken, and more than two years since she had left treatment.

"I went out for lunch with my girlfriend and had a glass of wine," the woman blurted.

"Okay," said Barnes. "Did you go home and continue drinking?"

"No," the woman said.

"Did you drink too much the day after?"

"No."

"I'm not sure I'm understanding," Barnes said.

"I relapsed! I drank!" the woman said, near tears.

"Let's get this straight," Barnes said. "When we met you drank two bottles of wine a day. You decided to change that habit, and you did. The other day you had a glass of wine with your girlfriend. One glass. This is not a 'relapse.' This is success."

When clients face challenging situations—weddings, parties, conventions—Wilson and Barnes encourage their clients to call for support with ideas about how to avoid falling into familiar patterns, no matter how long ago they wrapped up their sessions. They also suggest keeping a few doses of naltrexone around for a few years, in order to discourage binges.

•   •   •

Not everyone can drink in moderation. Most experts agree that some people, for whatever reason—a genetic vulnerability, as well as a combination of environmental, psychological, and physical factors—cannot drink in a controlled way.

"But that is a very, very small group of people," Barnes says. "Like so many other conditions, from asthma to eating disorders, there is a huge continuum for alcohol abuse."

It is not always easy to convince clients what conventional wisdom has held dear for the past eighty years—telling a woman she is not an alcoholic, and doesn't have to call herself one, seems almost as radical as hearing your mother tell you to ditch the sunscreen before heading to the beach. How to shift the way we understand alcohol and how to manage it for a varied population—and especially for women—will require some effort.

Since it was released in 2006, the COMBINE study appears to have made few inroads. Tim Norcross, the family doctor who treats Wilson's and Barnes's clients, had never heard of naltrexone when the psychologists approached him about working together in 2007—and he was just a few years out of medical school.

He wonders why nicotine addiction—which has been treated for twenty-five years with medicine—has such a different reputation. Ex-smokers don't call themselves "recovering smokers," and ads for Chantix, which blocks nicotine receptors so that smoking or chewing the drug can't activate them, fill medical journals. Anyone over eighteen can buy nicotine gum at the drugstore.

●　　●　　●

Barnes's and Wilson's program incorporates a number of methods that have been scientifically proven to reduce alcohol abuse, and they are among a growing number of practitioners who rely on science to treat their patients. I focused on Joanna because she was representative of the numerous women I've spoken to who were aware of the drawbacks of twelve-step treatment, and had researched an alternative approach that would be tailored to her. The last I spoke with her, in January 2013, she was happy, not drinking, and reported feeling healthier than she'd ever been.

In fact, there are many alternatives to Alcoholics Anonymous, including a group called Smart Recovery, which is a secular nonprofit organization that employs motivational and cognitive behavioral therapy in meetings and online support groups.

Ashley Phillips, a women's health leader and life coach in San Diego, found SMART online in the early 2000s. During a

painful divorce, Phillips began drinking several bottles of wine a day. Her alarmed friends and colleagues staged an intervention, and Phillips spent a month in rehab, grudgingly attending A.A. as part of her outpatient treatment afterward. But Phillips, who has devoted her career to strengthening women, was particularly unsettled by A.A.'s insistence that she was powerless, and that she submit her own will to God. Eventually, she felt so at odds with the program's principles that she explored other options.

She liked that the group was founded in 1994 by a team of people, primarily mental health professionals, who wanted to create a self-empowering, science-based, free mutual help addiction recovery group. The organization now has more than one thousand weekly meetings worldwide, and its handbook is available in eight languages.

Phillips found SMART's use of motivational interviewing particularly effective for her. It helps drinkers identify a sense of personal and intellectual discomfort as they look at the tension between their values and their drinking behavior. Together with other tools they can create their own incentives to quit. When an online SMART facilitator created a cost-benefit analysis of alcohol, Phillips concluded that the negative effects of her drinking far outweighed any benefit. "Having seen that in black and white, I was able to make healthy choices going forward," says Phillips, who has worked as a SMART facilitator since 2010.

Another organization, Rational Recovery, offers tools for alcohol and other substance abusers to recognize their own "addictive voice," and find abstinence on their own. It has no groups or meetings because it believes such gatherings merely reinforce the notion of a crippling lifelong disease.

Mark Willenbring, psychiatrist and former director of treatment research at the NIAAA, sees patients in private practice in Minneapolis. He has developed a new company, ALLTYR, which is dedicated to providing scientifically based treatment, and educating the public about twenty-first-century approaches to alcohol and drug abuse. Like Barnes and Wilson, he treats patients with individualized, personal therapy in his office for a fraction of the cost of rehab. "As taxpayers, as insurance policyholders, and insurance companies themselves," he says, "we're wasting tremendous amounts of money, and not getting anything out of what we spend. It just doesn't have to be this way."

Dee-Dee Stout, a California addictions counselor, agrees. In 2011, Stout cofounded AA2.org, an online self-help website that guides clients through evidence-based methods of recovery. Stout, the author of *Coming to Harm Reduction Kicking and Screaming: Looking for Harm Reduction in a 12-Step World*, travels globally to lecture on various approaches to alcohol abuse, including harm reduction. The concept brings together two seemingly opposite ideas: that people can be in recovery and yet continue to use substances responsibly. In 2007, Kenneth Anderson, a community organizer in Brooklyn, formed a group called HAMS, a peer-led support group that offers members guidance on harm reduction, abstinence, and moderation. Following scientific guidelines for harm reduction established by national health authorities in Canada, Australia, Hong Kong, and throughout the European Union as first-line treatment for alcohol and drug use, Anderson sets out a protocol that urges drinkers to give up all alcohol for thirty days, and reevaluate habits with a cost-benefit analysis of alcohol once that threshold has passed. (He provides a detailed set of strategies in his book, *How to Change Your Drinking: A Harm Reduction Guide to Alcohol*.)

I spoke to many women who employed harm-reduction techniques, but no one illustrated them quite so sharply as Jane, a fifty-four-year-old Virginia businesswoman who asked not to have her full name disclosed in order to protect her privacy. During the economic downturn, Jane found her business at a standstill—and her wine consumption ratcheting up from two glasses a night to an entire bottle. After a few months, she found that even a 750-milliliter wineglass couldn't mask her despair, and she switched to vodka, eventually downing a pint a night.

She knew she had to change her habits, and found HAMS on the Internet. Following its guidelines, she quit drinking for a month. That was a challenge, since drinking had become her only real source of relaxation during a period of high stress. But she read more books, cooked more, and ordered new guitar music. At first, falling asleep was difficult, but she soon realized that sleep that wasn't alcohol-induced was far more restful than waking up bleary-eyed ever could be.

Once the thirty days passed, Jane reintroduced alcohol, and began to take notes about her feelings as she drank. Reviewing them while sober, she realized that she felt good after the first and second drinks, but progressively worse after her third and fourth.

While drinking may have brought instant pleasure, Jane realized that it actually obscured activities that made her happy—playing the guitar and reading.

"I didn't always stick to my plan at first," she says. "It's a process. It took practice." Occasionally, she says, she'll have an evening where she goes over her two-drink limit, but that's rare. "I like having access to my brain," she says.

Likewise, Donna Dierker, a St. Louis neuroscientist, found that she was able to change her weekend binge drinking to a

more mindful pattern of moderation. In 2000, Dierker realized that on Friday nights and Saturdays she was plowing through a six-pack or more of beer, topped off by a half-bottle of wine. She knew something had to shift, and turned to Moderation Management, a secular nonprofit organization that uses peer-run support groups for nondependent problem drinkers who want to control their consumption.

M.M., founded in 1994 by a stay-at-home mother, Audrey Kishline, who hewed closely to the peer-reviewed studies of successful moderation, focuses on the individual's ability to make healthier decisions by using "self-monitoring." Its goal is to have members "accept personal responsibility for choosing and maintaining their own path, whether it be abstinence or moderation."

As a scientist, Dierker, fifty-one and a mother of two, was reassured by M.M.'s reliance on evidence-based practice, and through it has learned to tweak her habits. She alternates one month of abstention with two months of drinking by M.M.'s guidelines for women—no more than three drinks a day or nine a week. This has lowered her tolerance, and limited her concerns about the binge pattern in which she once found herself. "If you told me I could never drink again, that would be the only thing I thought about," says Dierker, who leads local M.M. discussions in St. Louis.

"M.M. taught me to drink more mindfully—to pay attention to how different effects correspond to different blood-alcohol levels," Dierker says. "You might appreciate the lifting of inhibitions after three or four drinks, but not the slurring, You might like the reduced social anxiety of three drinks, but miss the good intention to stop after two. The returns drop drastically after the first few drinks."

M.M. appears as an alternative resource on the NIAAA's "Rethinking Drinking" page, and the Substance Abuse and Mental Health Services Administration lists it in its national registry of evidence-based programs and practices. There are also moderation apps that studies have shown to be effective: one, developed by the moderation researchers Mark and Linda Sobell, is called iChange, and is downloadable on iTunes; another, based on M.M. guidelines, can be found at moderate drinking.com. M.M. also has a fifty-nine-dollar app that helps users track their drinking, and stay within moderate limits.

Stanton Peele, a New Jersey psychologist, lawyer, and author of nine books, has argued for decades that moderation is an acceptable goal for many problem drinkers. Peele is past the usual American retirement age, but for him slowing down is out of the question. He remains in demand as a lecturer, and in 2014 he published his twelfth book, a collaboration with the blogger Ilse Thompson.

The debate about abstinence rages on. Consider the case of Kishline herself, a problem drinker who struggled with A.A.'s concepts before founding M.M. The group says it doesn't suit all problem drinkers, and that abstinence for some is best.

In January 2000, Kishline posted a message saying that moderation didn't work for her, and that she would begin to attend A.A. and other abstinence-based groups. Two months later, having returned to A.A, with a blood-alcohol content of more than three times the legal limit, Kishline sped the wrong way on an icy highway in Washington State, killing a thirty-eight-year-old man and his twelve-year-old daughter. She served three and a half years of a four-and-a-half-year sentence.

This tragic accident has been used as irrefutable proof that for all problem drinkers, moderation is dangerous—and impossible.

Peele and others say that a single anecdote shouldn't decide treatments for large populations. The ultimate goal is an array of approaches for the array of patients.

Willenbring looks forward to the day when Americans view alcohol problems like they now see depression. Forty years ago, those who suffered from it had few choices. They could wait in agony for the hemorrhaging of tears to cease, the anxiety to dissipate. Families committed desperate patients— typically after suicide attempts—to psychiatric hospitals, where treatments were dubious and scary: around-the-clock sedation, isolation, and the full-scale seizures brought on by electroconvulsive therapy administered without anesthesia.

Since the advent of Prozac and its descendants, depression is part of the national conversation—and often a topic patients discuss with their primary-care doctors. In fact, the number of Americans treated with antidepressants between 1996 and 2007 went from 13.3 million to 27 million, according to a study of national mental health surveys. Of those patients, more than half were prescribed the drug by their primary-care doctors.

By contrast, Willenbring says, fewer than 10 percent of the twenty million Americans who suffer from an alcohol abuse disorder ever get specialized treatment for it—and that's usually only after they've suffered a serious physical or social consequence. Every week, Willenbring talks to female patients whose doctors refuse to prescribe medications that can help curb alcohol cravings. "They get referred to A.A., or rehab," he says.

"When a patient has high cholesterol, you don't wait for her to have a heart attack before you prescribe statins and make some dietary changes," he says. "When a patient has

mild asthma, you prescribe an inhaler. You don't wait until he can't breathe and then ship him off to the ICU. You intervene when the condition is mild."

He suggests that those who are concerned about their drinking seek evidence-based intervention if they can answer yes to the following three questions. "Do you set limits and repeatedly go over them? Do you have a persistent desire to quit or cut down and are unable to do it? Do you have frequent physical consequences, such as nausea or headaches, after time spent drinking?"

Yet fifty years after Jellinek distanced himself from the drinker's curve, conventional thinking about alcohol still retains its concepts. It's hard to imagine a realm of medicine in which the gap between science and practice is so great.

Change will take some doing. One useful step, Willenbring says, would be to distinguish more clearly between "at-risk drinking" and "alcohol dependence." At-risk drinking is drinking more than is medically advisable, and puts heavier drinkers at risk for developing an alcohol-use disorder. Alcohol dependence has a number of specific diagnostic criteria and professionals need to learn how to identify it. It's not clear that they do. Primary-care doctors do not always pick up on the signs of alcohol abuse until blood tests reveal a damaged liver. If medical schools want to train a generation of doctors who can handle this problem, they need to do more than shuffle their students off to meetings in church basements to learn about addiction. They need to teach doctors how to screen for and counsel at-risk drinkers and to treat patients with alcohol-use disorders medically.

Rather than entrust recovering drinkers as the first and last mechanism of support, we need to convince insurance com-

panies and federal insurance programs to reimburse doctors for their new role, and patients for expensive medication. The injectable form of naltrexone is the priciest—up to a thousand dollars a shot—but compared to rehab, it's cost effective even when it's combined with medical monitoring. When women learn that they can manage their drinking without the stigma, cost, and time of inpatient rehab, they might be willing to ask for help sooner.

•   •   •

If women need more reason to question the one-size-fits-all approach to alcohol abuse, they need only look at a map of the world. No one seems to agree, for one thing, on what the healthy daily dose of alcohol should be. From Sweden to Australia, Denmark to South Africa, drinking recommendations for women are twice the amount health officials suggest for American women. In Spain, Italy, and France, where wine is a revered national birthright, the suggested limits are even higher. Women in those countries live the longest of any other country in Europe, dying at around eighty-four. On the Greek island of Ikaria, which has one of the world's largest concentration of centenarians, wine consumption for both men and women is between two and four glasses a day. Of course, many women in these countries—particularly those in Greece—share a healthy diet that is rich in fish, olive oil, legumes, and greens.

And the manner of consumption is expected to be different, too. In Spain, for example, the recommendation for women is to consume no more than thirty grams of ethyl alcohol (roughly three five-ounce glasses of wine) a day. This con-

verts to a glass of wine at lunch, an aperitif with a snack, and a glass of wine at dinner. Having food—especially proteins, fats, and dense carbohydrates—slows down the absorption of alcohol into the bloodstream, giving the liver more time to process it.

In the United States, health officials suggest one drink a day for women, two for men. For women, heavy or "at-risk" drinking is anything more than three drinks in one day, or seven in one week. (For men, that figure is four drinks a day, or fourteen a week.) I'm not implying causation, but it's interesting to note that American women die sooner than their European counterparts. Hispanic women live the longest, until an average of eighty-two; white women, to an average of eighty-one; and black women, to an average of seventy-seven.

There are a number of reasons the U.S. recommendations are so low. According to Dr. Raul Caetano, dean of the School of Health Professions at the University of Texas Southwestern Medical School, in the United States and in northern Europe, people are aware that heavy drinking is not considered respectable. In these cultures especially, people naturally underreport their consumption. "Some people might forget or simply not know," he said during a phone interview. "But others underreport because they don't want to reveal how much they drink."

Some northern European studies show that there is a 50 percent difference between what people buy, Caetano says, and what they admit to actually drinking. So unless people are storing up their wine and vodka for Armageddon, chances are they shave off a few drinks.

I asked Dr. Caetano whether researchers in those countries would compensate for that by suggesting people drink less.

He answered the question indirectly: In cultures where alcohol has been integrated for millennia, health officials have a higher tolerance for its associated risks. Guidelines are also calculated according to what a nation considers a serious problem. For example, in the United States, where fifteen out of a hundred thousand deaths are in automobile accidents, researchers might be hoping to reduce the risk from alcohol-related car crashes. In the Netherlands, where auto deaths are rare, public health officials might be more concerned with preventing liver disease.

Fred Rotgers, a New Jersey clinical psychologist who is a pioneer in harm reduction and a cofounder of the online self-help group AA2.org, says there are also political motivations. Amid the "war on drugs," scientists who receive federal funding for alcohol research are unlikely to take liberal attitudes toward any aspect of substance use, he says. "You have legislators who view all alcohol consumption as morally wrong," he says. "They're not considering that the vast majority of people who consume alcohol do so responsibly. But if that's who controls your grant money, you've got to be careful." According to the Pew Research Center, about 27 percent of the 113th Congress belonged to religious groups that prohibit alcohol.

Many researchers agree that the restraint of U.S. guidelines stems in part from the many studies that suggest a link between breast cancer and even moderate alcohol consumption. As I was finishing my reporting for this book, another study showed an association. It was a worry that haunted many of my sources, and multitudes of my moderate-drinking friends.

On one hand, moderate alcohol consumption has been associated with lower rates of heart disease and stroke, certain types of cancers, dementia, and diabetes.

Yet a 2011 study of 106,000 women in the *Journal of the American Medical Association* found that women who drank between three and six drinks a week were about 15 percent more likely than nondrinkers to be diagnosed with breast cancer. Among women had two drinks a day, the risk rose to 51 percent. It made no difference whether the women drank wine, beer, or spirits.

The alarming percentage numbers were reported widely in the popular press, often without noting that, in fact, they translated to small increases in small numbers. But Dr. Steven A. Narod, a breast cancer scientist at the Women's College Research Institute in Toronto, noted in an accompanying *JAMA* editorial that, according to the data, women who routinely have a drink a day could expect their ten-year risk of breast cancer to increase from 2.8 percent to 3.5 percent. For women who have two drinks a day, that risk would rise from 2.8 percent to 4.1 percent. The numbers were adjusted for age, family history of the disease, smoking, and weight.

The study, led by Dr. Wendy Chen, an assistant professor of medicine at Harvard Medical School, analyzed lifelong consumption patterns of nearly 106,000 predominantly white nurses ages 30 to 55 between 1980 and 2008. They found that drinking both early in adult life and after age forty was associated with higher risk. The authors said that although the exact mechanism isn't known, it may involve alcohol's effects on a woman's estrogen levels. There is evidence that alcohol increases a woman's blood level of estrogen, and high levels of estrogen are a known risk factor for breast cancer.

Like many similar studies on alcohol's risks, the *JAMA* study was based on self-reports, which are not always reliable.

It lacked a control group and also found no evidence that giving up drinking lowers a woman's risk of breast cancer.

What's a wine lover to do? Experts cautioned against overreacting to the findings. Even Chen said women should weigh the risks and benefits of wine to prevent cardiovascular disease.

Dr. Lisa Schwartz, a professor of community and family medicine at Dartmouth Medical School, is skeptical of observed epidemiological studies, which she says share "an important weakness." While this study asked questions about drinking habits, Schwartz says, other factors might explain the findings. "We need to be humble about what observational studies tell us, since we can't randomly control for what we've observed."

In an editorial she cowrote for the *Journal of the National Cancer Institute,* Schwartz cited 2009 reports in the popular media warning women that a drink a day could raise their risk of breast cancer. But the coverage, based on a study published in the *JNCI,* didn't mention the magnitude of the risk. The researchers compared breast cancer rates among women who drank more than fifteen drinks a week to women who drank one or two drinks a week. The investigators observed a 0.6 percent increase in the risk of breast cancer diagnosis, from 2 percent to 2.6 percent. That's a tiny fraction of an increase, but it represents a 30 percent jump—and that's the figure that got reported.

Schwartz points out that the women who drink alcohol might be more health conscious, drinking one glass of wine a day for cardiovascular health. It's possible that those women are more likely to get more regular mammograms. "Maybe it's more screening that explains the higher breast cancer diagnosis—not the alcohol," Schwartz says. "To read the reports and even the press releases from the journals themselves, you're

led to believe that every drink makes a difference. That's just not what the data show," she says. "That's dramatically overstating the risks."

Such reports instill at once too much fear and too much hope: "There's inherent tension between wanting to tell people what might help them stay healthy versus being far too definitive and ramping up fear with things we're not sure about. I've never seen a randomized trial of high-risk women changing their habits and therefore being less likely to be diagnosed with breast cancer," she says. "This isn't like lung cancer and smoking."

The best approach, Schwartz says, is for researchers to be honest and say, "'We're really not sure, but with alcohol, at least, the risk is very small.'"

Some studies have shown that the nutrient folate, found in oranges, fortified grains, and green leafy vegetables, might protect against the increased risk of breast cancer associated with alcohol consumption because alcohol can reduce the cancer-protecting folate in the bloodstream. Scientists think that folate may be involved in how cells activate certain genes, and that low levels of folate can alter chemicals that affect DNA. This in turn might alter a cell's ability to repair itself, or divide incorrectly, and become cancerous.

Risk, after all, isn't destiny. Getting a flu shot lowers your risk of getting the flu, but it doesn't guarantee it. Exercising doesn't guarantee that you won't get heart disease, but it lowers the odds. Not drinking isn't going to prevent you from getting breast cancer, but it may lower your risk for developing certain kinds of it.

"Women need to be aware of the numbers," Schwartz says, "and decide for themselves."

Conclusion

American women's relationship with alcohol offers a fascinating window on how far we've come—and how far we haven't. The fact that we drink to excess far more often than our mothers is proof that we have passed a dubious milestone. Forget about boys will be boys. These days, many women have taken advantage of modern equality to behave just as stupidly as men at bachelorette parties, sporting events, and girls' nights out.

As with men's excesses, all this carousing may have benefits. In a few decades, maybe America's captains of industry will be drawn from members of the Old Girls Network who forged lifelong bonds overdoing it at sorority parties. After all, generations of men who dominated politics and business came of age as drinking buddies. But as a plethora of scientific studies have demonstrated in recent years, women *are*

different. When they match men beer for beer, they get drunk quicker. And when they end up in an A.A.-driven rehab, their needs are different. It's why so many women I interviewed felt that their trip to twelve-step treatment was a journey to a foreign land where they didn't speak the language or understand the local customs.

After years of speaking to women who have tried to cope with their drinking, a few simple findings emerge.

We need to take advantage of twenty-first-century science. We've learned a lot about how the brain works since the founding of A.A. in 1935. And we need to acknowledge what nearly every research study has found in recent years: One size could not possibly fit all. If alcoholism really is a medical condition—and there's plenty of evidence that addiction has a genetic component—then we should not blame the patient for failing to "work the program" when one type of treatment fails. We don't ask cancer patients to explain their "part" in a course of chemotherapy that didn't achieve the desired result.

For some, these words are heresy. Any questioning of the twelve-step dogma, they argue, threatens the lives of those who have tamed an otherwise intractable problem. That, of course, is not my intent. Women who have achieved success with A.A. or other twelve-step approaches should consider themselves lucky and keep attending meetings. But for those for whom it doesn't work—and that's the vast majority of people who try it—it's worth searching for other answers.

We can't know all the reasons women are drinking more, and by no means do I mean to suggest that it's the fault of women's progress in our society. Feminism is about gaining power, but when you take people out of one milieu and drop them in another, it changes them in unpredictable ways. Some

thrive. Others struggle. So it is with women in the postmodern universe. It's not that the trip there was a mistake, it's that the side effects need to be treated appropriately.

We consider alcohol a social equalizer, but we haven't been paying attention to the disparity of consequences. Women get drunk faster, and they suffer health problems from excess drinking faster, too.

Rather than spend resources after women have "hit bottom" like a group of midcentury white guys, we need to educate ourselves, our doctors, and our legal system about new approaches—ones that have nothing to do with surrendering control. That's something women have been experts in since the two genders began negotiating power.

Women are drinking more because they can. They have the means, and the freedom, to do it—and the stress that makes them feel they need to. They've provided a growth market for wine and spirits manufacturers in the United States, and are a bright spot for alcohol producers and importers in emerging economies from India to China, where women have typically drunk less than men. Indeed, in Uganda, the number of young women who identify themselves as "new drinkers" has edged out young men. Advertisers have taken note: In neighboring Tanzania, a beer ad shows a young couple marching down the aisle toward the altar. The groom reaches into his pocket for the bride's wedding ring, but can't find it. The bride's father glares, and the bride is disgusted. Then the beer's mascot, an animated leopard, appears out of nowhere with the glittering gold band. The bride reaches for the ring, elated, and joins the leopard in a beer-fueled wedding dance. The message is clear: Marriage will let you down, but you can count on the beer.

We're never going back to Prohibition, or the time not

so long ago when servers at the Ritz-Carlton ushered Betty Friedan from the bar and into the ladies' room lounge for her whiskey sour, since it just wasn't right for a woman to drink alone in public.

But maybe, just maybe, we can learn a thing or two from where we've been, and create a new approach to help women deal with a problem whose consequences in broken families, broken hearts, and broken futures, are all too real.

Acknowledgments

Sometimes when I see books on a bookshelf I think of the legions of people it takes to put them together: each one a small factory of thinkers, organizers, writers. This one is no different.

My first thanks go to Priscilla Painton, who suggested the idea of a book on women and alcohol on a wintry day when we both had colds. I sent her a proposal some weeks later, and we both thought it was a straightforward tale that would take me several months to put together. Her wisdom, keen eye, gifted pen, and infinite patience kept the book focused—and me calm. Michael Szczerban and Sydney Tanigawa are fabulous wordsmiths and technological mavens. (With such talent in ascendance, nobody should fear the End of Books.)

My agents, Glen Hartley and Lynn Chu, are tireless champions.

My reporting introduced me to women (and men) across the country who deepened my understanding of our country's relationship with alcohol, our regard for women who drink too much, and our health-care approach toward overdrinking altogether. Many thanks to the researchers and clinicians who work to employ science's answers for people who drink too much: Mary Ellen Barnes and Ed Wilson took endless hours to answer my questions, read my drafts, and hone my thinking. Dr. Mark Willenbring spoke to me many times, and read parts of the manuscript; Dr. Tim Norcross, Dee-Dee Stout, and Fred Rotgers were candid and unsparing about their experiences as treatment providers (and, in Dee-Dee's case, as a former drinker); Rick Grucza shared his research on current patterns; Sharon Wilsnack answered thousands of questions, including some I asked twice. She also described the mores surrounding women's drinking in the 1970s and helped me to understand how, despite the nation's current drinking patterns, some of those views can persist. Valerie Ramey added valuable insight on the American time deficit.

Lori Rotskoff read early chapters, and offered wisdom about the postwar climate in which A.A. flourished. Trysh Travis shared thoughts about her research into A.A.'s cultural impact, and Ron Roizen's questions improved my clarity. Madelon Powers debunked many myths.

I am grateful to all the women who spoke to me about this difficult subject, which remains, for so many, a shameful secret. Monica Richardson, Amy Lee Coy, and Jeannie Long laid bare their experiences, doubts, and battles. Ilse Thompson

shared her knowledge and sharp eyes. Pamela Pecs Cytron described how sympathy seemed to come more easily to friends and neighbors when she had breast cancer than when she had been in rehab. Joy spent hours to give me an accurate picture of her life, and the program that helped her. Joanna opened up her house—and salad provisions—to me as a complete stranger, and became a friend in the process. Louise welcomed me to Ohio, offered pithy commentary, and answered legal questions throughout.

I spoke and wrote to hundreds of women whose faulty shut-off valves plague them still, and I am deeply grateful for their willingness to talk to me. Their stories help demonstrate the complexity of female drinking today, and at least some of what drives it. Samantha, a retired federal prosecutor, described how wine and vodka helped her unwind from white-knuckled days trying some of her region's most unsavory criminals. Bridget, an intelligence officer in the early days of the Iraq war, told me about the bombing deaths of the civilians for whom she felt responsible. Merlot was the only thing that helped erase the gruesome images she saw on her desk. Sharon, an engineer at one of the nation's most demanding information technology firms, told me of her failed attempts at rehab—and spoke mournfully of losing custody of her three boys because of it. Cecilia, an environmental scientist in the Gulf of Mexico, was grieving her mother's death when the Deepwater Horizon catastrophe decimated the wildlife she so cherished and had dedicated her career to protecting. There were so many others: women who patiently answered questions that were surely uncomfortable to answer—about arrests while driving drunk; about jail time; about infidelities. Many described the

painful experiences of being abused at the hands of those they hoped would help them. Because so many wished to remain anonymous, their stories are woven into the background of much of what I wrote.

On my reporting trips, I had great hosts: Darieck Scott and Stephen Liacouras in San Francisco, and Michael Hawley in Los Angeles. In St. Helena, Pat Perini and Bob Long welcomed and fed me, and shared their own marvelous wines, and along with Harvey Posert and Margrit Biever Mondavi helped describe the vast changes taking place in their corner of the world in the 1970s and '80s. So, too, did Zelma Long, Axel Borg, and Ann Noble.

During the three years it took to put this together, my family was tolerant, patient, and encouraging even when I didn't reciprocate their courtesies. My daughters, Ilana, Moriah, and Dalia Engelberg, were kind, bright stars and impeccable culture-watchers, often spotting verities and memes I didn't even know existed. My sister, Michelle Glaser Jackson, listened to me talk, and helped me diagram, sometimes on place mats and used envelopes, patterns I hadn't seen myself. My sister-in-law, clinical psychologist Elizabeth Engelberg, shared her expertise about contemporary female struggles. My father-in-law, Edward Engelberg, watched out for the latest stories and studies on Americans and booze. My mother, Virginia Glaser, was a wise, kind, and thoughtful reader who gave me fabulous background on the social landscape of the 1950s, '60s, '70s, and '80s, and often challenged me to be clearer and more concise. My father, Steve Glaser, helped expand my palate—always with the moderation of which he is a model. I could not dream of better fortune than having them all in my orbit.

My neighbors and friends never told me to shut up even as I'm sure I bored them with booze talk. Thanks to Diana Arkoulakis, Martha Ann Overland, Val Thomas, Henry Reisch, Amy Putman, Nina Rosenstein, Dale Russakoff, Nomi Kehati, Netaya Anbar, Leslie Mitchel Bond, Tracy Weber, Nikole Hannah-Jones, Joyce Weatherford, Melissa Deutsch, Jennifer Dominguez, Cliff and Robin Kulwin. The great literary sage Flip Brophy listened, advised, and made soup.

I also had the great luck to marry a man who is brilliant, funny, and dazzlingly optimistic—especially when I'm not. Stephen Engelberg edited this manuscript many times, and talked me up from my book tunnel with alarming regularity. Thanks to him—for pretty much everything.

Notes

1: *Lush*

18 *In the same period, the rate for young men rose only 8 percent:* Aaron White et al, "Hospitalizations for Alcohol and Drug Overdoses in Young Adults Ages 18–24 in the United States, 1999–2008: Results from the Nationwide Inpatient Sample," *Journal of Studies on Alcohol and Drugs* 72 (September 2011): 774–86.

19 *In 2011, students at Rutgers University chose:* Gus Lubin, "State University Rutgers Paid Snooki $32,000 for a Speech about Partying and Tanning," *Business Insider* (April 4, 2011): http://articles .businessinsider.com/2011-04-04/news/29965833_1_snooki -budget-gap-commencement-address.

20 *In 2010, Gallup pollsters reported:* Gallup, "U.S. Drinking Rate Edges Up Slightly to 25-Year High" (July 30, 2010): www.gallup .com/poll/141656/drinking-rate-edges-slightly-year-high.asp.

20 *White women are more likely to drink:* Raul Caetano et al., "Socio-demographic Predictors of Pattern and Volume of Alcohol Consumption across Hispanics, Blacks, and Whites: 10-Year Trend (1992–2002)," *Alcoholism: Clinical and Experimental Research* 34, no. 10 (October 2010). This study did not examine Asian American women, who traditionally drink less than any group in the United States due in part to their inability to tolerate alcohol. Nor did it include Native American women, whose communities have been disproportionately devastated by the toxic effects of alcohol. I also interviewed Caetano by phone on March 16, 2011.

21 *Women are the wine industry's most enthusiastic:* This figure is well known in the wine industry, and documented in many surveys and papers, including Sharon Dean et al, "Women and Wine: An Analysis of This Important Market Segment" (paper, Fifth International Wine Business Research Conference, Auckland, New Zealand, February 8–10, 2010): http://academyofwinebusiness.com/wp-content/uploads/2010/04/ForbesCohenDean-Women-and-wine.pdf.

21 *Despite the recession or perhaps because of it:* WineMarketCouncil.com, http:/winemarketcouncil.com/?page_id=35.

21 *Not all that wine is being decorously sipped:* Centers for Disease Control and Prevention, "Binge Drinking," *Vital Signs* (January 10, 2012): www.cdc.gov/vitalsigns/bingedrinking.

21 *We often hear:* Interview, Dafna Kanny, senior scientist, Centers for Disease Control and Prevention, June 19, 2013.

21 *No surprise, then, that the number of women arrested for drunk driving: 2011 Annual Report of the California DUI Management Information System to the California Legislature:* www.dmv.ca.gov/about/profile/rd/r_d_report/Section%205/S5-233.pdf.

22 *There is evidence that alcohol dependence among women:* Richard A. Grucza et al, "Secular Trends in the Lifetime Prevalence of Al-

cohol Dependence in the United States: A Re-evaluation," *Alcoholism: Clinical and Experimental Research* 32, no. 5 (May 2008).

22   *Sharon Wilsnack, a psychologist at the University of North Dakota:* Sharon C. Wilsnack, interview with author, March 23, 2011. Wilsnack's quotes in this chapter come from that interview and a second interview on June 14, 2011.

23   *That dovetails with what Rick Grucza, an epidemiologist:* Richard A. Grucza, interview with author, May 15, 2009.

24   *Women of childbearing age are incessantly warned that alcohol poses a danger:* For reference on this or any other physical effects, see "Women and Alcohol: What You Need to Know," Harvard Health Publications, accessed September 12, 2012, www.helpguide .org/harvard/women_alcohol.htm.

24   *In California, the number of young women responsible for alcohol-related accidents jumped: Orange County Drinking and Driving 2008 Community Forum, Executive Summary,* accessed July 2, 2010, www.ochealthinfo.com/docs/public/adept/OCHCA-Executive -summary-2009.pdf.

24   *While the number of U.S. drunk-driving deaths fell:* National Highway Traffic Safety Administration, "Traffic Safety Facts, 2010 Data," accessed September 12, 2012, www-nrd.nhtsa.dot.gov/Pubs /811606.pdf.

24   *One way to measure the changes in women's drinking habits:* Substance Abuse Treatment Admissions by Primary Substance of Abuse, Office of Applied Statistics, Substance Abuse and Mental Health Services Administration, "Treatment Episode Data Set, January 7, 2010," accessed August 12, 2012, www.samhsa.gov/data/2k10/208/208Women Alc2k10web.pdf. The data are kept in files called the Treatment Episode Data Set, or TEDS. Of course, they reveal only the people who seek treatment, who represent a small percentage of people who actually have a drinking problem. Nevertheless, the statistics are telling.

2: *We Are Women, Hear Us Pour*

27 *Women are twice as likely to suffer from anxiety and depression:* Throughout my reporting, this fact was repeated frequently. See "Women and Alcohol: What You Need to Know," Harvard Health Publications, accessed September 12, 2012, www.helpguide.org /harvard/women_alcohol.htm.

28 *Until recently, nobody even thought to look at how differently alcohol:* F. Gerard Moeller, "Sex, Stress, and Drug Cues in Addiction," *American Journal of Psychiatry* (April 1, 2012): http://ajp .psychiatryonline.org/article.aspx?articleid=1090656. In this editorial, Moeller discusses several studies, including the 2012 Yale study. This is the study: Marc Potenza et al, "Neural Correlates of Stress-Induced and Cue-Induced Drug Craving: Influences of Sex and Cocaine Dependence," *American Journal of Psychiatry* (April 1, 2012): http://ajp.psychiatryonline.org/article.aspx?articleid=426881.

28 *In a study she conducted as a graduate student at Harvard:* Sharon C. Wilsnack, interview with author, March 23, 2011.

30 *Mrs. Kennedy praised their graceful simplicity: NBC News Time Capsule: Jacqueline Kennedy: The White House Tour,* February 14, 1962, accessed September 10, 2012, www.hulu.com/watch/5135. The number of viewers—56 million—was repeated frequently on the fiftieth anniversary of the tour. NPR's indomitable Sara Fishko repeated it on *On the Media,* accessed February 20, 2012, www.onthemedia .org/2012/feb/10/jacqueline-kennedys-white-house/transcript.

30 *But anybody could buy her crystal:* Jeffrey B. Snyder, "The Gavel: Morgantown Glass Graced the White House," accessed April 1, 2012, www.thegavel.net/morgan.html.

30 *When Letitia Baldrige, Mrs. Kennedy's social secretary:* Excerpt from Marie Smith, *Entertaining in the White House* (Washington, D.C.: Acropolis Books, 1967), accessed May 10, 2012, www.jfklibrary.org

/Research/Ready-Reference/JFK-Miscellaneous-Information /Entertaining-in-the-White-House.aspx. Baldrige herself describes the reaction of the press—and teetotaling politicians—to the free-flowing liquor in a number of recollections. One is in this memoir: Letitia Baldrige, *A Lady, First: My Life in the Kennedy White House and the American Embassies of Paris and Rome* (New York: Penguin, 2002), 171–72.

31 *Rick Grucza, the Washington University epidemiologist:* Richard A. Grucza, interview with author, May 15, 2009.

31 *Between 1940 and 1960, the number of women:* Claudia Goldin et al., "The Homecoming of American College Women: The Reversal of the College Gender Gap," *Journal of Economic Perspectives* 20, no. 4 (Fall 2006): 133.

31 *By 1963, Gallup pollsters found that 63 percent:* Frank Newport et al., "Long-Term Gallup Poll Trends: A Portrait of American Public Opinion Through the Century," Gallup News Service, December 20, 1999, www.gallup.com/poll/3400/LongTerm-Gallup -Poll-Trends-Portrait-American-Public-Opinion.aspx#1.

32 *By the mid-1970s, Gallup divided respondents:* Tracey Sugar, e-mail message to author, February 15, 2012. Sugar sent me some attachments that showed the gender breakdown of the poll from 1977, 1982, and 1987. In an e-mail message to me on February 2, 2012, Sugar told me that the company doesn't have archived tabulations of polls prior to the mid-1970s.

32 *At the end of the 1970s, nearly half of all women: Women in the Labor Force, 1970–2009,* U.S. Department of Labor, Bureau of Labor Statistics chart, January 5, 2011, www.bls.gov/opub/ted/2011 /ted_20110105_data.htm.

32 *Grucza calls this voyage to a new world:* Richard A. Grucza, interview with author, May 15, 2009.

33 *Harvey Posert, one of the industry's first marketers:* Harvey Pos-

ert, interview with author, February 3, 2010. Though we met three times, the recollections described here come from our second meeting, which took place on that date.

35   *A pamphlet the wine industry circulated to grocers:* This material comes from an undated pamphlet from the library of the Wine Institute in San Francisco. Posert guessed that it came from the late 1950s or early '60s.

36   *In California, where laws allowed the sale of wine in supermarkets:* Julia Flynn Siler, *The House of Mondavi: The Rise and Fall of an American Wine Dynasty* (New York: Gotham Books, 2007), 199.

37   *The University of California at Davis library has a vast collection:* UC Davis librarian Axel Borg is one of those superhuman people you feel lucky to meet. I met him for the first time on January 29, 2010, when he generously showed me the collections at the marvelous Peter Shields library. He is a giant ex-Marine with a shaved head and goatee, and an encyclopedic knowledge of California's food and wine history. The university honored him in 2011 at an awards ceremony you can read about here: http://dateline.ucdavis.edu/dl_detail.lasso?id=13748.

37   *The report, called "Wine and Women: A Ladies' Home Journal Reader Reaction":* The seventy-page report is titled simply "Wine and Women: A Ladies' Home Journal Reader Reaction Bureau Report." It lacks a date. In dozens of interviews at the University of California at Davis and in Napa and St. Helena, I met no one who could remember it.

38   *But it was clear the industry was seeking early adopters:* "Early adopters" is a phrase popularized by sociologist Everett M. Rogers in his 1962 book, *Diffusion of Innovations* (New York: Free Press, 2003). Now in its fifth printing, the book describes how new ideas disperse over time.

38   *By the early 1970s, wine was ubiquitous:* These headlines were compiled in Wine Institute Bulletins, 1970–1979. The Wine Institute Library in San Francisco kept detailed logs of wine's ap-

pearances and local news. I spotted "The Anti-Tension Diet" in *McCall's*, February 1977: 54.

38 *In the 1970s, sixty-two million newspapers were sold:* Pew Research Center's Project for Excellence in Journalism, "2004 Daily and Sunday Circulation," March 14, 2004, www.journalism.org/node/793.

39 *"Anything to get people to taste it, to familiarize themselves":* Harvey Posert, interview with author, May 18, 2010.

39 *For Margrit Biever, who would become Mondavi's second wife:* Margrit Biever Mondavi, interview with author, May 18, 2010.

40 *By the late 1970s, the quality of California wines:* At a 1976 blind tasting in Paris known as the "Judgment of Paris," a panel of judges selected a California chardonnay and a cabernet sauvignon as the top wines. The results surprised everybody.

40 *They helped put traditional little Napa on the map:* Statistics on U.S. wine consumption are from the Wine Institute, accessed June 1, 2012, www.wineinstitute.org/resources/statistics/article86.

41 *One was a young scientist named Zelma Long:* Zelma Long, interview with author, January 14, 2010.

42 *Taste tests from the early California whites:* Harvey Posert, interview with author, February 3, 2010.

42 *"For people who were new to wine, it had a rich":* Zelma Long, interview with author, September 1, 2010.

43 *depending on its alcohol content:* Vintner Bob Long, interview with author, February 2, 2010.

43 *Today, women buy nearly two-thirds of the 784 million gallons:* Andrew Adam Newman, "Marketing Wine as a Respite for Women's Many Roles," *New York Times* (August 29, 2012).

45 *Psychologist Bruce Alexander, a Canadian addiction expert:* Bruce K. Alexander, *The Roots of Addiction in Free Market Society* (Vancouver, B.C.: Canadian Center for Policy Alternatives, April 2001), 1. In this fascinating book, Alexander points to the rise of

addiction throughout the world—particularly when traditional tribal societies are crushed, or when an advanced one crumples.

48   *A few years ago, Valerie Ramey, an economist at the University of California:* Valerie Ramey, interview with author, October 27, 2010.

52   *By studying Bureau of Labor Statistics data from 1965 to 2007:* Garey Ramey and Valerie Ramey, "The Rug Rat Race," *Brookings Papers on Economic Activity* (Spring 2010): 129–76.

53   *In other words, the rise in child-care time resulted:* Ibid., 130.

54   *According to a 2009 study released by two Wharton School economists:* Betsey Stevenson and Justin Wolfers, "The Paradox of Declining Female Happiness," *American Economic Journal: Economic Policy 2009* 1, no. 2: 190–225, August. http://bpp.wharton .upenn.edu/betseys/papers/Female_Happiness.pdf.

55   *"Or," Stevenson and Wolfers conclude, "women may":* Ibid., 224.

3: *I Have to See a Man about a Dog*

58   *On frigid Sunday mornings, Puritan worshipers filed:* W. J. Rorabaugh, *The Alcoholic Republic: An American Tradition* (New York: Oxford University Press, 1979), 28.

59   *"It disperseth melancholly & causeth cheerfulness":* Karen Hess, transcriber, *Martha Washington's Booke of Cookery and Booke of Sweetmeats* (New York: Columbia University Press, 1996), 397.

59   *Capon Ale:* Ibid., 393.

60   *Betsy Ross's sister was expelled:* Marla R. Miller, *Betsy Ross and the Making of America* (New York: Henry Holt, 2010), 247.

60   *During the Revolutionary War, General Henry Knox:* Betty Sowers Alt and Bonnie Domrose Stone, *Campfollowing: A History of the Military Wife* (New York: Praeger, 1991), 55.

60   *Rush wrote a pamphlet about the effects of alcohol:* Rorabaugh, *The Alcoholic Republic,* 39–46.

61   *In his investigation of early American drinking:* Ibid., 8.

61   *Buffalo, transformed by the completion of the Erie:* Stephen R. Pow-
       ell, "Rushing the Growler: A History of Brewing and Drinking in
       Buffalo," accessed September 12, 2012, www.buffalonian.com
       /history/industry/brewing/growler/chapIII/buffsalooncapitol.html.

61   *New York State had a distillery for every:* For the number of dis-
       tilleries in New York State, see Rorabaugh, *The Alcoholic Repub-
       lic,* 87. For population figures, see *The State of New York Census
       of 1825,* New York State Library Online Catalog, accessed Sep-
       tember 14, 2012, http://128.121.13.244:8080/awweb/main.jsp?smd
       =2&did=79111&nt=browse5. Census figures show a population
       of 1.6 million, which results in one distillery per every fourteen
       hundred residents.

61   *"Bread is considered the staff of life":* Kenneth L. Holmes, ed.,
       *Covered Wagon Women: Diaries & Letters from the Western
       Trails,* vol. 8 (Glendale, CA: Arthur H. Clark, 1983), 252.

62   *From Tennessee to Alaska, there are nearly:* Geographical Names
       Information Service, U.S. Board on Geographic Names, accessed
       July 1, 2012, http://geonames.usgs.gov/pls/gnispublic/f?p=154:2:
       4397204383716030::NO:RP::.

64   *The most popular guidance came in a magazine:* Anne C. Rose,
       *Voices of the Marketplace: American Thought and Culture,
       1830–1860* (Lanham, MD: Rowman & Littlefield, 2004), 75. I also
       found information about *Godey's* and Hale at the University of
       Vermont's Godey's Lady's Book website: www.uvm.edu/%7Ehag
       /godey/contents.html.

64   *When she serialized T. S. Arthur's antialcohol novel:* T. S. Arthur,
       Ten Nights in a Bar-Room and What I Saw There (Bedford, MA:
       Applewood, 2000; originally published in Philadelphia by Lippin-
       cott, Grambo & Co., 1855). I had access to a hard copy, but I also
       found it on OpenLibrary.org, accessed May 2, 2012, http://archive

.org/stream/10nightsinabarroom00arthrich#page/n7/mode/2up.
For more, see Graham Donald Warder, "Selling Sobriety: How
Temperance Reshaped Culture in Antebellum America" (Ph.D.
diss., University of Massachusetts, Amherst, 2000), *Electronic
Doctoral Dissertations for UMass Amherst,* Paper AAI9960803;
http://scholarworks.umass.edu/dissertations/AAI9960803/.

64 *Meanwhile, a group of six ex-drinkers had formed:* The influence
of the Washingtonians on the U.S. attitude toward drinking should
not be underestimated. Mark Edward Lender and James Kirby
Martin discuss the Washingtonians in their wonderful overview of
American alcohol culture, *Drinking in America: A History* (New
York: Free Press, 1987), 74–79. Daniel Okrent does as well in *Last
Call: The Rise and Fall of Prohibition* (New York: Scribner, 2010),
9–12. William L. White also explores the group's history in *Slaying
the Dragon: The History of Addiction Treatment and Recovery in
America* (Bloomington, IL: Chestnut Health Systems, 1998), 8–14.

65 *In 1874, a group launched the Woman's Christian:* "Early History,"
WCTU.org, accessed May 1, 2012, www.wctu.org/earlyhistory.
Hundreds of historians have written about the WTCU's influence
on American society.

65 *The WCTU, which required that members be white:* Okrent, *Last
Call,* gives a lively overview in chapter 1, "Thunderous Drums and
Protestant Nuns." See also Andrew Sinclair, *Prohibition: The Era
of Excess* (London: Faber & Faber, 2009), first published in 1962.
Sinclair discusses the reformers' "textbook crusade" on pages 62
to 66. Finally, David Hanson, who blogs at *Alcohol: Problems and
Solutions,* has an excellent overview as well. He keeps a more cur-
rent log of temperance leaders here: www2.potsdam.edu/hansondj
/Controversies/1124913901.html, accessed September 12, 2012.

67 *Carry Nation, a manic middle-aged Kentuckian:* I first learned
about Carry Nation in Jerry Brenneman's AP history class in Al-

bany, Oregon, and was so fascinated by her fervor, I wrote my first-ever term paper on her. I refreshed my memory with Sinclair's *Prohibition*, Okrent's *Last Call*, and of course, Nation's florid 1905 autobiography, *The Use and Need of the Life of Carry A. Nation*. You can find a digital version here: www.gutenberg.org /dirs/etext98/crntn10.txt, accessed September 6, 2012.

68   *Over hearty chicken soup and the roar of some firefighters:* Madelon Powers, interview with author, December 4, 2010.

69   *Powers recounts the story of:* Madelon Powers, *Faces along the Bar: Lore and Order in the Workingman's Saloon, 1870–1920* (Chicago: University of Chicago Press, 1998), 210–11.

70   *Abstaining from alcohol didn't mean middle-class women:* Stephen R. Kandall, *Substance and Shadow: Women and Addiction in the United States* (Cambridge, MA: Harvard University Press, 1999), 22.

70   *They also made Lydia Pinkham a wealthy woman:* Okrent, *Last Call*, 194.

71   *Many Victorian-era women, including reformers:* Catherine Gilbert Murdock, *Domesticating Drink: Women, Men, and Alcohol in America, 1870–1940* (Baltimore: Johns Hopkins Press, 1998), 42–69.

71   *Twenty-one thousand American women had served as nurses:* "Women in the U.S. Army," www.army.mil/women/history.html.

71   *Tens of thousands more had attended college:* Claudia Goldin et al, "The Homecoming of American College Women: The Reversal of the College Gender Gap," *National Bureau of Economic Research*, NBER Working Paper Series (March 2006): 1, http://faculty.smu .edu/millimet/classes/eco7321/papers/goldin%20et%20al.pdf.

71   *It was so common for women to join:* "Running Wild: College Students in the 1920s," accessed April 2, 2012, www.flapperjane.c /September%2004/running_wild.htm.

72   *In* This Side of Paradise, *F. Scott Fitzgerald:* F. Scott Fit *This Side of Paradise* (New York: Modern Library, 200

73   *Women who, a few years before, would have blanched:* Frederick Lewis Allen, *Only Yesterday: An Informal History of the 1920s* (New York: Harper Collins, 1931), 111–12.

73   *In the first year, consumption was estimated:* Okrent, *Last Call*, p. 361.

74   *As Gilbert Murdock put it, the Eighteenth Amendment:* Gilbert Murdock, *Domesticating Drink*, p. 69.

75   *Karpman laid out his jaundiced view of female drinkers in his preface:* Benjamin Karpman, *The Alcoholic Woman: Case Studies in the Psychodynamics of Alcoholism* (Washington, D.C.: Linacre Press, 1948). These quotes, as well as the reaction to his 1934 talk, appear in the preface of the book, vii–x.

76   *He attributed the excess drinking of a patient named Frances:* Karpman dissects the poor woman in the chapter called "The Case of Mrs. Frances Elliott," Ibid., 119–223.

76   *Another patient, Vera, had a sadistic mother:* This comes from Karpman's analysis of Mrs. Vera Banchek, Ibid., 66–118.

77   *The third woman, Elizabeth, also had physically:* Karpman describes Miss Elizabeth Chesser, Ibid., 1–67.

78   *Colleagues revered Karpman, the author of dozens:* In the May 23, 1960, issue of *Time*, an unbylined article titled "Medicine: Criminal or Insane" described Karpman as "patriarchally bearded." They quoted him as saying: "Is the accused sick or not? You can't have mental illness and criminal responsibility in the same person at the same time?" When he died of a heart attack in 1962, death notices appeared in three journals, including the *American Journal of Psy-* The quoted obituary here was written by Bernard Cru-...rpman, 1886–1962." I found it here: http://ajp .../Journals/AJP/2663/1119.pdf, accessed ...ore, take a look at Karpman's Wikipedia ...dia.org/wiki/Benjamin_Karpman.

...*ist described the "Bistro Berthas":* These snip-

pets from the news appear in an excellent chapter in the anthology *Altering American Consciousness: The History of Alcohol and Drug Abuse in the United States, 1800–2000* (Amherst and Boston: University of Massachusetts Press, 2004). The chapter "Lady Tipplers: Gendering the Modern Alcoholism Paradigm, 1933–1960" was written by Michelle McClellan, an assistant professor of history at the University of Michigan.

79   *Noel Busch, a writer at* Life *magazine:* Noel F. Bush, "Lady Tipplers: Suggestions Are Offered for Improving Their Behavior," *Life* (April 14, 1947), 85. I found a paper copy that belonged to a collector friend, but you can see the piece for yourself here. It is a stunning reminder of how casually sexist U.S. society was: http://books .google.com/books?id=ik0EAAAAMBAJ&printsec=frontcover& source=gbs_ge_summary_r&cad=0#v=onepage&q&f=false.

79   *It went through several printings in the 1950s:* This information comes from Amazon.com, accessed April 7, 2012, www.amazon .com/The-Alcoholic-Woman-Benjamin-Karpman/dp/B000RT FUBS/ref=tmm_mmp_title_0.

4: *One Day at a Time: A.A. and Women*

81   *Founded by two men in the mid-1930s:* Many sources, on and off the record, referred openly to A.A.'s rocky early history with women; Marty Mann, the first woman who is said to have become sober in A.A., discussed it at Alcoholics Anonymous meeting in Toronto, July 1965. A recording is available at http://cpaulus .com/talks/OldTimers/MartyMann.mp3, accessed September 14, 2012. William L. White describes it in *Slaying the Dragon*, 158–62.

For this chapter, I consulted many Wilson biographies and films, as well as his own writings. They include *Alcoholics Anonymous,* Fourth Edition (New York: Alcoholics Anonymous World

Services, 2001); *As Bill Sees It* (New York: Alcoholics Anonymous World Services, 1967); Wilson's own *Alcoholics Anonymous Comes of Age* (New York: Alcoholics Anonymous World Services, 1957); and *Not-God: A History of Alcoholics Anonymous,* by Ernest Kurtz (Center City, MN: Hazelden, 1979). I also relied on these biographies: Francis Hartigan, *Bill W.: A Biography of Alcoholics Anonymous Cofounder Bill Wilson* (New York: Thomas Dunne Books, 2000); Susan Cheever, *My Name Is Bill: His Life and the Creation of Alcoholics Anonymous* (New York: Washington Square Press, 2004); and Nan Robertson, *Getting Better: Inside Alcoholics Anonymous* (New York: William Morrow, 1988).

Cheever has written about her own experiences with A.A., and is on the board of the National Council on Alcoholism and Drug Dependency, originally founded by Marty Mann. Hartigan served as Lois Wilson's personal secretary. Robertson, who died in 2009, was a journalist at the *New York Times* for four decades. I met her when I worked there as a news assistant the year she retired.

There is a great deal more less flattering information about Wilson on blogs that are critical of A.A., but even these biographies, from within the A.A. community, reveal untrustworthy traits in a man who encouraged others to be "rigorously honest."

82   *In more than 90 percent of the nation's rehab facilities:* Mark Willenbring, M.D., interview with author, May 13, 2011. Willenbring is a psychiatrist in private practice in the Twin Cities, and from 2004 to 2009 served as director of the Treatment and Recovery Research Division of the National Institute on Alcohol Abuse and Alcoholism/National Institutes of Health.

83   *Patients called the method, which had been developed:* Cheever, *My Name Is Bill,* 13.

84   *Like many innovators, Wilson was complicated:* Hartigan describes Wilson's paranormal and LSD experiments in *Bill W.,* pages 176 to

179, and describes his womanizing at length on pages 190 to 197. Robertson touches on his womanizing in *Getting Better,* pages 36, 40, and 84.

85 *As the group spread, Wilson and other early members:* The twelve steps of Alcoholics Anonymous are listed in Alcoholics Anonymous World Services, *Alcoholics Anonymous,* 59–60. The title of the chapter is "How It Works." The steps remain unchanged since the first edition.

THE TWELVE STEPS OF ALCOHOLICS ANONYMOUS

1. We admitted we were powerless over alcohol—that our lives had become unmanageable.
2. Came to believe that a Power greater than ourselves could restore us to sanity.
3. Made a decision to turn our will and our lives over to the care of God *as we understood Him.*
4. Made a searching and fearless moral inventory of ourselves.
5. Admitted to God, to ourselves, and to another human being the exact nature of our wrongs.
6. Were entirely ready to have God remove all these defects of character.
7. Humbly asked Him to remove our shortcomings.
8. Made a list of all persons we had harmed, and became willing to make amends to them all.
9. Made direct amends to such people wherever possible, except when to do so would injure them or others.
10. Continued to take personal inventory and when we were wrong promptly admitted it.
11. Sought through prayer and meditation to improve our conscious contact with God, *as we understood Him,* praying only for knowledge of His will for us and the power to carry that out.
12. Having had a spiritual awakening as the result of these Steps, we tried to carry this message to alcoholics, and to practice these principles in all our affairs.

86   *But in the A.A. worldview, a woman's most:* Alcoholics Anonymous World Services, *Alcoholics Anonymous,* chapter 5, "To Wives," 111. This chapter remains in the most recent edition. A.A.'s website maintains that Bill Wilson wrote the chapter against his wife Lois's wishes. Accessed February 15, 2012, www.aa.org/subpage.cfm?page=287#tres.

86   *"To my lot falls the rather doubtful distinction":* Florence R., "A Feminine Victory." This story appeared in the first edition of *Alcoholics Anonymous,* but later was omitted after she died, having returned to drinking. Her story can be found at http://fellowship12.com/index .php?option=com_content&view=article&id=110&Itemid=172, accessed September 13, 2012. Her biography appears on www .silkworth.net, "A New Light: The First Forty," accessed September 13, 2012, http://silkworth.net/dickb/thefirstforty.html.

86   *Records from the period show the men of A.A. worried:* Anonymous, "The Good Old Times," *Grapevine* 42, no. 1 (June 1985).

87   *But few men tolerated alcoholic women:* Sally Brown and David R. Brown, *A Biography of Mrs. Marty Mann: The First Lady of Alcoholics Anonymous* (Center City, MN: Hazelden, 2001), 116.

87   *To manage this potential distraction:* White, *Slaying the Dragon,* 158.

87   *Women-only meetings developed, too:* Ibid., 160.

87   *Her name was Marty Mann, and in 1939:* Brown and Brown, *A Biography,* gives a deeply researched and unvarnished view of Mann's life.

88   *To the men, Mann recalled, she was:* Marty Mann, Toronto speech, 1965.

89   *"This was a man's problem and A.A. was":* Ibid.

89   *As late as 1959, Mann noted disapprovingly:* Marty Mann, in a 1960 pamphlet called "For Men Only? AA Today: A Special Publication by the AA Grapevine Commemorating the 25th Anniversary of Alcoholics Anonymous" (New York: AA Grapevine, The International Journal of Alcoholics Anonymous, 1960): 33, www .barefootsworld.net/aaformenonlygvjune1960.html.

89 *"We hide," she said. "We do our drinking":* Mann, Toronto speech, 1965.

90 *Science could boost the movement, and so the research:* Ron Roizen, "The American Discovery of Alcoholism, 1933–1939" (Ph.D. diss., University of California, Berkeley, 1991), accessed September 14, 2012, www.roizen.com/ron/disshome.htm. Roizen's dissertation has been exceedingly helpful to me in this research, as has Roizen, who is a lively and generous conversationalist and even more energetic e-mailer. Roizen discusses the connection between brewers and early alcoholism studies on his blog, www.roizen .com/ron/sidetracked.htm.

90 *Mann attended the Yale summer school:* Ron Roizen delves into this here: www.roizen.com/ron/rr11.htm, accessed September 14, 2012. He explains it this way: Roizen queried University of Leipzig's archivist, K. Gaukel, about Jellinek's degrees. Gaukel found Jellinek's records as a linguistics and history student—but never a degree of any kind, and certainly not a medical one. I also checked with Stanford University, where Jellinek was working when he died of a heart attack in 1963, for confirmation of what Jellinek had claimed on his résumé before being hired. Drew Bourn, curator at the Stanford Medical History Center, Lane Medical Library & Knowledge Management Center, told me in an e-mail (May 13, 2011) that Jellinek's file listed the following institutions: University of Berlin 1908–1910; University of Grenoble, France, 1910–1911; University of Leipzig 1911–1914; M.Ed., 1913; Sc.D., 1936. Roizen dug up other interesting jobs, including stints at a hospital in Hungary for "nervous children"; as a currency trader; at a steamship line in Sierra Leone; and as a banana researcher for United Fruit in Honduras—all before turning to alcohol research. Like Roizen, I think that somebody ought to do a biography of the guy. Whatever you want to say, he had a fascinating life.

91   *Data for one of his early studies:* Trysh Travis, "Points: The Blog of the Alcohol and Drugs History Society: What Time Do You Want It to Be, Part Two, May 28, 2011," http://pointsadhsblog.wordpress .com/2011/05/28/what-time-do-you-want-it-to-be-part-two.

91   *This left ninety-eight self-selected white men:* E. M. Jellinek, "Phases in the Drinking History of Alcoholics: Analysis of a Survey Conducted by the Official Organ of Alcoholics Anonymous," *Quarterly Journal of Studies on Alcohol* (June 7, 1946): 1–88. You can also see a reprint of the 1946 paper here, including a footnote in which Jellinek explains why he tossed the female responses: http://silkworth.net/sociology/Soc04OCR.pdf.

91   *Over the next many years:* You can see a copy of an early rendering of the chart here: http://pointsadhsblog.wordpress.com/2011/05/28 /what-time-do-you-want-it-to-be-part-two.

Historians caution about the need to view documents and attitudes in the context of the period, but by the early 1940s researchers had developed penicillin and sulfa drugs; antihistamines; and vaccines that offered protection from typhus, yellow fever, and pertussis. So judging by those standards, it's hard to believe this was ever considered science.

British alcohol researcher Max Glatt published a study in which he concluded that group therapy was useful for alcoholics. It built on Jellenek's earlier work and chart, this time using a parabola. M. M. Glatt, "Group Therapy in Alcoholism," *The British Journal of Addiction,* vol. LIX, No. 2, January 1958.

92   *The misapplication of the word could only undermine:* E. M. Jellinek, "Phases of Alcohol Addiction," *Quarterly Journal of Studies on Alcohol* (December 13, 1952): 673–84.

92   *He acknowledged that his conclusions were:* E. M. Jellinek, *The Disease Concept of Alcoholism* (Mansfield, CT: Martino Publishing, 2010), 38.

92   *At a 1959 alcoholism conference at Columbia University:* Arthur
      H. Cain, "Alcoholics Anonymous: Cult or Cure?" *Harper's* (Feb-
      ruary 1963), 48. Cain was a psychologist who admired A.A. in its
      early days, but grew dismayed when it began to grow "ritualistic."
      He traced its popularity to a slew of positive magazine and news-
      paper stories in the 1940s.

93   *Jellinek wrote that "recovered alcoholics in Alcoholics Anonymous
      speak of ":* Jellinek, *The Disease Concept of Alcoholism,* 41.

93   *In his book* Alcohol: The World's Favorite Drug*:* Griffith Ed-
      wards, *Alcohol: The World's Favorite Drug* (New York: Thomas
      Dunne, 2000), 97.

94   *Marty Mann was remarkably gifted at spinning the bottle:* Marty Mann
      is a revered figure in the twelve-step community, and she certainly had
      a lot of guts. The Brown and Brown biography, *A Biography of Mrs.
      Marty Mann,* gives a reverential but clear-eyed view of her personal
      life. Ron Roizen draws a more complete picture, rounding out her
      professional aims (and compromises) in his blog: http://www.roizen
      .com/ron/mann.htm, accessed June 26, 2013. He points out some
      rather startling details about her massaging of facts in what endures, at
      least culturally, in our concept of alcoholism. I also read Mann's own
      books: *Marty Mann Answers Your Questions about Drinking and
      Alcoholism* (New York: Holt, Rinehart and Winston, 1970) and *Mar-
      ty Mann's New Primer on Alcoholism: How People Drink, How to
      Recognize Alcoholics and What to Do about Them* (New York: Holt,
      Rinehart and Winston, 1958). That title alone is a bold assertion about
      just how alcoholics could be *fixed.* Mine is a 1981 edition.

94   *In the 1940s, newspapers and national magazines:* There were
      many stories that sparked interest in the group, but perhaps the
      most important was written by Jack Alexander in the popular
      weekly *The Saturday Evening Post,* on March 1, 1941. His piece,
      "Alcoholics Anonymous: Freed Slaves of Drink, Now They Free

Others," generated thousands of letters to A.A.'s office in New York. Eight years after publication, Bill Wilson wrote to Alexander to request a follow-up that would give an "inside view" of the organization. Alexander complied, and wrote a second piece, "The Drunkard's Best Friend," that ran in the *Post* on April 1, 1950. The correspondence is available on A.A.'s website: www.aa.org/lang /en/subpage.cfm?page=472, accessed September 19, 2012.

94   *On radio and television shows, men poured out:* You can find a list of the appearances here: http://silkworth.net/aagrowth/mich_Detroit .html. Detroit media magnate William Edmund Scripps was an admirer of the group, and helped to publicize it in his outlets.

94   *In 1945, moviegoers turned* The Lost Weekend: As I was researching this chapter, for a couple of weeks my kids would come home from school and find me watching old movies. My youngest daughter was about eight or nine when she tiptoed into my room for a pencil, and whispered to a playmate that Mom was "working even if she didn't look like it." It hardly felt like it. *Some Like It Hot* (released 1959) is funny enough to "disperseth melancholly," and Richard Burton and Elizabeth Taylor soar in *Who's Afraid of Virginia Woolf?* ("Martha, rubbing alcohol for you?" "Sure. Never mix, never worry!" (released 1966). As a kid, I watched the *Thin Man* movies with my grandmother, who was a big fan of Myrna Loy. I was too young to really get the cocktail jokes, but it was so much fun to be with my giggling grandmother, I laughed alongside her. I watched parts of some of the films again, and was amazed at how stark the contrast was between the first *Thin Man* movie, in 1934, and *The Lost Weekend*, eleven years later. I'm hardly the first person to notice this, of course: Cultural historian Lori Rotskoff examines these films, along with gender and society, in her wonderfully titled *Love on the Rocks: Men, Women, and Alcohol in Post-World War II America* (Chapel Hill: University of North Carolina Press, 2002).

It is obvious but important to note that films in midcentury America were immensely influential. Long before our splintered universe of cable and the Web and tweets, we had movies, and their messages had impact. The *Thin Man* pictures debuted in 1934, the year after the repeal of Prohibition and in the midst of the Depression. The film *The Lost Weekend* appeared after a protracted, frightening war.

It's one tough slog of a movie, but it at least acquainted me with the work of Charles Jackson, author of the novel on which the film is based. Jackson became a star in A.A.—as long as he was sober. He was a frequent speaker at meetings throughout the 1950s, opening up to crowds about his hubris, hobnobbing with Judy Garland and Frank Sinatra, as well as his use of the barbiturate Seconal. (You can hear a 1959 speech he gave in Cleveland at www.xa-speakers.org/pafiledb.php?action=file&id=1797, accessed September 19, 2012.) He left the program for good, though, in the early '60s, and died alone in a Chelsea hotel room in 1968, OD'd on sleeping pills. For more on this sad history, see the rerelease of Jackson's short story collection, *The Sunnier Side: Arcadian Tales*, with an introduction by John W. Crowley (Syracuse, NY: Syracuse University Press, 1996).

95 *Director Blake Edwards later said he had quit drinking:* Steve Garbarino, "The Silver Panther Strikes Again," the *New York Times* (August 19, 2001).

96 *"Women Drunkards, Pitiful Creatures, Get Helping Hand":* Box 459, News and Notes From the General Service Office of A.A, "Welcome to Your General Service Office," vol. 49, 29, no. 2 (April–May 2003), accessed May 1, 2012, www.aa.org/en_pdfs/en _box459_april-may03.pdf.

96 *In 1946, the* Grapevine, *the group's monthly:* Grace O., "Women in AA Face Special Problems," *Grapevine*, 3, no. 5 (October 1946).

97   *A.A.'s most prominent initiative for women was Al-Anon:* Hartigan, *Bill W.,* 71. Eric Pace, "Lois Burnham Wilson, a Founder of Al-Anon Groups, Is Dead at 97," *New York Times* (October 6, 1988).

97   *Cultural historian Lori Rotskoff suggests:* Rotskoff, in *Love on the Rocks,* examines the role of A.A. in shaping marital politics in an especially lively and original chapter called "The Dilemma of the Alcoholic Marriage." The social worker's quote is found on page 154.

98   *Speaking to a Canadian audience celebrating:* Mann, Toronto speech, 1965.

5: *Rehab Nation*

99   *In 1970, the United States formally embraced:* NIH Almanac, accessed April 20, 2012, www.nih.gov/about/almanac/organization /NIAAA.htm.

99   *After addressing alcoholism, Congress declared war on cancer:* Office of Government and Congressional Relations website, National Cancer Institute, National Cancer Act of 1971, accessed April 20, 2012, http://legislative.cancer.gov/history/phsa/1971.

100   *In the years that followed, Mann's group:* NCADD.org, accessed April 20, 2012, www.ncadd.org/history/decade4.html.

100   *Government funding accounted for more:* Charles Bufe, *Alcoholics Anonymous: Cult or Cure?* (Tucson: Sharp Press, 1998), 110.

100   *At the same time, major insurers recognized alcoholism:* The government had come to accept alcoholism as an illness. Two federal appeals courts had dismissed charges of public inebriation against two men on the grounds that they were sick, and that conviction would be in violation of the Eighth Amendment, which prohibits the federal government from imposing cruel and unusual punishment. See more by Albert B. Logan, "May a Man Be Punished Because He Is Ill?" *American Bar Association Journal* 52, no. 10 (October 1966):

932–37. Also see Bufe, *A.A.: Cult or Cure?*, chapter 8, "A.A.'s Influence on Society," 105–28, accessed September 13, 2012, http://home.earthlink.net/~bbaa.library/AA_Cult_or_Cure.pdf.

101 *The counselors established a group:* Nancy Olson, *With a Lot of Help from Our Friends: The Politics of Alcoholism* (Lincoln, NE: Writers Club Press, 2003), 24–25.

101 *Consider this: In 1969, the outgoing Johnson administration:* Ibid., 72.

101 *In 1972, the NIAAA budget was:* Ibid., 192–96.

101 *In 1973, there were roughly 1,800 treatment:* National Admissions to Substance Abuse Treatment Services: The Treatment Episode Data Set (TEDS) 1992–1995, accessed March 12, 2012, www.samhsa.gov/data/DASIS/teds00/teds_rpt_2000_web.pdf, 6.

101 *By 2009, that number had jumped to more:* "2009 State Profile—United States National Survey of Substance Abuse Treatment Services," accessed March 12, 2012, wwwdasis.samhsa.gov/webt/state_data/US09.pdf.

101 *In 2012, the NIAAA's budget was $469 million:* National Institute of Alcohol Abuse and Alcoholism, accessed September 19, 2012, www.niaaa.nih.gov/about-niaaa/our-funding/congressional-budget-justification/fy-2012-congressional-budget.

101 *Government-supported researchers have discovered:* Bruce Booth, "Cancer Drug Targets: The March of the Lemmings," Forbes.com, accessed June 20, 2012, www.forbes.com/sites/brucebooth/2012/06/07/cancer-drug-targets-the-march-of-the-lemmings.

101 *Yet there are a mere:* Danish researchers discovered disuliram's emetic effects in the 1940s when they drank alcohol while testing the drug on themselves for antiparasitic abilities. The Food and Drug Administration approved it in 1951. Helge Kragh, "From Disulfiram to Antabuse: the Discorery of a Drug," *Bulletin for the History of Chemicals* 33, no. 2 (2008), accessed September 20, 2012, http://www.scs.illinois.edu/~mainzv/HIST/bulletin_open_access

/v33-2/v33-2%20p82-88.pdf. Naltrexone was synthesized in 1963 and used in clinical trials for addiction in 1973; the FDA approved it for alcohol treatment in 1994. "The Corporate, Political, and Scientific History of Naltrexone," accessed June 1, 2013, http://www.lowdosenaltrexone.org/gazorpa/History.html.

102 *As more Americans entered rehab:* Trysh Travis, *The Language of the Heart: A Cultural History of the Recovery Movement, from Alcoholics Anonymous to Oprah Winfrey* (Chapel Hill: University of North Carolina Press, 2009), 274.

102 *By 1968, females accounted for:* White, *Slaying the Dragon,* 161.

102 *Sociologists found that married American women:* Arlie Hochschild, *The Second Shift* (New York: Avon, 1989), 3.

102 *In national drinking surveys taken in 1967:* David J. Pittman and Helene Raskin White, eds., *Society, Culture, and Drinking Patterns Reexamined* (New Brunswick, NJ: Alcohol Research Documentation, Inc., Rutgers University, 1991), table 2, 164. I found this in chapter 5, "Changes in American Drinking Patterns and Problems, 1967–1984," by Michael E. Hilton and Walter B. Clark. The chapter was reprinted from the *Journal of Studies on Alcohol* 48 (1987), 515–22.

102 *And in that seventeen-year gap:* Pittman and White, *Society, Culture, and Drinking,* table 3, 166.

103 *There were other dramatic social changes:* National Center for Health Statistics, *Monthly Vital Statistics Report* 39, no. 12, supplement 2 (May 21, 1991).

103 *Though American women had begun to drink:* Marcia Russell, Maria Testa, and Sharon Wilsnack et al, "Alcohol Use and Abuse," in *Women & Health* (San Diego: Academic Press, 2000), 589–98. The book was edited by Marlene B. Goldman and Maureen C. Hatch.

103 *The discovery in the 1970s and '80s:* Elizabeth M. Armstrong and Ernest L. Abel, "Fetal Alcohol Syndrome: The Origins of a Moral Panic," *Alcohol and Alcoholism* 35, no. 3 (2000): 276–82.

104 *Mustering her courage, Wilsnack asked her professor:* Sharon C. Wilsnack, interview with author, March 23, 2011.

105 *Not far from Wilsnack's office, the authors of:* Information about *Our Bodies, Ourselves* comes from the authors' terrific website, accessed May 1, 2012, www.ourbodiesourselves.org/about/jamwa.asp.

106 *By 1976, the increasingly significant NIAAA:* Olson, *With a Lot of Help,* 306.

106 *"No single national data source covers":* Leigh Henderson, epidemiologist at the Substance Abuse and Mental Health Services Administration, e-mail message to author, June 16, 2011.

106 *In sociological surveys designed to test tolerance:* Florence Ridlon, *A Fallen Angel: The Status of the Female Alcoholic* (Cranbury, NJ: Associated University Presses, 1988), 25.

107 *In 1976, the Rand Corporation released results:* David J. Armor et al, *Alcoholism and Treatment* (Santa Monica, CA: Rand Corp., 1976). The introduction was enough to set off a firestorm (see pages v to vii). But read the whole thing, which people are still arguing about, even though it's science: accessed May 29, 2010, www.rand.org/content/dam/rand/pubs/reports/2007/R1739.pdf.

107 *Separately, two California researchers, Mark and Linda:* Stanton Peele, "Through a Glass Darkly," *Psychology Today* (April 1983): 38–42, www.peele.net/lib/glass.php.

108 *Prominent NCA board members tried to suppress:* Lender and Martin, *Drinking in America,* 201.

108 *In response to the criticism, Rand researchers:* J. Michael Polich et al, *The Course of Alcoholism: Four Years after Treatment* (Santa Monica, CA: Rand Corp., 1980), accessed May 29, 2010, www.rand.org/content/dam/rand/pubs/reports/2006/R2433.pdf.

108 *They were accused of fraud:* M. B. Sobell et al, "Alcohol Treatment Outcome Evaluation Methodology: State of the Art 1980–1984," *Addictive Behaviours* 12 (1987): 113–28.

108 *The root of the angry responses was obvious:* Alan G. Marlatt, interview with author, October 12, 2009.

109 *For proponents of twelve-step programs:* A.A. World Services, *Alcoholics Anonymous,* 31.

109 *At about the same time, another academic:* Biographical information on Jean Kirkpatrick comes from Jean Kirkpatrick, *Goodbye Hangovers, Hello Life* (New York: Atheneum, 1968), chapter 1. The quote is found on page xv.

110 *But what really rankled her was the notion:* Ibid., 111–69.

111 *Betty Ford left the White House:* Enid Nemy, "Betty Ford, Former First Lady, Dies at 93," *New York Times,* July 8, 2011, www.nytimes .com/2011/07/09/us/politics/betty-ford-dies.html?pagewanted=all.

111 *Elizabeth Taylor and Liza Minnelli told their:* Gioia Dillberto, "Stars in Rehab: Breaking the Cycle," *People,* August 6, 1984, www.people.com/people/archive/article/0,,20088392,00.html.

111 *Drew Barrymore checked in as a teenager:* "Rehabbed Stars: How Betty Ford Helped," accessed July 13, 2011, www.people.com /people/gallery/0,,20509577_20986930,00.html.

111 *Elsewhere, Ann Richards campaigned for governor:* Maura Casey, "Ann R., Alcoholic," *New York Times,* September 16, 2006, www .nytimes.com/2006/09/16/opinion/16sat4.html.

111 *Between 1968 and 1989, the number of women:* White, *Slaying the Dragon,* 161.

111 *In 1990, Ms. magazine published:* Charlotte Kasl, "The Twelve-Step Controversy," *Ms.,* November/December 1990, 30–31.

112 *In the early days of A.A., Bill Wilson:* A.A. World Services, *Alcoholics Anonymous,* xvi.

112 *Results are released to researchers sporadically:* Don McIntire, "How Well Does A.A. Work? An Analysis of Published A.A. Surveys (1968–1996) and Related Analyses/Comments," *Alcoholism Treatment Quarterly* (December 2000), 1–18.

113   *Actor Charlie Sheen even mentioned it:* Jeannine Stein and Mary Forgione, "Charlie Sheen Claims A.A. Has a 5% Success Rate— Is He Right?" *Los Angeles Times,* March 3, 2011, http://articles .latimes.com/2011/mar/03/news/la-heb-sheen-aa-20110302.

113   *"The problem with the conclusions drawn":* Don McIntire, "How Well Does A.A.Work?," 5.

113   *She identified herself as Carol McIntire:* Carol McIntire, interview with author, July 7, 2011.

113   *"He kept his work to himself":* Carol McIntire, interview with author, July 7, 2011.

114   *A.A.'s most recent member survey:* Alcoholics Anonymous, 2011 Membership Survey, accessed September 24, 2012, www.aa.org /pdf/products/p-48_membershipsurvey.pdf.

114   *In it, they wrote:* Arthur S., Tom E., and Glenn C., "Alcoholics Anonymous Recovery Outcome Rates: Contemporary Myth and Misinterpretation," January 1, 2008, accessed July 12, 2011, http://hindsfoot.org/recout01.pdf.

115   *The first time I went, the place felt like Lourdes:* I visited the GSO building several times in 2010. The first scene I describe took place on May 7, 2010.

116   *On the second visit, I was with:* This meeting and the quotes come from the interview with Joy. on June 11, 2010.

117   *In part because of this, Trysh Travis:* Travis, *The Language of the Heart,* 11.

117   *"Many people revere the idea of experience":* Trysh Travis, interview with author, March 21, 2012.

118   *At the end of her life, Elizabeth Taylor was:* Brooks Barnes, "Gay Bar Mourns Elizabeth Taylor," *New York Times,* March 24, 2011.

118   *"It's like trying to study the 'effectiveness' of yoga":* Mark Willenbring, interview with author, May 13, 2011.

119   *A comprehensive analysis in the* Cochrane Review: M. Ferri et.

al, "Alcoholics Anonymous and Other 12-Step Programmes for Alcohol Dependence," *Cochrane Database System Review* (July 2006). I have a hard copy, but the abstract is available here: www .ncbi.nlm.nih.gov/pubmed/16856072. Not everyone was pleased with the report. In an August 2008 letter to the editor of the journal *Addiction,* Lee Ann Kaskutas, a senior scientist at the Alcohol Research Group in Emeryville, California, called the Cochrane report "misleading," accessed September 24, 2012, http://onlinelibrary .wiley.com/doi/10.1111/j.1360-0443.2008.02240.x/full.

119 *Psychologist and author Stanton Peele noted:* Stanton Peele, interview with author, September 7, 2011.

119 *Alan Marlatt called it "poorly conceived":* Bruce Bower, "Alcoholics Synonymous: Heavy Drinkers of All Stripes May Get Comparable Help from a Variety of Therapies," *Science News,* January 25, 1997, http://lifering.org/1997/08/alcoholics-synonymous-heavy -drinkers-of-all-stripes-may-get-comparable-help-from-a-variety -of-therapies.

119 *In a reanalysis of the data published:* Robert Cutler and David Fishbain, "Are Alcoholism Treatments Effective? The Project MATCH data," *BMC Public Health* (July 2005), www.biomedcentral.com /1471-2458/5/75.

119 *And, as Willenbring pointed out, the studies were largely:* Mark Willenbring, interview with author, September 22, 2011.

120 *As more and more women entered twelve-step programs:* Cheever, *My Name Is Bill,* 231.

A note: As I began my research on this sexual predation in A.A. in 2010, I consulted many Wilson biographies, and spoke to a number of "old-timers." I drew my own conclusions, but in 2012, while reading the *Orange Papers,* an online analysis of A.A., I noticed that Orange, the site's curator, had cited many of the same details. You can read them here: www.orange-papers.org/orange

-otherwomen.html#ftnt03, accessed March 15, 2012. The site is amazingly comprehensive. In a January 19, 2011, e-mail, Orange, as he is called, told me that he gets about a million hits a month.

6: *The Thirteenth Step*

121 *For years, Monica Richardson, a singer and actress:* I first spoke to Richardson by phone in the winter of 2011. February 2010 began a vivid e-mail and phone correspondence, and we met in person in July 2012. Her notes of her time in A.A. are extensive, and she read many versions of this chapter for accuracy.

121 *"We are like men who have lost their legs":* A.A. World Services, *Alcoholics Anonymous,* 30.

123 *A.A. discourages sexual relationships between longtime members:* A.A World Services, *Alcoholics Anonymous: Twelve Steps & Twelve Traditions* (New York: Alcoholics Anonymous World Services, 1952), 119, accessed May 1, 2012, www.aa.org/twelveandtwelve/en _copyright.cfm. It suggests that members get together romantically only when they are "solid" A.A.s who have known each other long enough to know that their "compatibility at spiritual, emotional and mental levels is a fact and not wishful thinking."

126 *Some researchers have found that women:* Sharon C. Wilsnack et al, "Childhood Sexual Abuse and Women's Substance Abuse: National Survey Findings," *Journal of Studies on Alcohol and Drugs* (May 1997): 264–71. This research has been replicated many times, and Wilsnack, in several telephone conversations, reiterated its importance.

126 *Psychologist Charlotte Davis Kasl writes that:* Charlotte Davis Kasl, *Many Roads, One Journey: Moving beyond the 12 Steps* (New York: Harper, 1992), discusses this phenomenon in detail in chapter 10, "Boundaries and Sexual Exploitation, or Why Do I Have This Knot in My Gut?," which begins on page 230.

126 *Since the group's first days in Akron:* A.A. pamphlet, *Questions and Answers on Sponsorship,* 9, accessed May 2, 2012, www.aa.org/pdf /products/p-15_Q&AonSpon.pdf. Also in A.A. World Services, *Alcoholics Anonymous Twelve & Twelve,* 119.

127 *A 2010 sociology journal found that:* Jolene M. Sanders, "Acknowl- edging Gender in Women-Only Meetings of Alcoholics Anony- mous," *Journal of Groups in Addiction & Recovery* 5, no. 1 (2010), 17–33. I did a random search on A.A. websites for women-only meetings in northern New Jersey, the greater Boston area, Atlanta, and metropolitan Seattle. Of the thousands of meetings listed in each area, roughly 6 percent were women-only.

127 *Four percent said they had been raped by:* Cathy J. Bogart, "'13th-Stepping': Why Alcoholics Anonymous Is Not Always a Safe Place for Women," *Journal of Addictions Nursing: A Journal for the Prevention and Management of Addictions* 14, no. 1 (2003): 43–47. I also spoke with Bogart by phone on November 28, 2011. She told me that she had submitted the study to several journals, but that it was only accepted by one. "Everybody acknowledges this exists," she told me that day, "but few people want to face it."

128 *I also read the creepy diary of Sean:* Brandon Hanson, "Sex Of- fender Sent to Jail for Preying on Women in A.A.," *Lake Coun- ty Leader Advertiser,* April 6, 2012, http://leaderadvertiser.com /news/article_201455de-7e9f-11e1-9514-0019bb2963f4.html.

128 *This, too, fits a pattern, and manipulators:* Kasl, *Many Roads, One Journey,* 233–34.

129 *When she first joined A.A., Gwen said:* "Sexual and Financial Pred- ators in A.A., Parts 1 and 2," *Safe Recovery,* Richardson's Internet radio show, Blogtalkradio.com, episodes 41 and 43, May 10, 2011, and May 24, 2011. On these shows, the two women recalled their first meeting in 2009. I use a pseudonym to protect Gwen's identi- ty, but she used her real name on these shows.

130   *She found several blogs that were critical:* Richardson saw the *Orange Papers* (www.orange-papers.org) for the first time, as well as two articles: Marc Fisher, "Midtown Group: AA Group Leads Members Away from Traditions," *Washington Post,* July 22, 2007, www.washingtonpost.com/wp-dyn/content/article/2007/07/21/AR2007072101356_pf.html; and Nick Summers, "A Struggle Inside A.A," *Newsweek,* May 6, 2007, www.thedailybeast.com/newsweek/2007/05/06/a-struggle-inside-aa.html.

For additional information on this story, I spoke with Fisher on November 8, 2011. We also exchanged e-mails that day.

131   *"I pimped [them] out":* Fisher, "Midtown Group."

131   *While A.A. instructs members not to "play doctor":* Pamphlet, *The AA Member—Medications and Other Drugs* (New York: A.A. World Services, Inc., 2011), accessed May 7, 2012, www.aa.org/pdf/products/p-11_aamembersMedDrug.pdf.

132   *I asked A.A.'s General Service Office:* I met Mary C., the public information officer at A.A. in person for an interview on July 13, 2010, but I asked this question by e-mail on December 10, 2011. I received a response on December 20, 2011.

132   *When ex-Midtown members contacted:* Fisher, "Midtown Group," and Summers, "A Struggle Inside A.A."

133   *It warned that "the organization has the potential to become":* Gerard Seenan "Drink Advice Service Confronts Sex Abuse," *The Guardian,* July 4, 2000, www.guardian.co.uk/uk/2000/jul/05/gerardseenan?INTCMP=SRCH.

133   *In the leaked documents, A.A. nonalcoholic trustee:* Letter by Alcoholics Anonymous General Service Board trustee, "Reason for Topic and Additional Background Information: Predators in A.A.," July 29, 2007. You can see it on the *Orange Papers,* accessed September 22, 2011, www.orange-papers.org/ATTACHMENT_TO_TOPIC_002-PREDATORS.pdf. In communications with

the trustee, who verified the document, I agreed to maintain his anonymity.

134 *The British behavioral guidelines include:* "Personal Conduct Matters," *Guidelines for A.A. in Great Britain*, no. 17 (April 2002): 63–65.

134 *Written against the backdrop of the* Washington Post: A.A. trustee, "Reason for Topic and Additional Background."

135 *It was written by a woman whose:* Letter to *Grapevine*, July 1993.

136 *In October 2009, more than two years:* General Service Board, Subcommittee on Vulnerable Members in A.A., *Final Subcommittee Report* (October 27, 2009). Also in the *Orange Papers*, accessed September 22, 2011, www.orange-papers.org/ATTACHMENT _TO_TOPIC_002-PREDATORS.pdf.

137 *Here's the key passage:* General Service Board, *Final Subcommittee Report*.

137 *The Alcoholics Anonymous groups oppose no one:* The Big Book Online, Appendices, www.aa.org/bigbookonline/en_appendicei .cfm, accessed January 15, 2013.

140 *Richardson was stunned when:* Mary Vorsino, "Murder-Suicide Leaves 3 Dead," *Honolulu Star-Advertiser*, August 21, 2010, www .saradvertiser.com/news/20100821_Murder-Suicide_leaves_3_dead .html?id=101217004. Rob Perez, "Red Flags Missed," *Honolulu Star-Advertiser*, November 7, 2010, www.staradvertiser.com/news /20101107_Red_flags_missed.html?id=106. Brooks Baehr, "Combat Stress and Rejected Marriage Proposal May Have Triggered Rage," August 21, 2010, www.hawaiinewsnow.com/global/story .asp?s=13024225.

141 *The former trustee:* Former trustee, interview with author, December 6, 2011.

141 *But some of his friends did:* Marc Fisher, e-mail, November 8, 2011.

141 *Ellen Dye, a Washington-area psychologist:* Ellen Dye, Ph.D., interview with author, October 4, 2011.

142 *"Who's going to believe a drunk girl":* Amy Lee Coy, interview with author, July 16, 2011.

142 *She likens it to the Penn State sex abuse:* Louise, e-mail, September 26, 2012.

142 *In a forum on the anti-A.A. blog:* "A.A. and 13th-Step Victims," June 13, 2011, post on www.orange-papers.org/forum/node/150.

142 *"What was 'my part'":* Safe Recovery Online Radio, May 24, 2011, www.blogtalkradio.com/saferecovery.

143 *"Thirteenth stepping is a big problem":* Comment made to me during my tour of the General Service Office, June 11, 2010.

144 *The Boy Scouts, for instance, issued guidelines:* "Open Letter to Our Parents," accessed September 26, 2012, www.scouting.org /sitecore/content/BSAYouthProtection/BSA_Communications /parent_letter.aspx.

144 *Victor Vieth, a former Minnesota prosecutor:* Victor Vieth, interview with author, April 26, 2012.

144 *As Mary C. . . . wrote:* Mary C., e-mail, December 20, 2011.

144 *In April 2012, Richardson posted an accounting:* "Leaving A.A.," accessed April 24, 2012, http://leavingaa.com/?p=858#comment-4223.

7: *Twenty-First-Century Treatment*

147 *Joanna made two big decisions when she turned fifty:* Joanna's narrative comes from repeated interviews in person, by e-mail, and on the phone, with Joanna herself, though that is not her real name. All other details are correct, but because she lives in a small Pennsylvania town where she and her husband are business owners, she prefers to maintain her privacy. I met her through Ed Wilson and Mary Ellen Barnes, who approached her about telling her story. She readily agreed, and I met her for the first time at her home on July 14, 2010. The quotes and narrative attributed to her come from

that interview and ones that followed over the next two years. Like Monica Richardson, Joanna, Mark Willenbring, Ed Wilson, and Mary Ellen Barnes read and vetted everything written about them.

150 *Immediately Joanna liked what she read:* Like Joanna, I found Barnes and Wilson by typing the same thing into Google: www .non12step.com. I met them for the first time at their office on May 19, 2010.

151 *Addictions counseling licensing requirements:* Basic Level Certification, NAADAC, Association for Addiction Professionals, accessed June 10, 2011, www.naadac.org/certification/535.

153 *The morning of their first meeting:* Dr. Tim Norcross, interview with author, August 4, 2011.

153 *If the client is in good health:* National Center for Biotechnology Information Bookshelf, "Oral Naltrexone at a Glance," accessed August 11, 2011, www.ncbi.nlm.nih.gov/books/NBK64042.

154 *In 2006, the NIAAA released the results:* Raymond F. Anton et al., "Combined Pharmacotherapies and Behavioral Interventions for Alcohol Dependence/The COMBINE Study: A Randomized Controlled Trial," *Journal of the American Medical Association* 295, no. 17 (May 2006): 2003–17, http://jama.jamanetwork.com /article.aspx?articleid=202789.

155 *The FDA approved acamprosate, used extensively:* "FDA Approves New Drug for Treatment of Alcoholism: FDA Talk Paper," July 29, 2004, http://web.archive.org/web/20080117175319 /http://www.fda.gov/bbs/topics/answers/2004/ANS01302.html.

155 *Topiramate, an anticonvulsant:* Bankole Johnson et al., "Topiramate for Treating Alcohol Dependence," *Journal of the American Medical Association* 298, no. 14 (October 7, 2007): 1641–651, http://jama.ama-assn.org/content/298/14/1641.full.

155 *Meta-analyses have shown that oral:* There have been many. Here is a recent one: S. Rosner et al., "Opioid Antagonists for Alco-

hol Dependence," *Cochrane Library* 12 (2010), accessed September 27, 2012, www.thecochranelibrary.com/details/file/884765 /CD001867.html.

155 *In a study of the use of extended-release naltrexone:* S. S. O'Malley and P. G. O'Connor, "Medications for Unhealthy Alcohol Use: Across the Spectrum," *Journal of the National Institute on Alcohol Abuse and Alcoholism* 33, no. 4 (2011), accessed September 24, 2012, http://pubs.niaaa.nih.gov/publications/arh334/300-312 .htm.

155 *But some small studies have reported that naltrexone:* B. E. Setiawan et al., "The Effect of Naltrexone on Alcohol's Stimulant Properties and Self-Administration Behavior in Social Drinkers: Influence of Gender and Genotype," *Alcoholism: Clinical and Experimental Research Journal* 35, no. 6 (June 2011): 1134–41. You can see the abstract here: www.ncbi.nlm.nih.gov/pubmed/21410481, accessed June 10, 2012. A team of Spanish researchers found optimistic signs for the gene marker as well: A. J. Chamorro et al., "Association of μ-Opioid Receptor (OPRM1) Gene Polymorphism with Response to Naltrexone in Alcohol Dependence: A Systematic Review and Meta-Analysis," *Addiction Biology* 17, no. 3 (May 2012): 505–12, www.ncbi.nlm.nih.gov/pubmed/22515274.

156 *Another study showed promising signs for naltrexone's:* Jennifer Tidey et al, "Moderators of Naltrexone's Effects on Drinking, Urge and Alcohol Effects in Non-Treatment Seeking Heavy Drinkers in the Natural Environment," *Alcoholism: Clinical and Experimental Research Journal* 32, no. 1 (January 2008): 58–66, www.ncbi.nlm .nih.gov/pmc/articles/PMC2743136. This study found the drug reduced drinking days among those with a gene called DRD4-L, but did not moderate effects for those with the OPRM1 gene. This was a small study, however, and I include it because of the drug's notable effects on women.

156 *In Finland, however, an American doctor:* John David Sinclair, "Evidence about the Use of Naltrexone and for Different Ways of Using It in the Treatment of Alcoholism," *Alcohol and Alcoholism* 36, no. 1 (2001): 2–10. You can also find an explanation of Sinclair's methods at his website: http://thecureforalcoholism.com, accessed September 27, 2012.

157 *But he says it helps to prepare a problem drinker:* Ed Wilson, interview with author, October 26, 2010.

157 *Joanna wasn't looking for magic, though:* Again, this narrative comes from repeated interviews with Joanna, Mary Ellen Barnes, and Ed Wilson in 2011, as well as an interview with Tim Norcross, to whom I spoke on August 4, 2011.

158 *Wilson administers one designed in the 1970s:* Jane Loevinger, ed., *Technical Foundations for Measuring Ego Development* (Mahwah, NJ: Erlbaum, 1998), 53. Susanne R. Cook-Greuter further developed Loevinger's stage theory. For more information, see www.stillpointintegral.com/docs/cook-greuter.pdf, accessed September 27, 2012. For a brief background on Loevinger, see "Women's Intellectual Contributions to the Study of Mind and Society," accessed October 26, 2010, www.webster.edu/~woolflm/loevinger.html.

162 *Like Joanna, Wilson's and Barnes's clients:* These numbers come from Ed Wilson, interview with author, September 21, 2011. He and Barnes follow up with their clients by phone and e-mail regularly.

164 *Often, they are also dedicated exercisers:* M. T. French et al, "Do Alcohol Consumers Exercise More? Findings from a National Survey," *American Journal of Health Promotion* 24, no. 1 (September–October 2009): 2–10, http://ajhpcontents.org/doi/abs/10.4278/ajhp.0801104.

167 *Tim Norcross, the family doctor who treats:* Tim Norcross, interview with author, August 4, 2011.

167 *Ashley Phillips, a women's:* I spoke to and emailed Ashley many

times over the summer of 2013, once the book had been published. Many of the book's readers pointed out that while I included the names of alternative methods of recovery, I didn't describe how they worked for individual women. The additions of Phillips, as well as Jane and Donna Dierker below, is an attempt to rectify that. This is a condensed version of Phillips's story, as she recounted it to me from July 2013 to November 2013.

169 *Mark Willenbring, psychiatrist and former director:* Mark Willenbring, interview with author, May 13, 2011. His website is http://mattsub.blogspot.com/2011/02/alltyr-is-born.html.

169 *In 2011, Stout cofounded AA2.org:* Dee-Dee Stout, interview with author, February 24, 2011. Stout's book *Coming to Harm Reduction Kicking and Screaming: Looking for Harm Reduction in a 12-Step World* (Bloomington, IN: Author House, 2009) offers a new look at the different modes of recovery from alcohol and drug abuse. You can learn more about her group at www.aa2.org.

169 *Ken Anderson, a community organizer in Brooklyn:* Ken Anderson, interview with author, January 10, 2012.

170 *During the economic downturn . . . "my brain," she says:* I spoke and emailed Jane many times over the fall of 2013, once my book had been published. This is a condensed version of Jane's experience, as recounted to me in September, October, and November 2013.

170 *Likewise, Donna Dierker:* I emailed and spoke to Dierker many times over the fall of 2013, and she explained the M.M. method in great detail.

172 *M.M. appears as an alternative:* National Institute for Alcohol Abuse and Alcoholism, "Rethinking Drinking," accessed December 10, 2013: http://rethinkingdrinking.niaaa.nih.gov/Tools Resources/Resources.asp. Here, it appears on the Substance Abuse and the Mental Health Services Administration lists it in its National Registry of Evidence-Based Programs and Practices.

Accessed December 10, 2013: http://www.nrepp.samhsa.gov
/ViewAll.aspx?selChar=M.

172 *Stanton Peele, a New Jersey psychologist:* Stanton Peele, interview
with author, September 7, 2011.

172 *Consider the case of Audrey Kishline:* The tragedy of Audrey Kishline inspires continued debate. I first learned of her in an *NBC
Dateline* episode called "Road to Recovery" that aired September
1, 2006. For a transcript see www.msnbc.msn.com/id/14627442
/ns/dateline_nbc/t/road-recovery/, accessed September 21, 2011.
You can also see some of the online debate about her, including
Peele's comment, on Dr. Alexander DeLuca's website, "Addiction, Pain, and Public Health Website," www.doctordeluca.com
/Documents/KishlineToldMM.htm, accessed September 21, 2011.

173 *Willenbring looks forward to the day when Americans:* Mark Willenbring, interview with author, September 22, 2011.

173 *In fact, the number of Americans:* Mark Olfson and Steven C.
Marcus, "National Patterns in Antidepressant Medication Treatment," *Archives of General Psychiatry* 66, no. 8 (August 2009),
http://archpsyc.jamanetwork.com/article.aspx?articleid=483159.

173 *Of those patients, more than half:* Nancy Shute, "Antidepressant Use Grows, As Primary Care Doctors Do the Prescribing,"
"Shots," Health News from National Public Radio, August 4, 2011,
www.npr.org/blogs/health/2011/08/06/138987152/antidepressant
-use-climbs-as-primary-care-doctors-do-the-prescribing.

173 *By contrast, Willenbring says, fewer than 10 percent:* Mark Willenbring, interview with author, September 22, 2011.

175 *From Sweden to Australia, Denmark to South Africa:* International
Center for Alcohol Policies, "International Drinking Guidelines," accessed June 6, 2012, www.icap.org/PolicyIssues/DrinkingGuidelines.
ICAP is a nonprofit organization in Washington, D.C., that is funded
by a number of large alcohol producers.

175 *Women in those countries live the longest:* European Commission, *Mortality and Life Expectancy Statistics,* accessed October 24, 2012, http://epp.eurostat.ec.europa.eu/statistics_explained/index .php/Mortality_and_life_expectancy_statistics.

175 *On the Greek island of Ikaria:* Dan Buettner, "The Island Where People Forget to Die," *New York Times Magazine,* October 24, 2012, www.nytimes.com/2012/10/28/magazine/the-island-where -people-forget-to-die.html?src=me&ref=general.

176 *American women, meanwhile, die sooner:* Sabrina Tavernese, "Life Span Shrinks for Less-Educated Whites in the U.S.," the *New York Times,* September 20, 2012, www.nytimes.com/2012/09/21 /us/life-expectancy-for-less-educated-whites-in-us-is-shrinking .html?pagewanted=all.

176 *According to Dr. Raul Caetano:* Raul Caetano, interview with author, March 16, 2011.

177 *Fred Rotgers, a New Jersey clinical psychologist:* Fred Rotgers, interview with author, December 11, 2011.

177 *According to the Pew Research Center:* Pew Forum on Religious and Public Life, "Faith on the Hill: The Religious Composition of the 113th Congress," analysis, accessed January 12, 2013, http:// www.pewforum.org/government/faith-on-the-hill--the-religious -composition-of-the-113th-congress.aspx#new. Of the 533 members, 128 were evangelical Christians whose denominations forbid alcohol, including Baptists, Methodists, Holiness, Adventist, and Congregationalist; 15 were Mormon; 2 were Muslim.

178 *Yet a 2011 study of 106,000 women in the* Journal of the American Medical Association*:* Wendy Y. Chen et al., "Moderate Alcohol Consumption during Adult Life, Drinking Patterns, and Breast Cancer Risk," *Journal of the American Medical Association* 306, no. 17 (November 2, 2011): 1884–890.

178 *But Dr. Steven A. Narod:* Steven A. Narod, "Alcohol and Risk of

Breast Cancer," editorial, *Journal of the American Medical Association* 306, no. 17 (November. 2, 2011), 1920–1921. http://jama .jamanetwork.com/article.aspx?articleid=1104569.

179   *Dr. Lisa Schwartz, a professor of community:* Quotes are from Dr. Lisa Schwartz, interview with author, December 19, 2011. Schwartz's editorial, "Promoting Healthy Skepticism in the News: Helping Journalists Get it Right," appeared in *Journal of the National Cancer Institute* 101, no. 23 (November 20, 2009): 1596–99. She wrote it with Steve Woloshin and Barnett S. Kramer.

Conclusion

183   *They've provided a growth market for:* Annabel Jackson, "Why Women Drink Wine: A Survey by Vinexpo Exposes the Gender Politics behind a Glass of Vino in Asia," June 25, 2010, www .cnngo.com/hong-kong/women-and-wine-asia-430659. For information in India, see Pavos Kakaviatos, "Indian Women Drive Surge in Wine Consumption," November 7, 2011, www.decanter .com/news/wine-news/529492/indian-women-drive-surge-in -wine-consumption.

183   *Indeed, in Uganda, the number of young:* Sharon C. Wilsnack, interview with author, March 30, 2012. Wilsnack studies women and alcohol around the globe.

183   *Advertisers have taken note:* Video, Serengeti Beer, accessed March 30, 2012, www.youtube.com/watch?v=0zU5s6t29tA.

183   *We're never going back to Prohibition:* Gail Collins describes this story in *When Everything Changed: The Amazing Journey of American Women from 1960 to the Present* (New York: Little, Brown, 2009), 24.

Permissions

Index

A118G gene, 156
AA2.org, 169, 177
abstinence:
    and A.A., 84, 91, 93, 110,
      112, 169
    and naltrexone, 155, 156
    and one's definition of
      success, 151
    organizations offering support
      for, 110, 167, 168, 169
    and research, 60, 107, 155
    and temperance societies,
      64–67, 74, 91
    and underground drinkers, 74
acamprosate, 154
accidents, alcohol-related, 24,
    174

accountability, 92
Adams, John, 59
addiction:
    and A.A., 83, 97, 172, 173
    as adaptation to life's
      pressures, 46
    and rehab centers, 111,
      151
    and research, 25, 45, 46, 119,
      155, 167, 182
    self-help website, 169
    and societal change, 46
aging, 47
Al-Anon: 97–98
alcohol:
    absorbed more rapidly by
      women, 24, 27–28, 122,

126, 144, 182, 183
advertisements for, 79, 183
in bloodstream, 17
and breast cancer, 165,
   178–80
in colonial America, 57–60
death rates from, 24
and drug use, 18
gender differences in effects
   of, 28, 104–5, 181–82, 183
high tolerance of, 177
and immigrant cultures,
   65–66
and Prohibition, 70–75
religion vs., 63, 177
safe amounts of, 9, 157,
   175–79
self-reporting statistics on,
   17, 22–23, 176
as socially acceptable, 15,
   29–31, 58, 65
surveys on women and, 20–
   23, 31–32, 37–38, 104–5,
   156, 178, 179
taxes on, 73
toxic effects of, 24
U.S. consumption of, 21, 23,
   40, 61, 70, 73, 177
in U.S. culture, 13–14, 18–19,
   26, 29–31, 44–45, 47–48
alcohol abuse:
   predisposition toward, 27–28
   treatment for, 18, 25–26
   triggers of, 45–46
   see also alcoholism
Alcohol and Drugs History
   Society, 117

alcohol dehydrogenase, 24
alcohol dependence, 22, 23, 24,
   174
alcoholic:
   recovered, 93
   use of term, 92
"alcoholic marriage," 98
*Alcoholics Anonymous: The
   Story of How More Than
   One Hundred Men
   Have Recovered from
   Alcoholism* (A.A.), 85–86
Alcoholics Anonymous (A.A.),
   15
   abstinence as necessary in,
      84, 91, 93, 110, 112, 122,
      169
   alcoholism as illness in, 83,
      84, 88, 89, 91–94, 109, 182
   alternate opinions struck
      down by, 93–94, 132, 182
   alternatives to, 167–70, 182
   anonymity as rule in, 89, 112,
      134, 135
   author's visits to, 115–16
   beginnings of, 81–82, 83–84
   Big Book of, 82, 88, 109, 121
   British code of conduct in,
      133–34
   closed minds in, 118, 132–35,
      136, 143
   and community development
      model, 101, 115
   court-ordered referrals to,
      82, 139–40, 144
   data provided by, 112–14,
      116

decentralized structure of, 144–45
developed by men for men, 25, 82, 85–87, 89, 124–25
doctor referrals to, 148–49, 173
double standard in, 89, 96, 123–24, 142
dropouts from, 113, 145
as faith-based group, 25, 82–84, 88, 90, 123
family support for (Al-Anon), 97–98, 158
General Service Office (GSO) of, 91, 115–16, 132, 136, 143
general service representatives (GSRs), 129, 132
as gold standard, 112
growth of, 85, 102
as ill-suited to women, 25, 81, 82, 85–89, 96–97, 182
Kirkpatrick's experience with, 109–12
members learning a new way to live, 116–17, 118
members ordered off medication, 131–32
Midtown chapter, 130–32, 135, 141, 142
mutual support of members in, 84, 88–89, 107, 112, 117, 133, 140
ninety-day trial period of, 114
outside issues of, 137–38
as pickup joint, 128

and popular culture, 94–98
powerlessness promoted by, 82, 83, 84, 88, 93, 110, 123, 124, 130
refusal to accept sex abuse data, 132–40, 143
and rehab industry profits, 82, 100–102
and Richardson, *see* Richardson, Monica
scientific study impossible in, 112, 118–20
sponsors in, 117, 124, 127, 131, 149
structure offered by, 115, 159
Subcommittee on Vulnerable Members, 134, 136
success in, 112–13, 114, 116, 182
survey (1940s), 90–94, 107
"thirteenth-stepping" in, 120, 121–45
twelve-step program, 25, 82, 83, 84, 88, 98, 99–100, 109, 111, 113, 114, 119, 167
Twelve Traditions, 123, 132, 137
volunteer positions in, 132
women as members of, 84, 87–88, 96–97, 102, 127–29, 131
women-only meetings of, 87, 127, 149
women sexually abused in, 124–39, 141–43, 145
Alcoholics Anonymous World Services, 100, 137

alcoholism:
  and accountability, 92
  alternative solutions for,
    167–73
  and behavior modification,
    108, 119, 167
  and codependence, 97–98
  cold turkey as treatment of,
    107
  and controlled drinking,
    107–9, 157, 166–67
  data nonexistent for women
    and, 106
  drugs for treatment of,
    101–2
  effectiveness of treatment,
    117–19
  evidence-based research on,
    82–83, 119
  evidence-based treatment for,
    25, 150–75
  and families, 87, 97–98, 164
  gender differences in
    recovery from, 98, 110–11,
    182
  and harm reduction, 112,
    172, 177
  as illness, 83, 84, 88, 89, 91–
    94, 99, 100, 109, 117, 182
  and individualized therapy,
    150–67, 169
  and lapse prevention, 157
  and legislation, 99–100
  as lifelong condition, 107
  medical cures for, 90
  medical management of,
    153–57
  and motivational
    enhancement, 119, 168
  NIAAA treatment programs
    for, 100, 101, 106, 107,
    108, 119, 154
  Project MATCH, 119–20
  public image of, 92–93
  "purge and puke" treatment
    of, 83
  and relapse, 165–66
  and religion, 94
  as social problem, 103
  spectrum of, 151
  stages of, 91–92
  triggers of, 45–46, 107, 115,
    165, 166
  twelve-step treatments of,
    25, 82, 83, 84, 88, 97, 98,
    99–100, 101, 109, 111, 113,
    114, 119, 120, 126, 142,
    168, 182
*Alcoholism Treatment
  Quarterly,* 112–13
alcohol studies:
  and anonymity, 118–20
  COMBINE study, 154, 167
  contrasted with cancer
    studies, 101
  evidence-based, 107–9,
    119–20
  federal funding for, 177
  funded by alcohol
    companies, 90
  gap between science and
    practice in, 176–77
  growing field of, 75–79,
    90–94

Index

by Jellinek, 90–94, 107, 174
and legislation, 100, 104–8
and media reports, 179
public rejection of results,
    108–9
random control absent in,
    179
self-reporting in, 17, 22–23,
    102–3, 156, 176, 178
subjective results of, 118–20,
    156
women ignored in, 91, 104–6,
    108
Yale University, 90–91
Alexander, Bruce, 45–46
Allen, Frederick Lewis, 73
ALLTYR, 169
American Indians, alcohol used
    by, 61
American Medical Association
    (AMA), 99, 153
Anderson, Ken, 169
Antabuse, 102
Anthony, Susan B., 67
antianxiety medication, 158
antidepressants, 173
anti-German sentiment, 70
Anti-Saloon League, 70
anxiety, 27, 47–48, 54, 115, 160,
    163
aqua mirabilis, 59
Arthur, T. S., *Ten Nights in a
    Bar-Room and What I
    Saw There*, 64, 70, 93
autism, 78, 93
auto accidents, 11, 12, 18, 32,
    177

Baldrige, Letitia, 30–31
Ball, Lucille, 33
Barnes, Mary Ellen, 150–52,
    159, 160, 162, 163–67
Barrymore, Drew, 111
beer, 33
    in colonial America, 57, 58,
        60
    in growlers, 69
    in nineteenth century, 65,
        69, 70
    and Prohibition, 71
behavior modification, 108, 119,
    167, 169
belladonna, 90
Bening, Annette, 20
Bettelheim, Bruno, 78
Betty Ford Center, 111
Biever Mondavi, Margrit,
    39–40
Big Brothers and Big Sisters of
    America, 143
Booze-Free Brigade, 14
boredom, 28
Borg, Axel, 37
Boy Scouts of America (BSA),
    143, 144
brain damage, 24
brain studies, 182
    gender differences in, 28–29
brandy, 57
breast cancer, 165, 177–80
Brown, Geoffrey, 133–34
Buffalo, New York, saloons in,
    61
bulimia, 28
Busch, Noel, 79

cabernet sauvignon, 42
Caetano, Raul, 176–77
Calahan, Sean, 128
California wine industry,
    32–43
  tweaking the product, 40–43
  wine tastings, 34, 37, 38, 39
  winners at Paris
    competitions, 40
cancer studies, 101, 165, 177–80
Capon Ale (recipe), 59–60
cardiovascular disease, 179
Carmen, 162–63
Cass, Kristine, 139–40
Catholic Church, scandals in,
    133, 134, 143, 144
CDC, 21
cells, self-repair of, 180
central nervous system, 28
Chantix, 167
chardonnay, 42–43
Chen, Wendy, 178–79
Child, Julia, 35
child care, time dedicated to,
    52–55, 102, 103
children:
  autistic, 78, 93
  education of, 66
  of immigrants, 66
cider, 57, 58, 59
cirrhosis of the liver, 24
Cochrane Review, 119
cocktail hour, 29–31
coffee, 70
cognitive behavioral therapy,
    119, 150, 167
COMBINE study, 154, 167

*Comprehensive Alcohol
    Abuse and Alcoholism
    Prevention, Treatment,
    and Rehabilitation Act*
    [Hughes Act] (1970), 99–
    100, 102, 104, 105, 106–7
Conley, Clayborne, 139–40
consistency, 41
Cougar Town, 20
Cox, Courteney, 20
Coy, Amy Lee, *From Death Do
    I Part*, 142
crack babies, 93
cruises to nowhere, 74
cultural shift, 10
Cutler, Robert, 119

Days of Wine and Roses, The
    (movie), 95
dementia, 175
depression, 27, 115, 173
diabetes, 177
Didion, Joan, 27
Dierker, Donna, 170–71
disulfiram, 154
divorce rate, 103
doctors, primary-care, 174–75
Drinkard, Martha Ann, 61
drinking:
  as act of rebellion, 26
  at-risk, 174
  binge, 21
  in colonial America, 57–61
  controlled, 107–9, 157, 166–67
  as disease, 75
  gender differences in, 104–5,
    181–82, 183

government guidelines for, 9
intentional, 23
for maximum effect, 23
minimum age for, 32
in moderation, 6, 60, 108,
  155, 157, 166–67, 169
national surveys of, 102–3
in nineteenth century, 62–70
and Prohibition, 70–75
as release valve, 45
safe quantities of, 9, 175–80
as shameful sin, 26, 46, 64–
  67, 176, 177
slipping into a habit, 9
and socioeconomic status,
  20–21, 72
triggers for, 13, 27–28, 32,
  45–46, 55, 104, 107, 115,
  165, 166
underreporting, 176
drugs:
  and alcohol abuse, 18
  in public image, 105
  sold via Sears catalogue, 70
  and stress, 28
drunk driving, 21–22, 24
Dye, Ellen, 141

early adopters, 38
Edwards, Blake, 95
Edwards, Griffiths, *Alcohol:
  The World's Favorite
  Drug,* 93–94
Emerson, Ralph Waldo, 110
employee assistance programs,
  100, 144
endorphins, 154, 157

Erie Canal, 61
estrogen, 178
ethyl alcohol, 175
Europe:
  life expectancy in, 175
  traditional wine drinking in,
    175–76, 177
  traditional wine-making in,
    40–41
exercise, and health, 180

fetal alcohol syndrome (FAS),
  24, 103
Fields, W. C., 94–95
Fishbain, David, 119
Fisher, Marc, 141
Fitzgerald, F. Scott, *This Side of
  Paradise,* 72
flavor, preserving, 41
flu shot, 180
folate, 180
food writers, 38–39
Ford, Betty, 111
France, study in, 5–6
Franklin, Ben, "The Drinker's
  Dictionary," 58
Franzen, Jonathan, *Freedom,* 20
French Chef, The (TV), 35
Friedan, Betty, 184

Godey's Lady's Book, 64
government guidelines, 9
Grapevine, 96, 135, 138
Great Depression, 83
Grucza, Rick, 23, 31, 46
Gwen (A.A. member), 129–30,
  142

Hale, Sarah, 64
HAMS, 169, 170
happiness survey, 54–55
harm reduction, 112, 169, 177
Hayward, Susan, 95
heart disease, 177, 180
Henderson, Leigh, 106
Henry Hudson Parkway, New
    York, auto accident on, 12
heroin, sold by Sears catalogue, 70
history, 45–47
Hochschild, Arlie, *The Second
    Shift*, 102
Hughes, Harold, 99, 101
Hughes Act (1970), 99–100, 102,
    104, 105, 106–7

iChange, 172
Ikaria, Greece, 175
I'll Cry Tomorrow (movie), 95
immigrants:
    anti-German sentiment, 70
    cultural traditions of, 65–66
Industrial Revolution, 62–63

Jackson, Charles, 95
jazz, 73
Jefferson, Thomas, 59
Jellinek, E. M., 90–94, 107, 174
Joanna (in treatment), 147–50,
    157–63, 167–68
Joy (A.A. member), 116

Karpman, Benjamin, *The Alco-
    holic Woman: Case Studies
    in the Psychodynamics of
    Alcoholism*, 75–79

Kasl, Charlotte Davis, 111, 126,
    128
Ken (pseud.), 122–24
Kennedy, Jacqueline, 29–31
Kids Are All Right, The (movie),
    20
Kirkpatrick, Jean, 109–12
Kishline, Audrey, 171–72
Klonopin, 158
Knox, Henry, 60
Kristen (A.A. member), 131

Ladies' Home Journal, 37–38
Lareau, Annette, 48
Lemmon, Jack, 95
life expectancy, 175, 176
Lincoln, Abraham, 64
liver damage, 24, 174, 176, 177
Loevinger, Jane, 158–59
Long, Zelma, 41–42
Lost Weekend, The (movie),
    94–95
Louise (lawyer), 142
Louv, Richard, *Last Child in the
    Woods*, 48
Loy, Myrna, 95
LSD, 85

malolactic fermentation, 42
Mann, Horace, 87
Mann, Marty, 87–89, 90, 94, 98,
    100, 108, 124
Marlatt, Alan, 108, 109, 119
Mary C. (A.A. officer), 132, 144
Masson, Paul, 35
May, Cliff, 35
Mayflower, 57

McIntire, Don, 112–14
McSorley's Ale House, 68
mead, 59
media reports, 179–80
medical management, 154, 175
medicine:
    Americans' faith in, 94
    drugs for alcoholism
        treatment, 101–2
    men in charge of, 105, 106
    primary-care doctors,
        174–75
men:
    and A.A., *see* Alcoholics
        Anonymous
    alcohol dehydrogenase in, 24
    and double standard, 89, 96,
        123–24, 142
    and drinking as illness, 75
    as drinking buddies, 181
    and fatherhood, 52
    financial responsibility of, 54,
        62–63, 97
    gender differences in
        research, 28–29
    as primary researchers, 17
    statistics flat, 18, 23, 24
    surveys on drinking in U.S.,
        23
    and wine, 34–35
Minnelli, Liza, 111
moderation, 172–73
Moderation Management
    (M.M.), 171–72
Moms Who Need Wine
    (Facebook), 19
Mondavi, Robert, 35–36

Mondavi Winery, 35–36, 39–40
    female wine makers in, 41–42
Morrison, Toni, 19
*MotherF**ker with the Hat,
    The,* 145
motivational enhancement
    therapy, 119, 150, 167
Mr. X, 133, 134–36, 138–39
Ms., 111
Murdock, Catherine Gilbert, 74

naltrexone, 102, 153–57, 158,
    160, 166, 167, 175
Narod, Steven A., 178
Nation, Carry, 67–68
National Association of
    Alcohol Counselors and
    Trainers, 101
National Council on
    Alcoholism, 89, 100, 108
National Institute for Alcohol
    Abuse and Alcoholism
    (NIAAA), 100, 101, 106,
    107, 108, 119–20, 154
    and employee assistance
        programs, 100
    and Hughes Act, 100, 101,
        102, 106
    and research, 106, 108, 119–
        20, 154
    treatment programs funded
        by, 100, 101, 106, 107, 108,
        119, 154
New York, distilleries in, 61
niacin, as mood regulator, 85
nicotine addiction, 167
nicotine gum, 167

Norcross, Tim, 153, 157–58, 167

Nurse Jackie (TV), 55

O'Connor, Sandra Day, 43

O'Malley, Stephanie, 155

"OMG, I So Need a Glass of Wine or I'm Gonna Sell My Kids," 19

opiates, public use of, 70

opioid receptors, 154, 155–56

OPRM1 gene, 155–56

Orange Papers, 142, 145

Oregon Trail, 61–62

Our Bodies, Ourselves, 105

Oxford Group, 83–84

Peele, Stanton, 119, 172–73

   The Diseasing of America, 172

Penn State sex abuse case, 142, 144

perry, from pears, 57

Phillips, Ashley, 167–68

Pilgrims, 57

Pinkham, Lydia, 70–71

Pinsky, Drew, 113

Poppy (granddad), 4–5

poppy seeds, 59

Posert, Harvey, 33–34, 36–37, 38, 39

potassium, 38

Powell, William, 95

Powers, Madelon, 68, 69

Powers, Tom, 120

Prohibition, 70–71

   cultural effects of, 73

   defiance of, 72–73

   drinking habits changed by, 74–75

   economic effects of, 73–74

   and organized crime, 73

   repeal of, 32, 33, 41, 73–74, 75

   and ships to nowhere, 74

   and speakeasies, 73–74

Project MATCH, 119–20

Prozac, 173

psychiatric hospitals, referrals to, 173

Puritans, 58

Quinones, Michael, 131, 141

Race to Nowhere (movie), 48

Ramey, Garey, 49, 51–53, 54

Ramey, Valerie, 48–53, 54

Rand Corporation, 107, 108–9

Rankin, Florence, 86

Rational Recovery, 168

Real Housewives, 20

recipe: Capon Ale, 59–60

recovery movement, 117–18

rehab, 100–102

   celebrities in, 111

   community development model of, 101

   and controlled drinking, 107–9

   gender differences ignored in, 110–11

   nonprofessional staffs for, 100–101, 119

profitability of, 101, 108
records destroyed by, 153
study of patients in, 107–9,
119–20
twelve-step programs in, 82,
100
women in, 24–25
religion:
A.A. as faith-based, 25, 82–
84, 88, 90, 123
and alcoholism, 94
and Congress, 177
and immigration, 65–66
"let go and let God," 97
and morality lessons, 63–67
and sex scandals, 133, 134,
143, 144
and wine, 33
religious revivals, 63
Remick, Lee, 95
Revere, Paul, 59
Richards, Ann, 111
Richardson, Dorothy, 69
Richardson, Monica, 121–45
and A.A. double standard,
123–24
as A.A. member, 122–23, 127,
145
and A.A. refusal to act, 136–
40, 143
adolescence of, 121–22
childhood sexual abuse of,
125–26
commitment to A.A., 128–
29, 132, 140, 145
Internet radio show of, 142
and Ken, 122–24

leaving A.A., 145
and Mr. X, 133, 134–36,
138–39
researching thirteenth step,
130–35
as service representative,
128–29, 140
singing career of, 125, 133
and *Stop13stepinaa.com*,
139
in therapy, 125–26
trying to stop the abuse,
134–39, 140, 143–45
Ride, Sally, 43, 44
risk, living with, 180
Rock, Chris, 145
Roe v. Wade, 102
Rorabaugh, W. J., 61
Rosado, Leandra, 12
Ross, Betsy, 60
Rotgers, Fred, 177
Roth, Lillian, 95
Rotskoff, Lori, 97
rum:
in colonial times, 57, 58, 59,
60
"Demon Rum," 68
Rush, Benjamin, 60, 84
Rutgers University, 19

saloons, 58, 61, 68–70, 79
Schuler, Diane, 11
Schwartz, Lisa, 178–80
Sears, Roebuck, 70
Second Great Awakening, 63
self-awareness, 159
sensory science, 41

sexual abuse, 115
  A.A. "thirteenth-stepping,"
    120, 121–45
  Penn State case, 142, 144
  as risk factor for women
    alcoholics, 28
Sheen, Charlie, 113, 114
Silkworth, William, 83
Sinclair, David, 156
slavery, and alcohol, 61
SMART, 167–68
Smart Recovery, 145, 167
Smashed (movie), 20
Smith, Anne, 97
Smith, Bob, 84
Snooki, 19
Sobell, Mark and Linda, 107–8,
    172
soda pop, 33, 42
speakeasies, 73–74
sports, 46–47, 50
Stanton, Elizabeth Cady, 67
Stevenson, Betsey, 54, 55
Stossel, Ludwig, 35
Stout, Dee-Dee, 169
stress, 27, 28, 32, 45, 183
stroke, 177
suffragists, 67
suicide, 24, 173
Swiss Colony wine, 35

Taconic Parkway, New York,
    auto accident on, 11
tannins, 42
taverns:
  in colonial America, 58
  as "men's clubs," 79

saloons, 61, 68–70
Taylor, Elizabeth, 111, 118
teetotaler, derivation of term, 66
temperance movement, 67–68,
    74, 91, 93
terroir, 41
Thin Man, The (movie), 95
Thompson, Ilse, 172
time, use of, 48
Title IX, 102
topiramate, 154–55
Towns, Charles, 93
Travis, Trysh, *Language of the
    Heart*, 117–18
Twitter, 114

University of California at
    Davis, 37, 41

Vieth, Victor, 144
Vietnam War, 32
vulnerabilities, 24, 46

Wakefield, Andrew, 93
Washington, George, 59
Washington, Martha, 59
Washingtonians, 137
Washingtonian Total Abstinence
    Society, 64–65
Washington University Sentence
    Completion Test, 158–59
wassail, 58
water:
  clean, for drinking, 63, 70
  contaminated, 59
Waters, Alice, 35
whiskey distillery, 59

Wilder, Billy, 94
Wilder-Taylor, Stefanie, 14
Willenbring, Mark, 118, 169,
    173–74
Wilsnack, Richard, 22–23
Wilsnack, Sharon, 22–23, 28,
    104–5
Wilson, Bill, 25, 81–82, 83,
    84–86, 88, 107, 112
Wilson, Ed, 150–52, 157, 159–
    60, 163–67
Wilson, Lois, 85, 97
wine:
    California wine industry, 32–43
    calories in, 43
    in colonial America, 57–58
    as the drink of the poor, 33
    and food, 176
    and health, 173
    immigrants' use of, 65–66
    as man's realm, 34–35
    marketing of, 35–39, 43
    and Prohibition, 71
    recommended daily intake
        of, 38, 60, 175
    and relaxation, 103
    religious use of, 33
    and seltzer, 43
    U.S. consumption of, 21, 40
    as women's beverage of
        choice, 19, 21, 32, 42–43
wine surveys, 37–38
wine tastings, 34, 37, 38, 39
Wolfers, Justin, 54, 55
women:
    and A.A., *see* Alcoholics
        Anonymous

advertising geared to, 38–39
in American West, 61–62
blaming the victim, 86–87,
    89, 142
changing expectations of,
    44–45, 71–73, 78
college attendance by, 31, 32,
    37, 43, 71–72, 102
in colonial times, 57–61,
    62–63
death rates of, 24
and double standard, 89, 96,
    106, 123–24, 142
education of, 64
and equality, 181, 182
fearing they drink too much,
    12, 14, 122
gender differences in
    research, 17–18, 23, 27–29,
    106
and gender roles, 43–44, 46,
    63, 78–79, 97, 102
help sought by, 24–25
hidden drinkers, 14–15, 74–75
increased alcohol use by,
    17–18, 23
independence of, 72, 78, 102,
    111
intolerance of, in A.A., 82
lack of confidence in, 110,
    128
leaving their jobs, 50, 52, 53
leisure time of, 72
middle-aged, 19, 25
and motherhood, 12, 28, 44,
    49, 52–55, 78, 102, 163–64
in nineteenth century, 62–70

women (*cont.*)
  as nurses in wartime, 71
  on-line confessions of, 12–13, 14
  and public opinion, 103
  regular drinkers, 20
  risk factors for, 115, 126
  "safe" guidelines for wine consumption, 9, 177–80
  in saloons, 69
  scrutiny of, 12
  sexual predation of, in A.A., 120, 121–45
  as single parents, 54
  and social change, 103
  suffragists, 67
  surveys on alcohol and, 20–23, 31–32, 37–38, 104–5, 156, 177–78, 179
  as teachers, 66
  vulnerability to alcohol, 24, 27–28, 122, 126, 144, 182, 183
  and wine, 19, 21, 32, 42–43
  working, 32, 66, 67, 71–72, 102
  young, risky habits of, 18
Women for Sobriety, 110, 150
Women's Christian Temperance Union (WCTU), 65–67, 70
women's rights, 43
World War I, 70, 71
  postwar years, 78
Wynn, Helen, 85

Yale Center for Alcohol Studies, 90–91
YMCA, 143
Your Empowering Solutions, 150–67

About the Author

Gabrielle Glaser is the author of *The Nose: A Profile of Sex, Beauty, and Survival* and *Strangers to the Tribe: Portraits of Interfaith Marriage.* She is an award-winning journalist whose work on the intersection of health and culture has appeared in the *New York Times,* the *New York Times Magazine,* the *Economist,* and many other publications. She lives with her family in Montclair, New Jersey.

Glaser, Gabrielle, author.
Her best-kept secret : why
women drink-- and how they
can regain control